YOU ARE READING THE WRONG WAY

Black Torch reads from right to left, starting in the upper-right corner. Japanese is read from right to left, meaning that action, sound effects, and word-balloon order are completely reversed from English order.

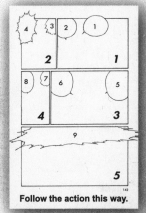

Follow the action this way.

DRAGON BALL SUPER

STORY BY **Akira Toriyama**   ART BY **Toyotarou**

Goku's adventure from the best-selling classic manga _Dragon Ball_ continues in this new series written by Akira Toriyama himself!

Ever since Goku became Earth's greatest hero and gathered the seven Dragon Balls to defeat the evil Boo, his life on Earth has grown a little dull. But new threats loom overhead, and Goku and his friends will have to defend the planet once again!

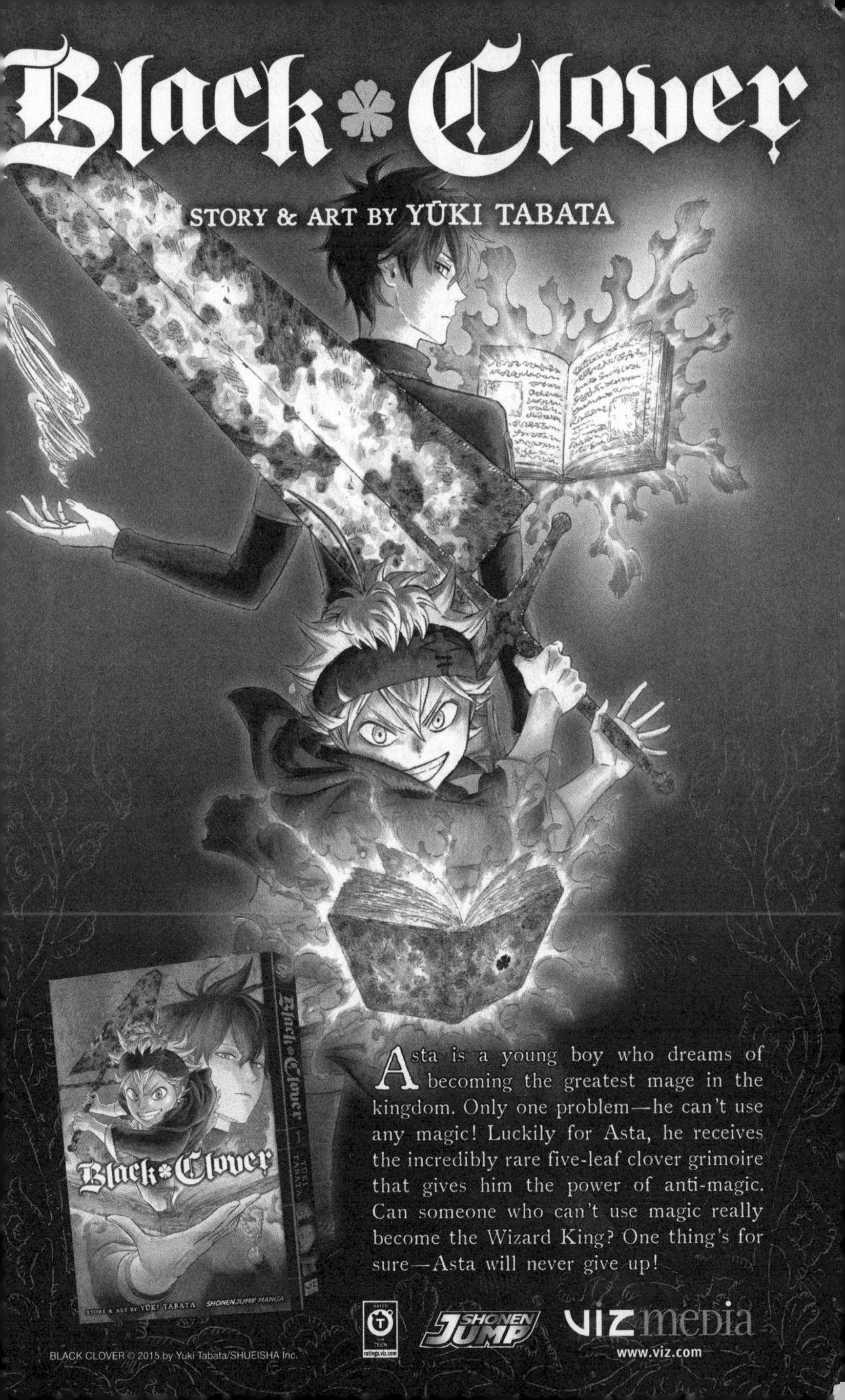
Black Clover
STORY & ART BY YŪKI TABATA
Asta is a young boy who dreams of becoming the greatest mage in the kingdom. Only one problem—he can't use any magic! Luckily for Asta, he receives the incredibly rare five-leaf clover grimoire that gives him the power of anti-magic. Can someone who can't use magic really become the Wizard King? One thing's for sure—Asta will never give up!
Black Clover
STORY & ART BY YŪKI TABATA
SHONEN JUMP MANGA
SHONEN JUMP
VIZ media
www.viz.com
ratings.viz.com
BLACK CLOVER © 2015 by Yuki Tabata/SHUEISHA Inc.

BLACK TORCH

VOLUME 1

SHONEN JUMP Manga Edition

STORY AND ART BY **TSUYOSHI TAKAKI**

Translation/Toshikazu Aizawa and Colin Leigh
Touch-Up Art & Lettering/Annaliese Christman
Design/Julian [JR] Robinson
Editor/Marlene First

Published by VIZ Media, LLC
P.O. Box 77010
San Francisco, CA 94107

Printed in the U.S.A.

10 9 8 7 6 5 4 3 2 1
First printing, August 2018

viz.com

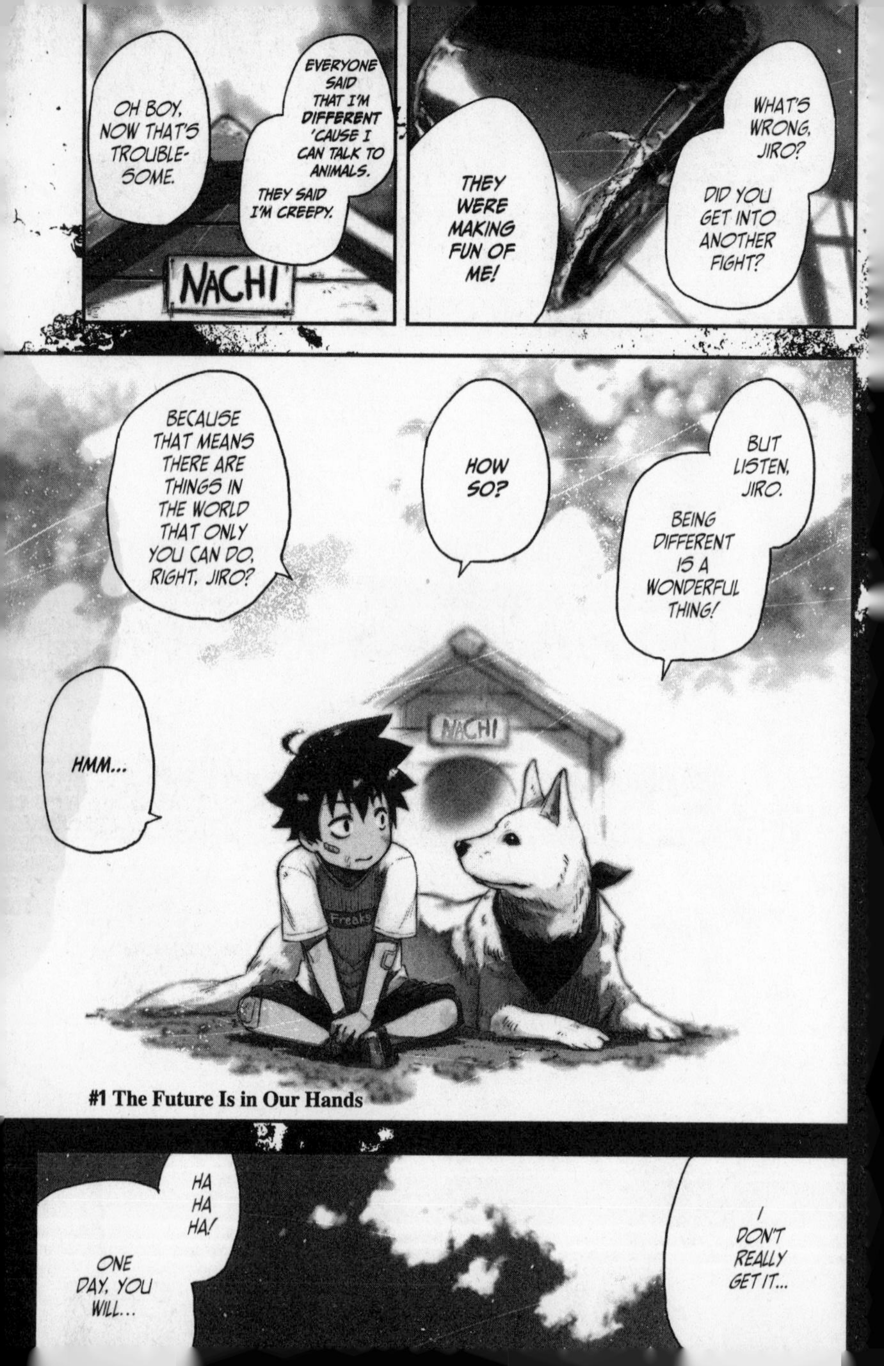
WHAT'S WRONG, JIRO?
DID YOU GET INTO ANOTHER FIGHT?
THEY WERE MAKING FUN OF ME!
EVERYONE SAID THAT I'M DIFFERENT 'CAUSE I CAN TALK TO ANIMALS.
THEY SAID I'M CREEPY.
OH BOY, NOW THAT'S TROUBLE-SOME.
NACHI
BUT LISTEN, JIRO.
BEING DIFFERENT IS A WONDERFUL THING!
HOW SO?
BECAUSE THAT MEANS THERE ARE THINGS IN THE WORLD THAT ONLY YOU CAN DO, RIGHT, JIRO?
NACHI
HMM...
Freaks
#1 The Future Is in Our Hands
I DON'T REALLY GET IT...
HA HA HA!
ONE DAY, YOU WILL...

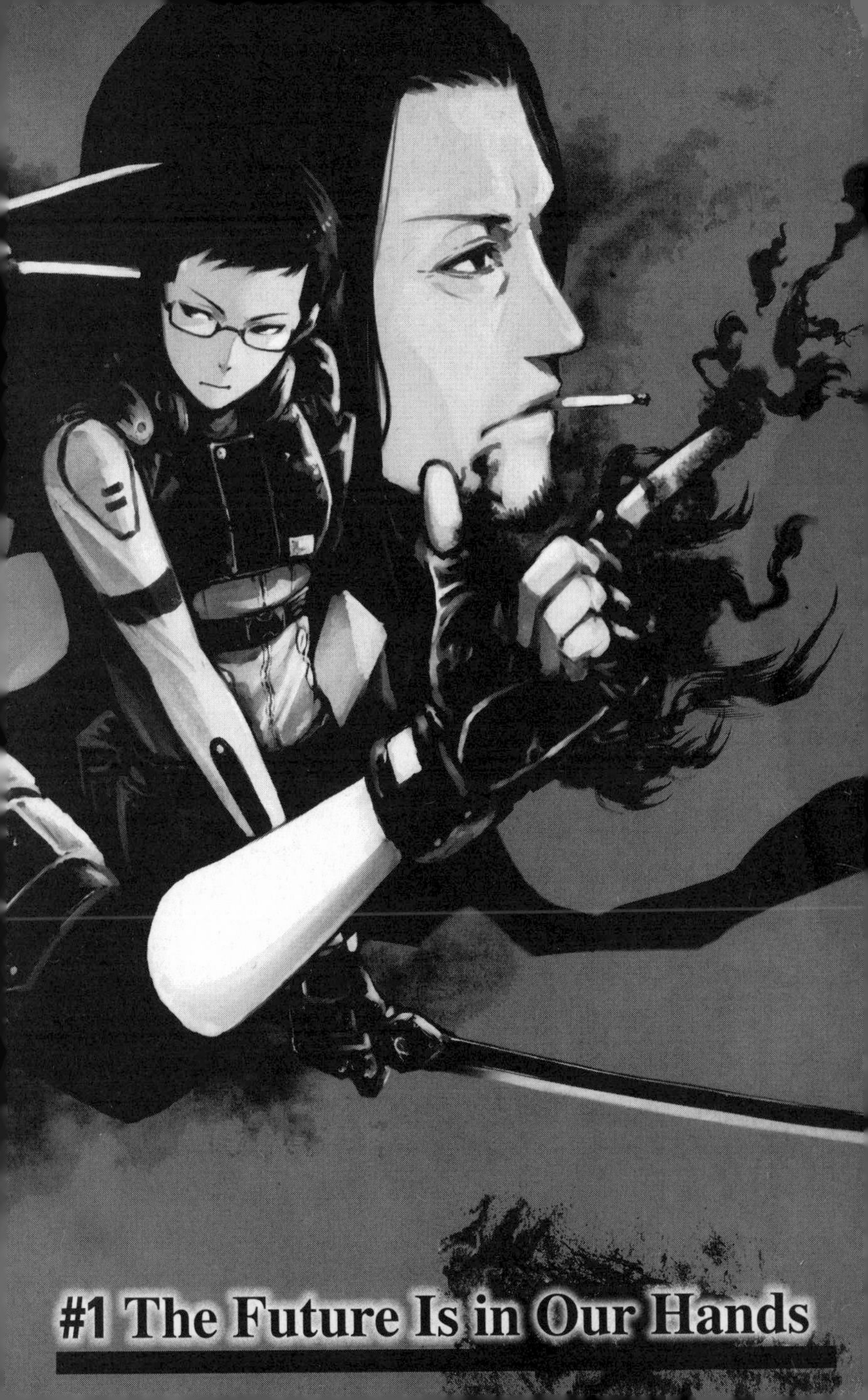

#1 The Future Is in Our Hands

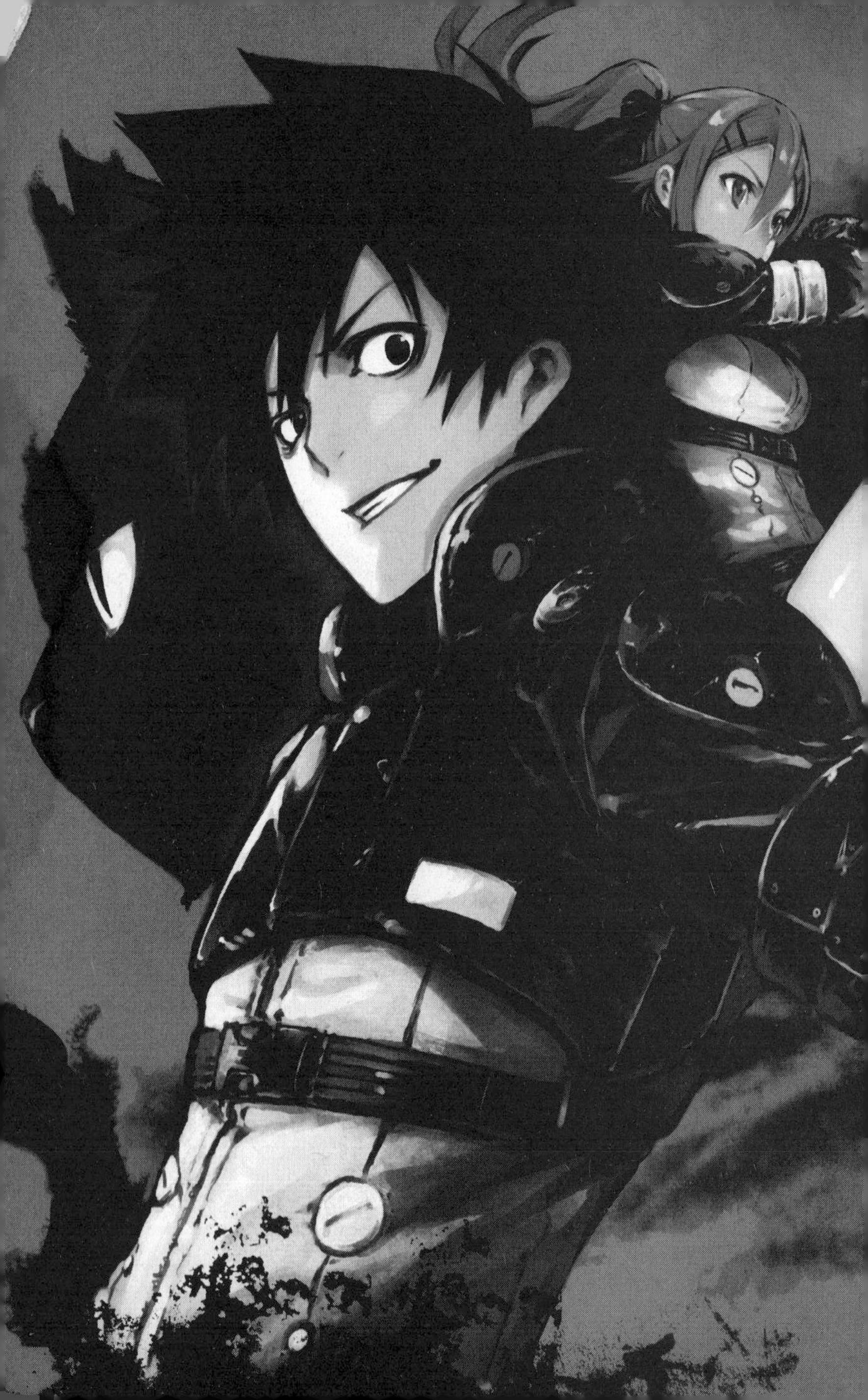

BLACK TORCH

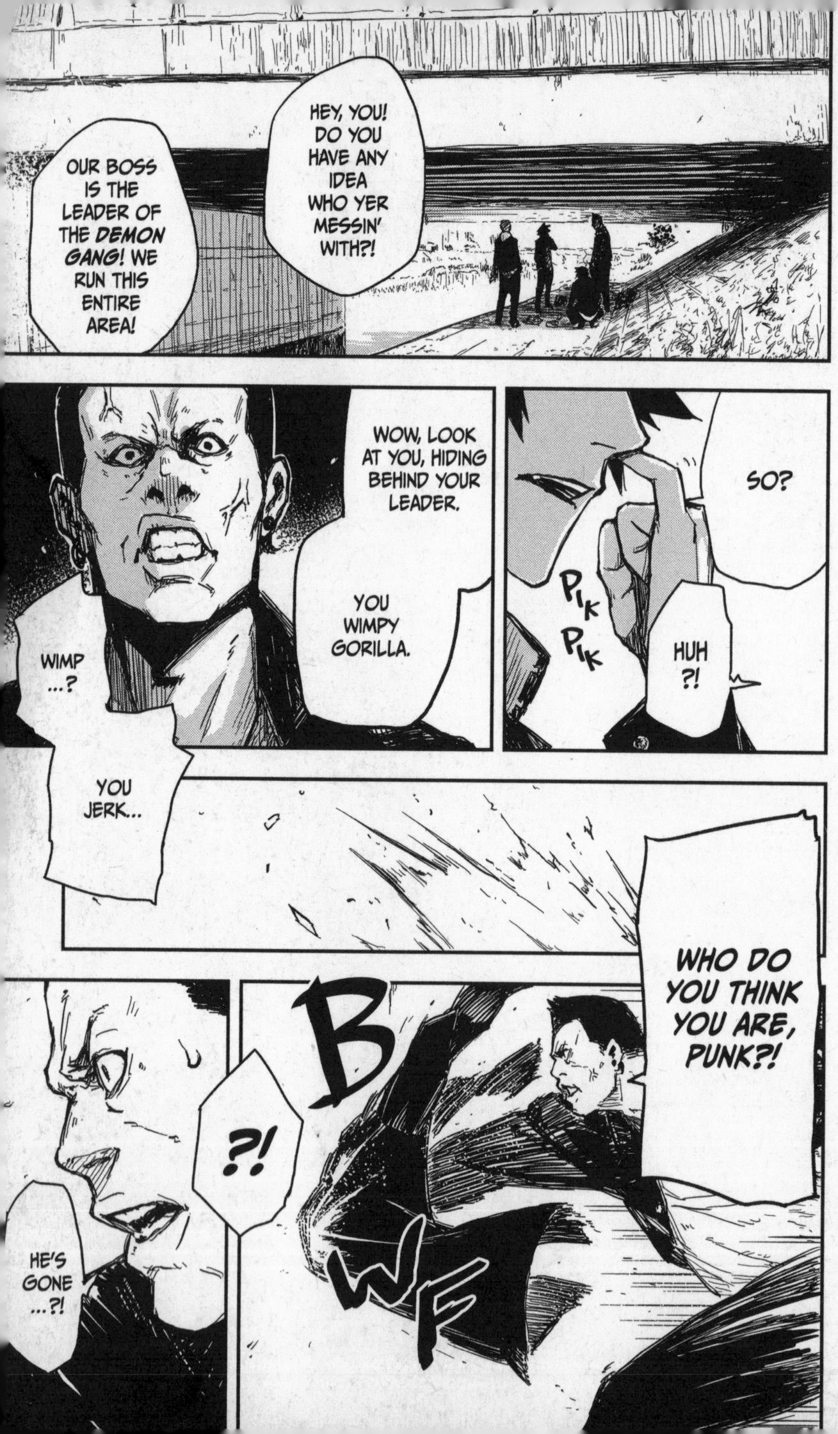
HEY, YOU! DO YOU HAVE ANY IDEA WHO YER MESSIN' WITH?!
OUR BOSS IS THE LEADER OF THE *DEMON GANG!* WE RUN THIS ENTIRE AREA!
SO?
PIK PIK
HUH?!
WOW, LOOK AT YOU, HIDING BEHIND YOUR LEADER.
YOU WIMPY GORILLA.
WIMP...?
YOU JERK...
WHO DO YOU THINK YOU ARE, PUNK?!
B
WF
?!
HE'S GONE...?!

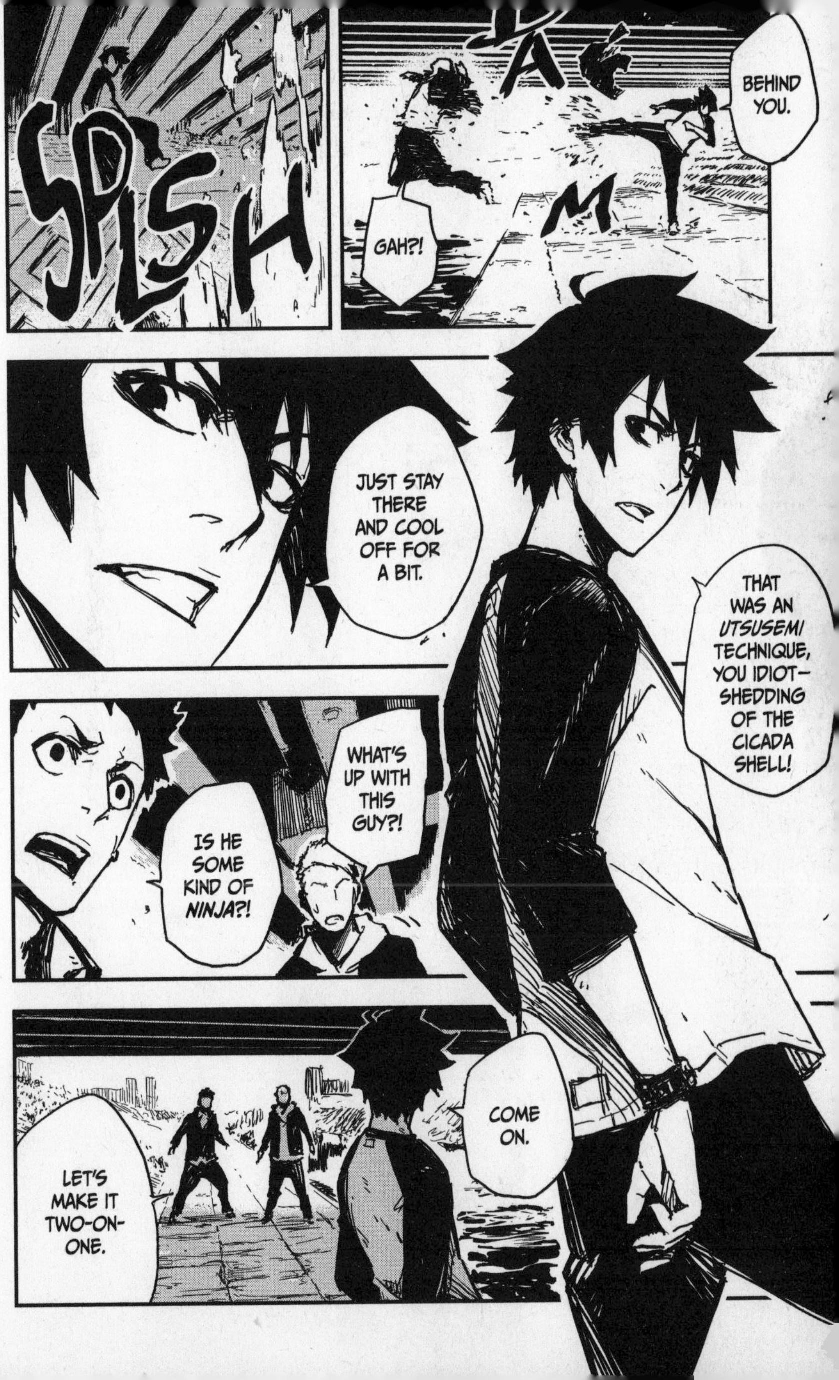
BEHIND YOU.
GAH?!
SPLSH
THAT WAS AN *UTSUSEMI* TECHNIQUE, YOU IDIOT—SHEDDING OF THE CICADA SHELL!
COME ON.
JUST STAY THERE AND COOL OFF FOR A BIT.
WHAT'S UP WITH THIS GUY?!
IS HE SOME KIND OF *NINJA*?!
LET'S MAKE IT TWO-ON-ONE.

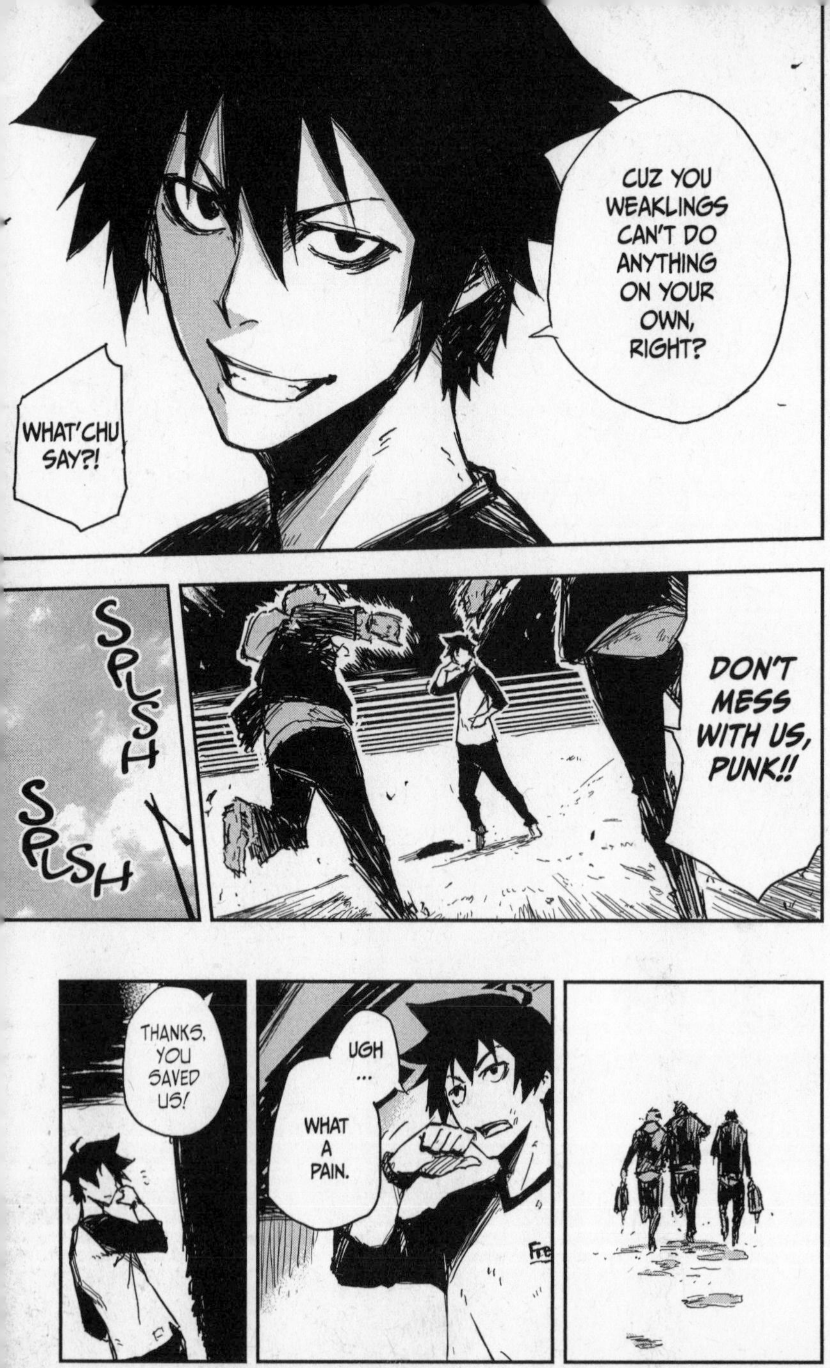
CUZ YOU WEAKLINGS CAN'T DO ANYTHING ON YOUR OWN, RIGHT?
WHAT'CHU SAY?!
DON'T MESS WITH US, PUNK!!
SPLSH
SPLSH
UGH ...
WHAT A PAIN.
THANKS, YOU SAVED US!

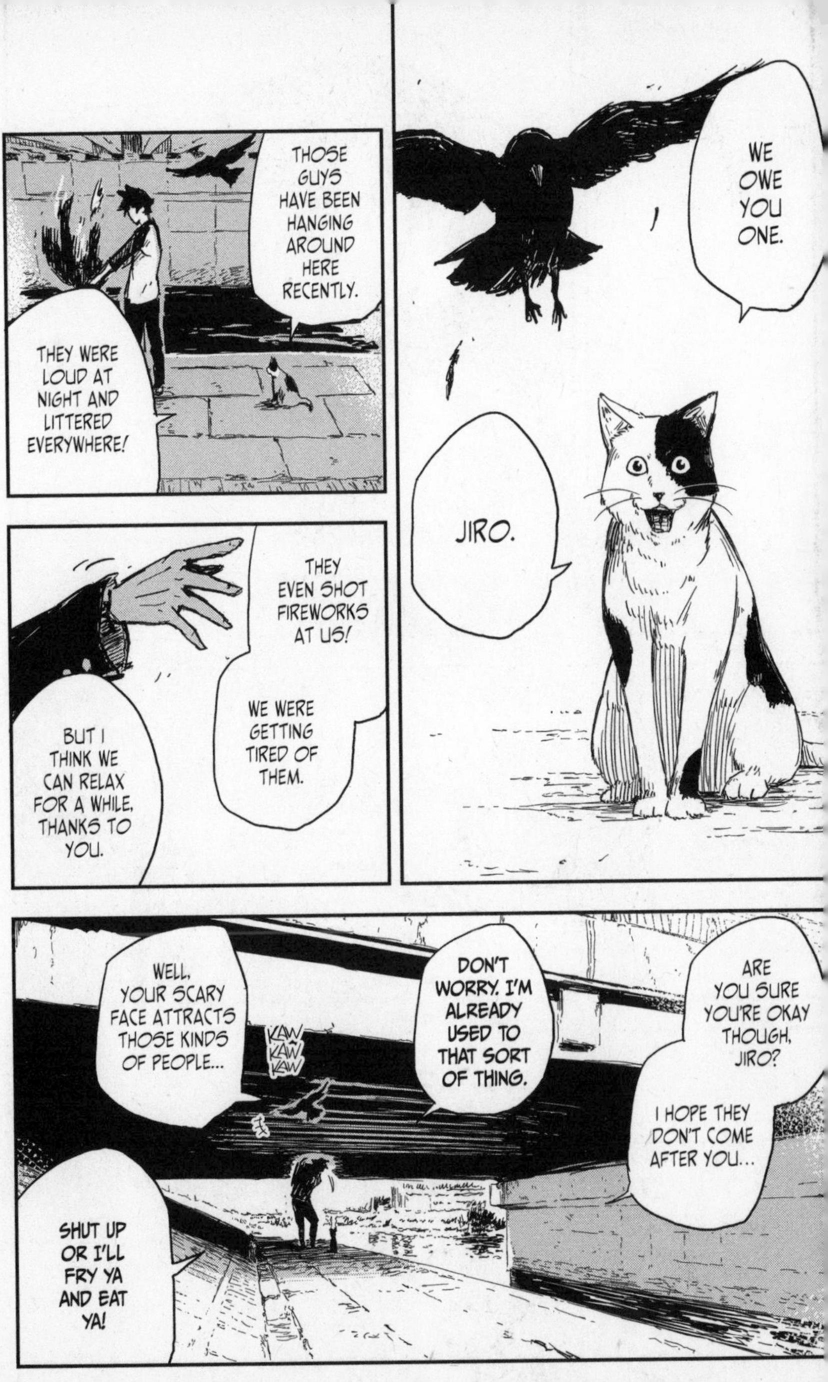
WE OWE YOU ONE.
JIRO.
THOSE GUYS HAVE BEEN HANGING AROUND HERE RECENTLY.
THEY WERE LOUD AT NIGHT AND LITTERED EVERYWHERE!
THEY EVEN SHOT FIREWORKS AT US!
WE WERE GETTING TIRED OF THEM.
BUT I THINK WE CAN RELAX FOR A WHILE, THANKS TO YOU.
ARE YOU SURE YOU'RE OKAY THOUGH, JIRO?
I HOPE THEY DON'T COME AFTER YOU...
DON'T WORRY. I'M ALREADY USED TO THAT SORT OF THING.
KAW KAW KAW
WELL, YOUR SCARY FACE ATTRACTS THOSE KINDS OF PEOPLE...
SHUT UP OR I'LL FRY YA AND EAT YA!

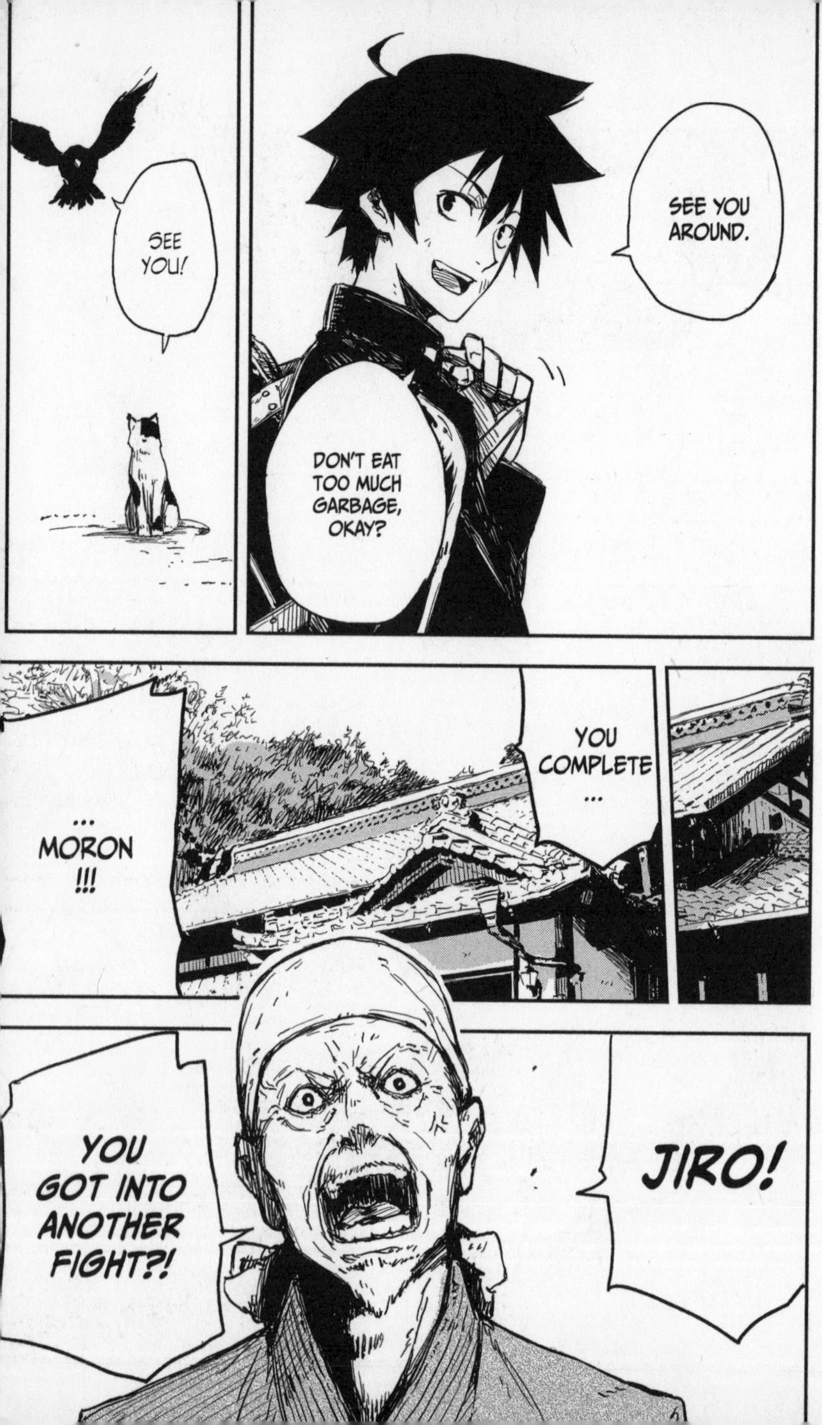
SEE YOU AROUND.
DON'T EAT TOO MUCH GARBAGE, OKAY?
SEE YOU!
YOU COMPLETE ...
... MORON !!!
JIRO!
YOU GOT INTO ANOTHER FIGHT?!

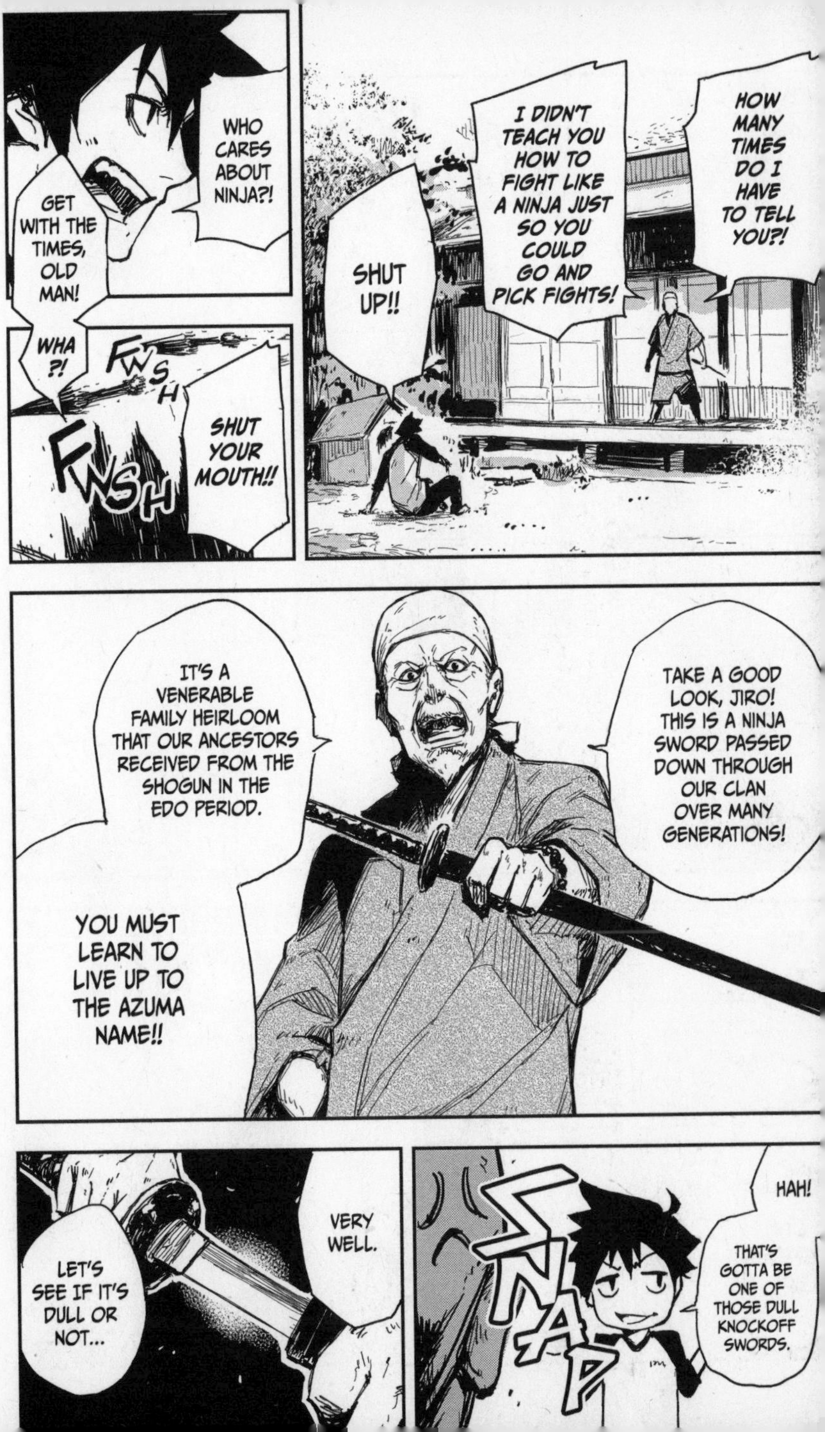
HOW MANY TIMES DO I HAVE TO TELL YOU?!
I DIDN'T TEACH YOU HOW TO FIGHT LIKE A NINJA JUST SO YOU COULD GO AND PICK FIGHTS!
SHUT UP!!
WHO CARES ABOUT NINJA?!
GET WITH THE TIMES, OLD MAN!
WHA?!
FWSH
SHUT YOUR MOUTH!!
FWSH
TAKE A GOOD LOOK, JIRO! THIS IS A NINJA SWORD PASSED DOWN THROUGH OUR CLAN OVER MANY GENERATIONS!
IT'S A VENERABLE FAMILY HEIRLOOM THAT OUR ANCESTORS RECEIVED FROM THE SHOGUN IN THE EDO PERIOD.
YOU MUST LEARN TO LIVE UP TO THE AZUMA NAME!!
HAH!
THAT'S GOTTA BE ONE OF THOSE DULL KNOCKOFF SWORDS.
SNAP
VERY WELL.
LET'S SEE IF IT'S DULL OR NOT...

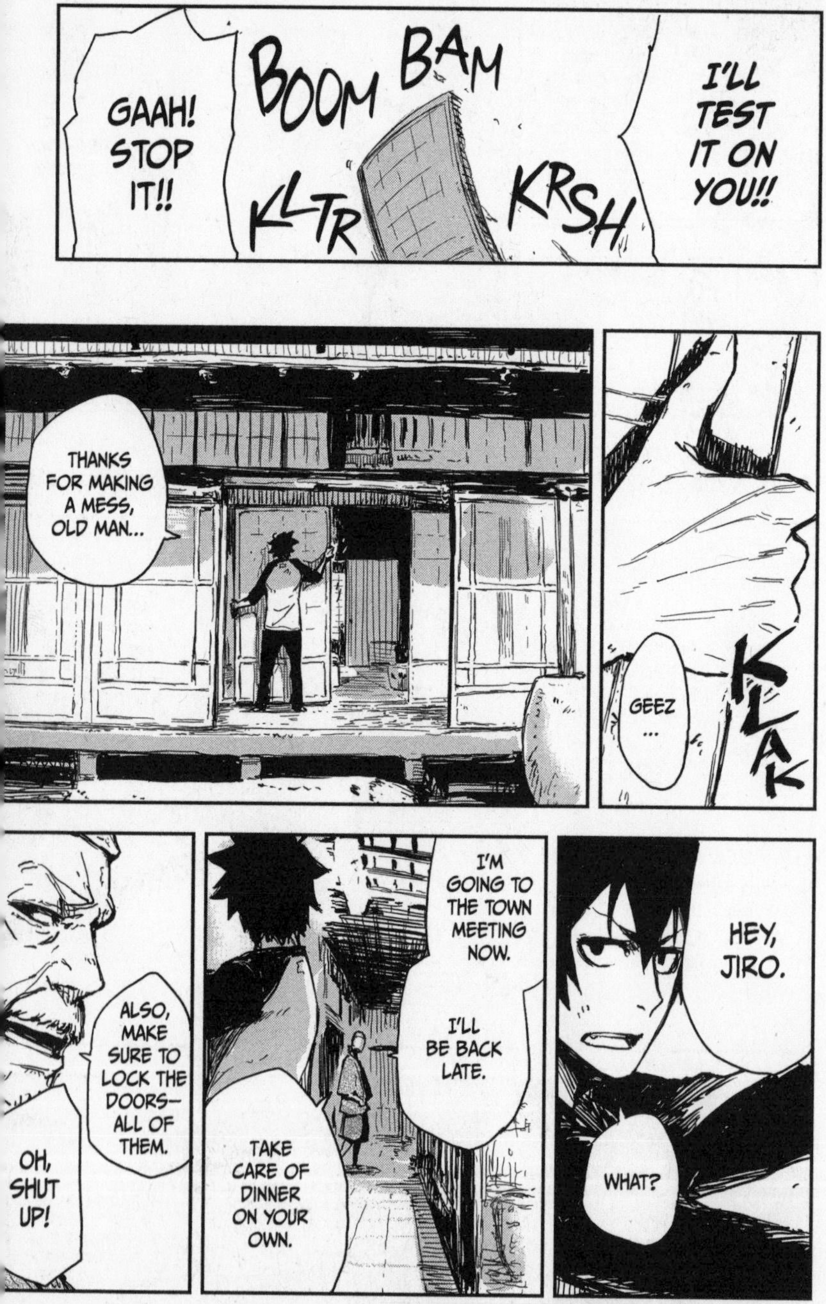
I'LL TEST IT ON YOU!!
BAM
BOOM
KRSH
KLTR
GAAH! STOP IT!!
KLAK
GEEZ...
THANKS FOR MAKING A MESS, OLD MAN...
HEY, JIRO.
WHAT?
I'M GOING TO THE TOWN MEETING NOW.
I'LL BE BACK LATE.
TAKE CARE OF DINNER ON YOUR OWN.
ALSO, MAKE SURE TO LOCK THE DOORS—ALL OF THEM.
OH, SHUT UP!

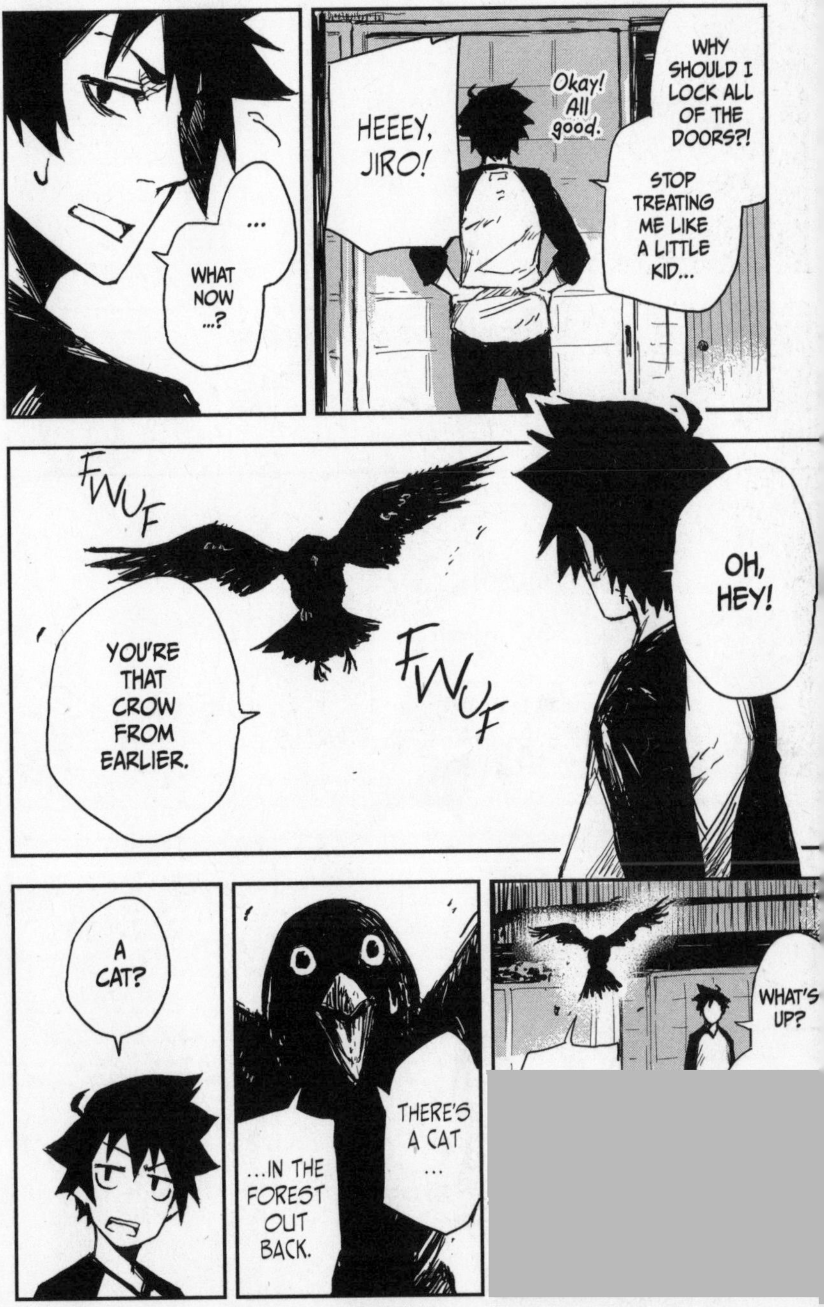
WHY SHOULD I LOCK ALL OF THE DOORS?!
STOP TREATING ME LIKE A LITTLE KID...
Okay! All good.
HEEEY, JIRO!
...
WHAT NOW ...?
OH, HEY!
FWUF
FWUF
YOU'RE THAT CROW FROM EARLIER.
WHAT'S UP?
THERE'S A CAT ...
...IN THE FOREST OUT BACK.
A CAT?

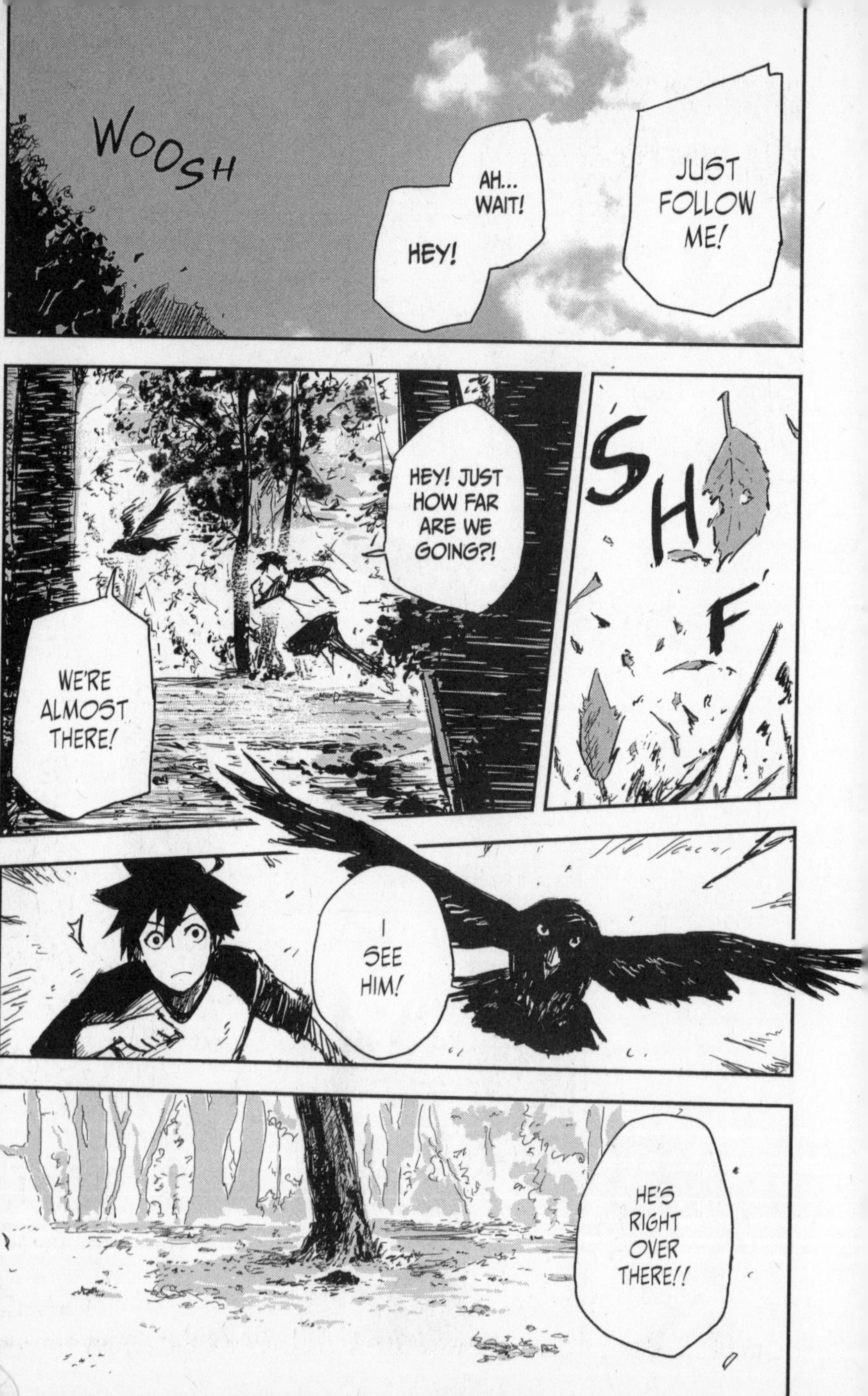
JUST FOLLOW ME!
AH... WAIT!
HEY!
WOOSH
SHF
HEY! JUST HOW FAR ARE WE GOING?!
WE'RE ALMOST THERE!
I SEE HIM!
HE'S RIGHT OVER THERE!!

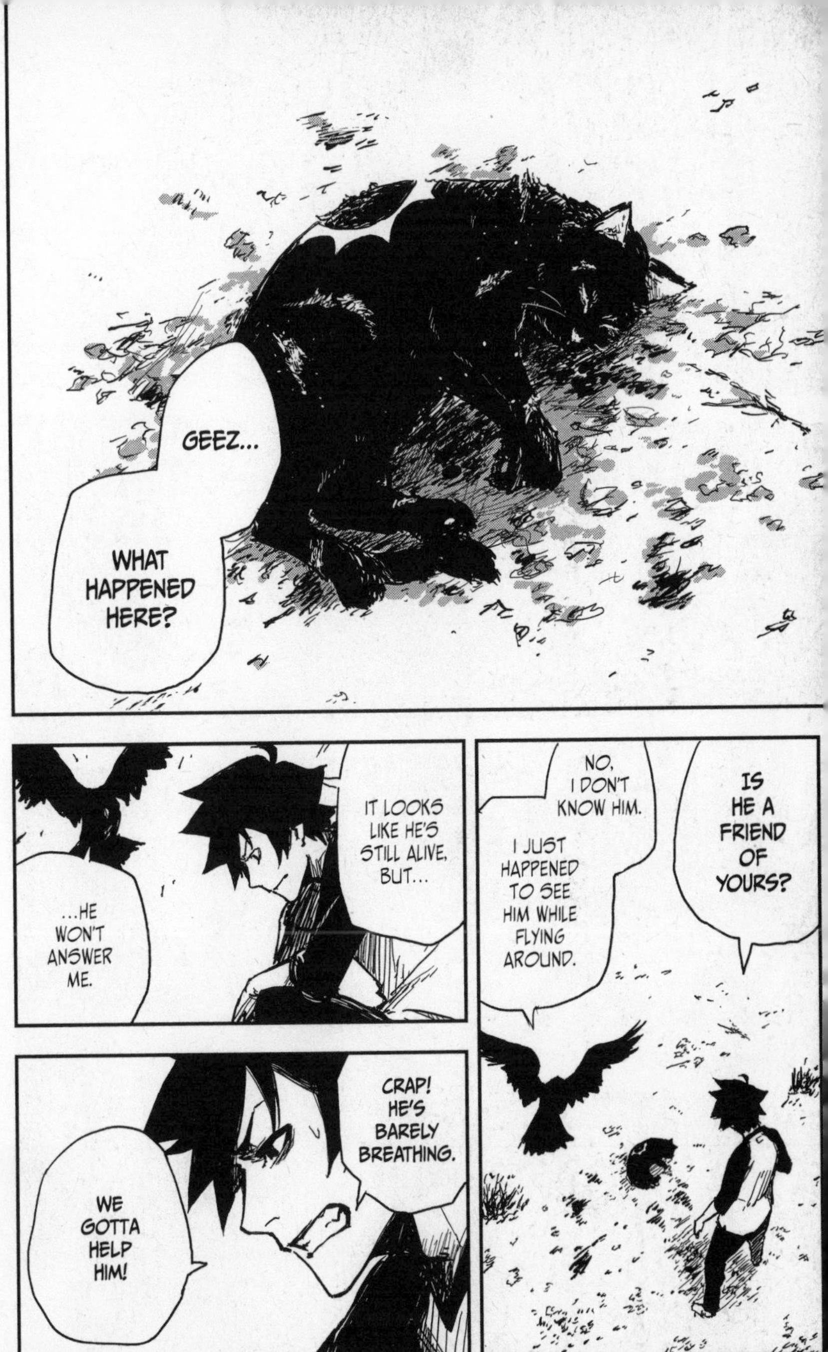
GEEZ...
WHAT HAPPENED HERE?
IS HE A FRIEND OF YOURS?
NO, I DON'T KNOW HIM.
I JUST HAPPENED TO SEE HIM WHILE FLYING AROUND.
IT LOOKS LIKE HE'S STILL ALIVE, BUT...
...HE WON'T ANSWER ME.
CRAP! HE'S BARELY BREATHING.
WE GOTTA HELP HIM!

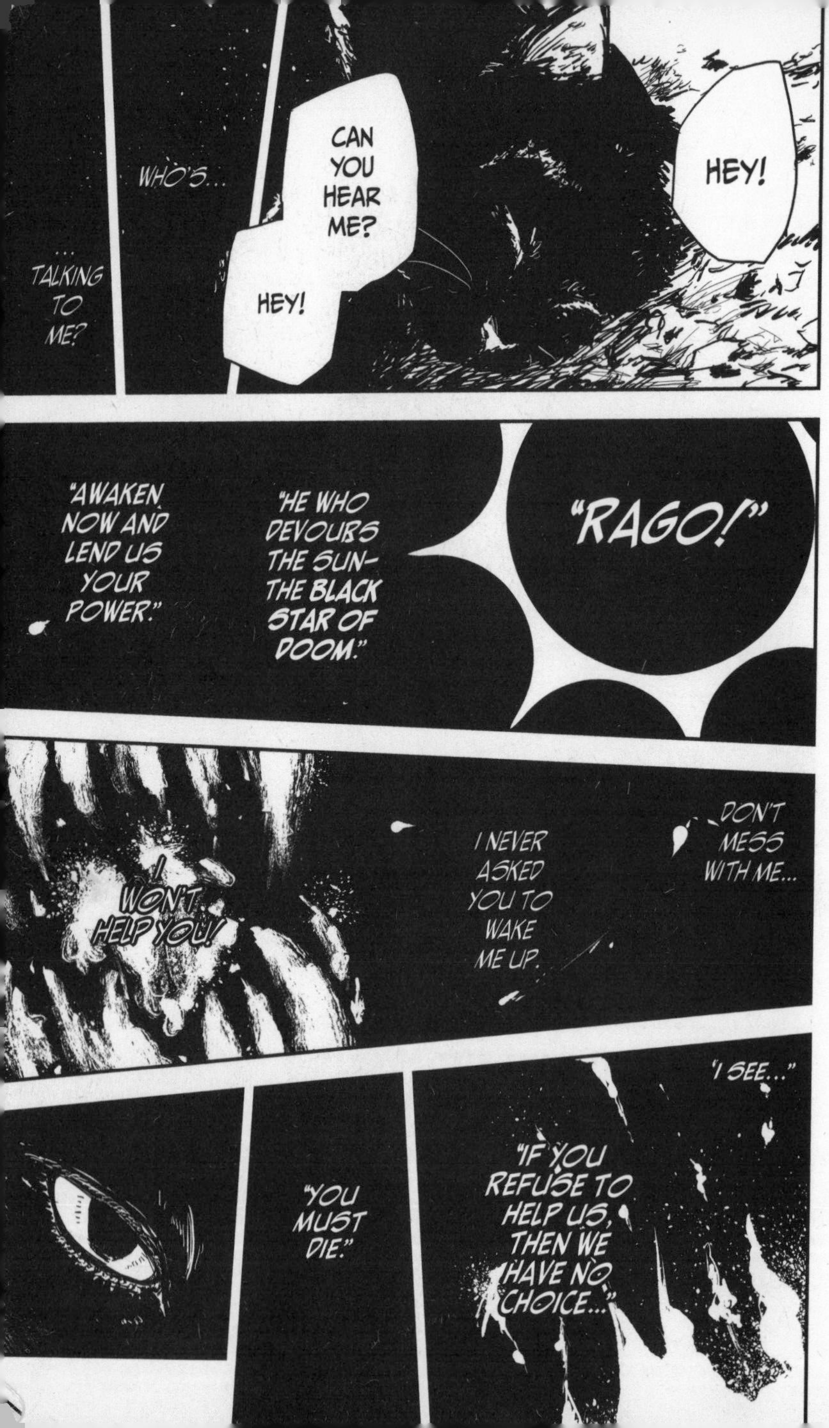
HEY!
CAN YOU HEAR ME?
HEY!
WHO'S...
...TALKING TO ME?
"RAGO!"
"HE WHO DEVOURS THE SUN—THE BLACK STAR OF DOOM."
"AWAKEN NOW AND LEND US YOUR POWER."
DON'T MESS WITH ME...
I NEVER ASKED YOU TO WAKE ME UP.
I WON'T HELP YOU!
"I SEE..."
"IF YOU REFUSE TO HELP US, THEN WE HAVE NO CHOICE..."
"YOU MUST DIE."

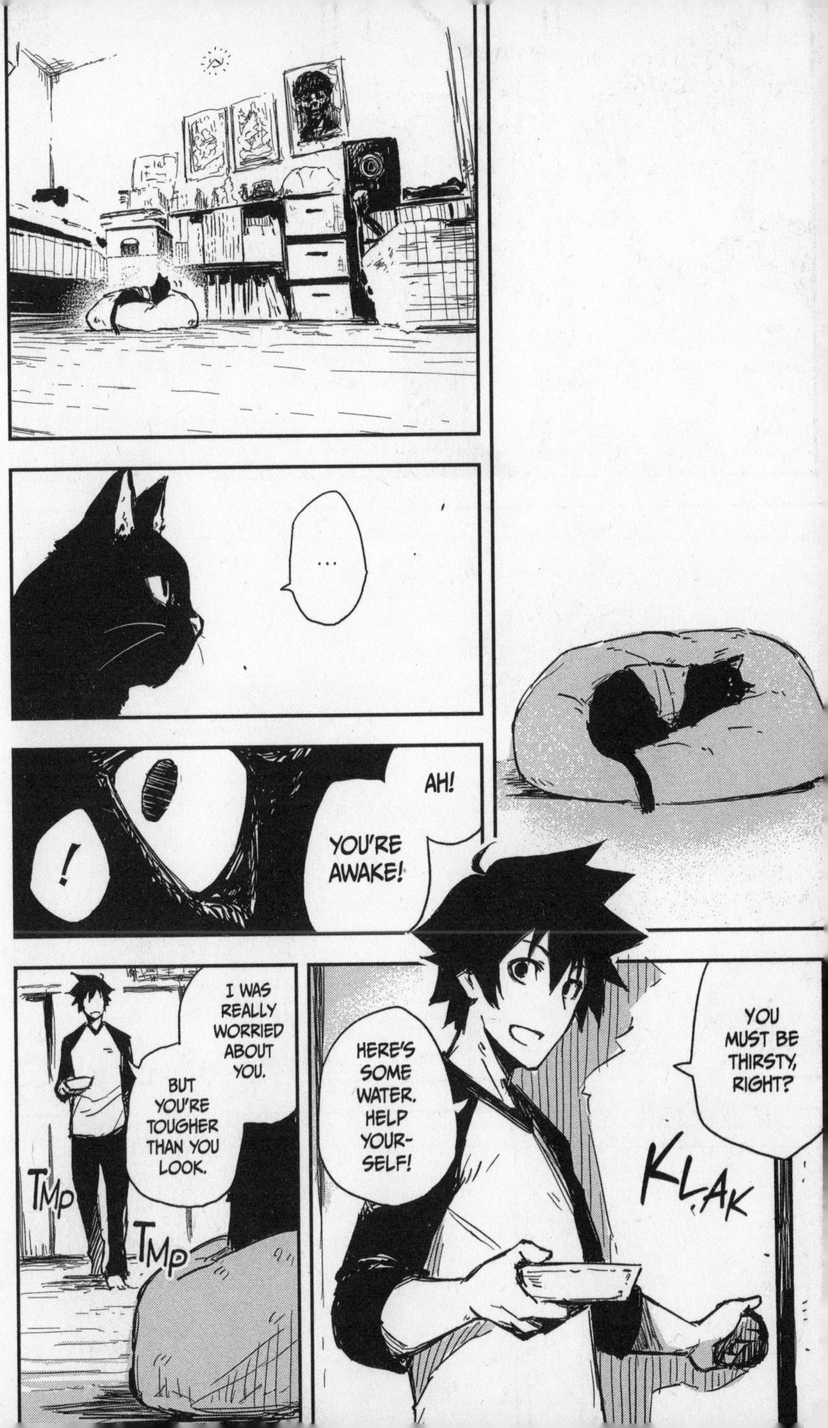
...
AH!
YOU'RE AWAKE!
!
YOU MUST BE THIRSTY, RIGHT?
KLAK
HERE'S SOME WATER. HELP YOURSELF!
I WAS REALLY WORRIED ABOUT YOU.
BUT YOU'RE TOUGHER THAN YOU LOOK.
TMP
TMP

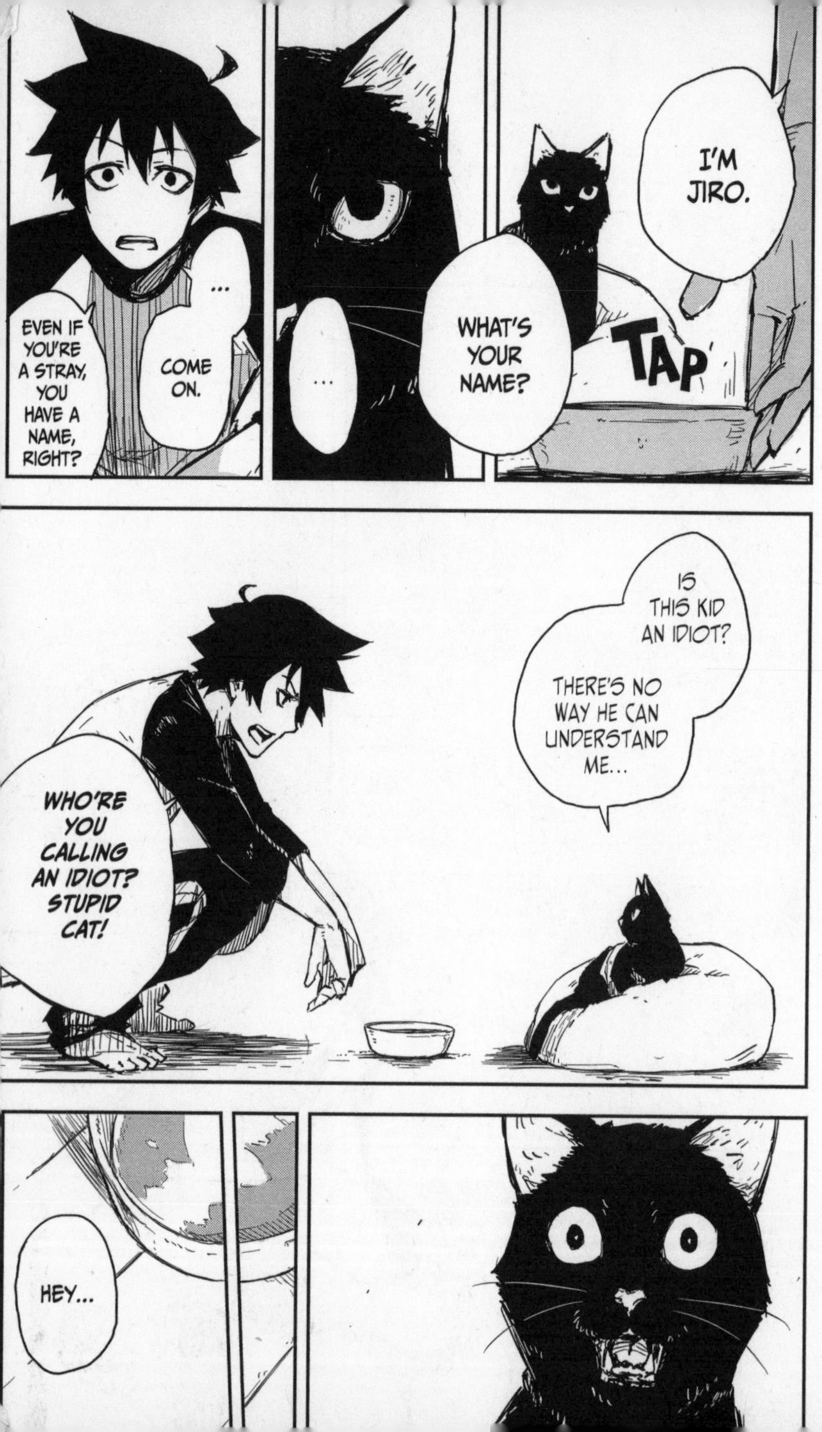
I'M JIRO.
WHAT'S YOUR NAME?
TAP
...
...
COME ON.
EVEN IF YOU'RE A STRAY, YOU HAVE A NAME, RIGHT?
IS THIS KID AN IDIOT?
THERE'S NO WAY HE CAN UNDERSTAND ME...
WHO'RE YOU CALLING AN IDIOT? STUPID CAT!
HEY...

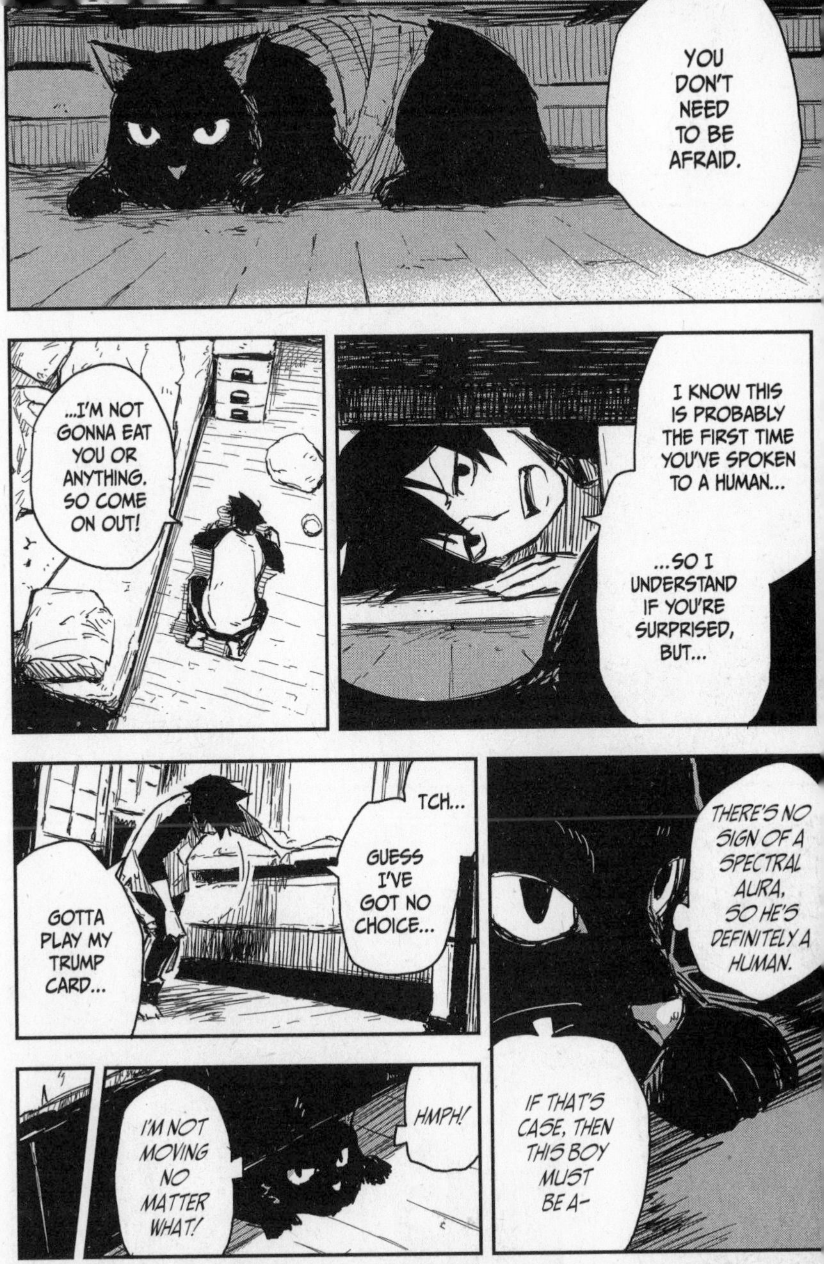
YOU DON'T NEED TO BE AFRAID.
I KNOW THIS IS PROBABLY THE FIRST TIME YOU'VE SPOKEN TO A HUMAN...
...SO I UNDERSTAND IF YOU'RE SURPRISED, BUT...
...I'M NOT GONNA EAT YOU OR ANYTHING. SO COME ON OUT!
THERE'S NO SIGN OF A SPECTRAL AURA, SO HE'S DEFINITELY A HUMAN.
IF THAT'S CASE, THEN THIS BOY MUST BE A-
TCH...
GUESS I'VE GOT NO CHOICE...
GOTTA PLAY MY TRUMP CARD...
HMPH!
I'M NOT MOVING NO MATTER WHAT!

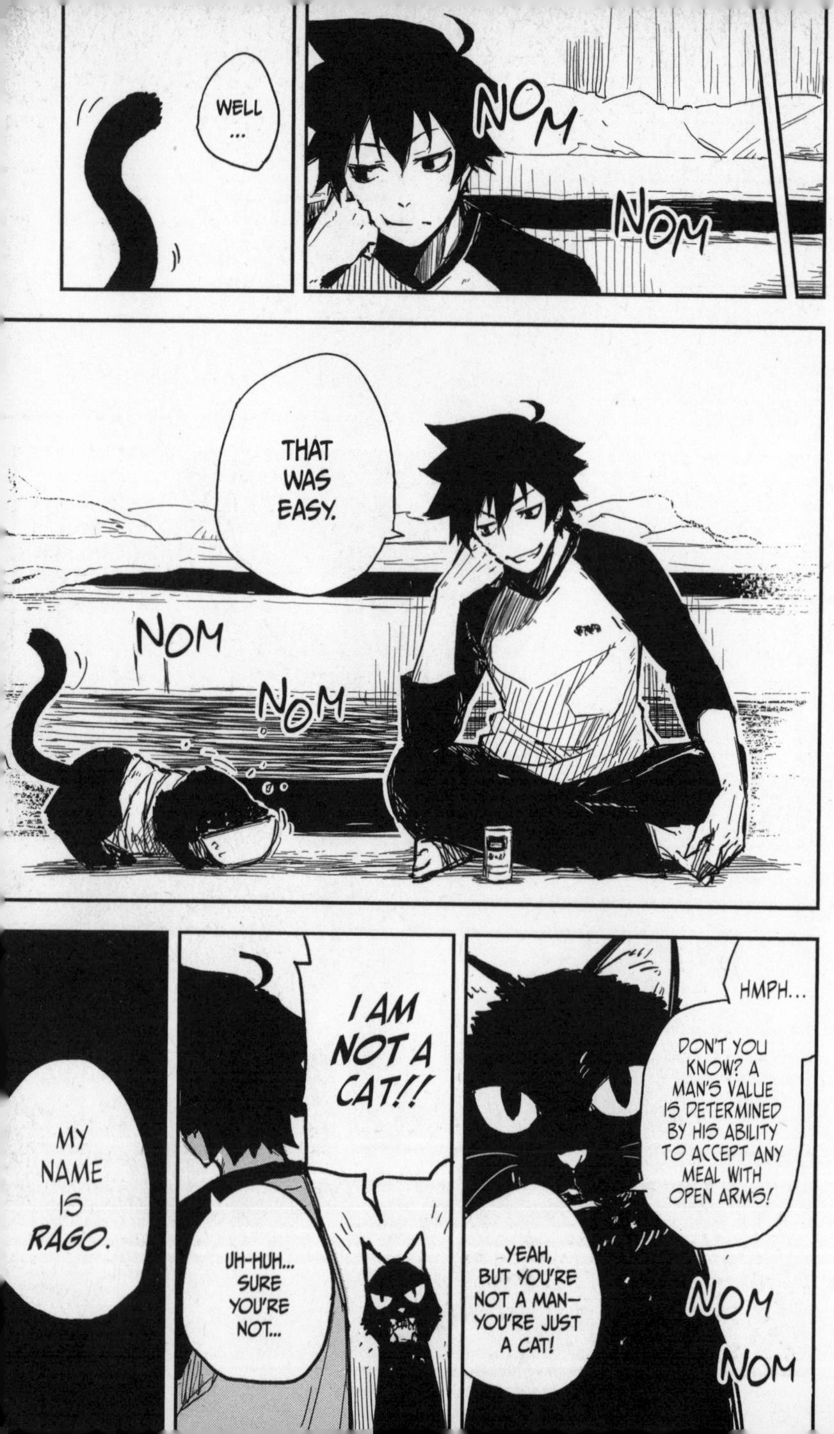
NOM NOM
WELL...
THAT WAS EASY.
NOM NOM
HMPH...
DON'T YOU KNOW? A MAN'S VALUE IS DETERMINED BY HIS ABILITY TO ACCEPT ANY MEAL WITH OPEN ARMS!
NOM NOM
YEAH, BUT YOU'RE NOT A MAN—YOU'RE JUST A CAT!
I AM NOT A CAT!!
UH-HUH... SURE YOU'RE NOT...
MY NAME IS RAGO.

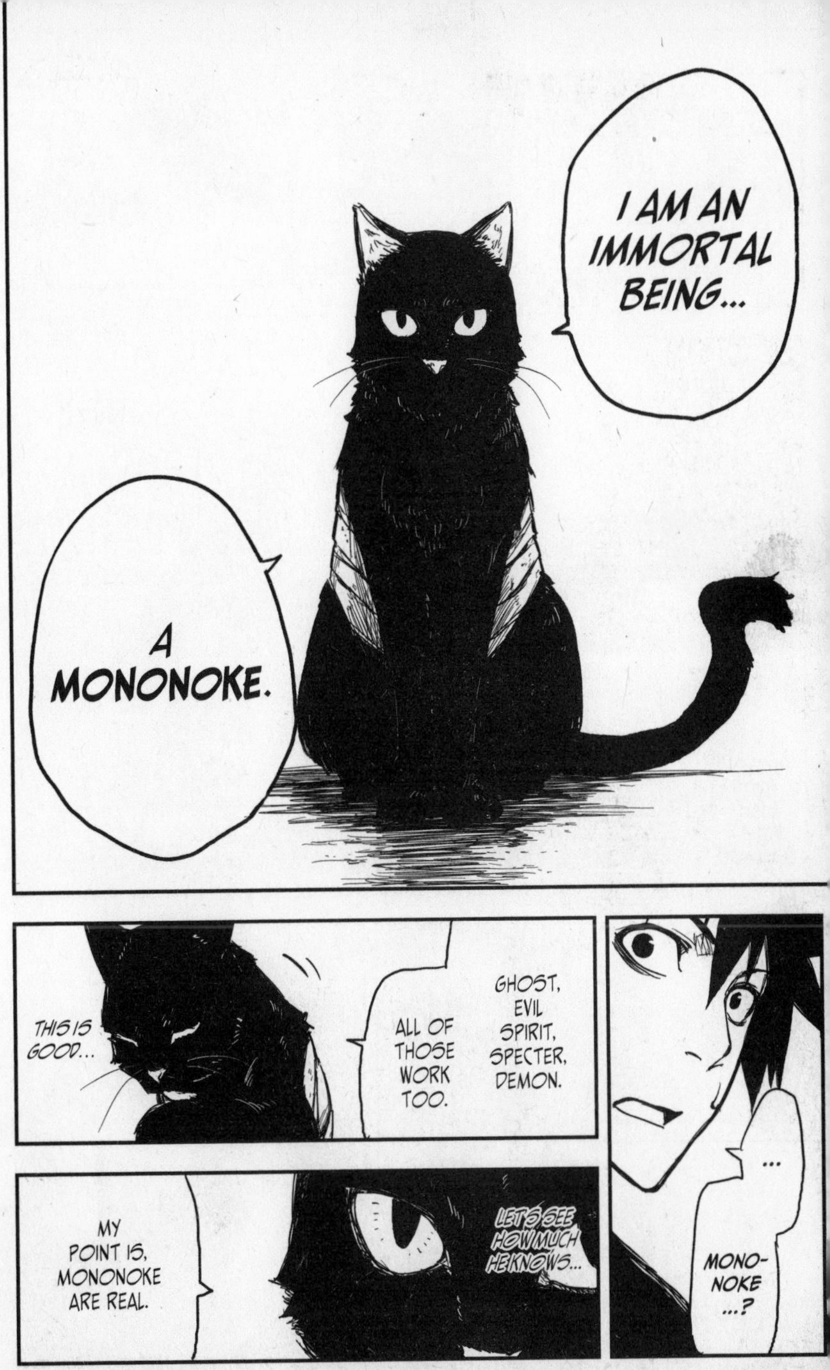
I AM AN IMMORTAL BEING...
A MONONOKE.
...
MONO-NOKE ...?
GHOST, EVIL SPIRIT, SPECTER, DEMON.
ALL OF THOSE WORK TOO.
THIS IS GOOD...
LET'S SEE HOW MUCH HE KNOWS...
MY POINT IS, MONONOKE ARE REAL.

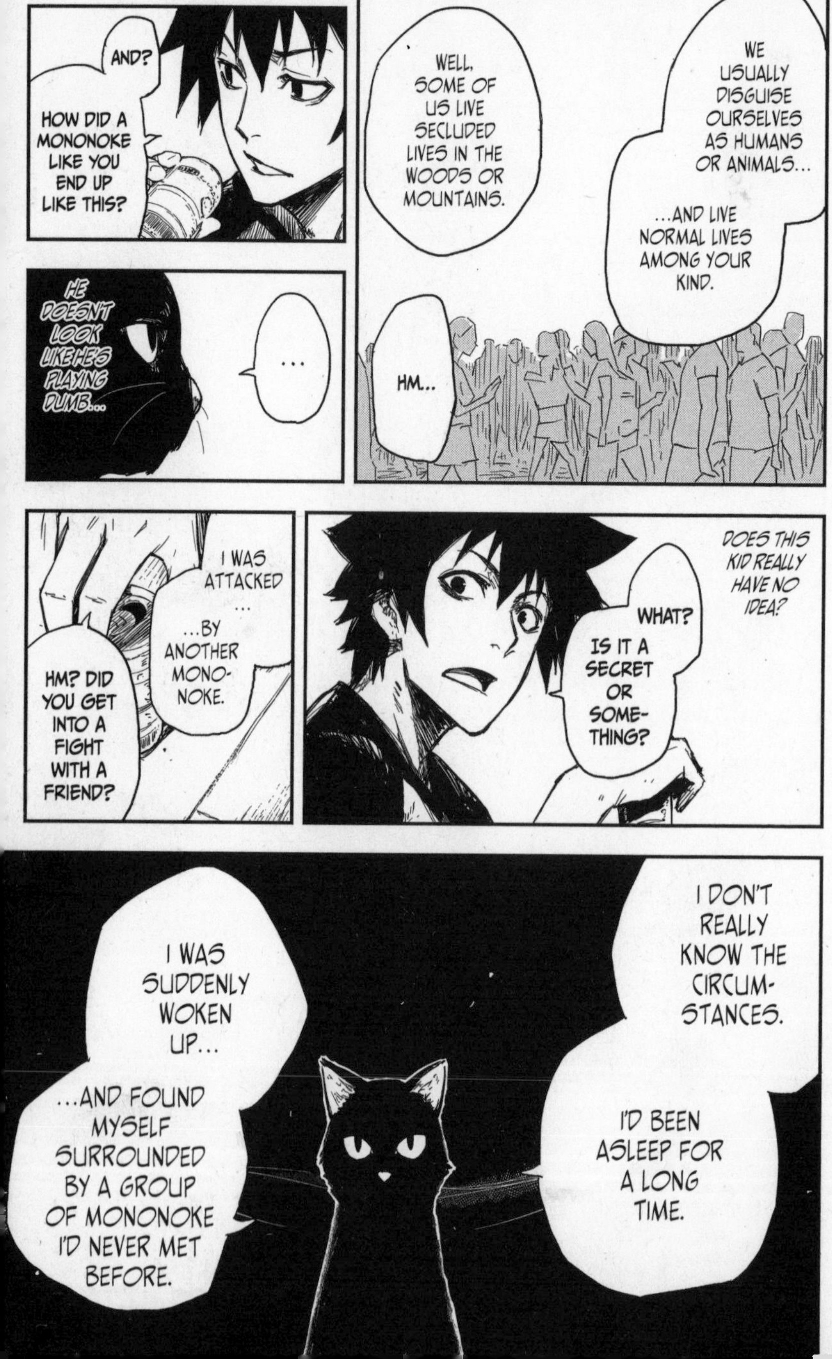
WE USUALLY DISGUISE OURSELVES AS HUMANS OR ANIMALS...
...AND LIVE NORMAL LIVES AMONG YOUR KIND.
WELL, SOME OF US LIVE SECLUDED LIVES IN THE WOODS OR MOUNTAINS.
HM...
AND?
HOW DID A MONONOKE LIKE YOU END UP LIKE THIS?
HE DOESN'T LOOK LIKE HE'S PLAYING DUMB...
...
DOES THIS KID REALLY HAVE NO IDEA?
WHAT?
IS IT A SECRET OR SOMETHING?
I WAS ATTACKED...
...BY ANOTHER MONONOKE.
HM? DID YOU GET INTO A FIGHT WITH A FRIEND?
I DON'T REALLY KNOW THE CIRCUMSTANCES.
I'D BEEN ASLEEP FOR A LONG TIME.
I WAS SUDDENLY WOKEN UP...
...AND FOUND MYSELF SURROUNDED BY A GROUP OF MONONOKE I'D NEVER MET BEFORE.

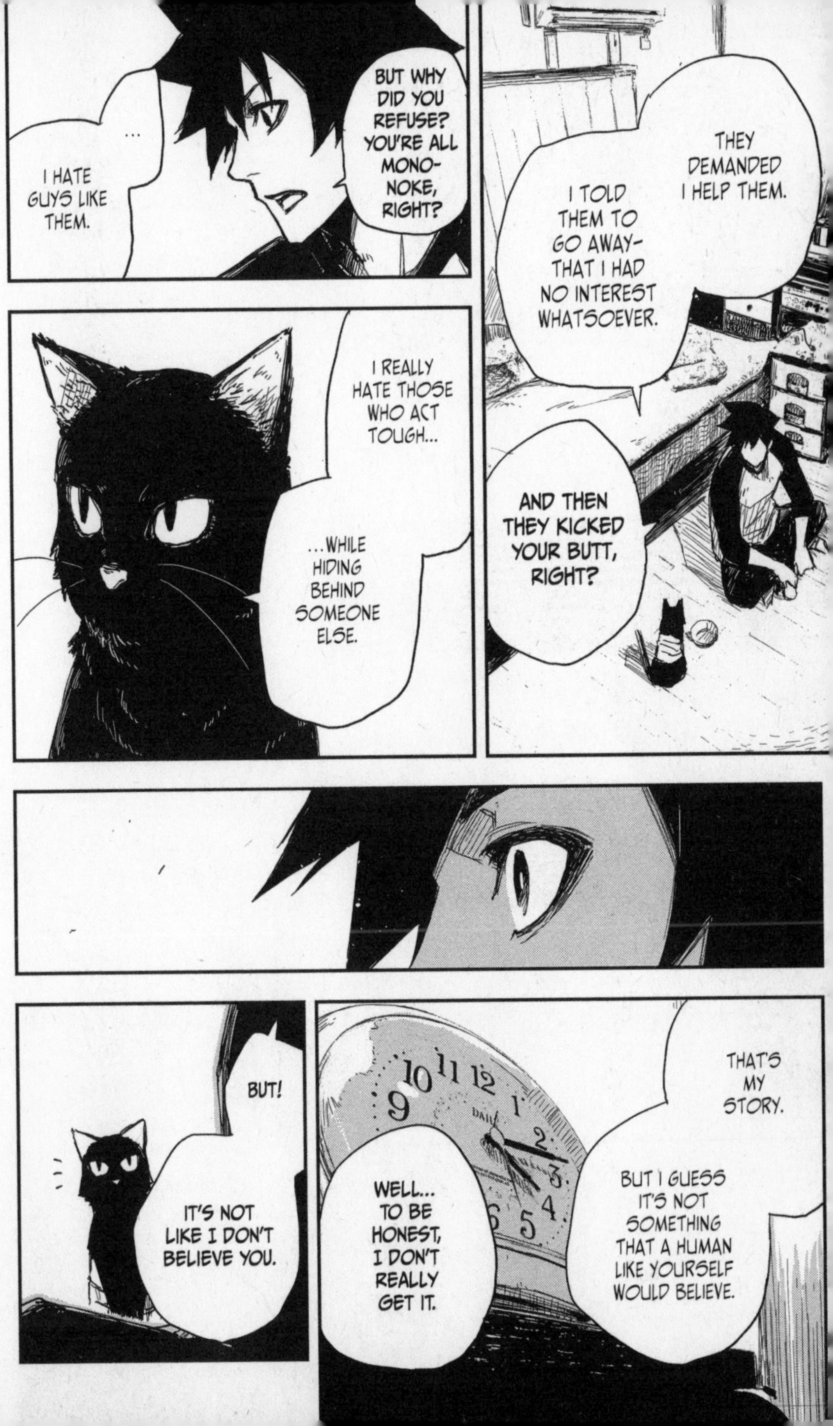
THEY DEMANDED I HELP THEM.
I TOLD THEM TO GO AWAY- THAT I HAD NO INTEREST WHATSOEVER.
AND THEN THEY KICKED YOUR BUTT, RIGHT?
BUT WHY DID YOU REFUSE? YOU'RE ALL MONO-NOKE, RIGHT?
...
I HATE GUYS LIKE THEM.
I REALLY HATE THOSE WHO ACT TOUGH...
...WHILE HIDING BEHIND SOMEONE ELSE.
THAT'S MY STORY.
BUT I GUESS IT'S NOT SOMETHING THAT A HUMAN LIKE YOURSELF WOULD BELIEVE.
WELL... TO BE HONEST, I DON'T REALLY GET IT.
BUT!
IT'S NOT LIKE I DON'T BELIEVE YOU.

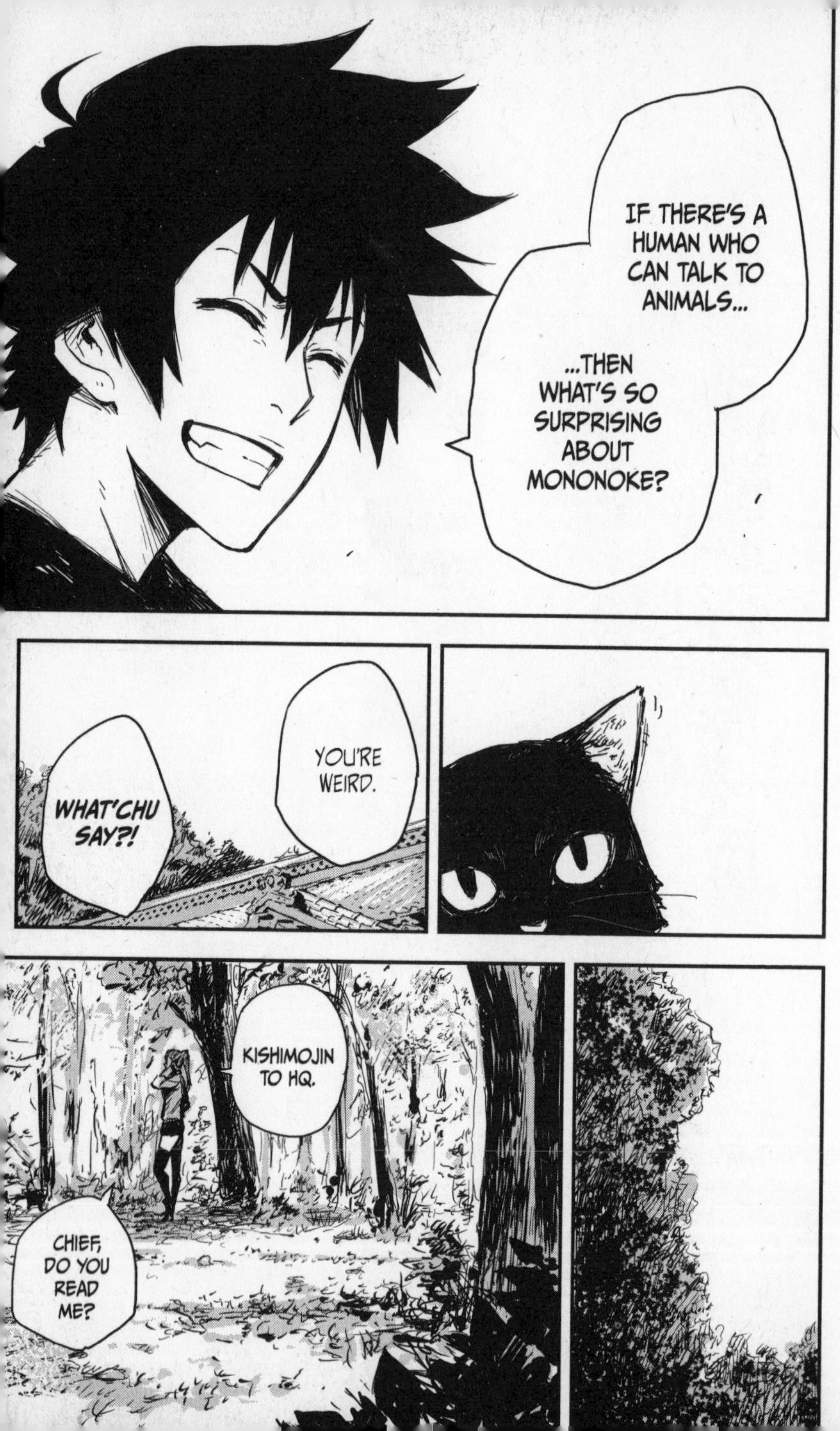
IF THERE'S A HUMAN WHO CAN TALK TO ANIMALS...
...THEN WHAT'S SO SURPRISING ABOUT MONONOKE?
YOU'RE WEIRD.
WHAT'CHU SAY?!
KISHIMOJIN TO HQ.
CHIEF, DO YOU READ ME?

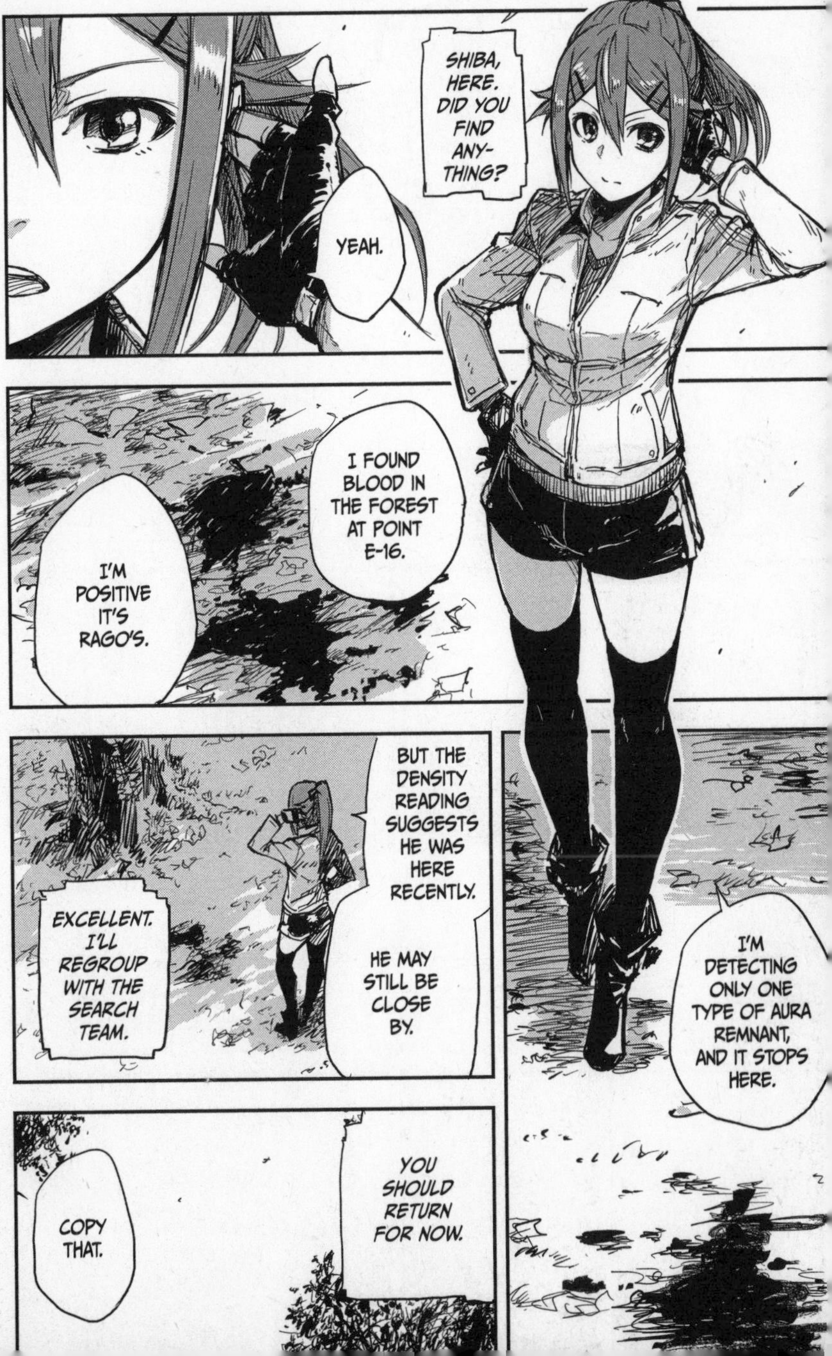
SHIBA, HERE. DID YOU FIND ANY-THING?
YEAH.
I FOUND BLOOD IN THE FOREST AT POINT E-16.
I'M POSITIVE IT'S RAGO'S.
I'M DETECTING ONLY ONE TYPE OF AURA REMNANT, AND IT STOPS HERE.
BUT THE DENSITY READING SUGGESTS HE WAS HERE RECENTLY.
HE MAY STILL BE CLOSE BY.
EXCELLENT. I'LL REGROUP WITH THE SEARCH TEAM.
YOU SHOULD RETURN FOR NOW.
COPY THAT.

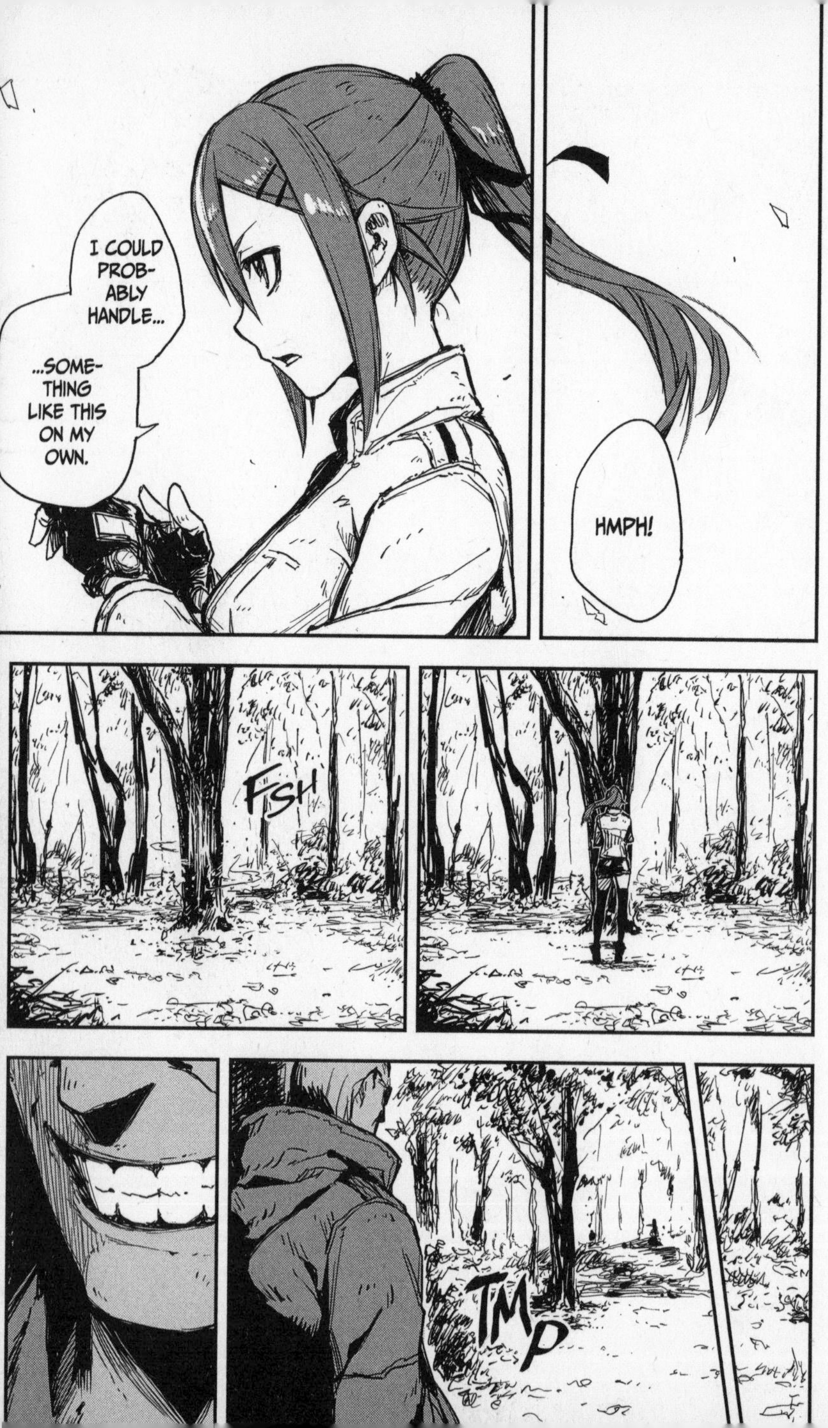
HMPH!
I COULD PROB- ABLY HANDLE...
...SOME- THING LIKE THIS ON MY OWN.
FSH
TMP

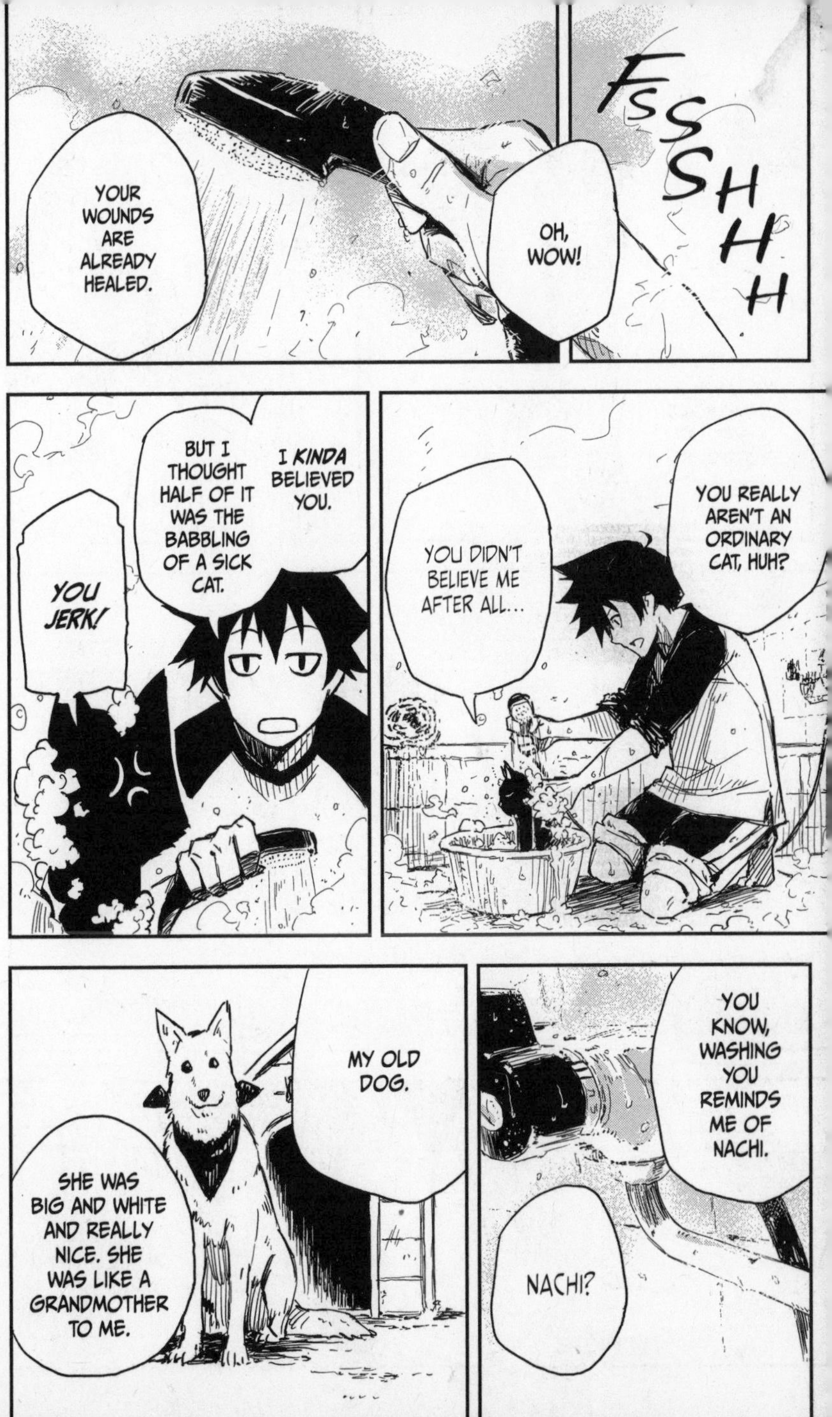
FSSHHH
OH, WOW!
YOUR WOUNDS ARE ALREADY HEALED.
YOU REALLY AREN'T AN ORDINARY CAT, HUH?
YOU DIDN'T BELIEVE ME AFTER ALL...
I *KINDA* BELIEVED YOU.
BUT I THOUGHT HALF OF IT WAS THE BABBLING OF A SICK CAT.
YOU JERK!
YOU KNOW, WASHING YOU REMINDS ME OF NACHI.
NACHI?
MY OLD DOG.
SHE WAS BIG AND WHITE AND REALLY NICE. SHE WAS LIKE A GRANDMOTHER TO ME.

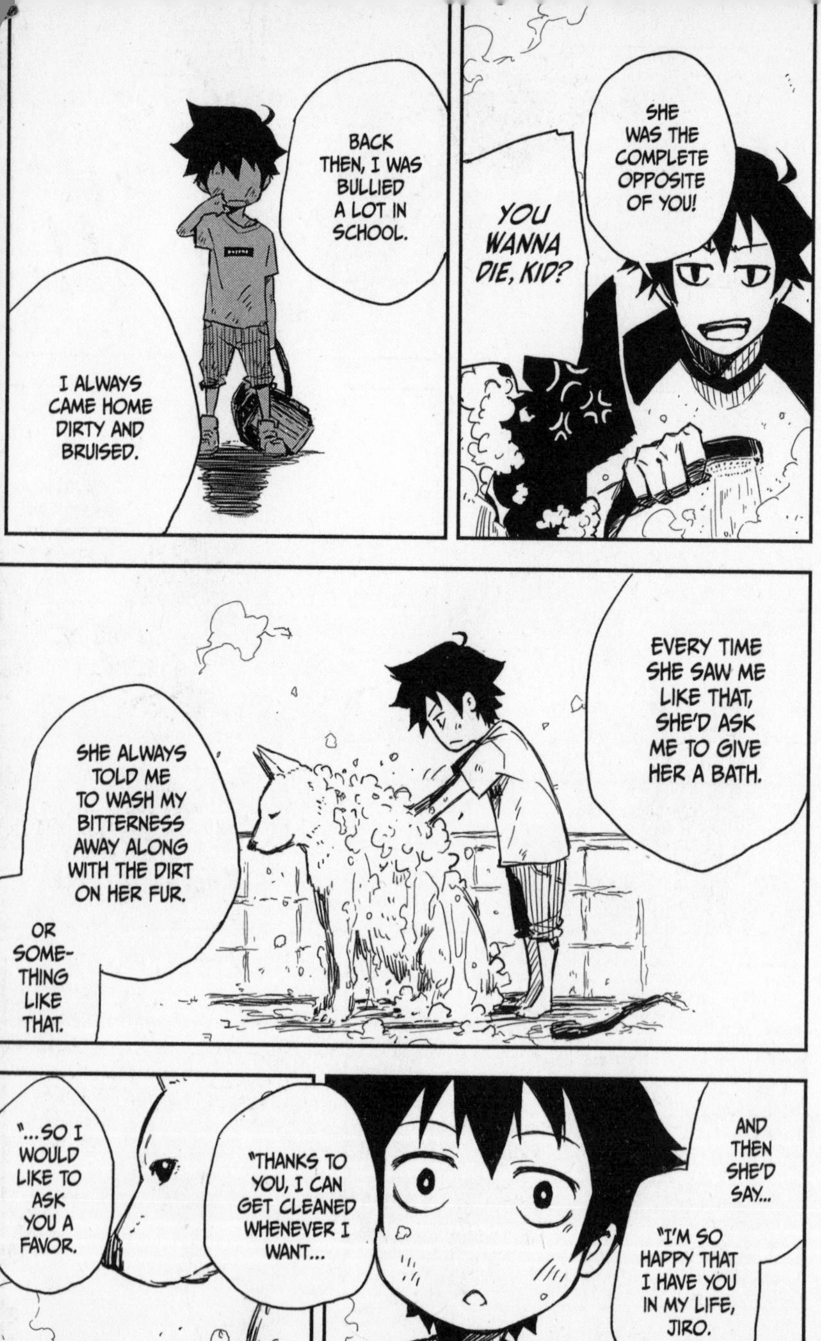
SHE WAS THE COMPLETE OPPOSITE OF YOU!
YOU WANNA DIE, KID?
BACK THEN, I WAS BULLIED A LOT IN SCHOOL.
I ALWAYS CAME HOME DIRTY AND BRUISED.
EVERY TIME SHE SAW ME LIKE THAT, SHE'D ASK ME TO GIVE HER A BATH.
SHE ALWAYS TOLD ME TO WASH MY BITTERNESS AWAY ALONG WITH THE DIRT ON HER FUR.
OR SOME-THING LIKE THAT.
AND THEN SHE'D SAY...
"I'M SO HAPPY THAT I HAVE YOU IN MY LIFE, JIRO.
"THANKS TO YOU, I CAN GET CLEANED WHENEVER I WANT...
"...SO I WOULD LIKE TO ASK YOU A FAVOR.

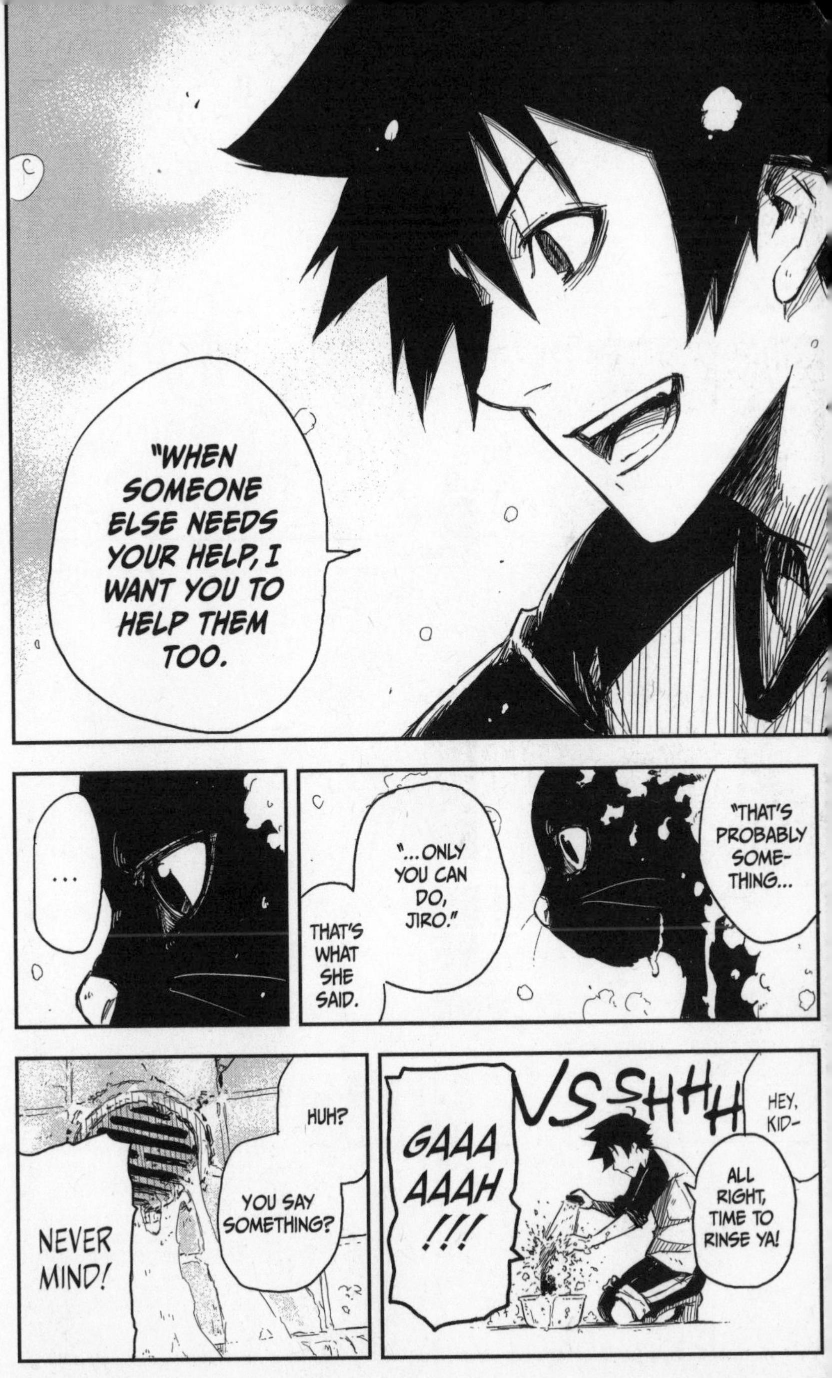
"WHEN SOMEONE ELSE NEEDS YOUR HELP, I WANT YOU TO HELP THEM TOO.
"THAT'S PROBABLY SOMETHING...
"...ONLY YOU CAN DO, JIRO."
THAT'S WHAT SHE SAID.
...
VSSHHH
HEY, KID-
ALL RIGHT, TIME TO RINSE YA!
GAAAAAAH!!!
HUH?
YOU SAY SOMETHING?
NEVER MIND!

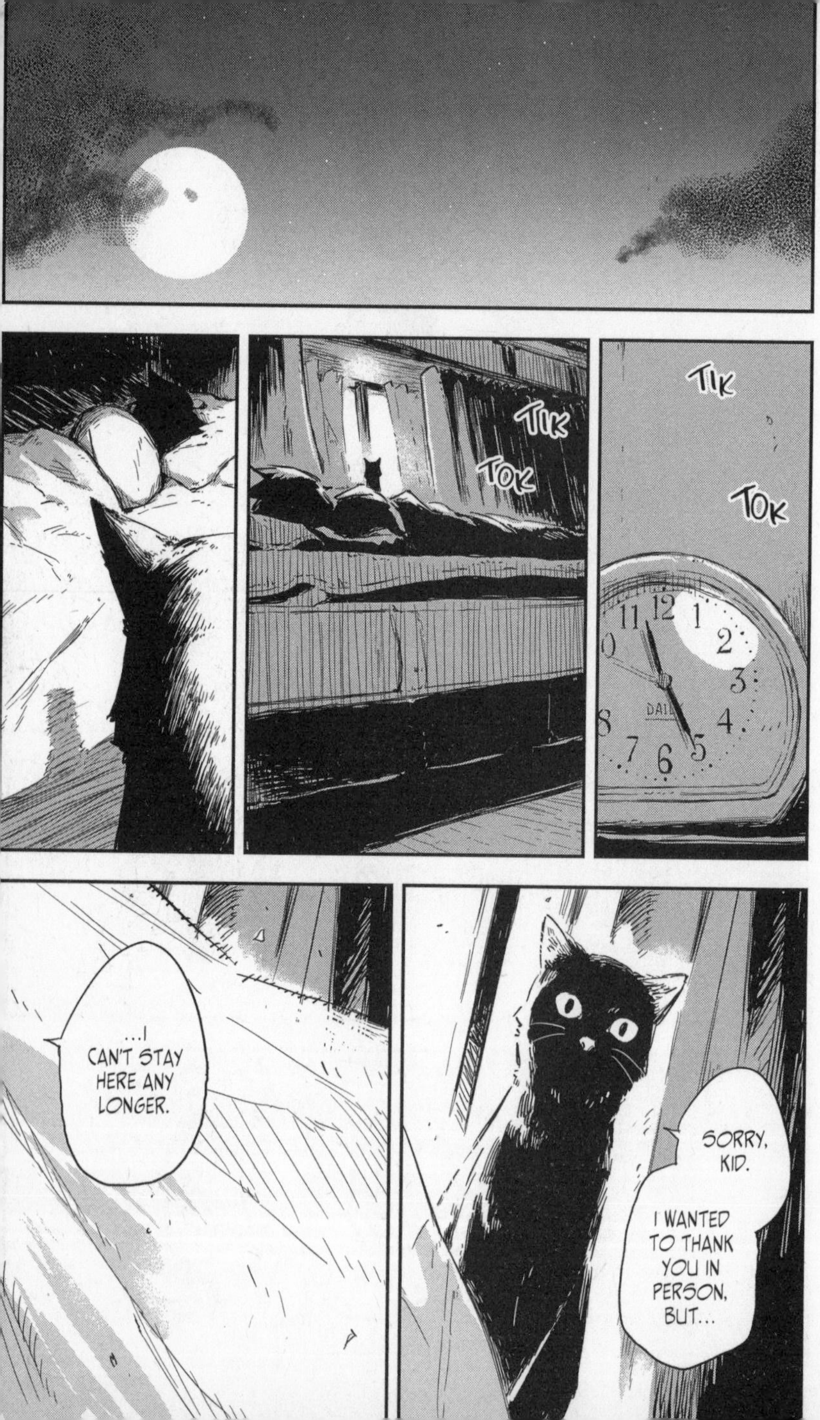
TIK
TOK
TIK
TOK
SORRY, KID.
I WANTED TO THANK YOU IN PERSON, BUT...
...I CAN'T STAY HERE ANY LONGER.

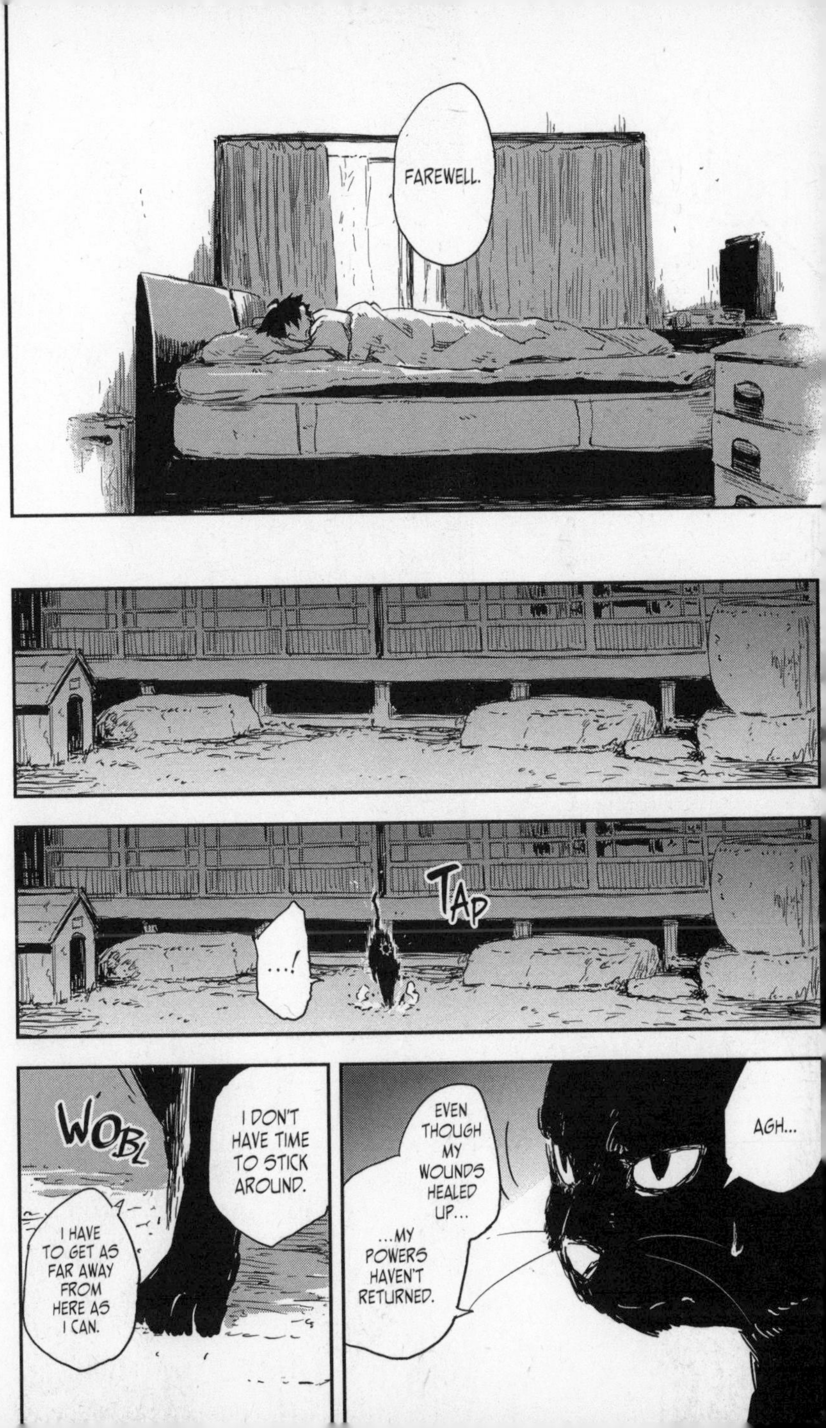
FAREWELL.
TAP
...!
AGH...
EVEN THOUGH MY WOUNDS HEALED UP...
...MY POWERS HAVEN'T RETURNED.
I DON'T HAVE TIME TO STICK AROUND.
WOBL
I HAVE TO GET AS FAR AWAY FROM HERE AS I CAN.

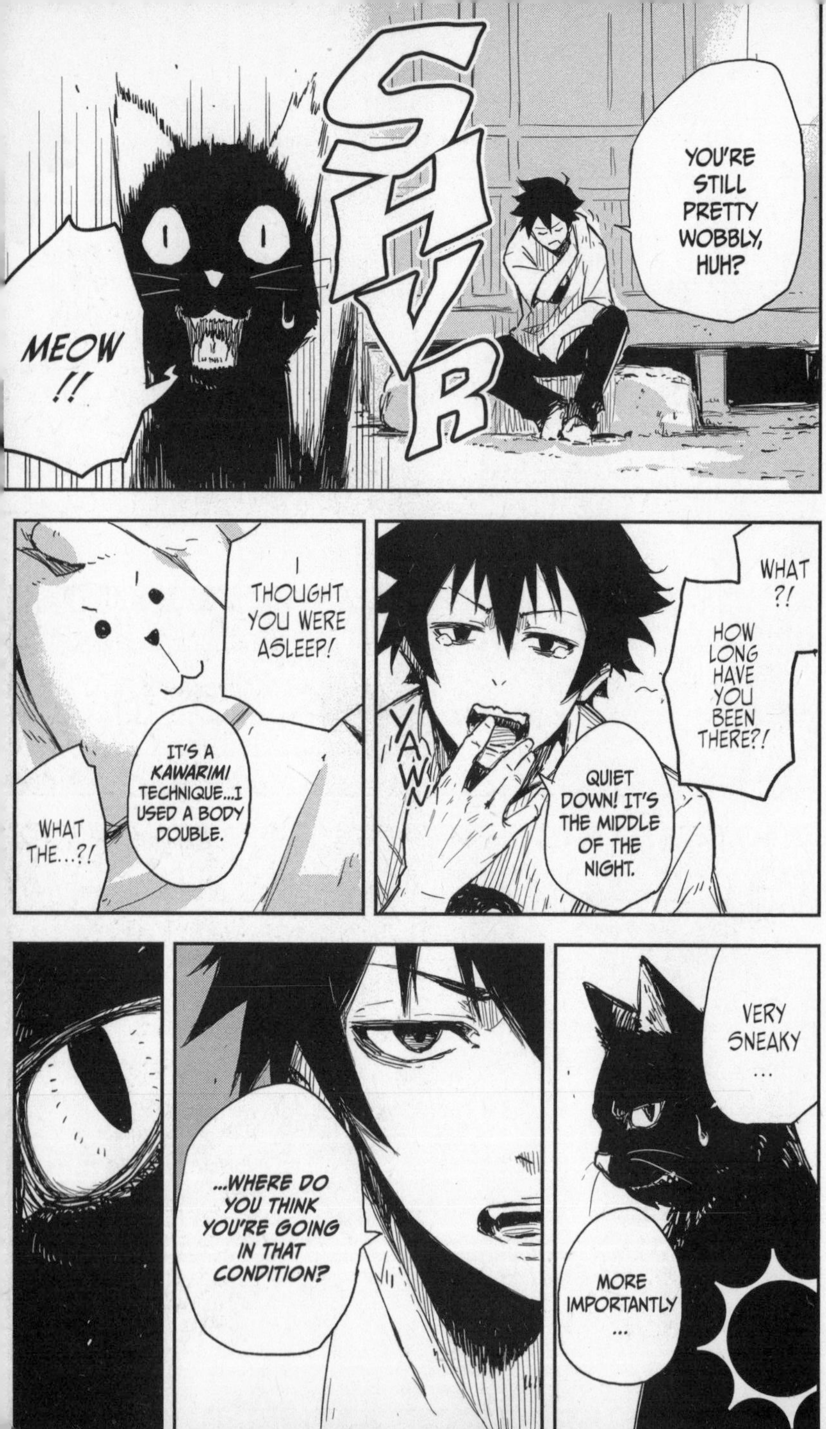
YOU'RE STILL PRETTY WOBBLY, HUH?
SHVR
MEOW!!
WHAT?!
HOW LONG HAVE YOU BEEN THERE?!
YAWN
QUIET DOWN! IT'S THE MIDDLE OF THE NIGHT.
I THOUGHT YOU WERE ASLEEP!
IT'S A KAWARIMI TECHNIQUE...I USED A BODY DOUBLE.
WHAT THE...?!
VERY SNEAKY...
MORE IMPORTANTLY...
...WHERE DO YOU THINK YOU'RE GOING IN THAT CONDITION?

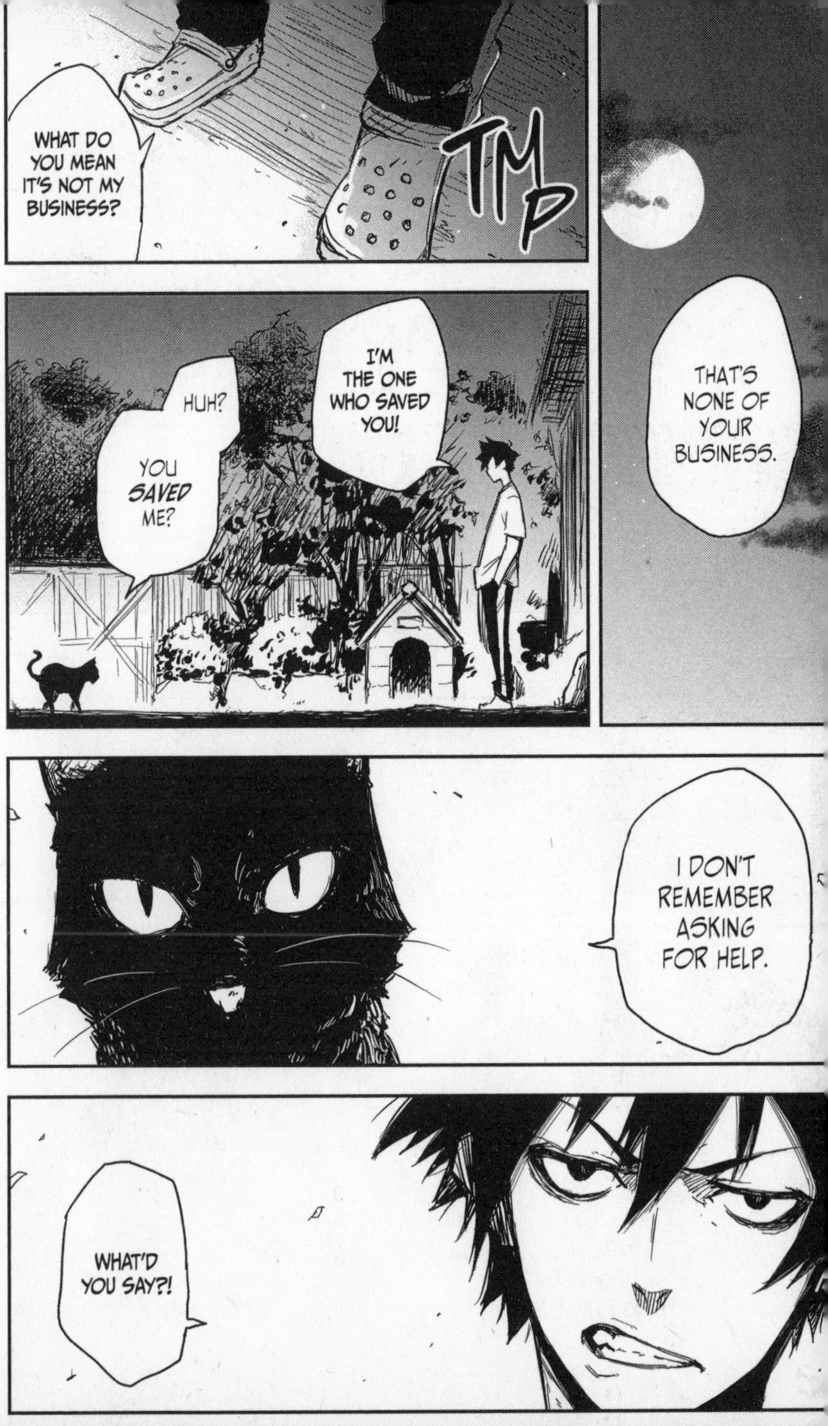
THAT'S NONE OF YOUR BUSINESS.
TMP
WHAT DO YOU MEAN IT'S NOT MY BUSINESS?
I'M THE ONE WHO SAVED YOU!
HUH?
YOU SAVED ME?
I DON'T REMEMBER ASKING FOR HELP.
WHAT'D YOU SAY?!

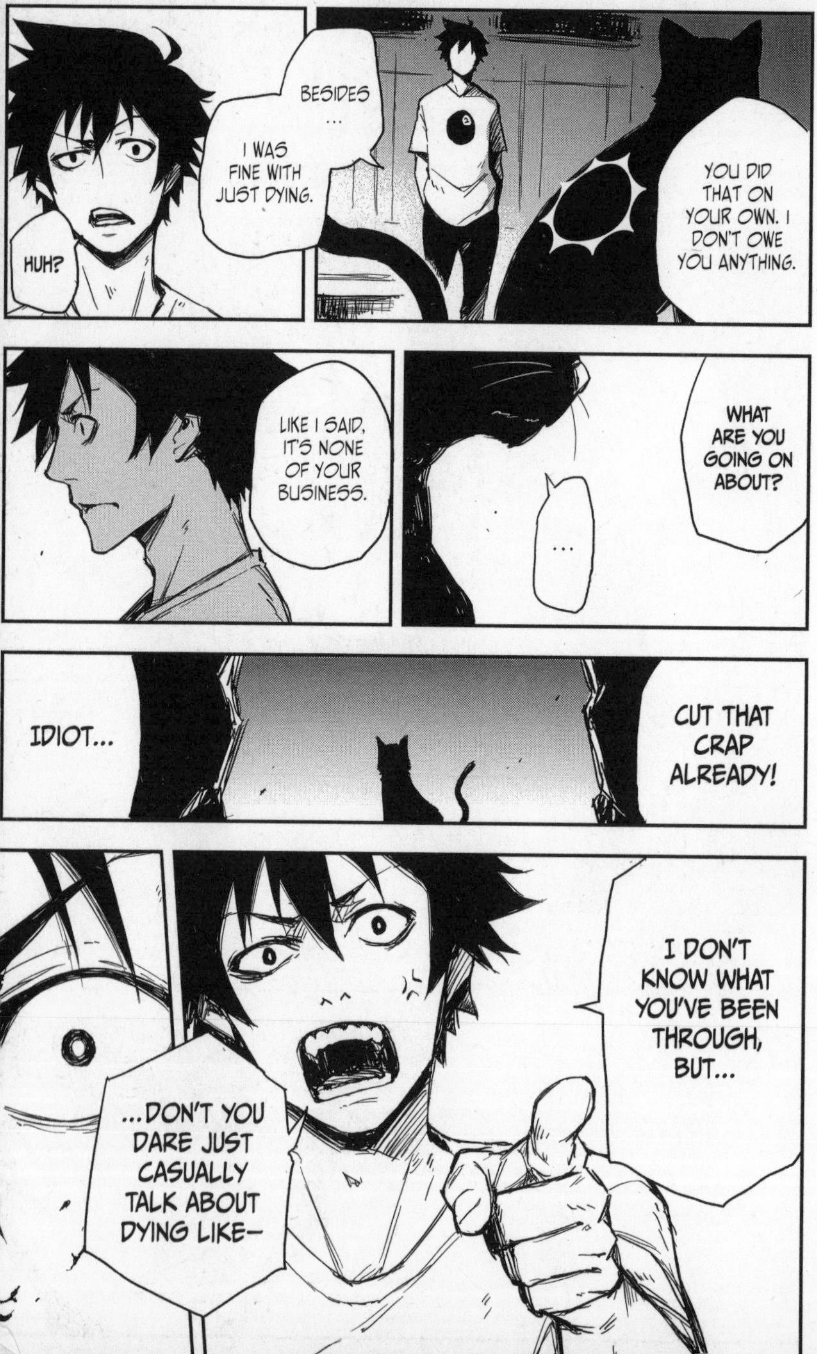
YOU DID THAT ON YOUR OWN. I DON'T OWE YOU ANYTHING.
BESIDES ... I WAS FINE WITH JUST DYING.
HUH?
WHAT ARE YOU GOING ON ABOUT?
...
LIKE I SAID, IT'S NONE OF YOUR BUSINESS.
CUT THAT CRAP ALREADY!
IDIOT...
I DON'T KNOW WHAT YOU'VE BEEN THROUGH, BUT...
...DON'T YOU DARE JUST CASUALLY TALK ABOUT DYING LIKE–

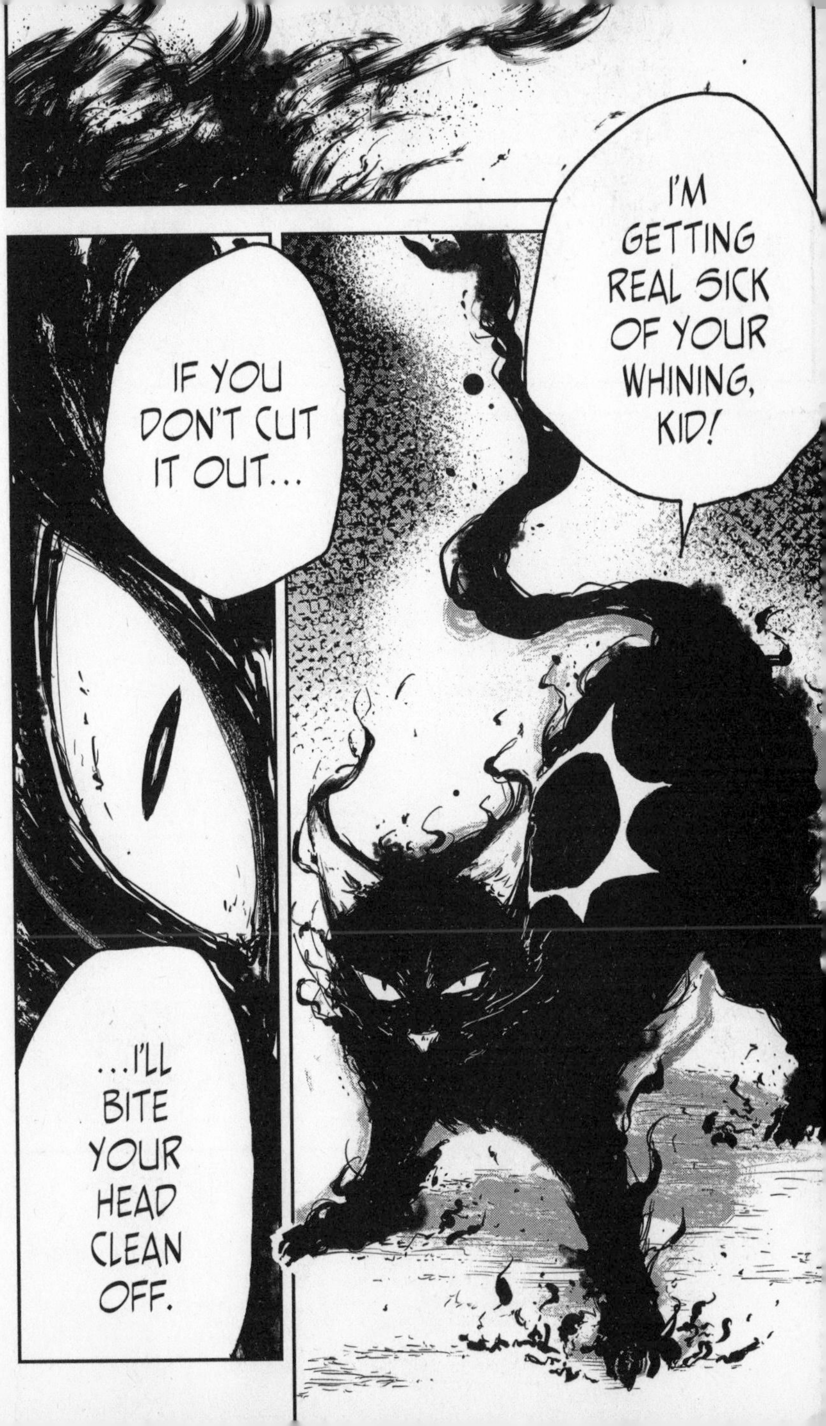
I'M GETTING REAL SICK OF YOUR WHINING, KID!
IF YOU DON'T CUT IT OUT...
...I'LL BITE YOUR HEAD CLEAN OFF.

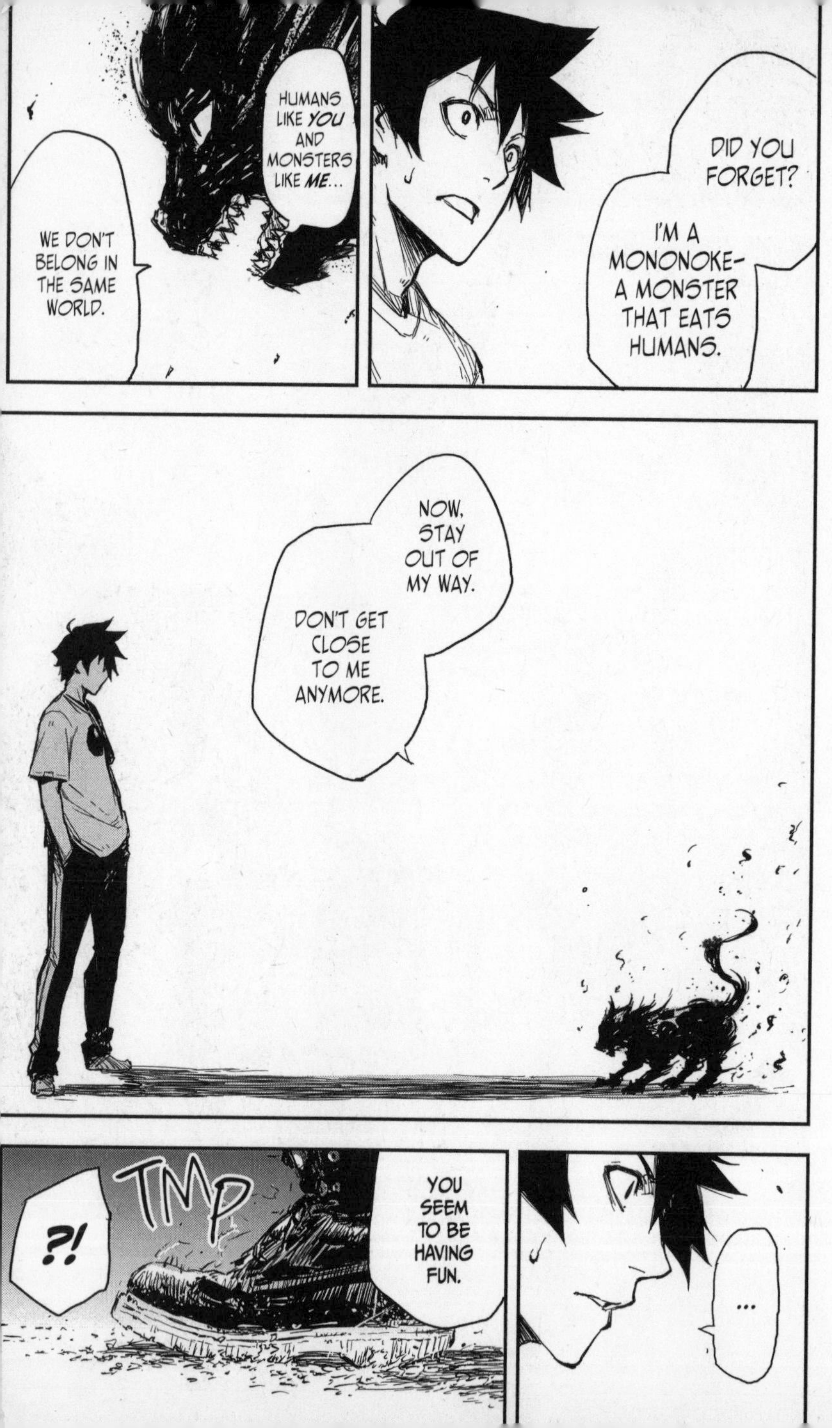
DID YOU FORGET?
I'M A MONONOKE- A MONSTER THAT EATS HUMANS.
HUMANS LIKE *YOU* AND MONSTERS LIKE *ME*...
WE DON'T BELONG IN THE SAME WORLD.
NOW, STAY OUT OF MY WAY.
DON'T GET CLOSE TO ME ANYMORE.
...
YOU SEEM TO BE HAVING FUN.
TMP
?!

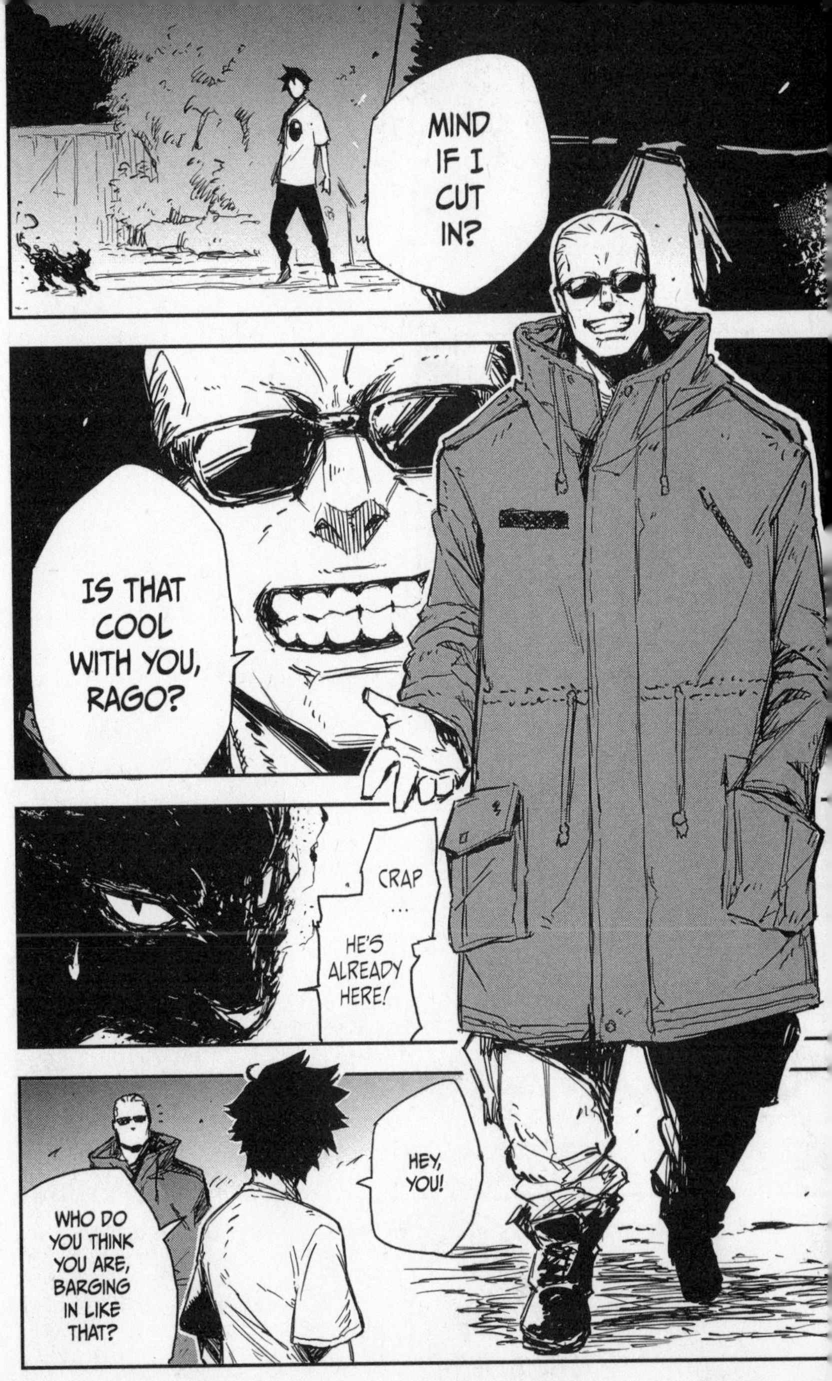
MIND IF I CUT IN?
IS THAT COOL WITH YOU, RAGO?
CRAP ...
HE'S ALREADY HERE!
HEY, YOU!
WHO DO YOU THINK YOU ARE, BARGING IN LIKE THAT?

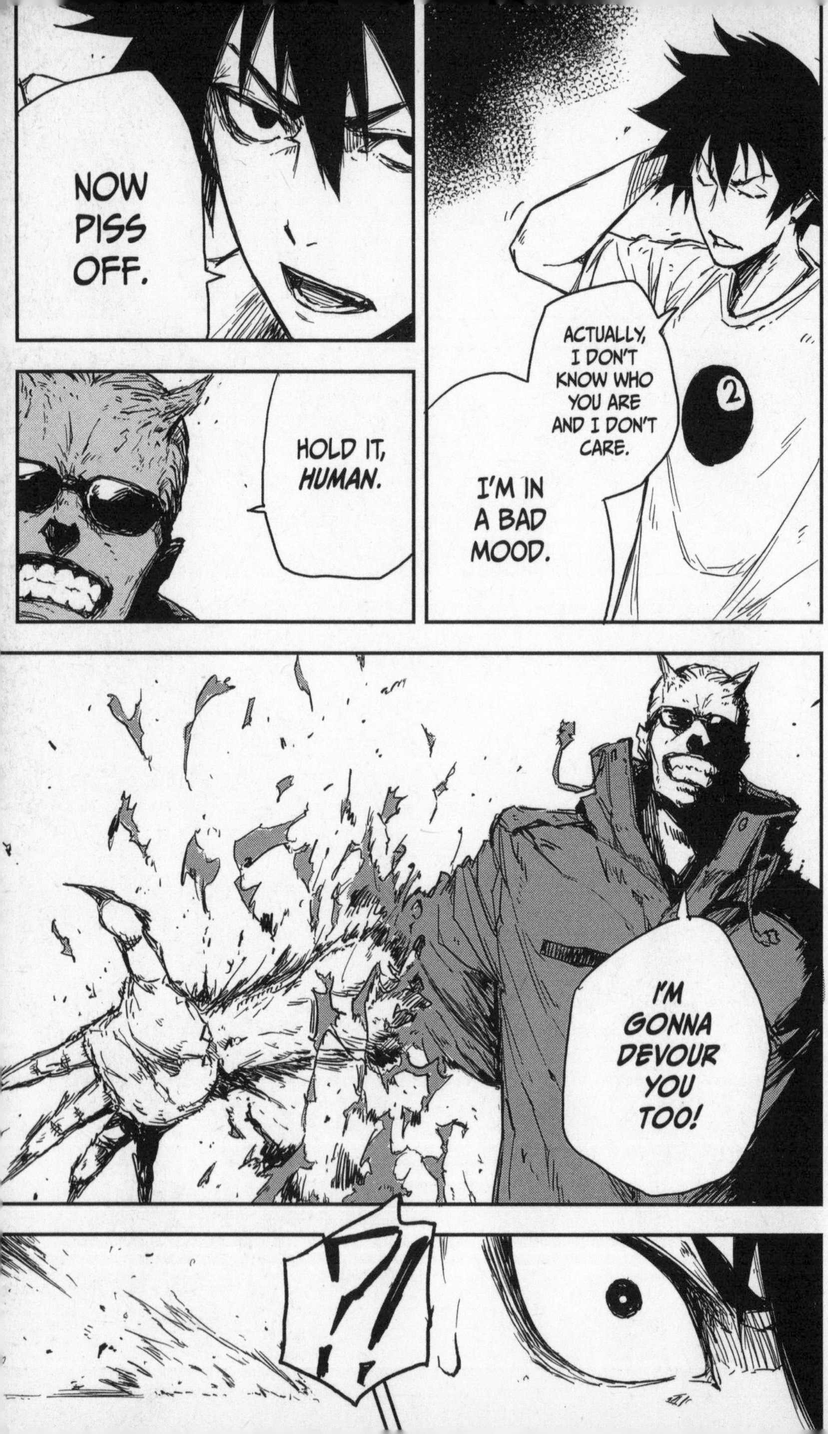
ACTUALLY, I DON'T KNOW WHO YOU ARE AND I DON'T CARE.
I'M IN A BAD MOOD.
NOW PISS OFF.
HOLD IT, *HUMAN.*
I'M GONNA DEVOUR YOU TOO!
!?

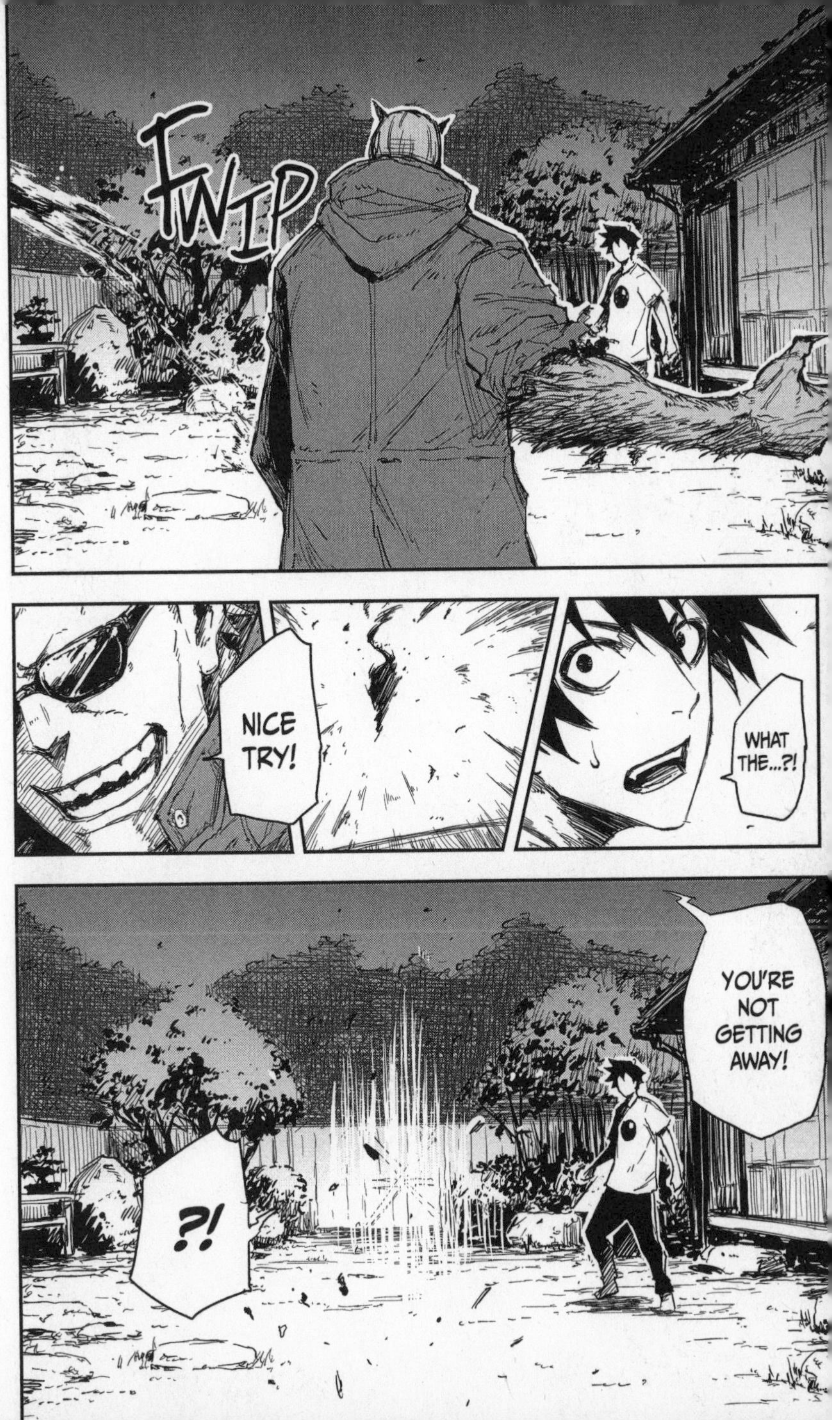
FWIP
WHAT THE...?!
NICE TRY!
YOU'RE NOT GETTING AWAY!
?!

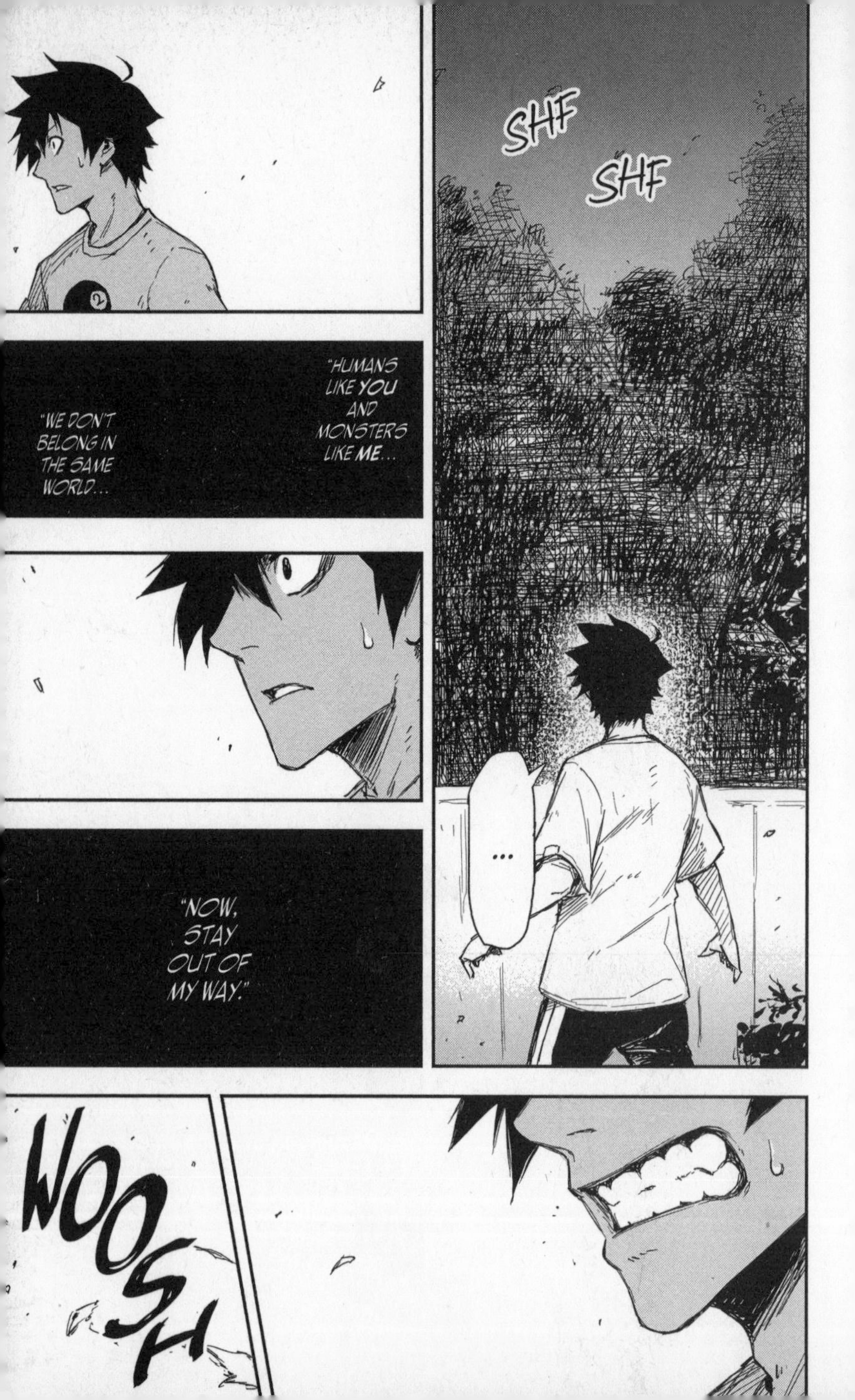
SHF
SHF
...
"HUMANS LIKE YOU AND MONSTERS LIKE ME...
"WE DON'T BELONG IN THE SAME WORLD...
"NOW, STAY OUT OF MY WAY."
WOOSH

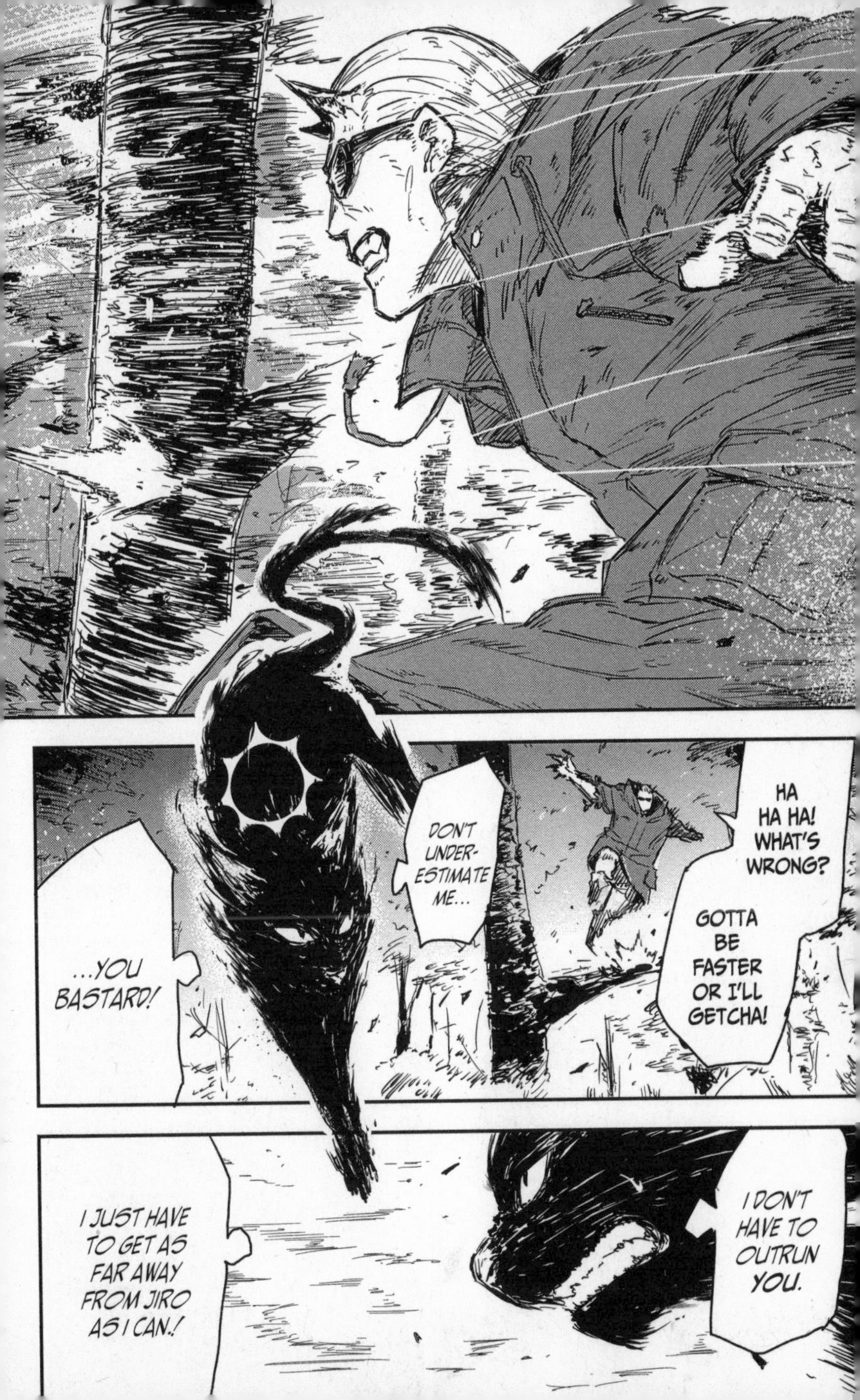
HA HA HA! WHAT'S WRONG?
GOTTA BE FASTER OR I'LL GETCHA!
DON'T UNDER-ESTIMATE ME...
...YOU BASTARD!
I DON'T HAVE TO OUTRUN YOU.
I JUST HAVE TO GET AS FAR AWAY FROM JIRO AS I CAN!

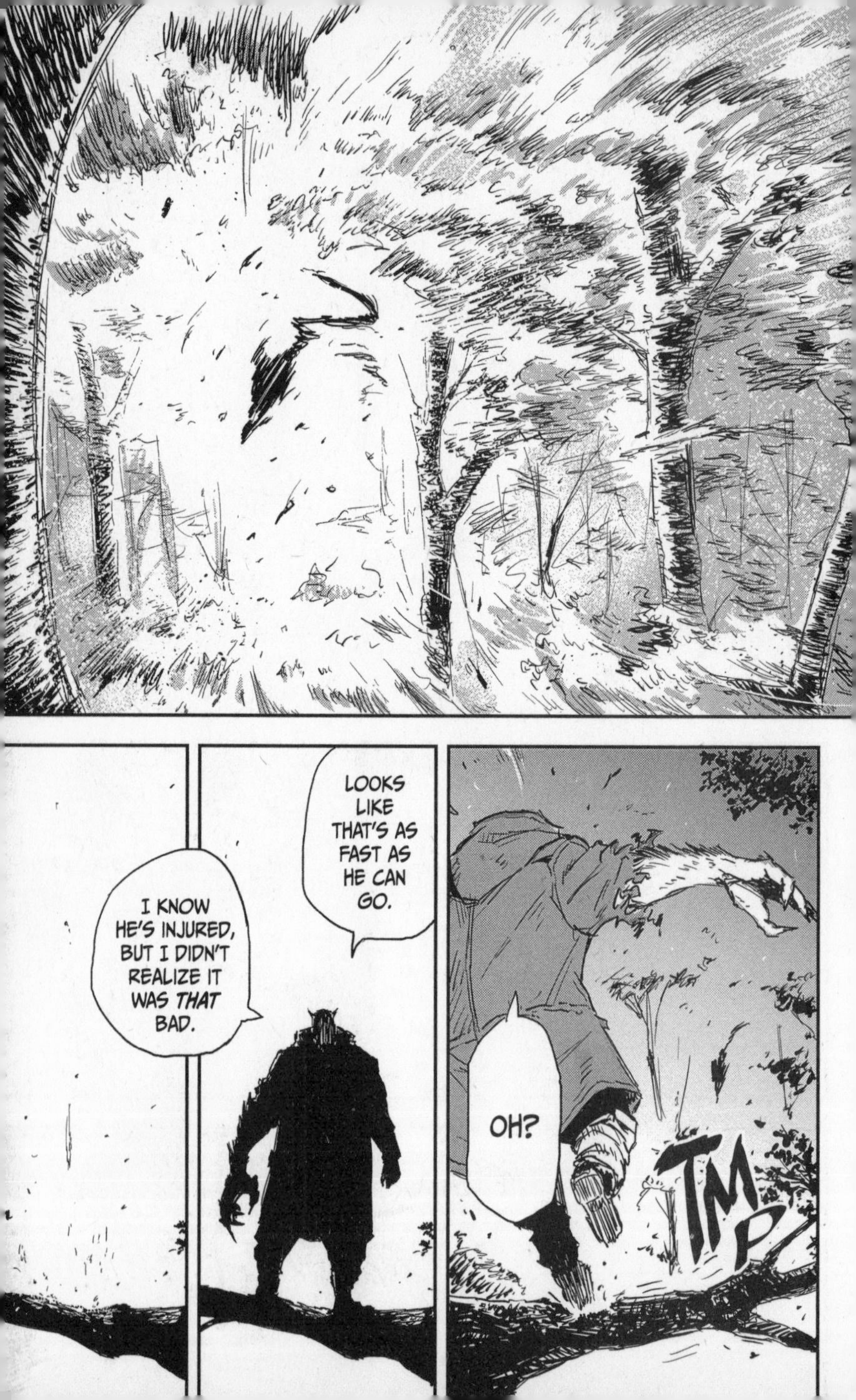
OH?
TMP
LOOKS LIKE THAT'S AS FAST AS HE CAN GO.
I KNOW HE'S INJURED, BUT I DIDN'T REALIZE IT WAS *THAT* BAD.

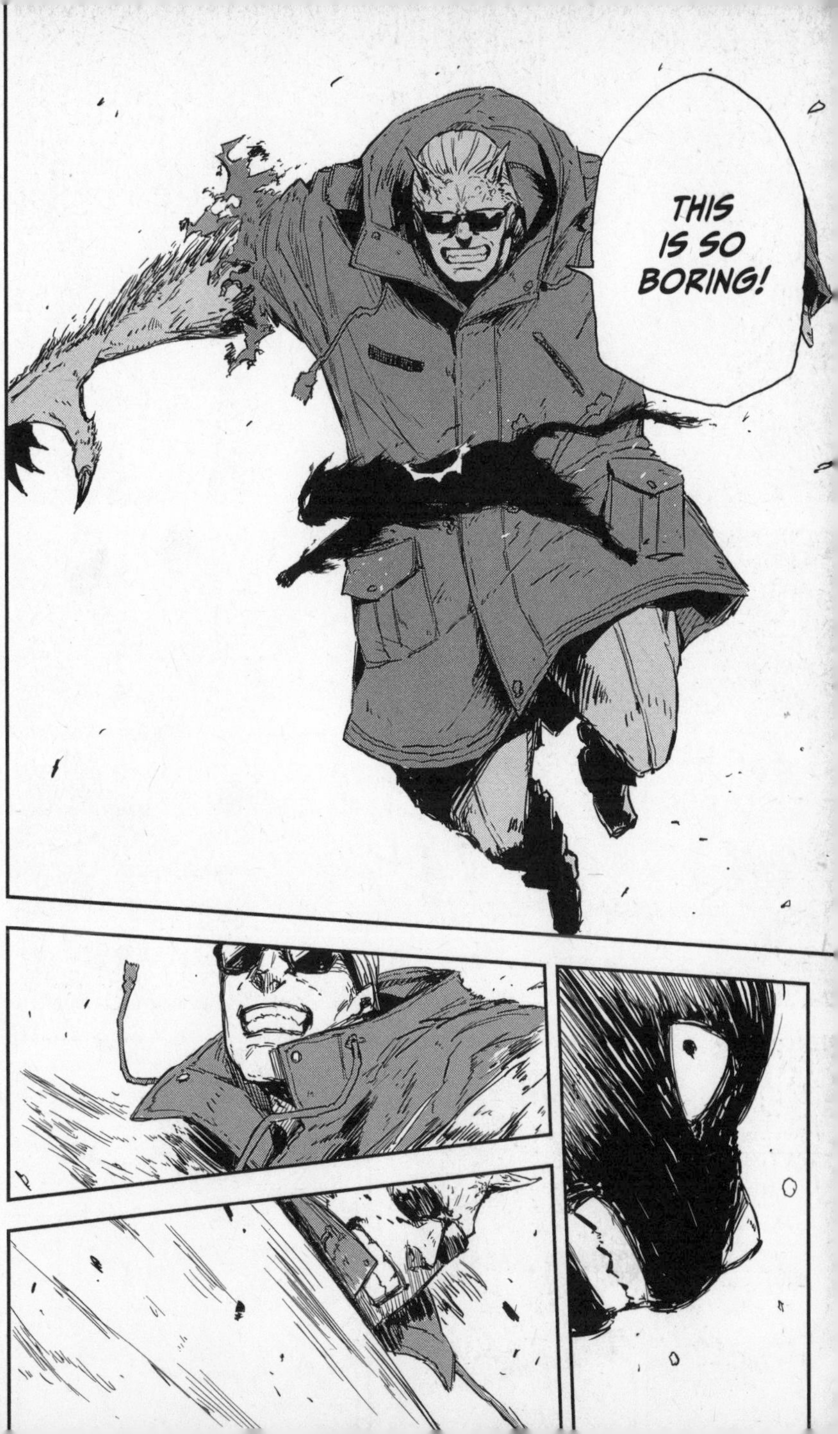
THIS IS SO BORING!

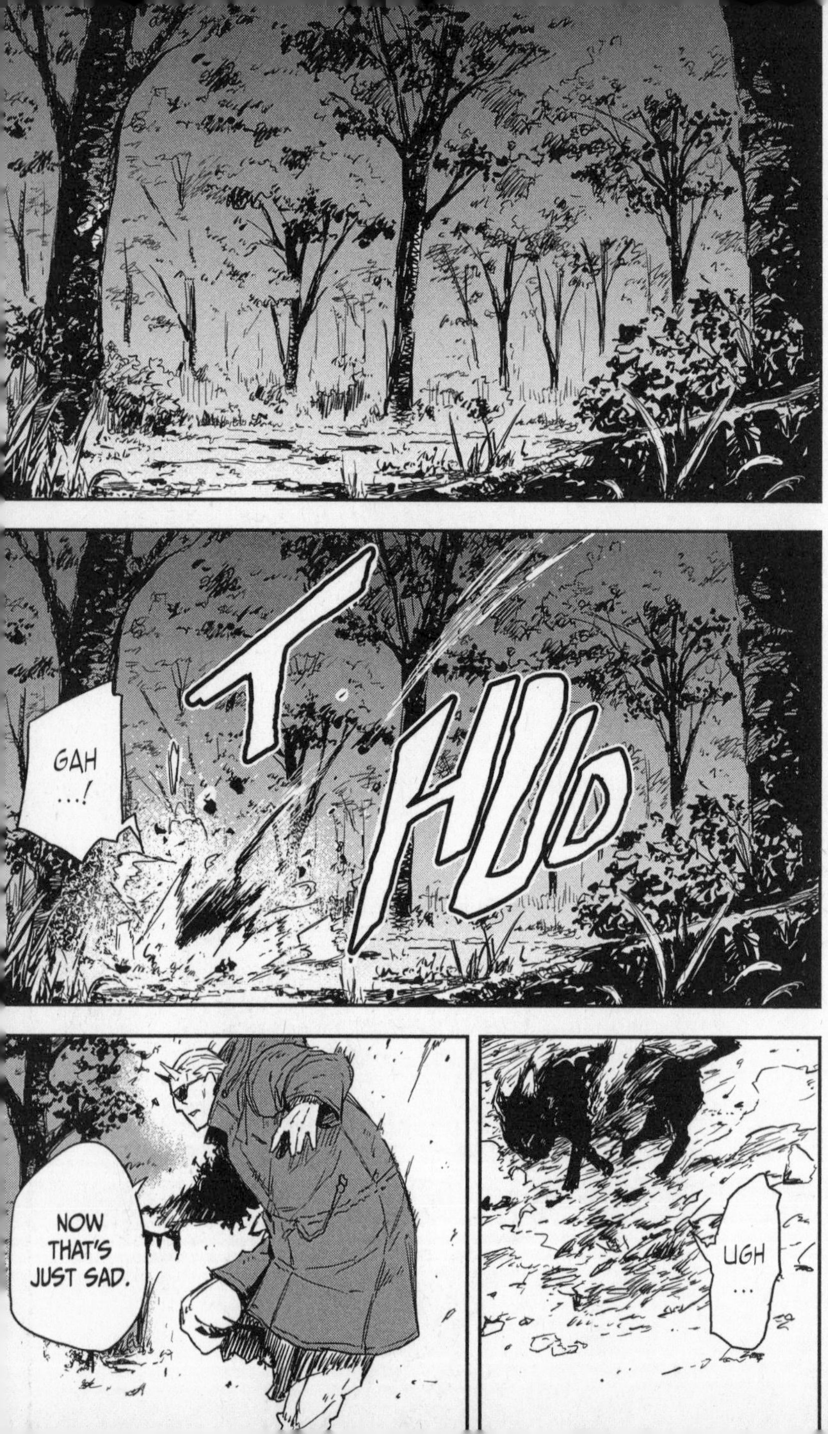
THUD
GAH ...!
UGH ...
NOW THAT'S JUST SAD.

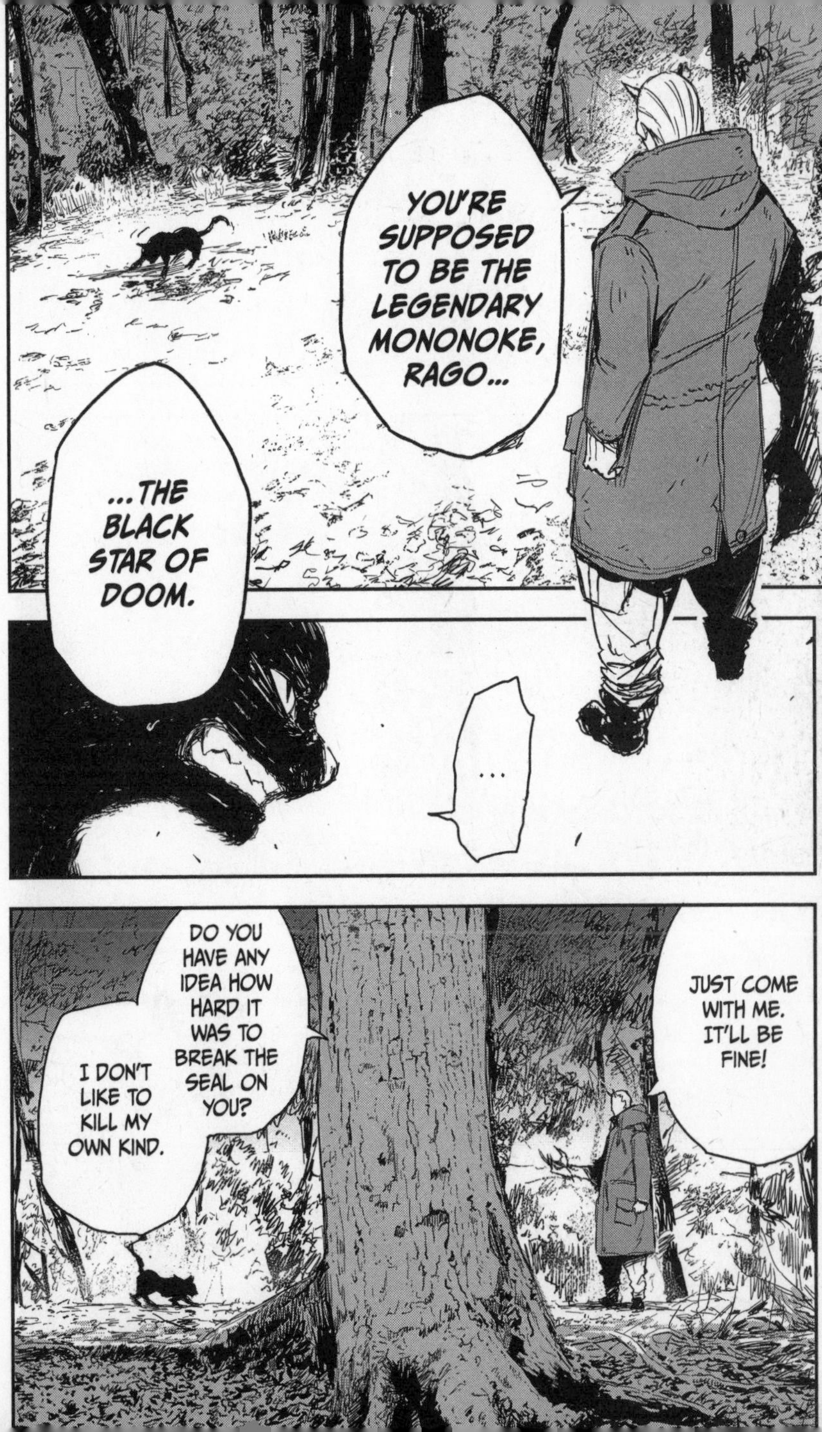
YOU'RE SUPPOSED TO BE THE LEGENDARY MONONOKE, RAGO...
...THE BLACK STAR OF DOOM.
...
JUST COME WITH ME. IT'LL BE FINE!
DO YOU HAVE ANY IDEA HOW HARD IT WAS TO BREAK THE SEAL ON YOU?
I DON'T LIKE TO KILL MY OWN KIND.

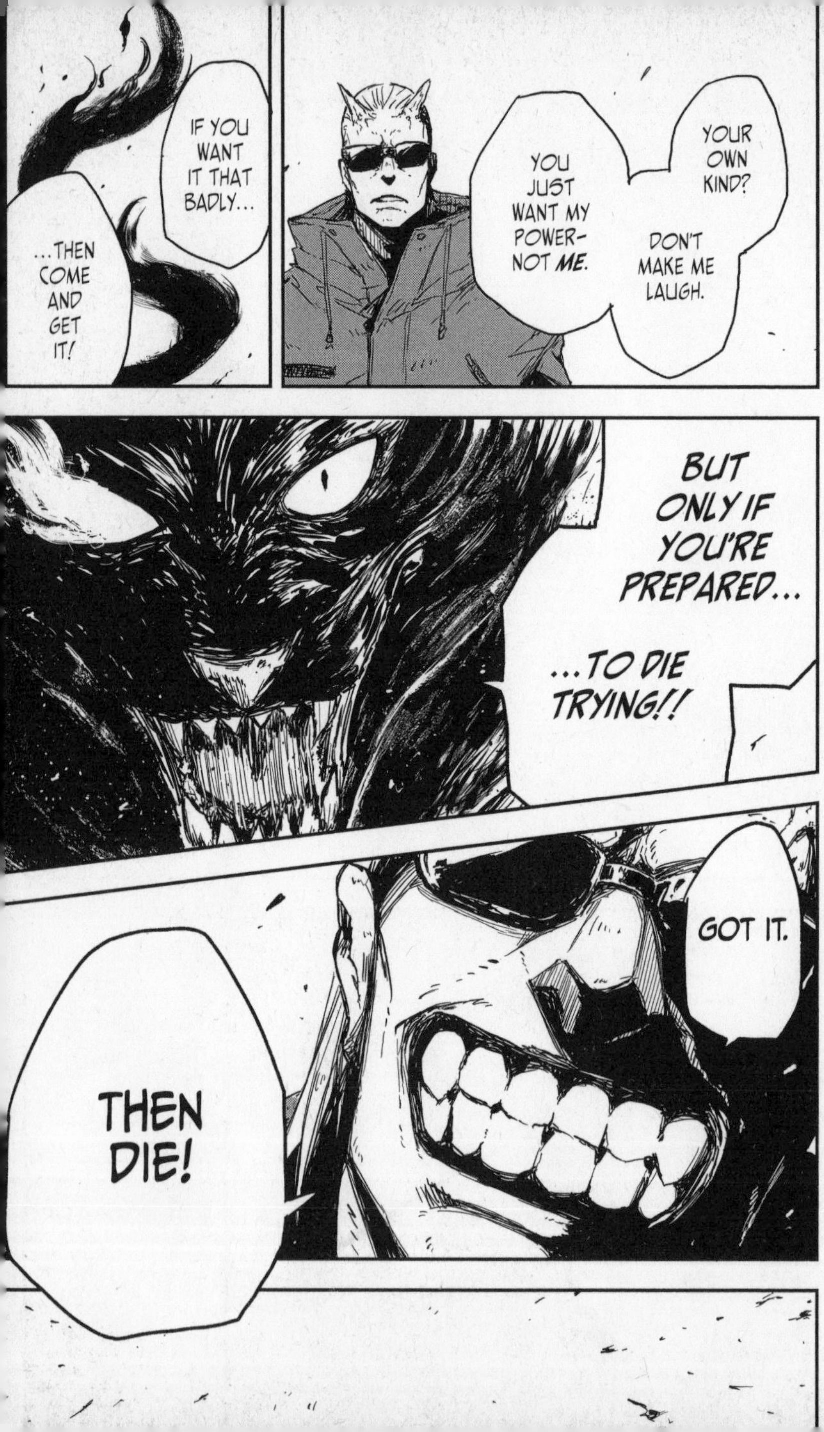
YOUR OWN KIND?
DON'T MAKE ME LAUGH.
YOU JUST WANT MY POWER-NOT *ME*.
IF YOU WANT IT THAT BADLY...
...THEN COME AND GET IT!
BUT ONLY IF YOU'RE PREPARED...
...TO DIE TRYING!!
GOT IT.
THEN DIE!

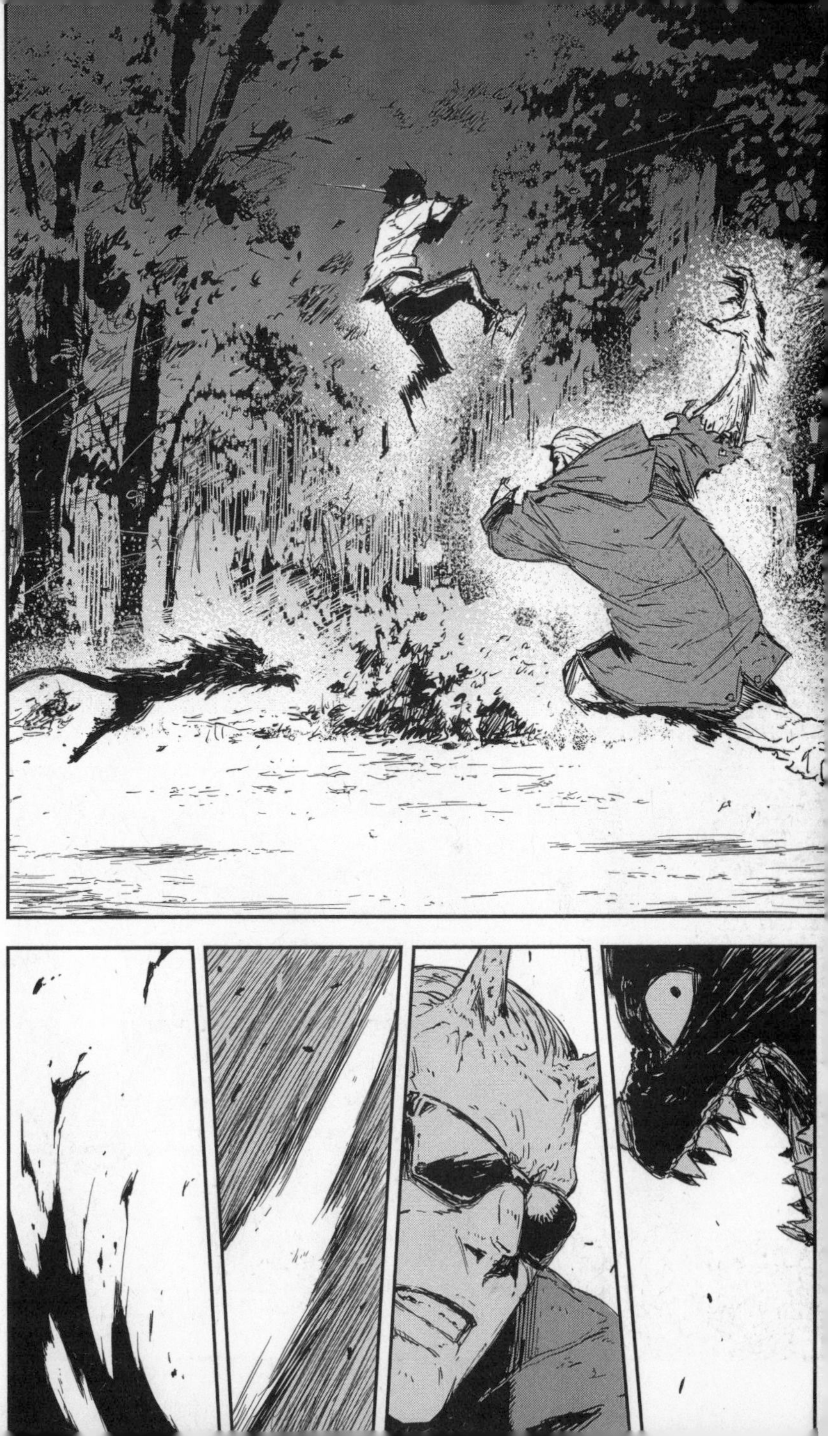

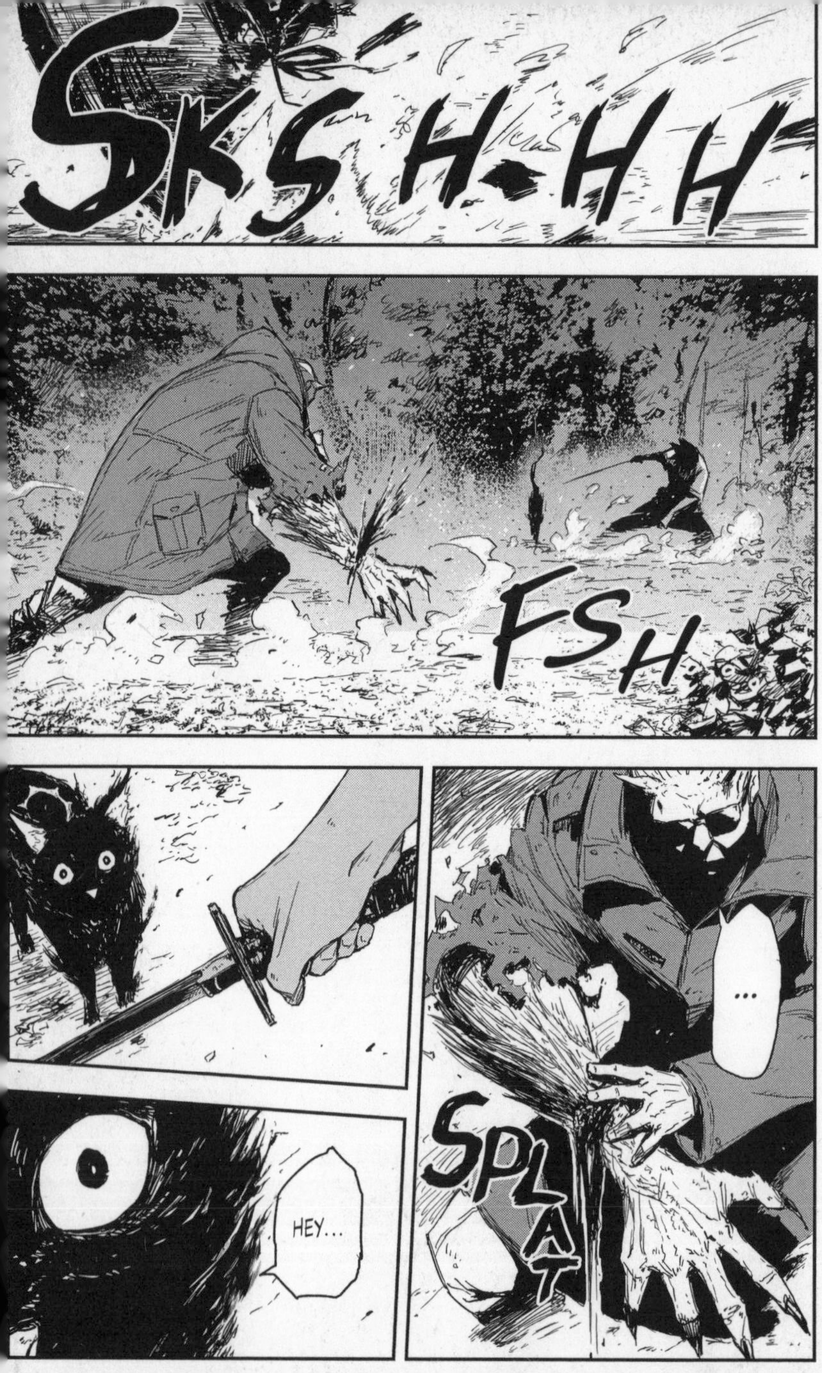
SKSH-HH
FSH
...
SPLAT
HEY...

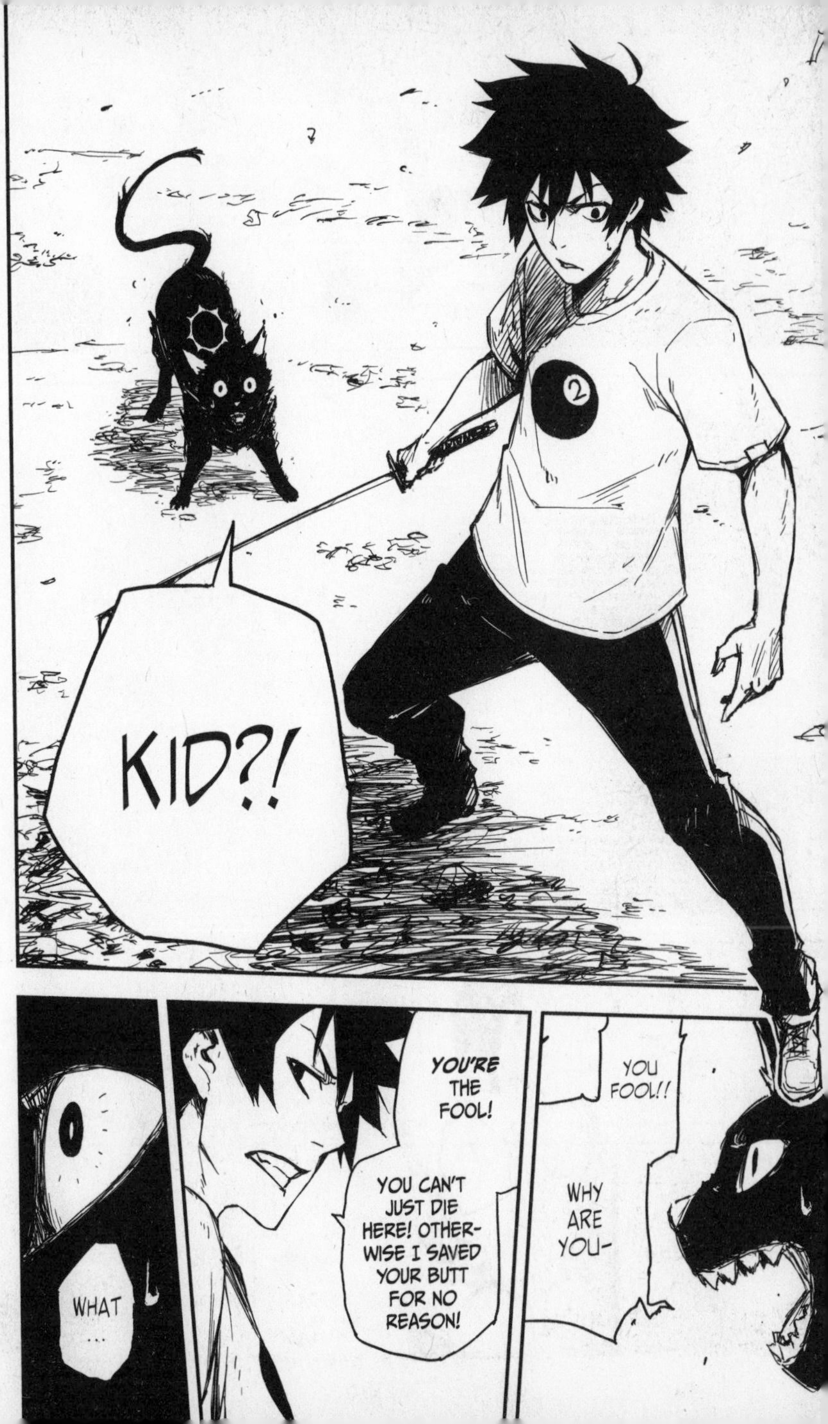
KID?!
YOU FOOL!!
WHY ARE YOU-
YOU'RE THE FOOL!
YOU CAN'T JUST DIE HERE! OTHER-WISE I SAVED YOUR BUTT FOR NO REASON!
WHAT ...

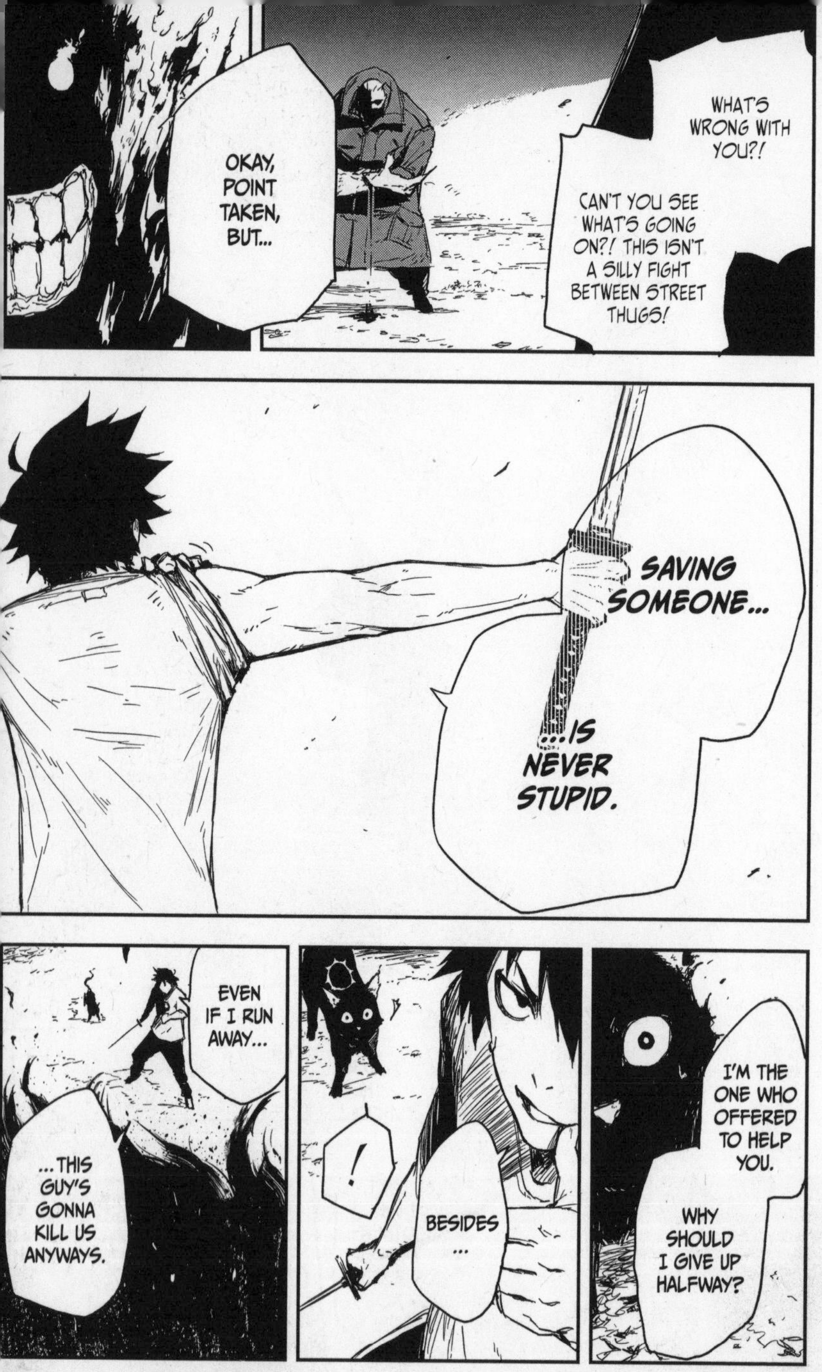
WHAT'S WRONG WITH YOU?!
CAN'T YOU SEE WHAT'S GOING ON?! THIS ISN'T A SILLY FIGHT BETWEEN STREET THUGS!
OKAY, POINT TAKEN, BUT...
SAVING SOMEONE...
...IS NEVER STUPID.
I'M THE ONE WHO OFFERED TO HELP YOU.
WHY SHOULD I GIVE UP HALFWAY?
!
BESIDES...
EVEN IF I RUN AWAY...
...THIS GUY'S GONNA KILL US ANYWAYS.

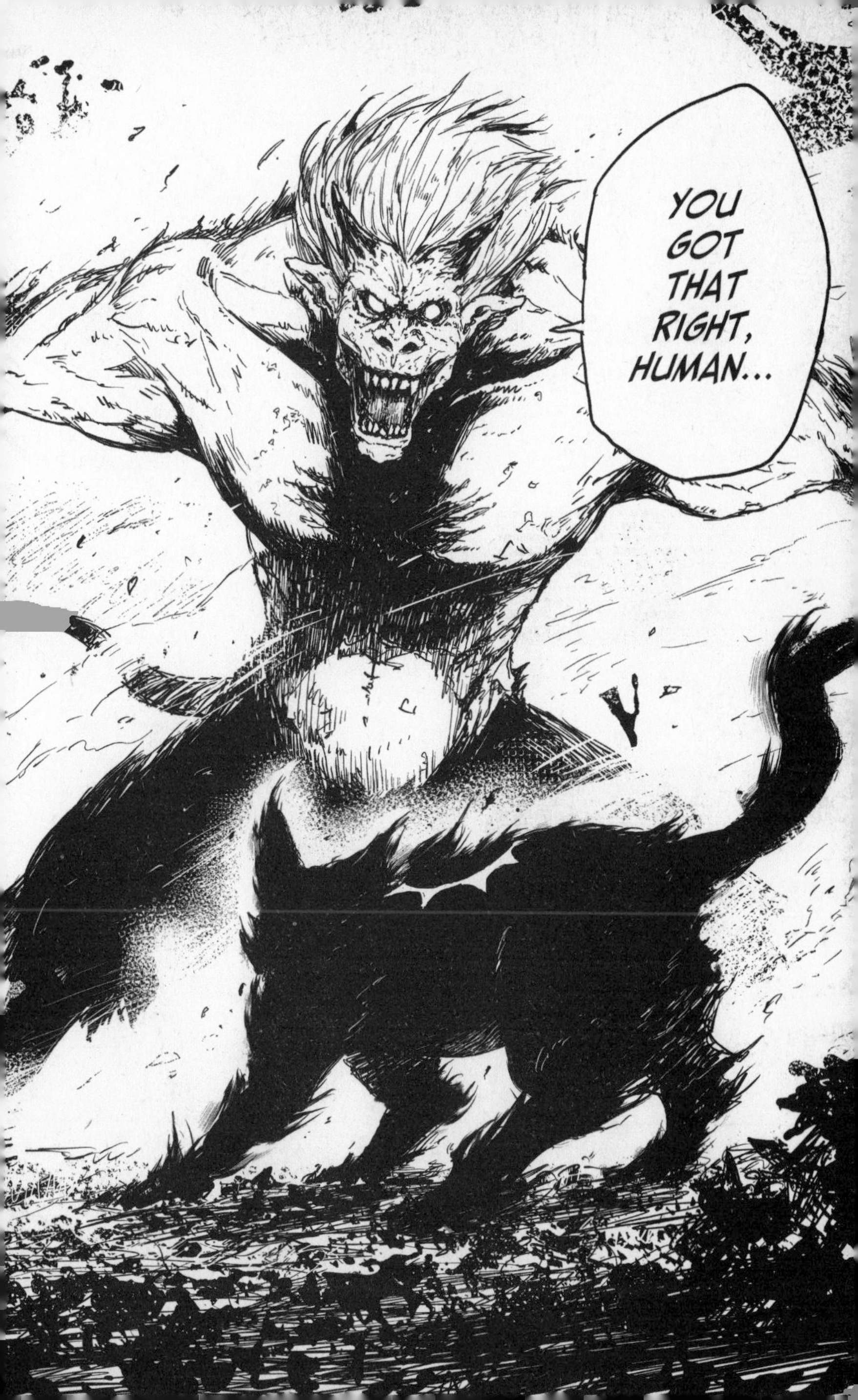
YOU GOT THAT RIGHT, HUMAN...

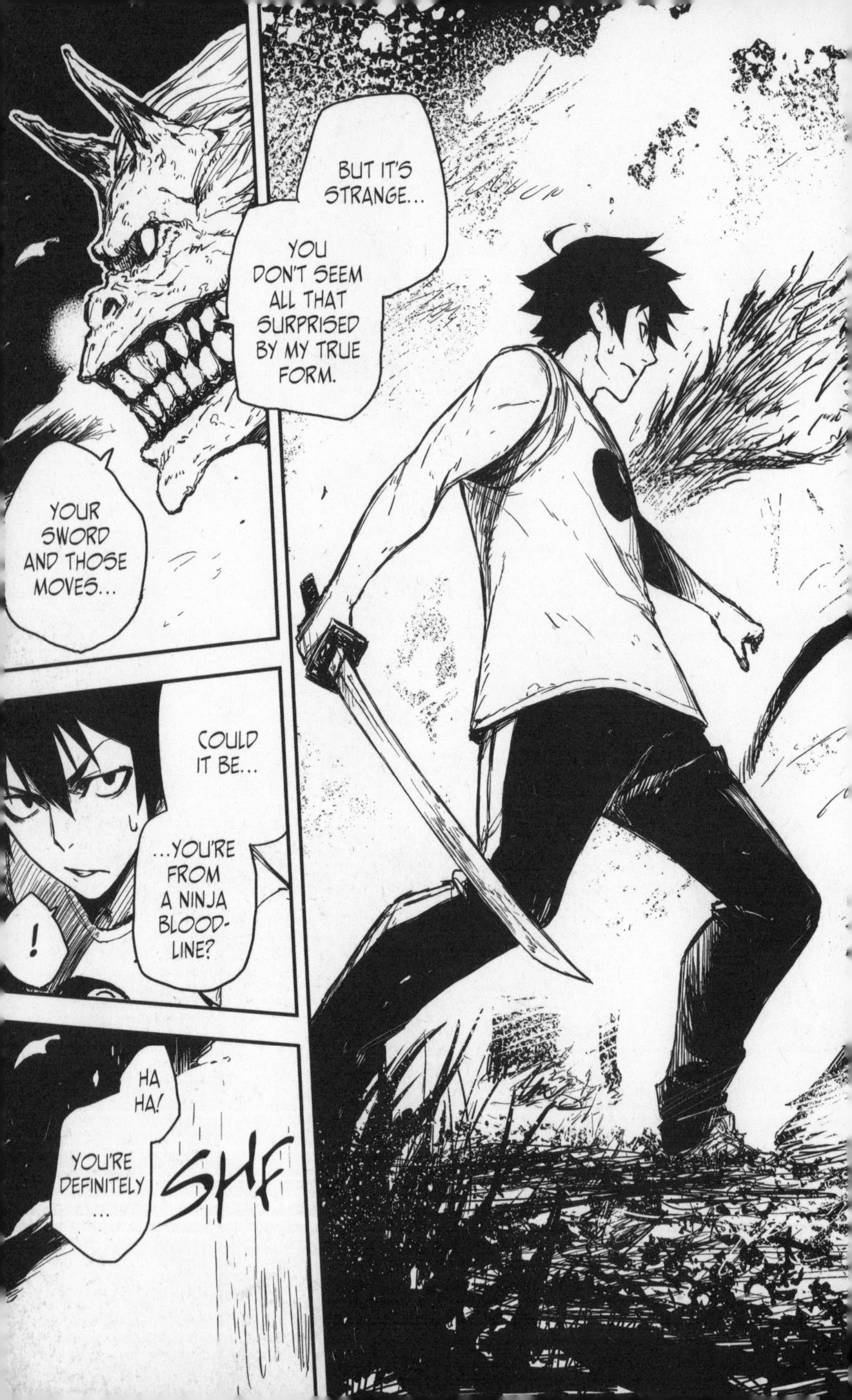
BUT IT'S STRANGE...
YOU DON'T SEEM ALL THAT SURPRISED BY MY TRUE FORM.
YOUR SWORD AND THOSE MOVES...
COULD IT BE...
...YOU'RE FROM A NINJA BLOOD-LINE?
!
HA HA!
SHF
YOU'RE DEFINITELY...

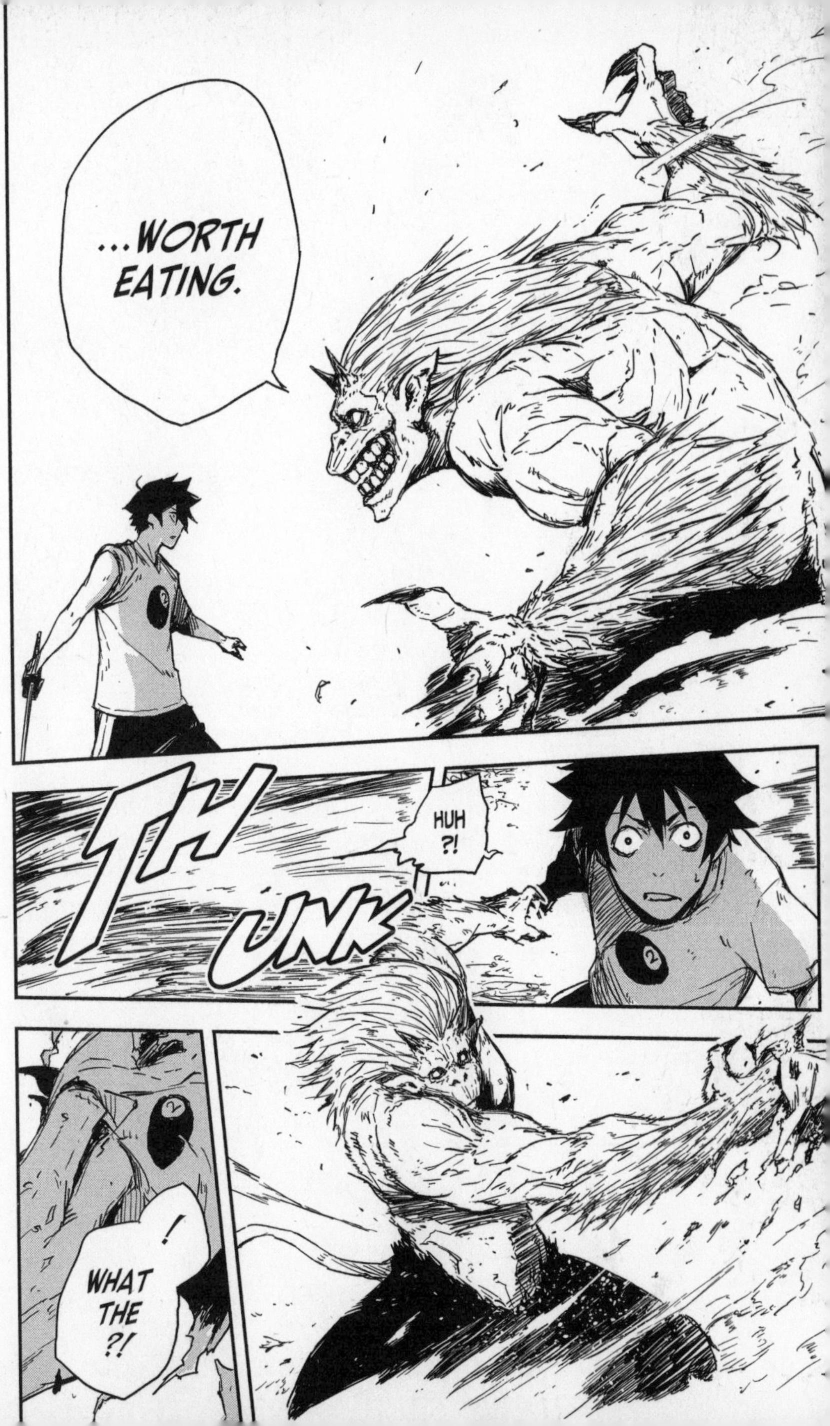
...WORTH EATING.
HUH ?!
THUNK
!
WHAT THE ?!

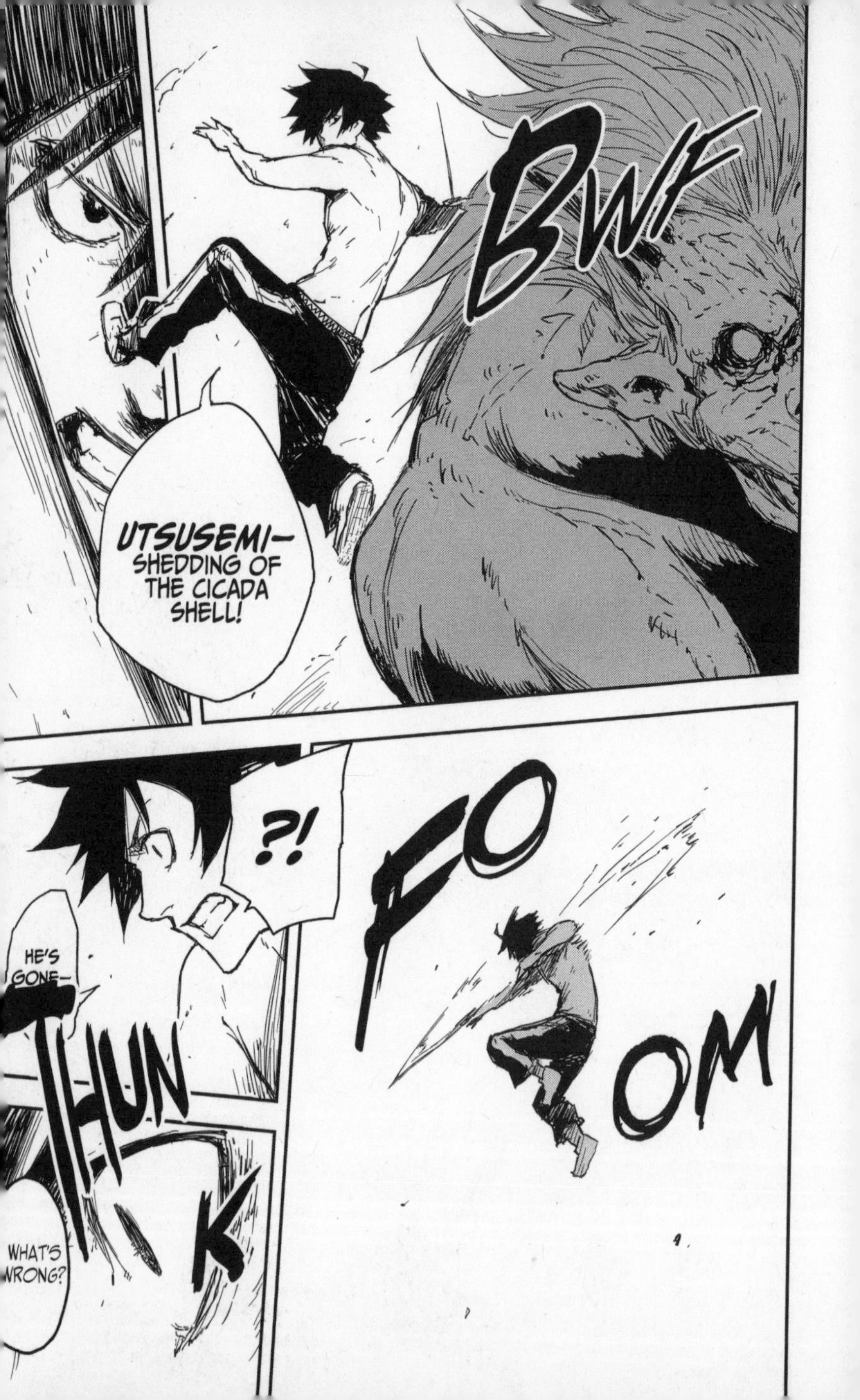
BWF
UTSUSEMI— SHEDDING OF THE CICADA SHELL!
FOOM
?!
HE'S GONE—
THUNK
WHAT'S WRONG?

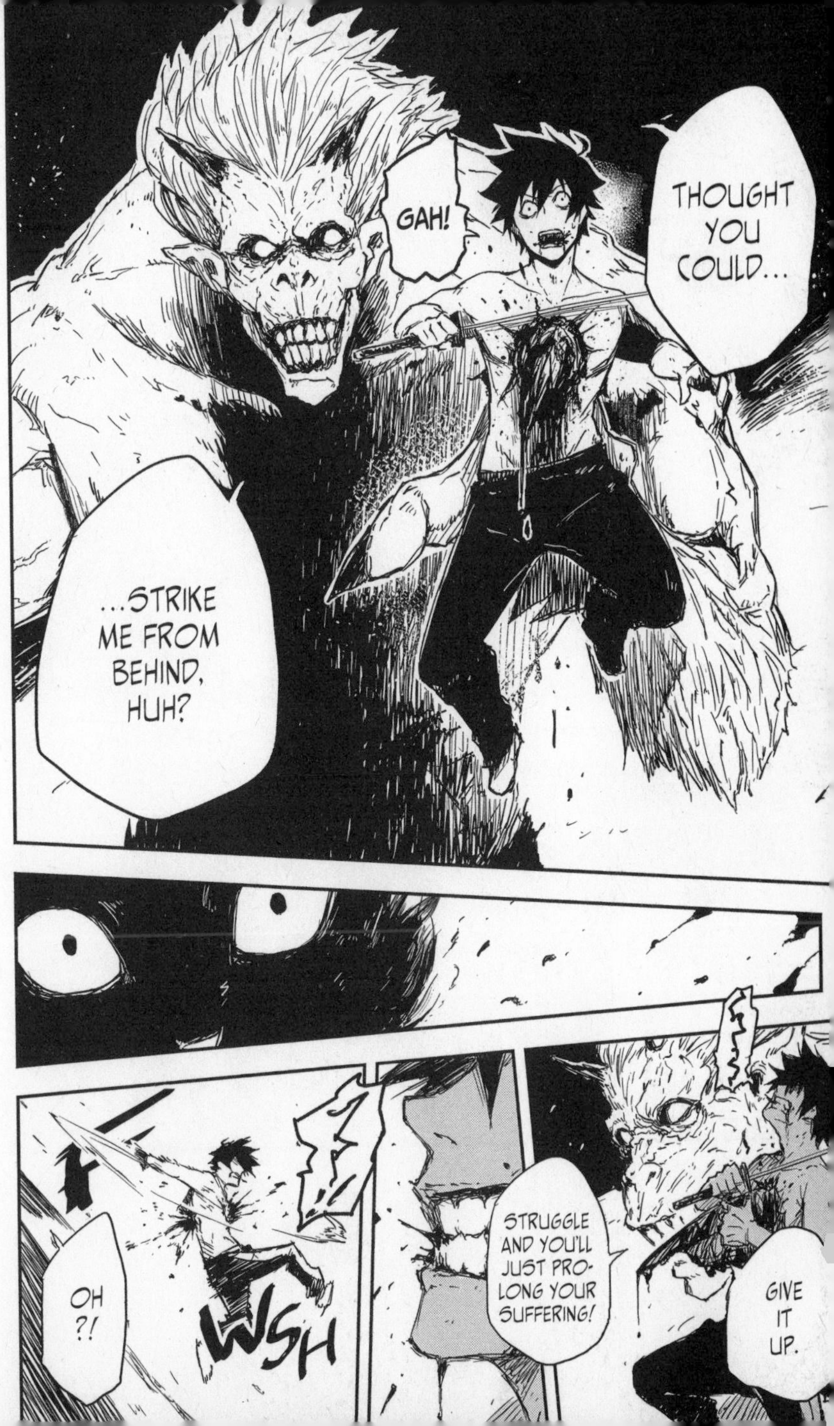

THOUGHT YOU COULD...
GAH!
...STRIKE ME FROM BEHIND, HUH?
GIVE IT UP.
STRUGGLE AND YOU'LL JUST PRO-LONG YOUR SUFFERING!
OH ?!
WSH

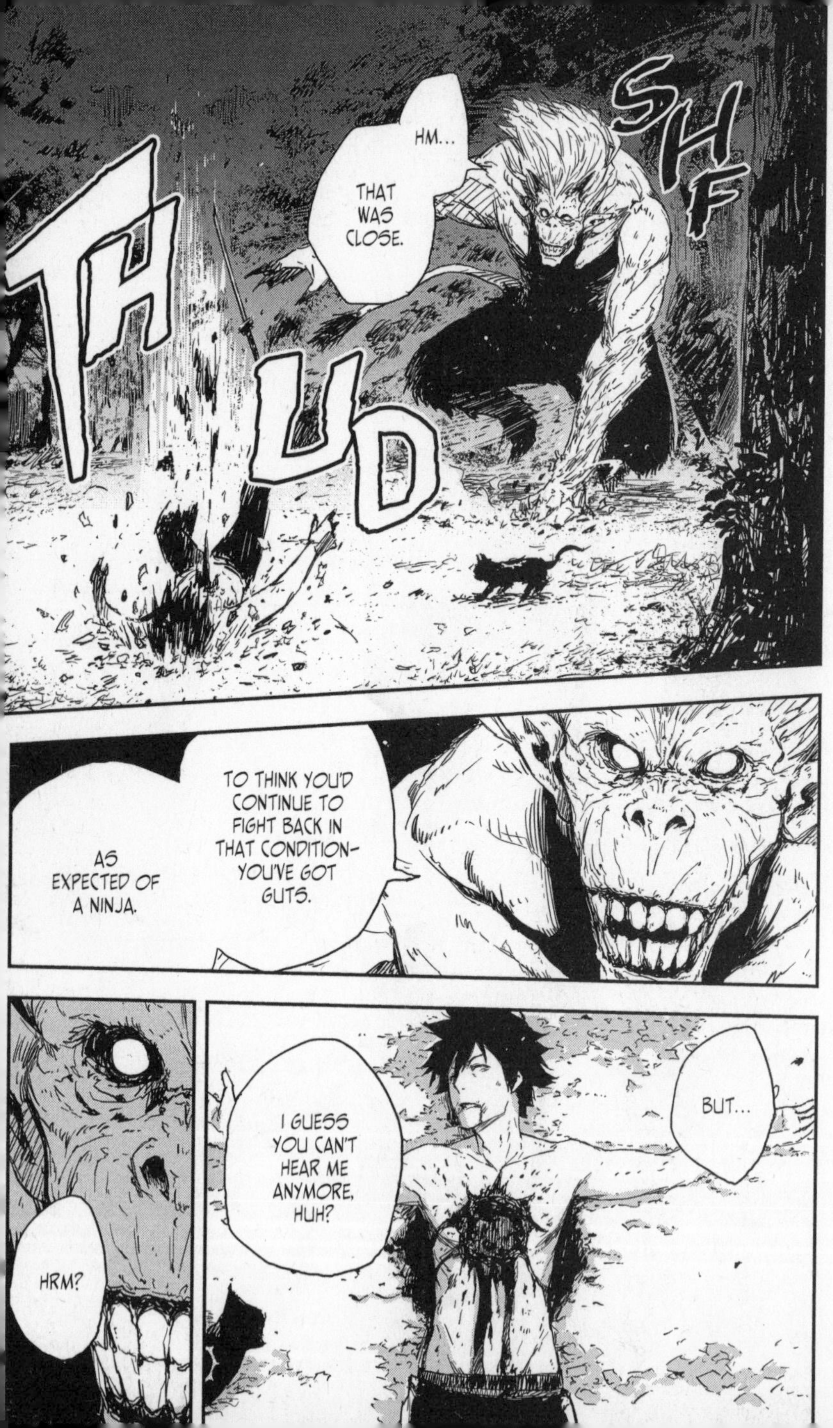
SHF
HM...
THAT WAS CLOSE.
THUD
TO THINK YOU'D CONTINUE TO FIGHT BACK IN THAT CONDITION- YOU'VE GOT GUTS.
AS EXPECTED OF A NINJA.
BUT...
....
I GUESS YOU CAN'T HEAR ME ANYMORE, HUH?
HRM?

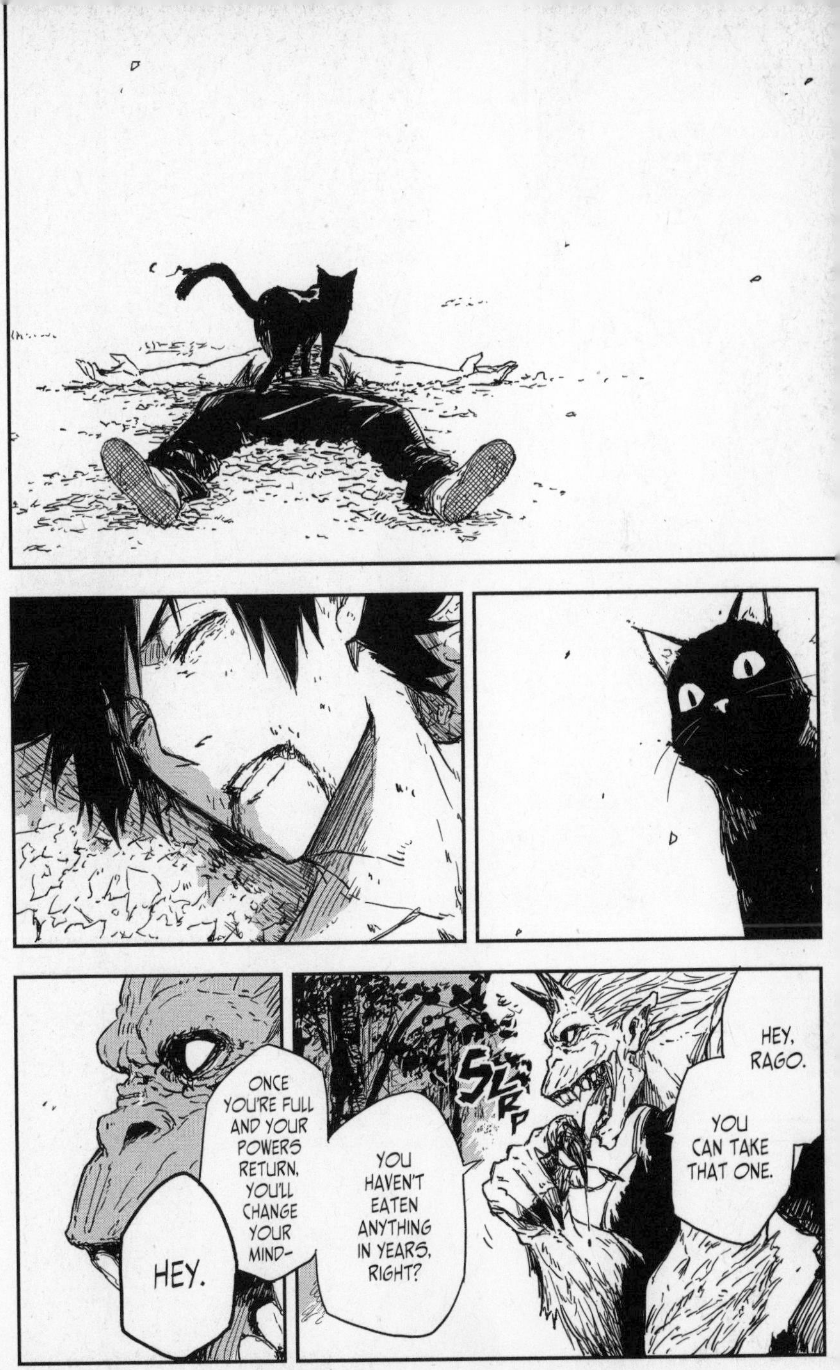
HEY, RAGO.
YOU CAN TAKE THAT ONE.
SLRP
YOU HAVEN'T EATEN ANYTHING IN YEARS, RIGHT?
ONCE YOU'RE FULL AND YOUR POWERS RETURN, YOU'LL CHANGE YOUR MIND–
HEY.

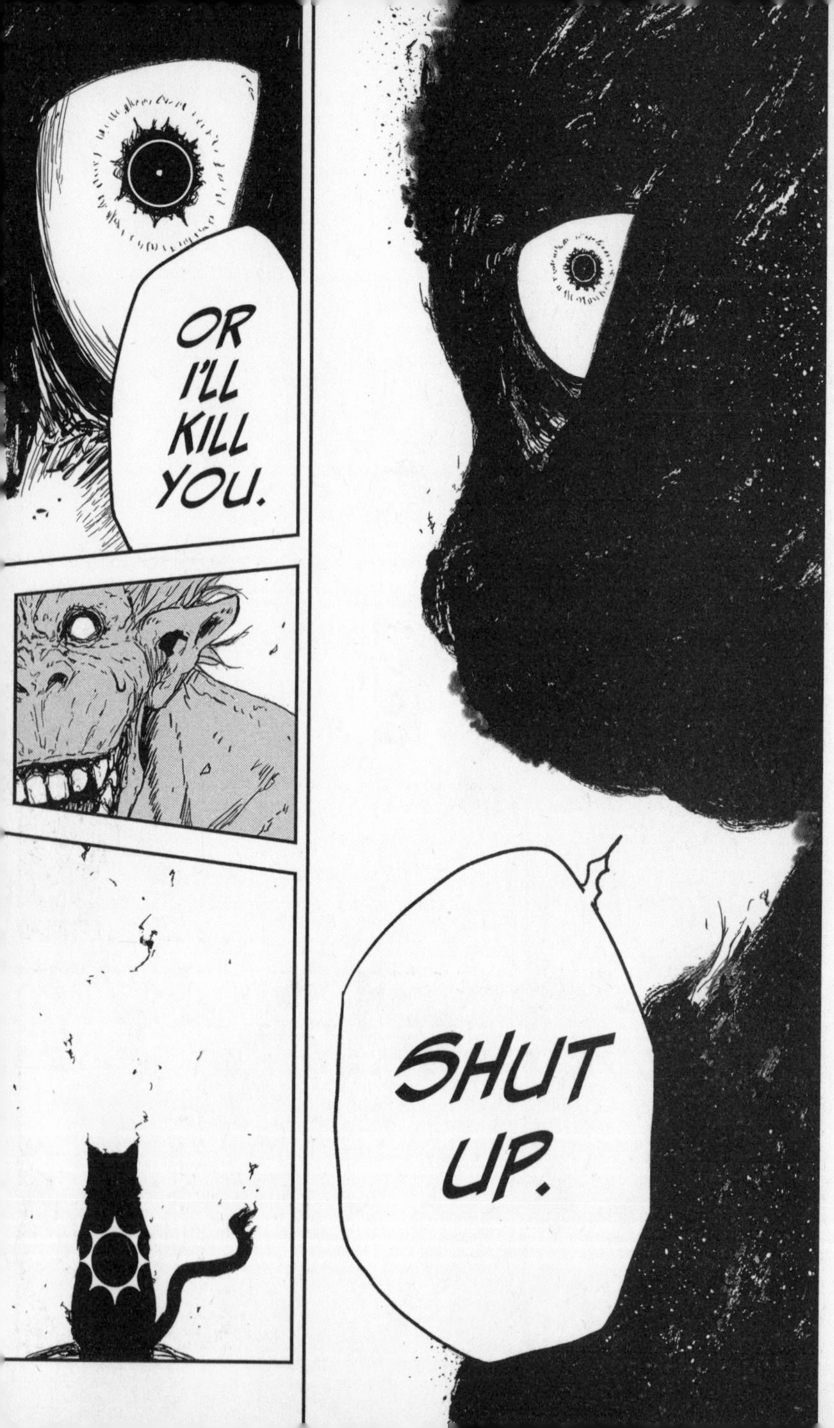
SHUT UP.
OR I'LL KILL YOU.

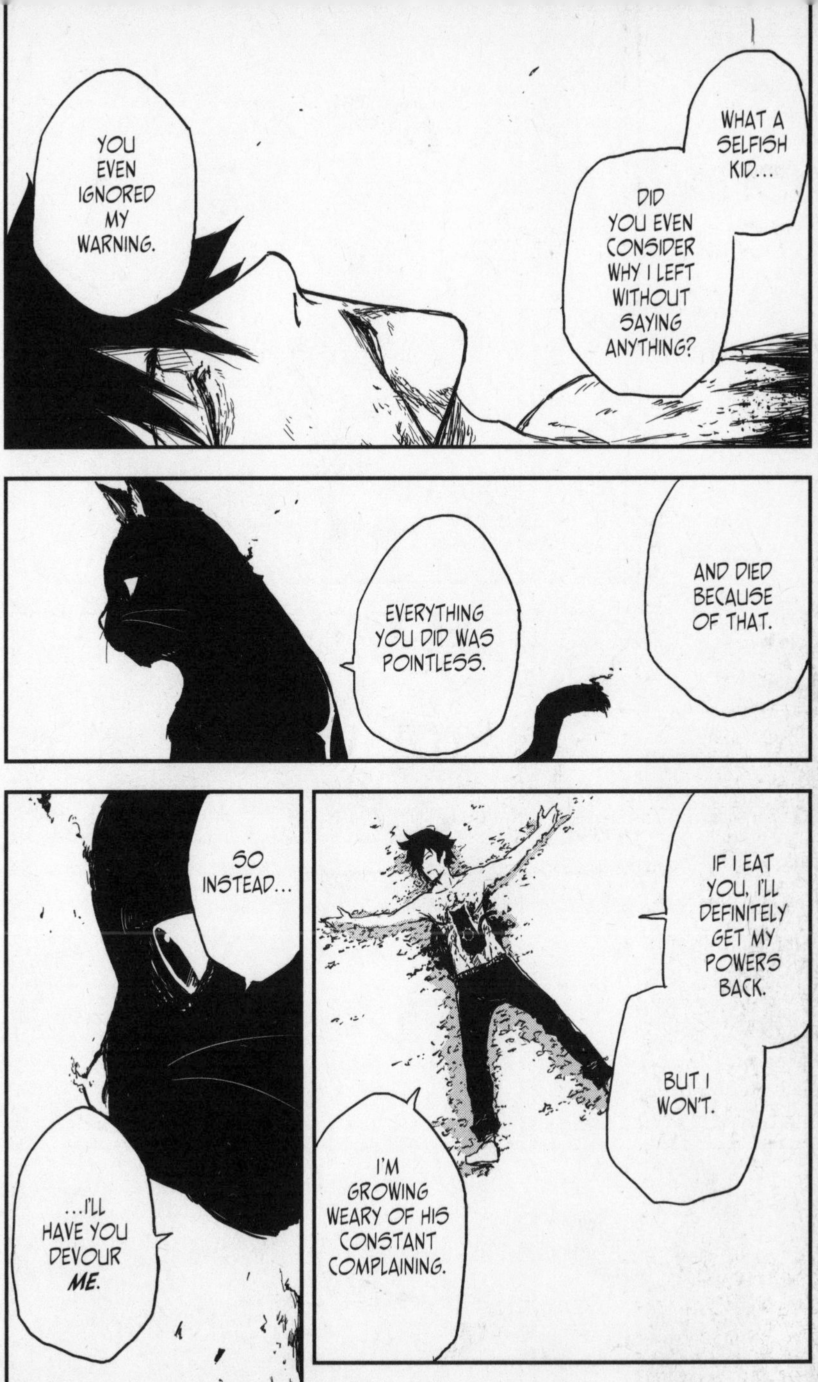
WHAT A SELFISH KID...
DID YOU EVEN CONSIDER WHY I LEFT WITHOUT SAYING ANYTHING?
YOU EVEN IGNORED MY WARNING.
AND DIED BECAUSE OF THAT.
EVERYTHING YOU DID WAS POINTLESS.
IF I EAT YOU, I'LL DEFINITELY GET MY POWERS BACK.
BUT I WON'T.
I'M GROWING WEARY OF HIS CONSTANT COMPLAINING.
SO INSTEAD...
...I'LL HAVE YOU DEVOUR *ME*.

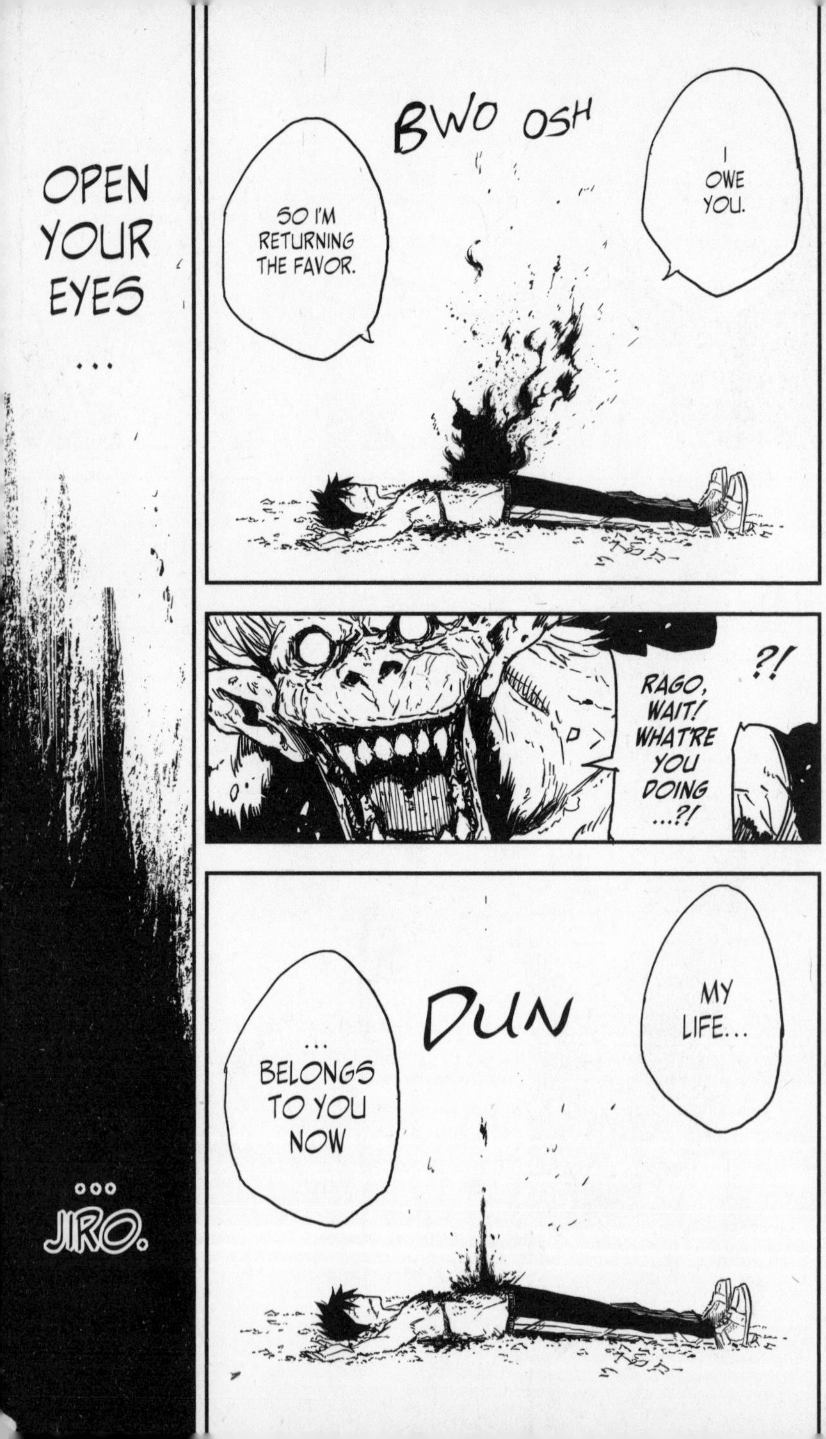
I OWE YOU.
BWO OSH
SO I'M RETURNING THE FAVOR.
?!
RAGO, WAIT! WHAT'RE YOU DOING ...?!
MY LIFE...
DUN
... BELONGS TO YOU NOW
OPEN YOUR EYES ...
... JIRO.

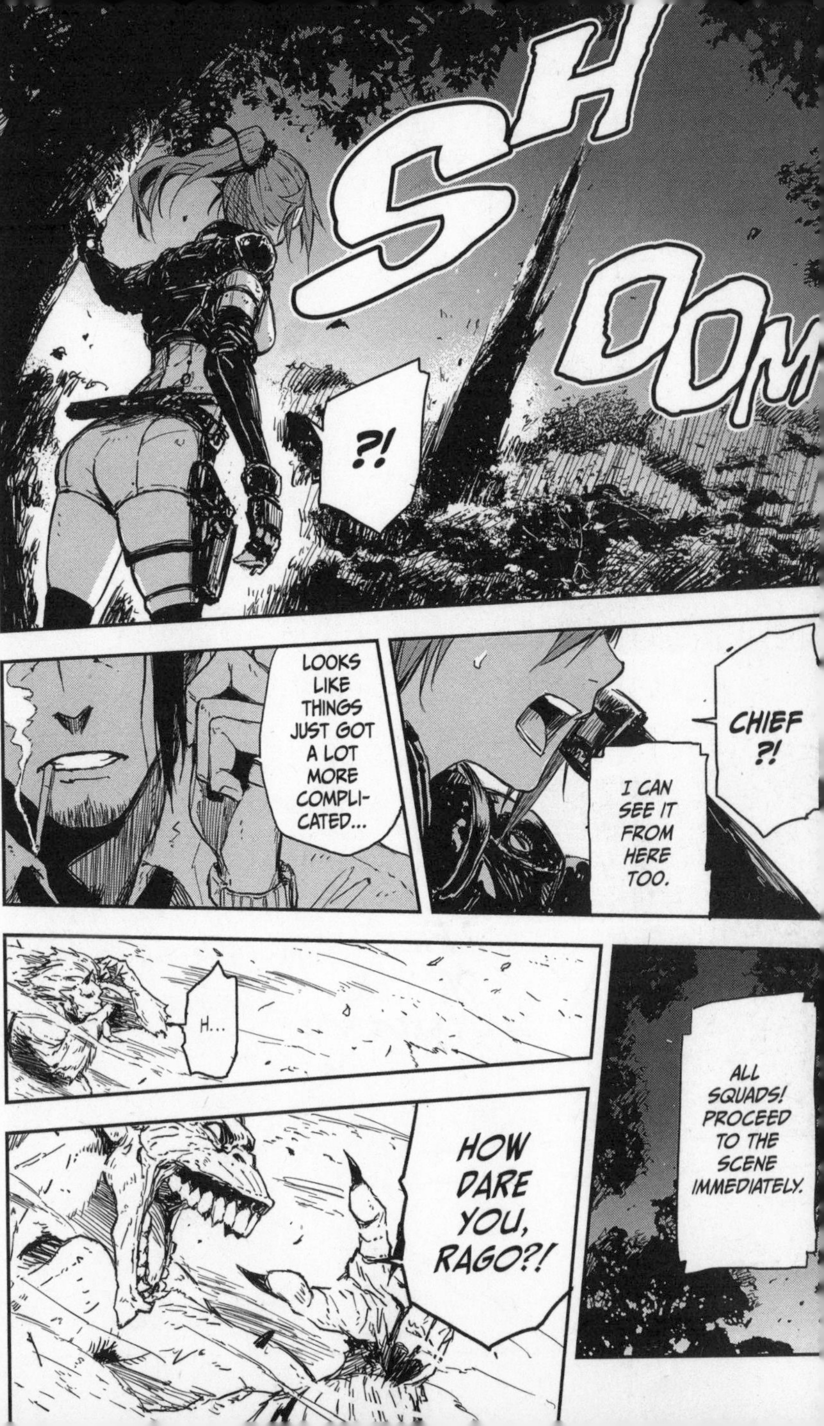
SHDOOM
?!
CHIEF ?!
I CAN SEE IT FROM HERE TOO.
LOOKS LIKE THINGS JUST GOT A LOT MORE COMPLICATED...
ALL SQUADS! PROCEED TO THE SCENE IMMEDIATELY.
H...
HOW DARE YOU, RAGO?!

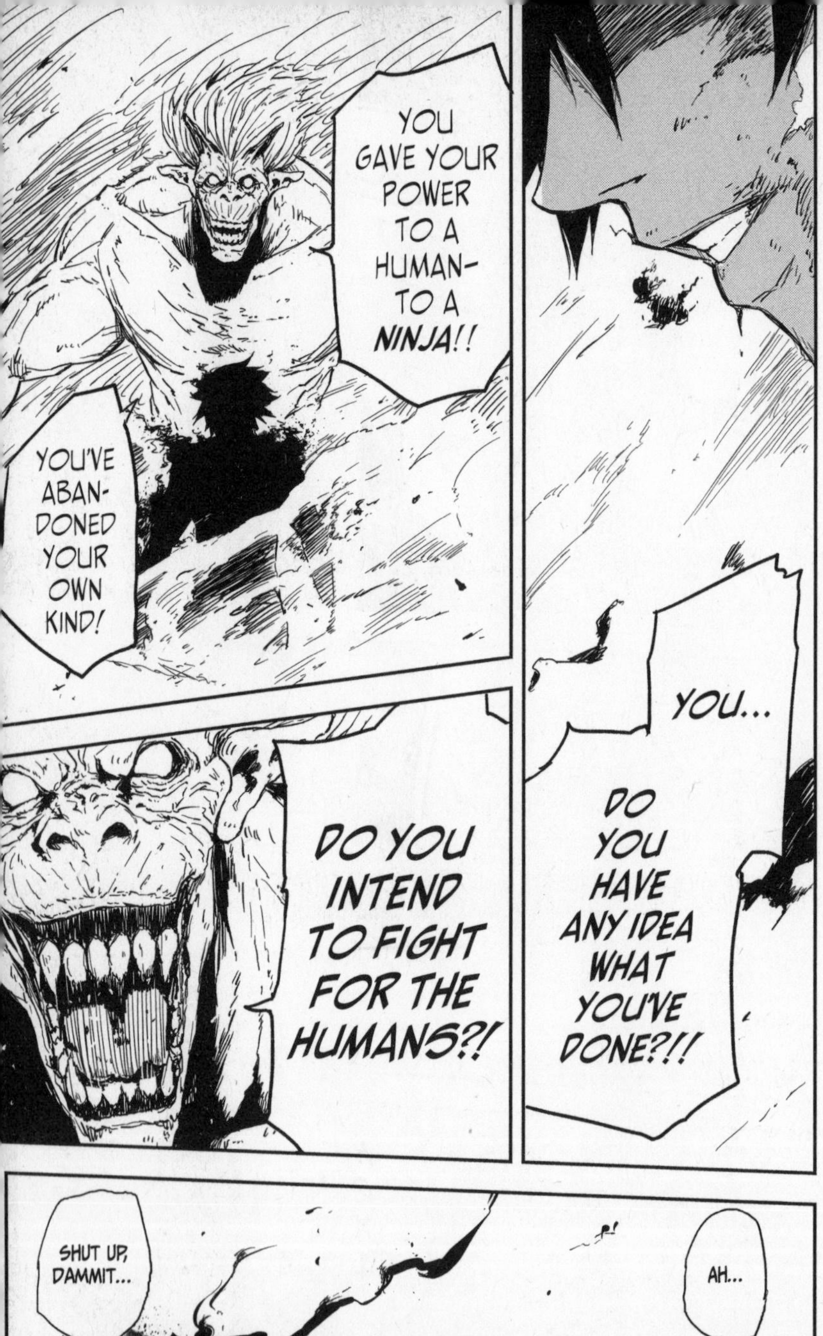
YOU...
DO YOU HAVE ANY IDEA WHAT YOU'VE DONE?!!
YOU GAVE YOUR POWER TO A HUMAN-TO A NINJA!!
YOU'VE ABANDONED YOUR OWN KIND!
DO YOU INTEND TO FIGHT FOR THE HUMANS?!
AH...
SHUT UP, DAMMIT...

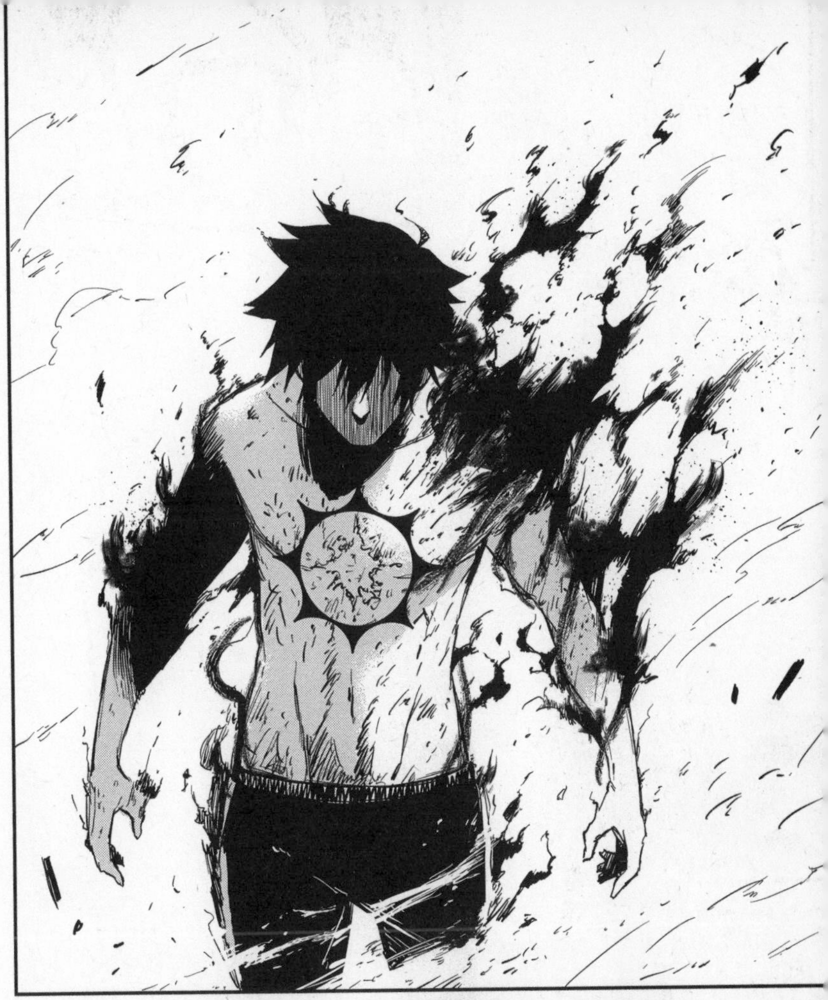

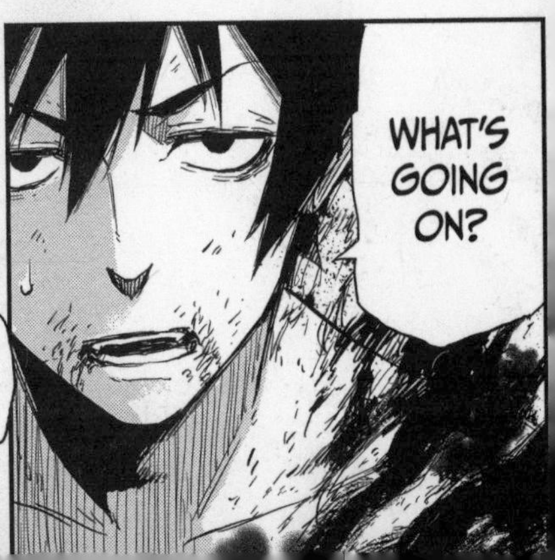
WHAT'S GOING ON?

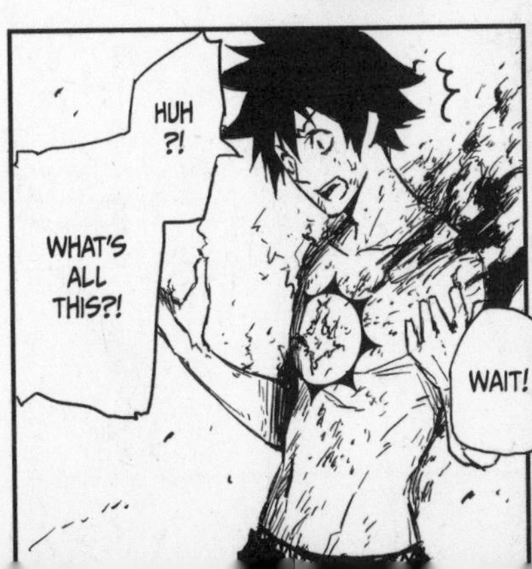
HUH?!
WHAT'S ALL THIS?!
WAIT!

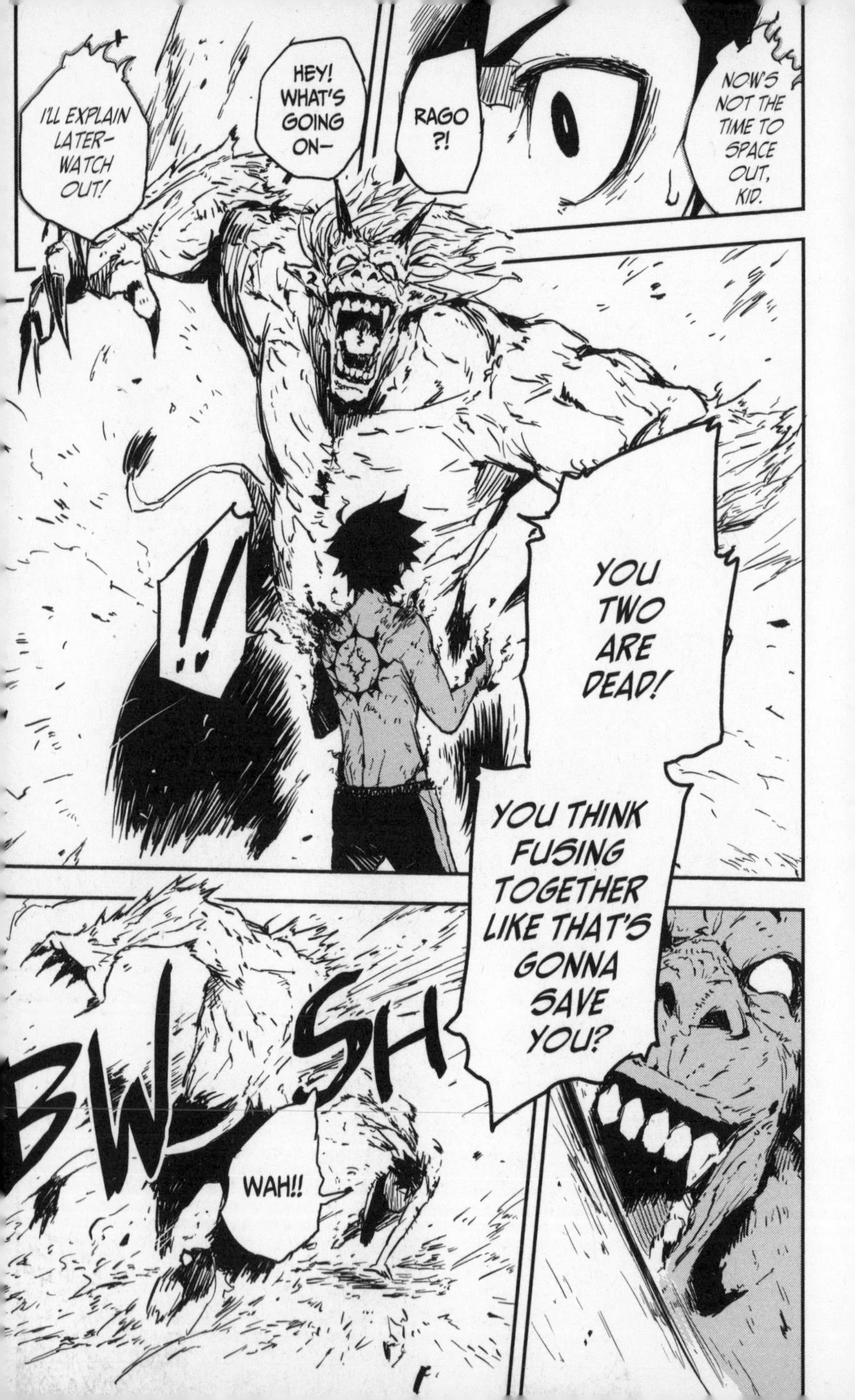
NOW'S NOT THE TIME TO SPACE OUT, KID.
RAGO ?!
HEY! WHAT'S GOING ON—
I'LL EXPLAIN LATER—WATCH OUT!
YOU TWO ARE DEAD!
!!
YOU THINK FUSING TOGETHER LIKE THAT'S GONNA SAVE YOU?
BWSH
WAH!!

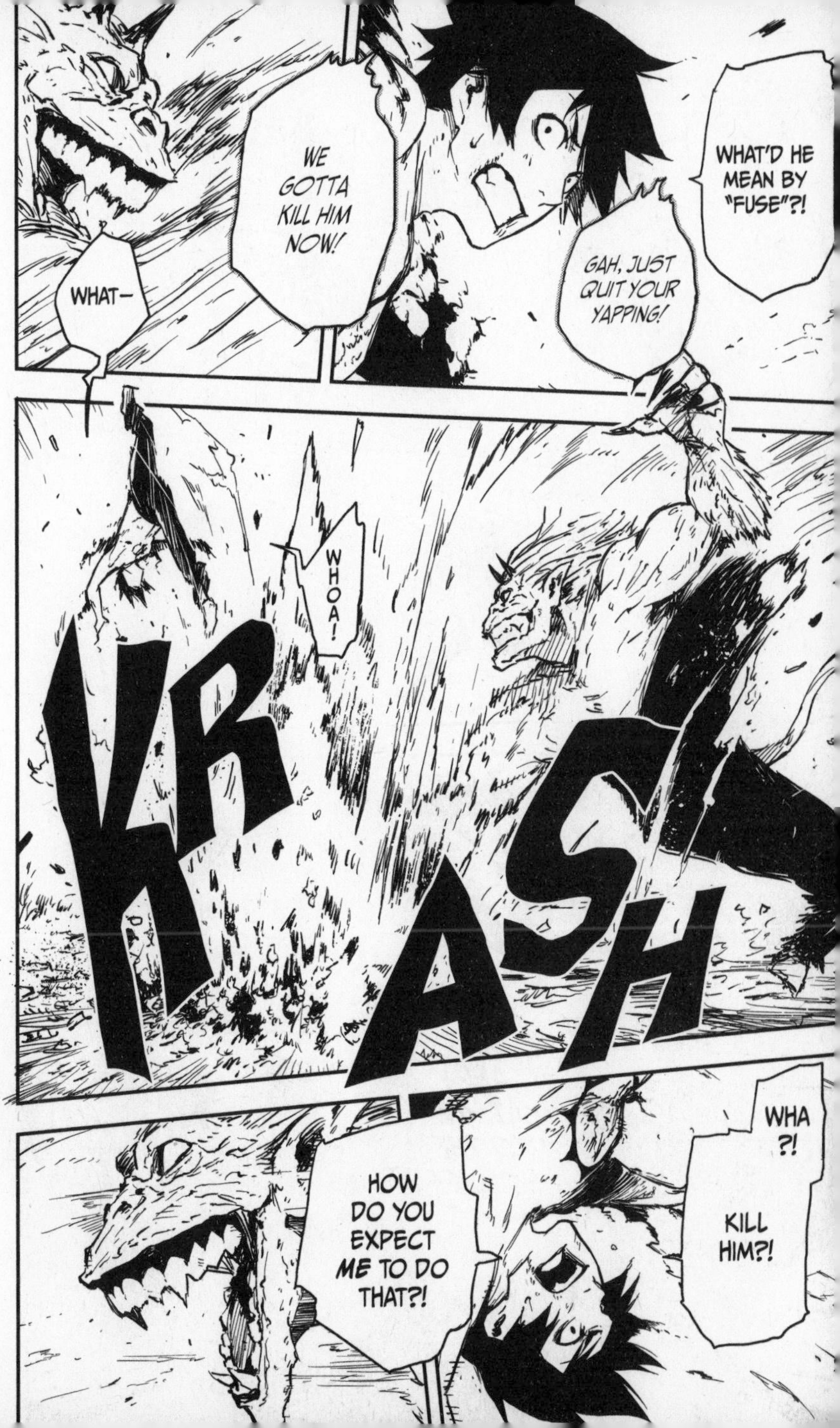
WHAT'D HE MEAN BY "FUSE"?!
GAH, JUST QUIT YOUR YAPPING!
WE GOTTA KILL HIM NOW!
WHAT—
WHOA!
KRASH
WHA?!
KILL HIM?!
HOW DO YOU EXPECT ME TO DO THAT?!

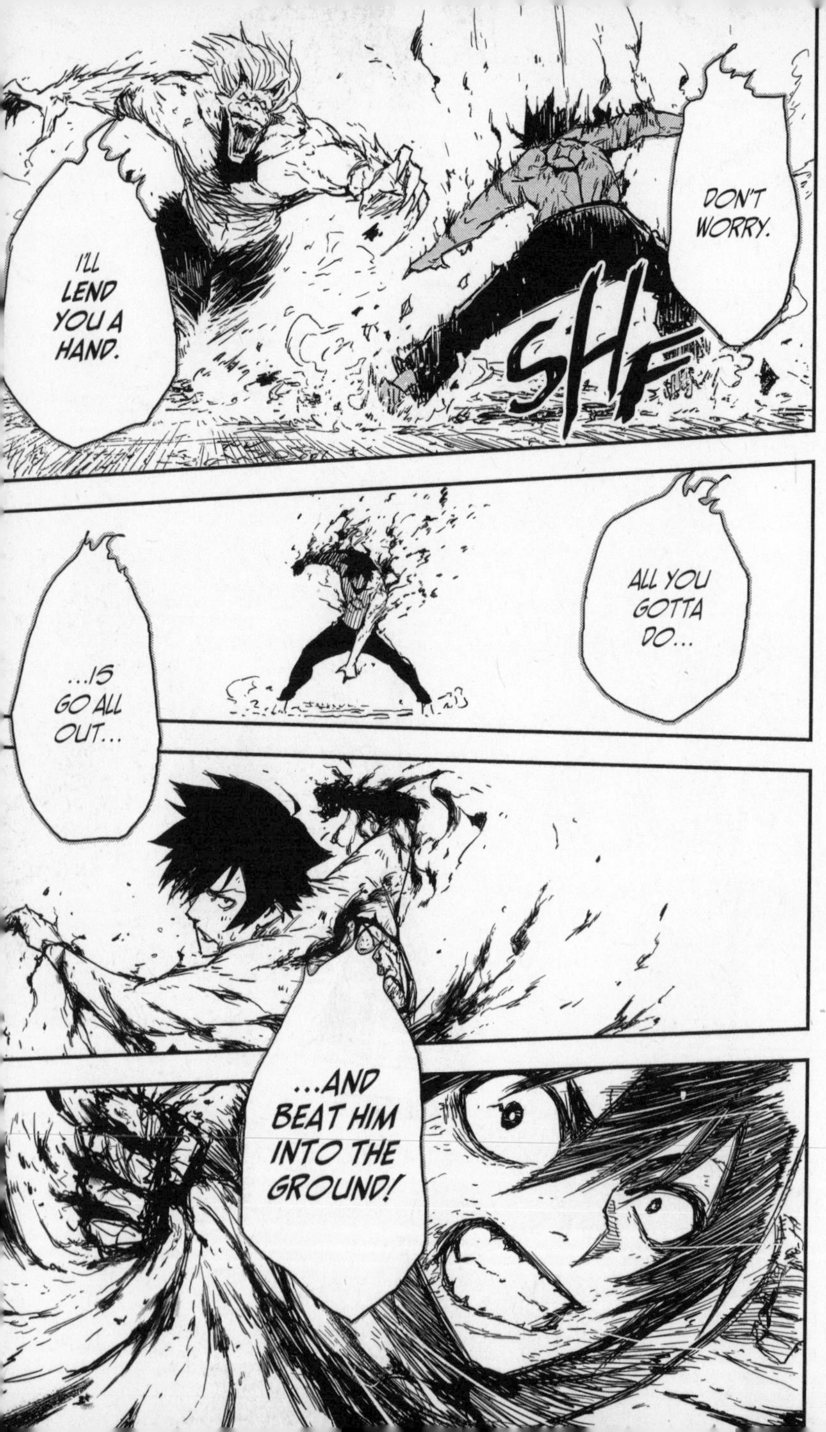
DON'T WORRY.
SHF
I'LL LEND YOU A HAND.
ALL YOU GOTTA DO...
...IS GO ALL OUT...
...AND BEAT HIM INTO THE GROUND!

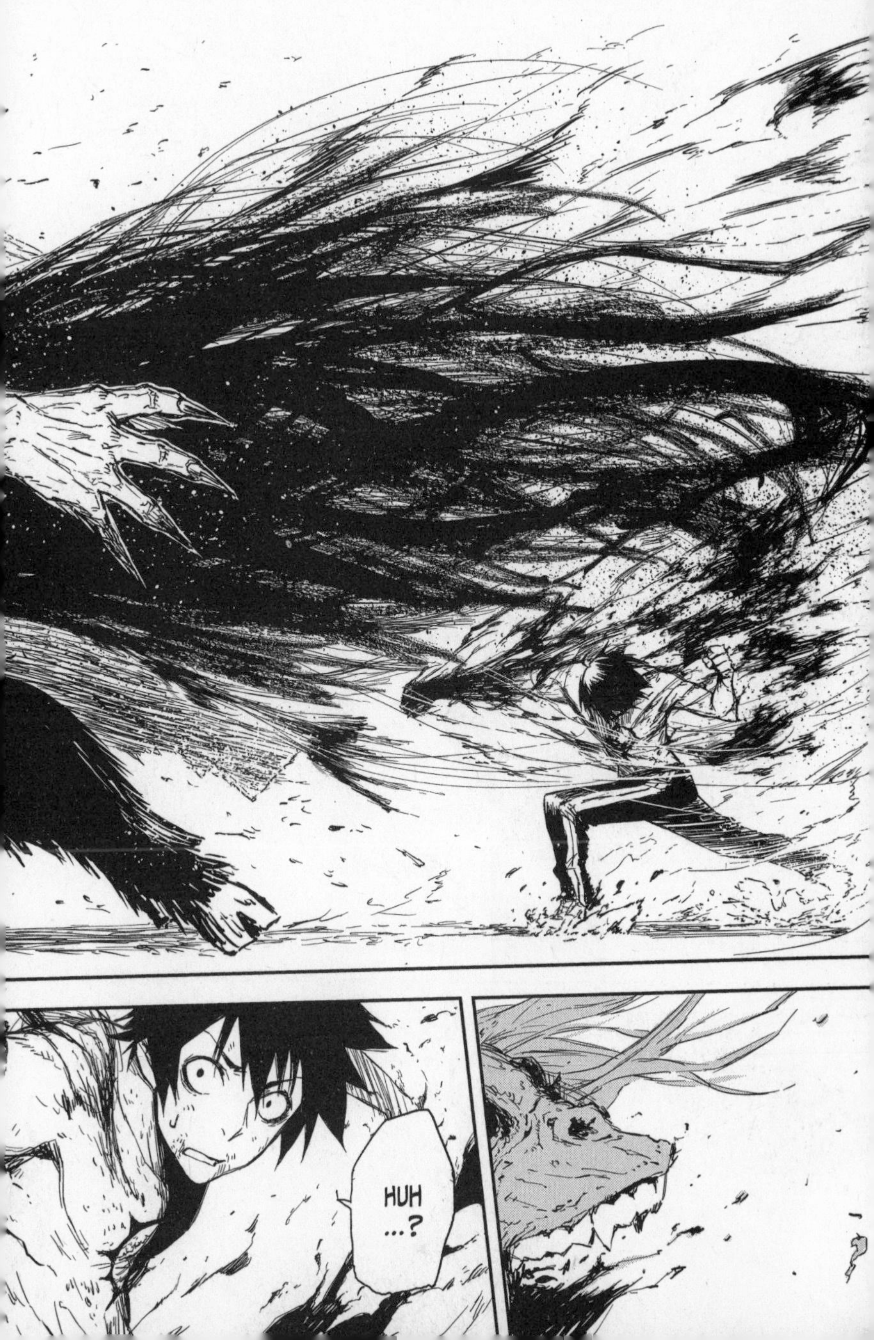
HUH ...?

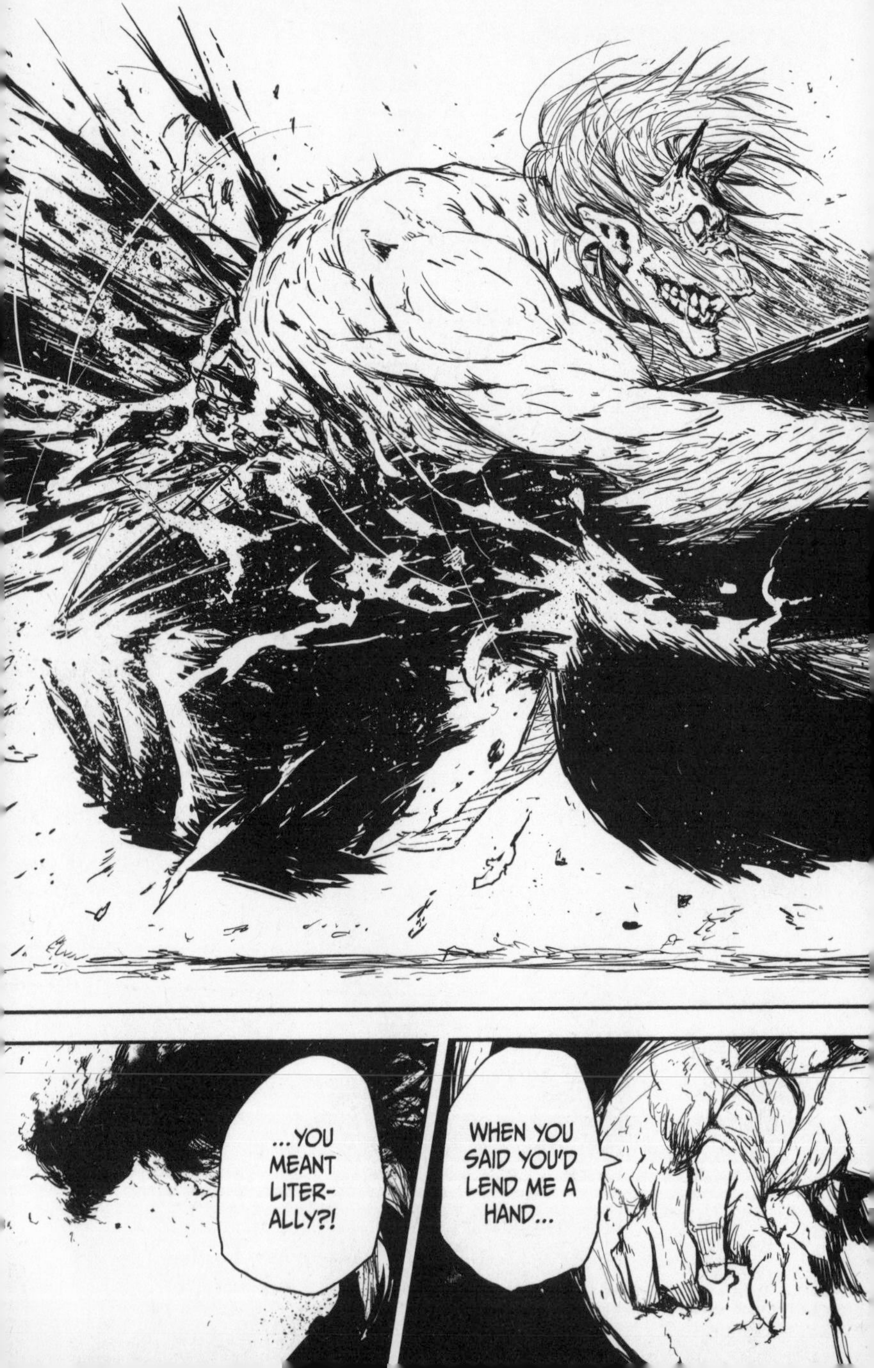
WHEN YOU SAID YOU'D LEND ME A HAND...
...YOU MEANT LITER-ALLY?!

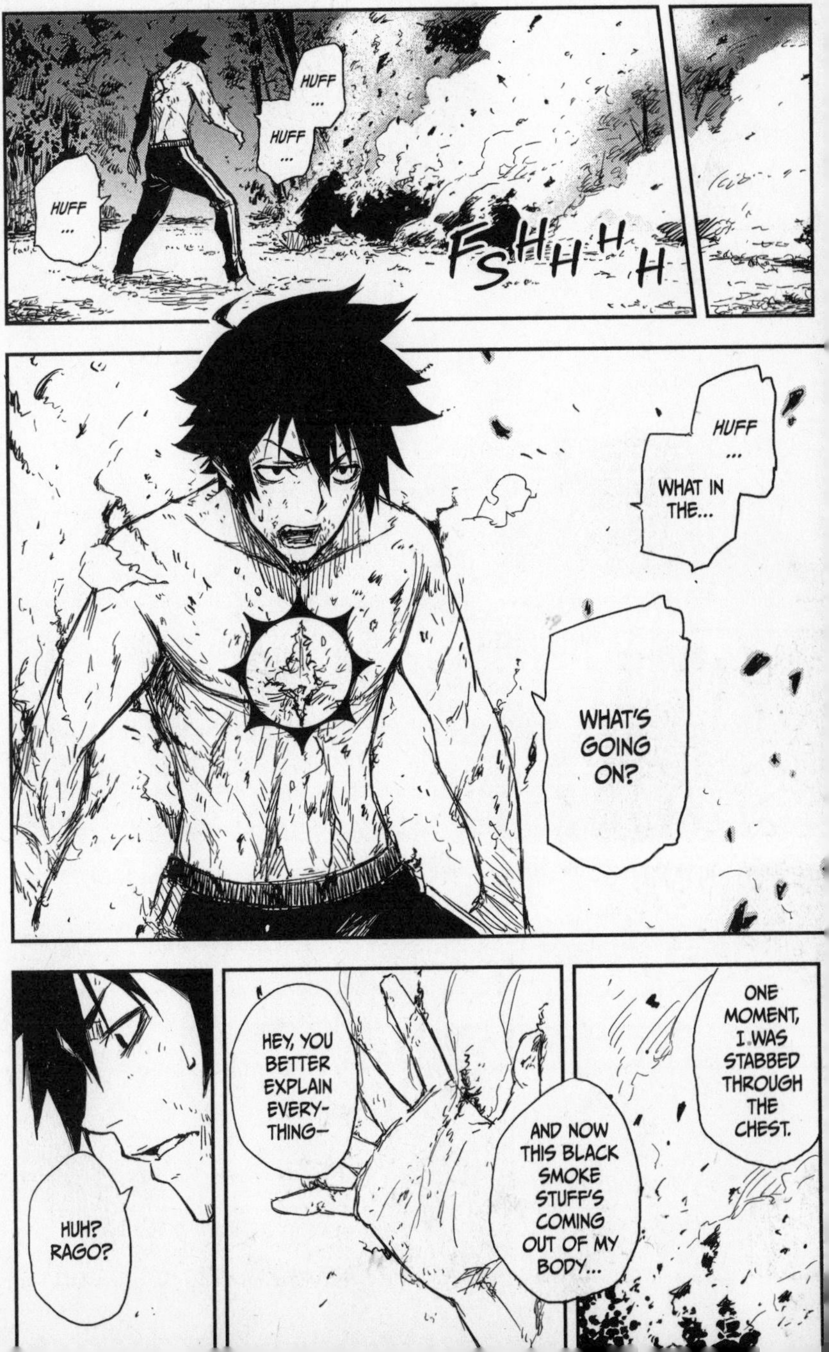
HUFF ...
HUFF ...
HUFF ...
FSHHHHH
HUFF ... WHAT IN THE...
WHAT'S GOING ON?
ONE MOMENT, I WAS STABBED THROUGH THE CHEST.
AND NOW THIS BLACK SMOKE STUFF'S COMING OUT OF MY BODY...
HEY, YOU BETTER EXPLAIN EVERY-THING—
HUH? RAGO?

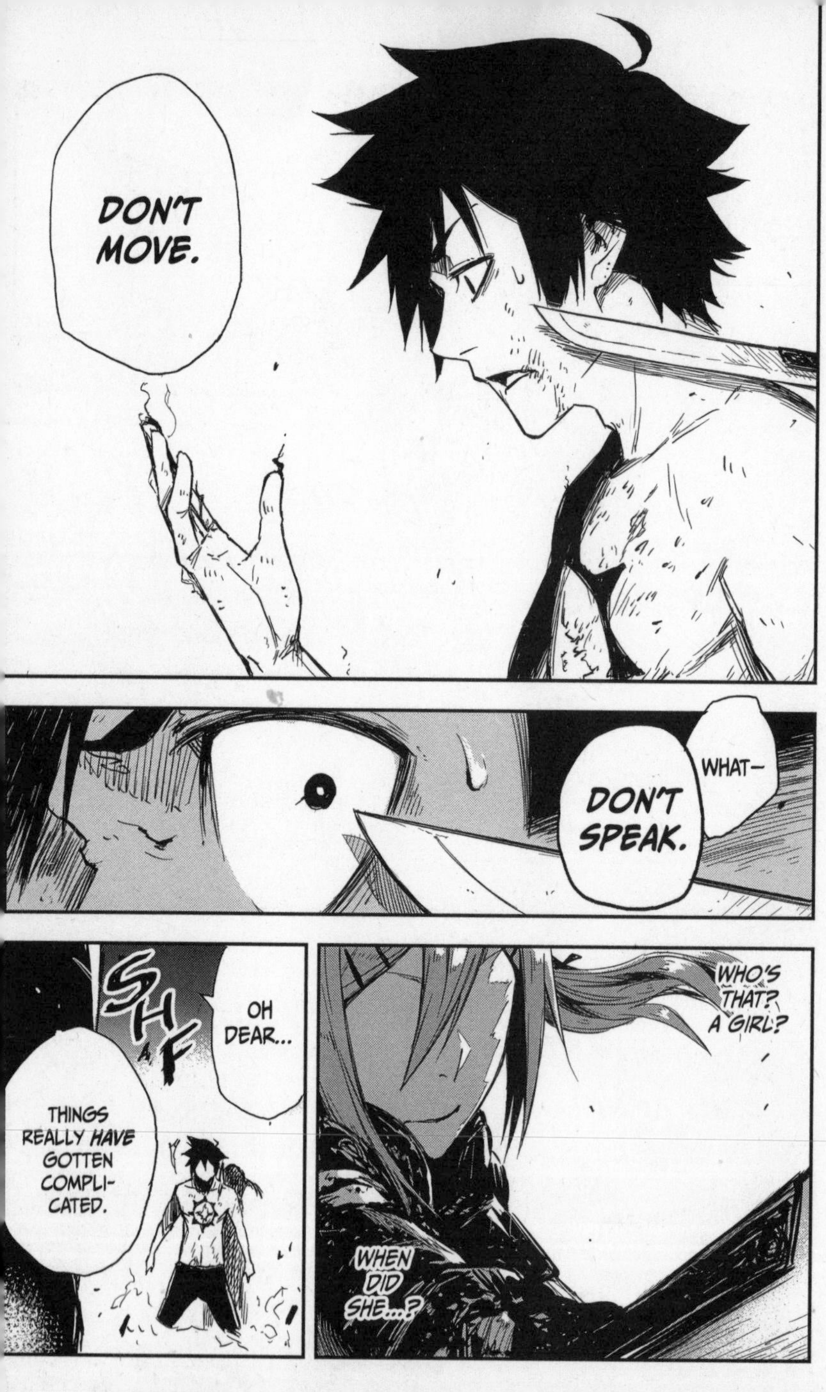
DON'T MOVE.
WHAT—
DON'T SPEAK.
WHO'S THAT? A GIRL?
WHEN DID SHE...?
SHF
OH DEAR...
THINGS REALLY HAVE GOTTEN COMPLI-CATED.

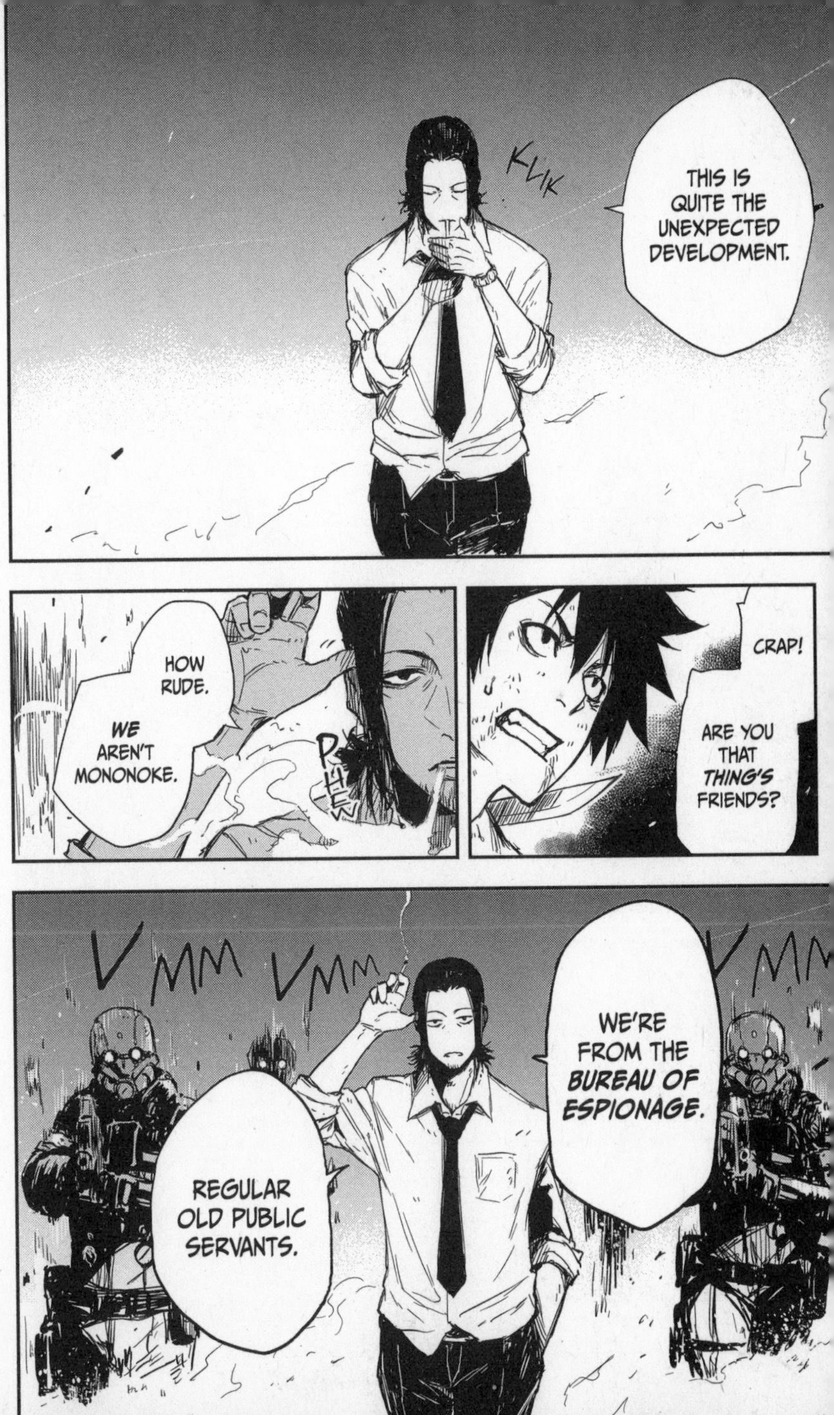
KLIK
THIS IS QUITE THE UNEXPECTED DEVELOPMENT.
CRAP!
ARE YOU THAT *THING'S* FRIENDS?
PHEW
HOW RUDE.
WE AREN'T MONONOKE.
VMM VMM VMM
WE'RE FROM THE *BUREAU OF ESPIONAGE.*
REGULAR OLD PUBLIC SERVANTS.

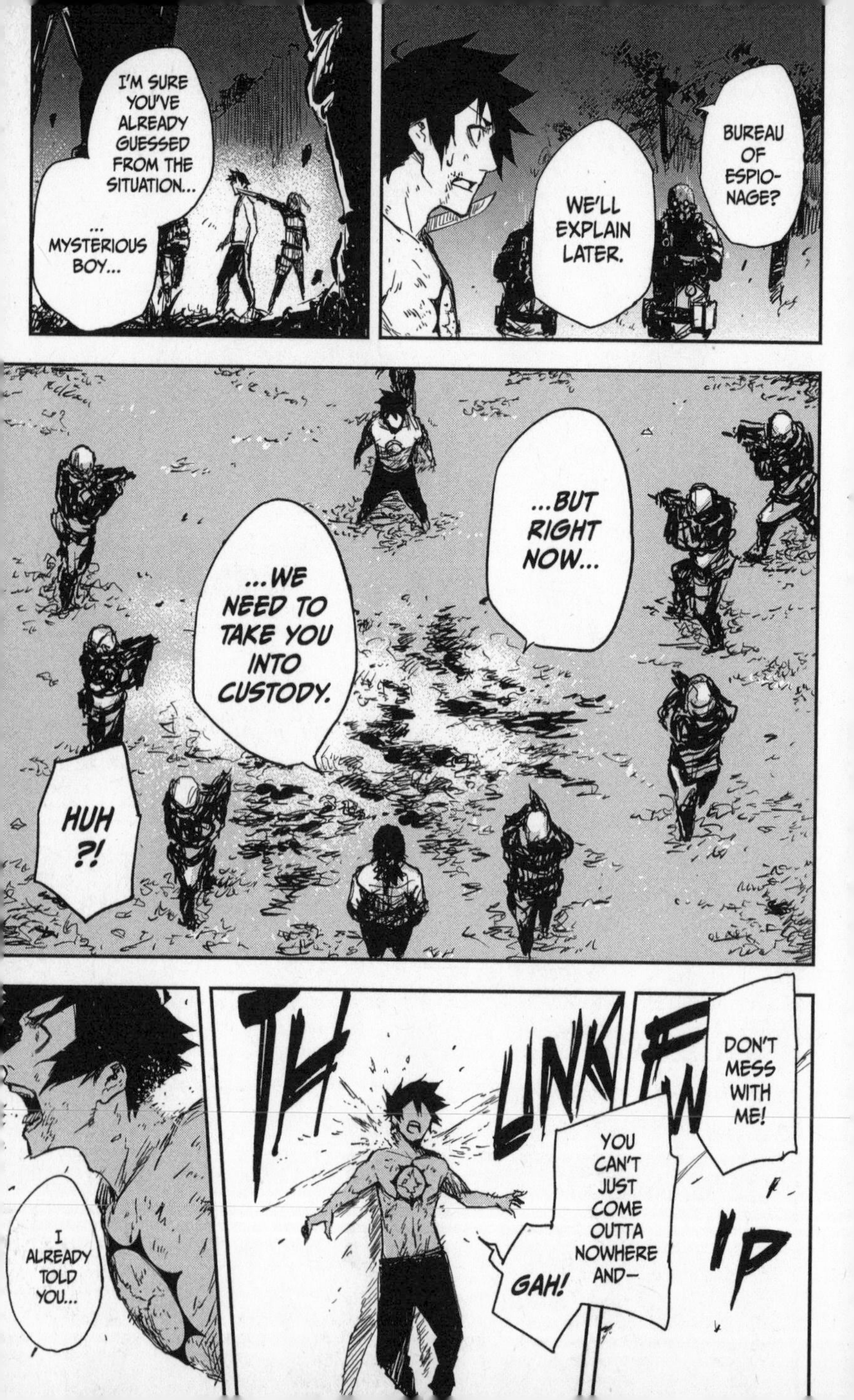
BUREAU OF ESPIO-NAGE?
WE'LL EXPLAIN LATER.
I'M SURE YOU'VE ALREADY GUESSED FROM THE SITUATION...
...MYSTERIOUS BOY...
...BUT RIGHT NOW...
...WE NEED TO TAKE YOU INTO CUSTODY.
HUH?!
DON'T MESS WITH ME!
YOU CAN'T JUST COME OUTTA NOWHERE AND—
FWIP
THUNK
GAH!
I ALREADY TOLD YOU...

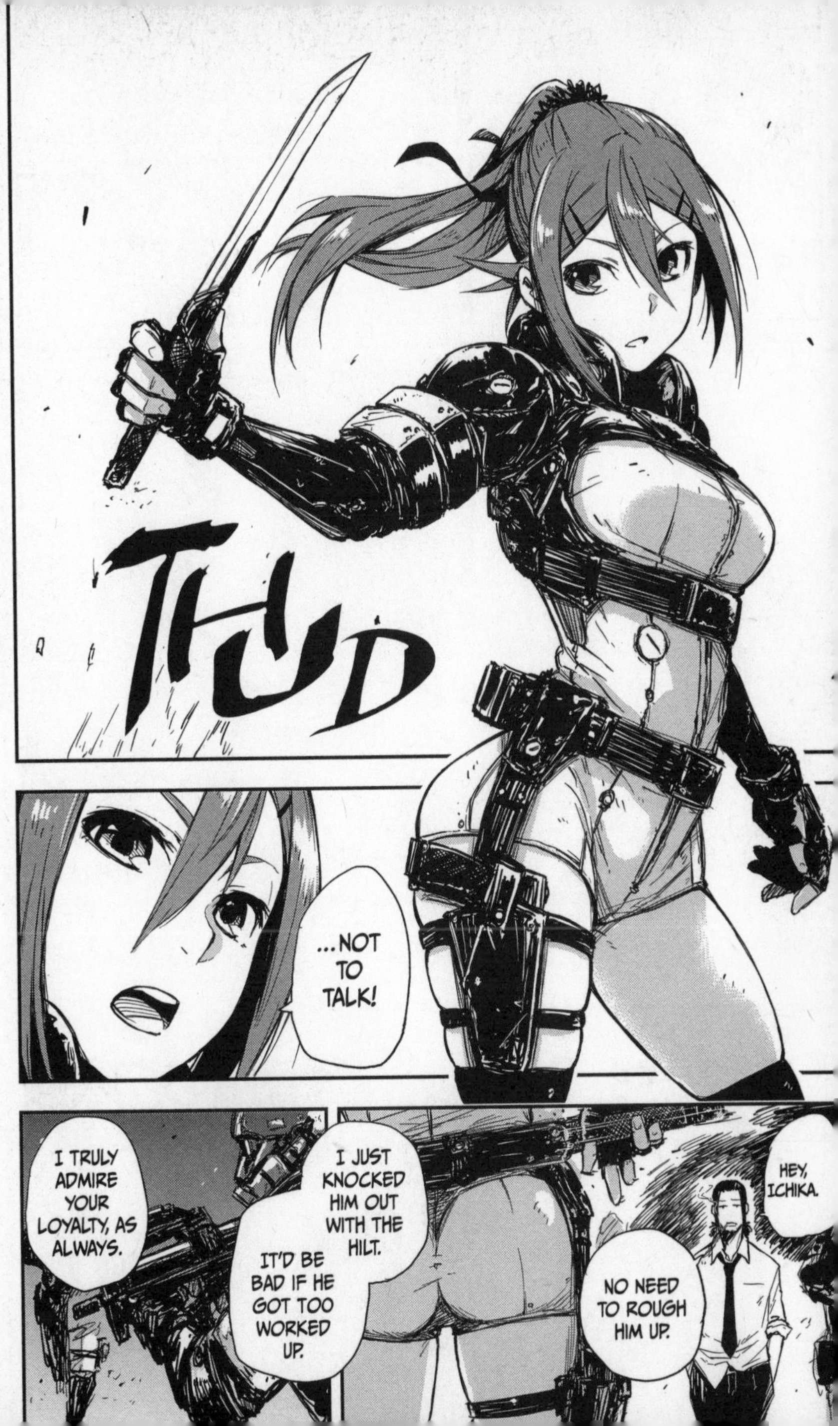
THUD
...NOT TO TALK!
HEY, ICHIKA.
NO NEED TO ROUGH HIM UP.
I JUST KNOCKED HIM OUT WITH THE HILT.
IT'D BE BAD IF HE GOT TOO WORKED UP.
I TRULY ADMIRE YOUR LOYALTY, AS ALWAYS.

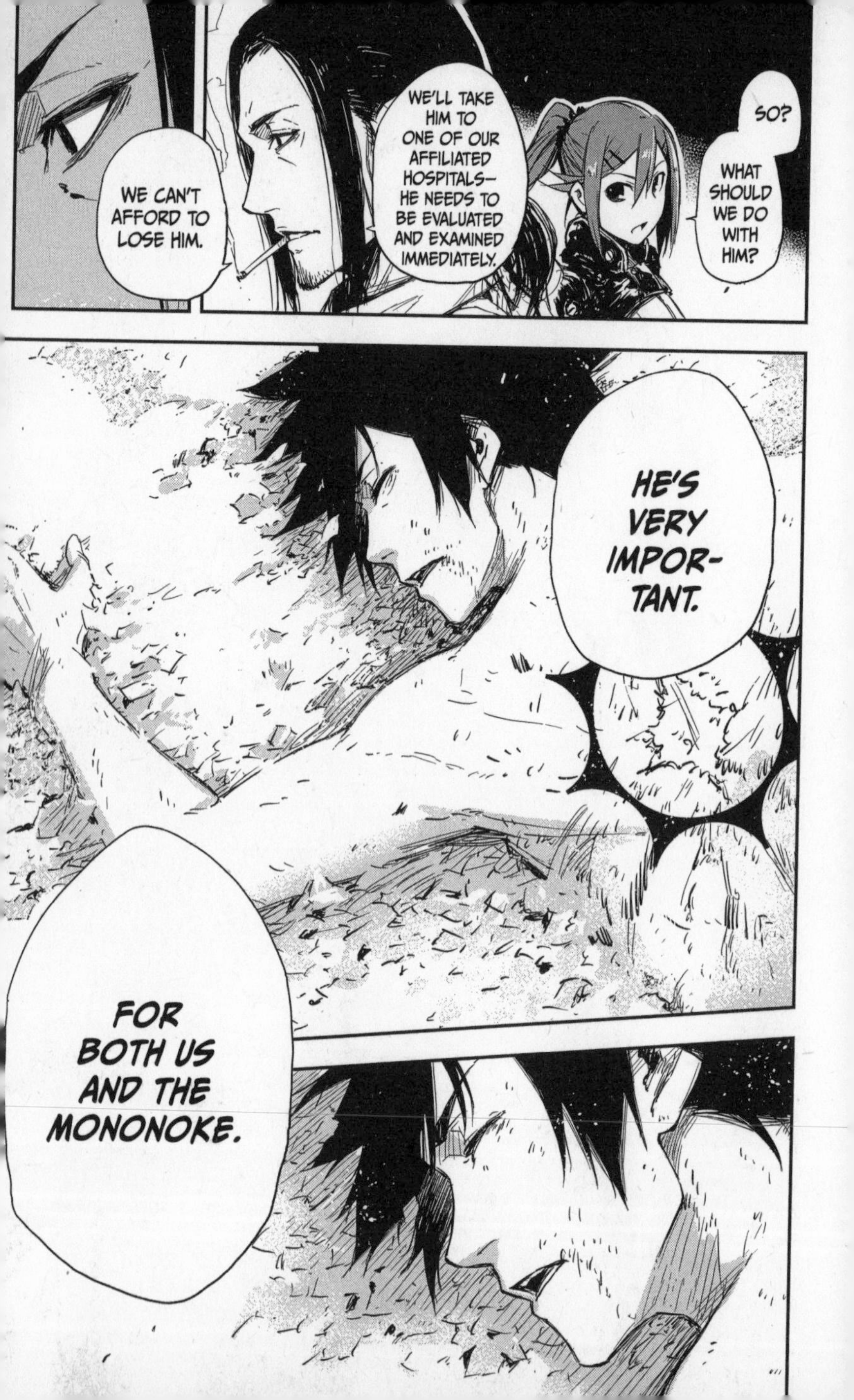
SO?
WHAT SHOULD WE DO WITH HIM?
WE'LL TAKE HIM TO ONE OF OUR AFFILIATED HOSPITALS— HE NEEDS TO BE EVALUATED AND EXAMINED IMMEDIATELY.
WE CAN'T AFFORD TO LOSE HIM.
HE'S VERY IMPOR-TANT.
FOR BOTH US AND THE MONONOKE.

BLACK TORCH

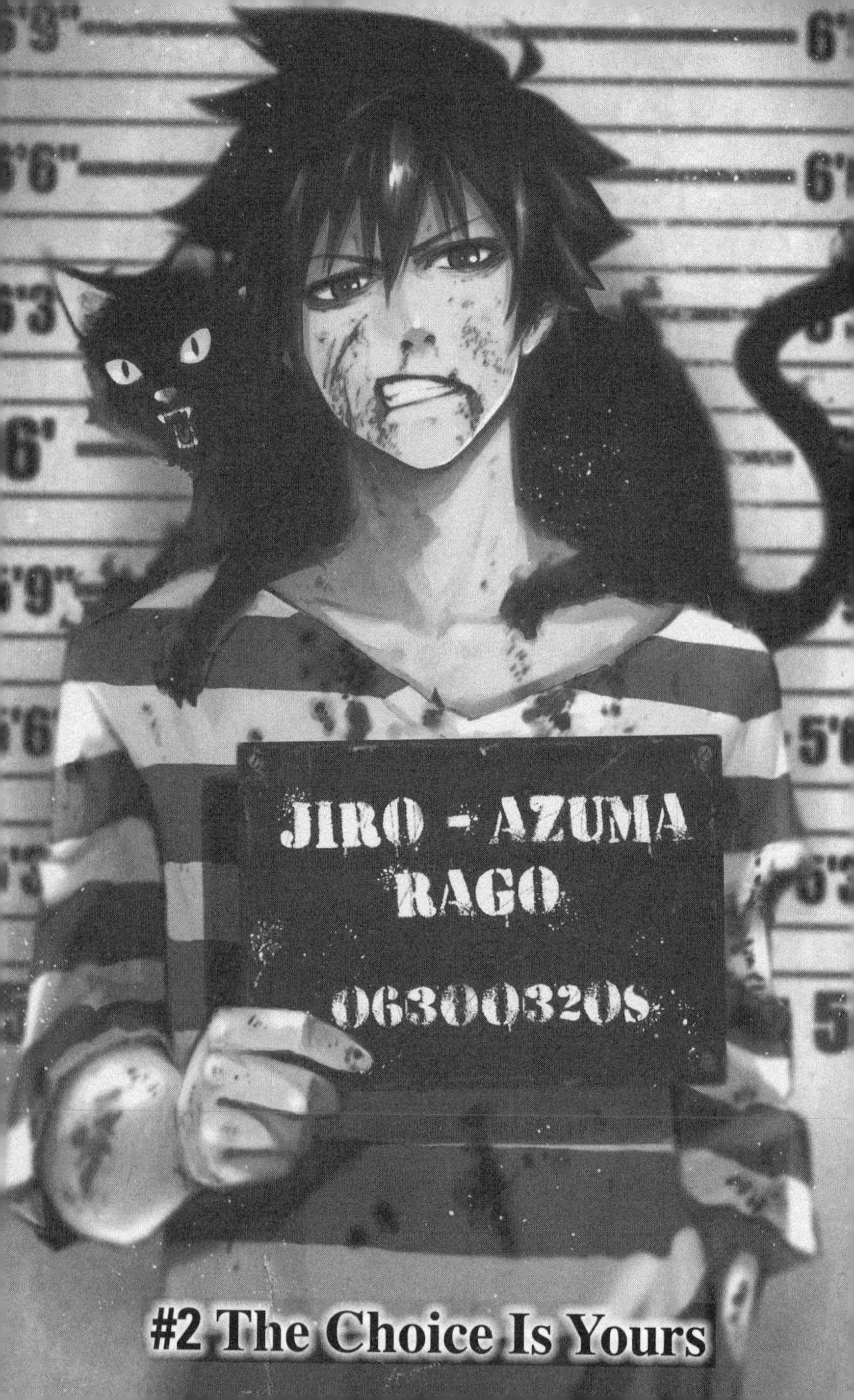
JIRO - AZUMA
RAGO
06300320S

#2 The Choice Is Yours

BLACK TORCH

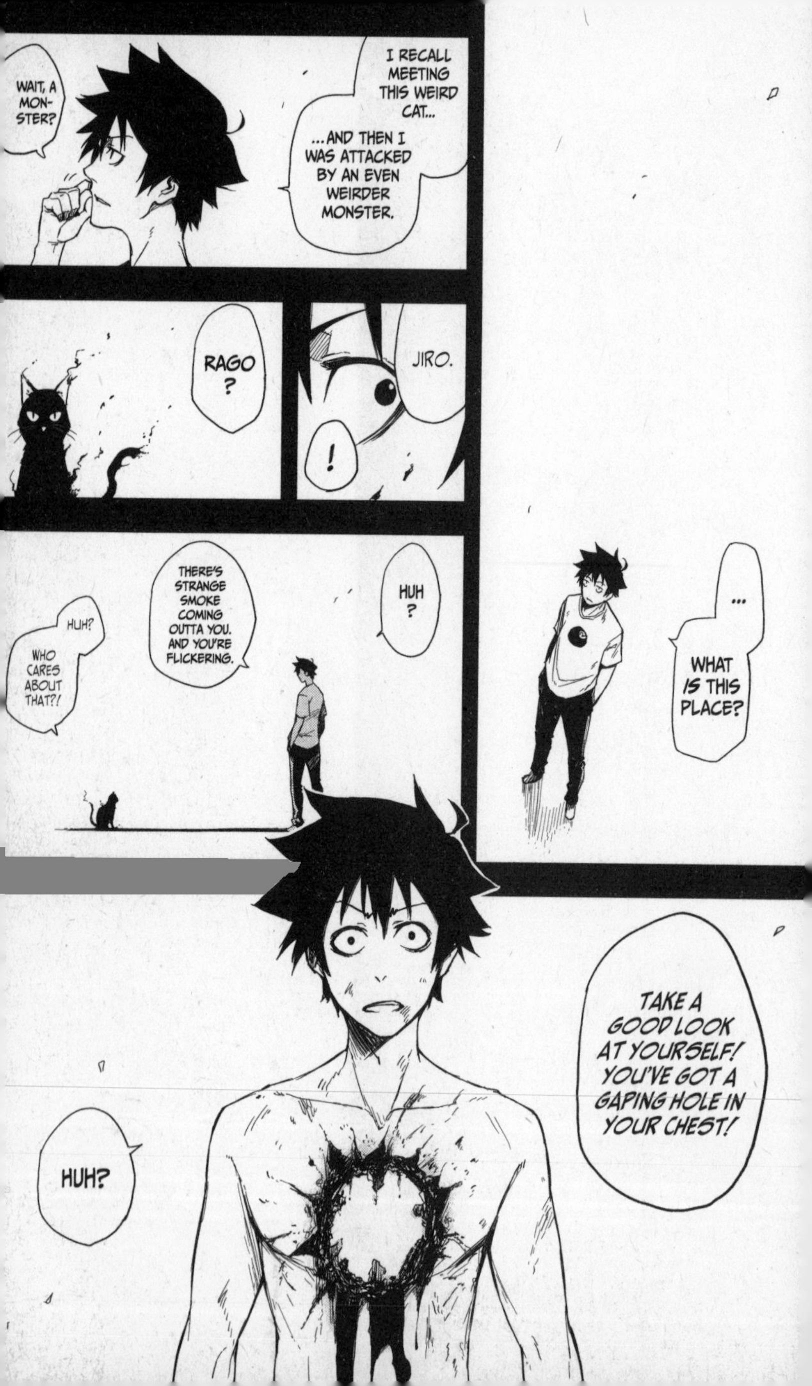
...
WHAT IS THIS PLACE?
I RECALL MEETING THIS WEIRD CAT...
...AND THEN I WAS ATTACKED BY AN EVEN WEIRDER MONSTER.
WAIT, A MONSTER?
JIRO.
!
RAGO?
HUH?
THERE'S STRANGE SMOKE COMING OUTTA YOU. AND YOU'RE FLICKERING.
HUH?
WHO CARES ABOUT THAT?!
TAKE A GOOD LOOK AT YOURSELF! YOU'VE GOT A GAPING HOLE IN YOUR CHEST!
HUH?

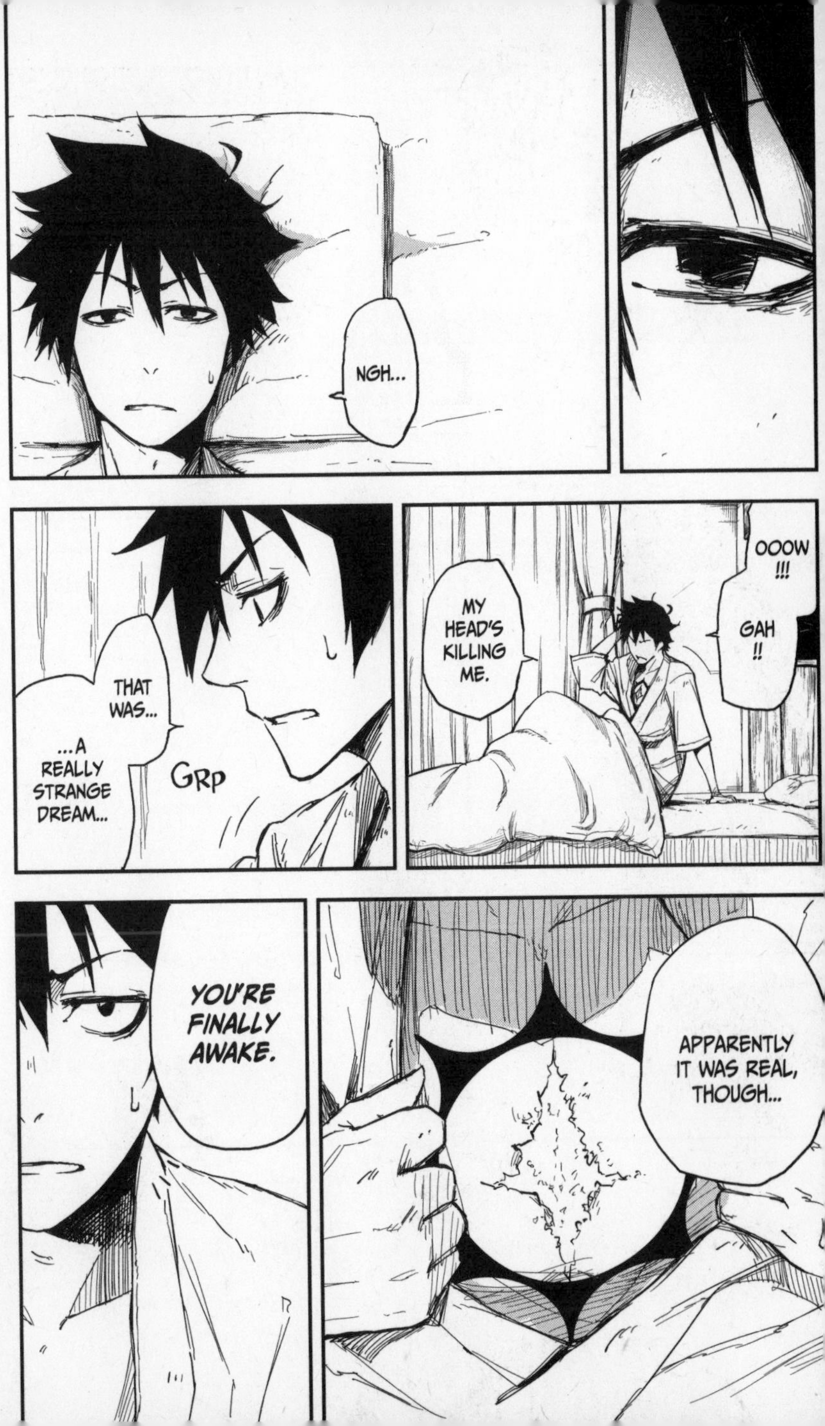
NGH...
OOOW!!!
GAH!!
MY HEAD'S KILLING ME.
THAT WAS...
...A REALLY STRANGE DREAM...
GRP
APPARENTLY IT WAS REAL, THOUGH...
YOU'RE FINALLY AWAKE.

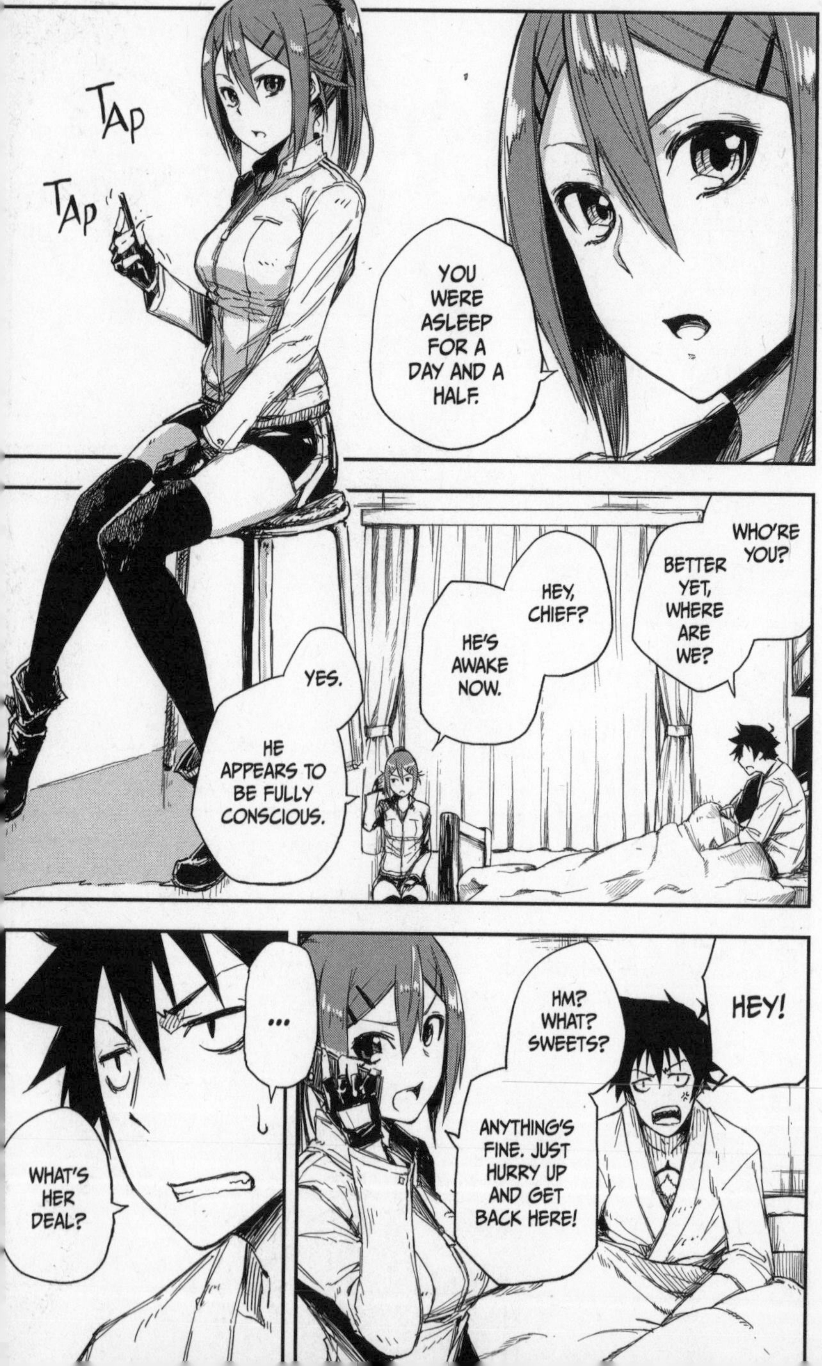
YOU WERE ASLEEP FOR A DAY AND A HALF.
WHO'RE YOU?
BETTER YET, WHERE ARE WE?
HEY, CHIEF?
HE'S AWAKE NOW.
YES.
HE APPEARS TO BE FULLY CONSCIOUS.
TAP
TAP
HEY!
HM? WHAT? SWEETS?
ANYTHING'S FINE. JUST HURRY UP AND GET BACK HERE!
...
WHAT'S HER DEAL?

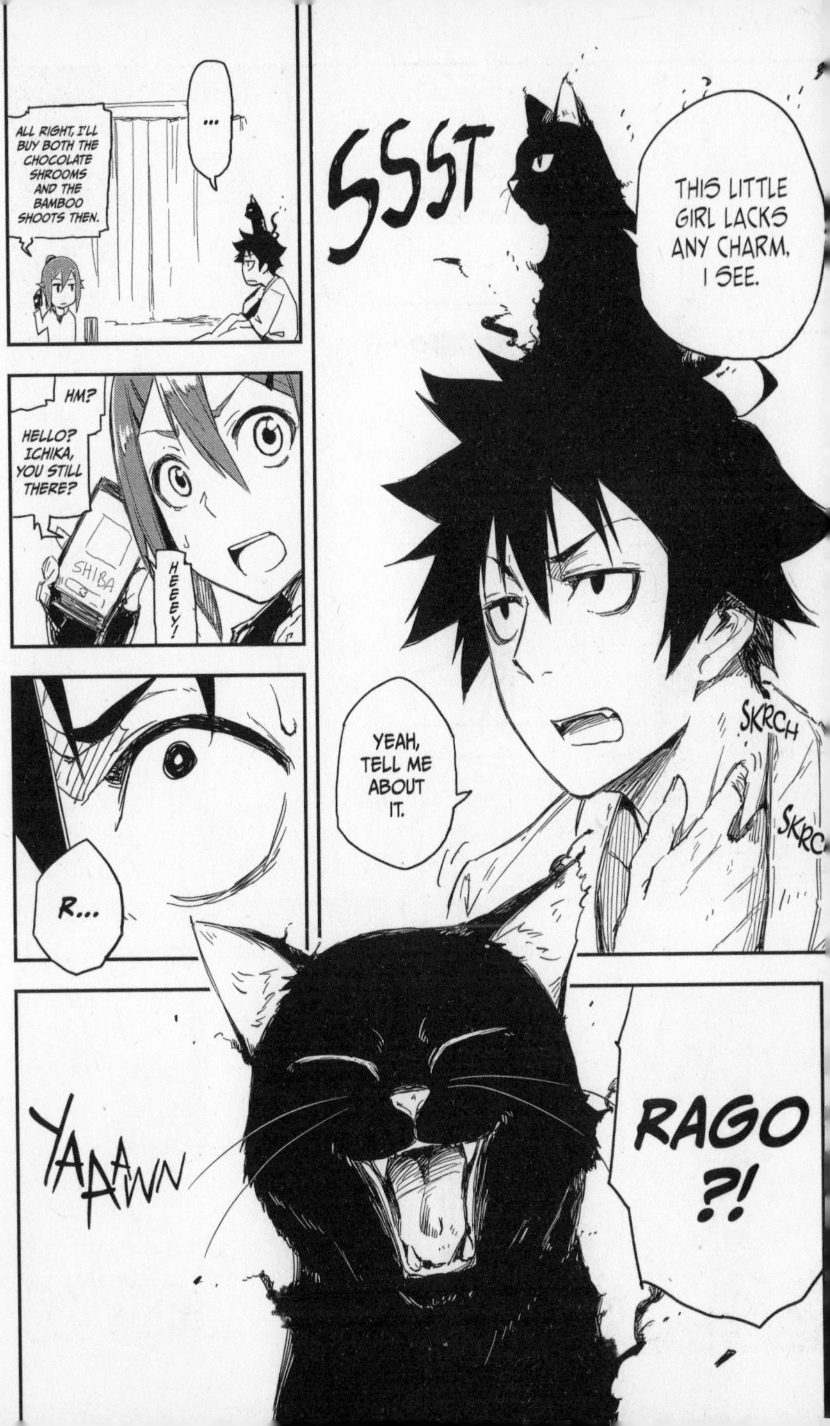
THIS LITTLE GIRL LACKS ANY CHARM, I SEE.
SSST
SKRCH
SKRC
YEAH, TELL ME ABOUT IT.
...
ALL RIGHT, I'LL BUY BOTH THE CHOCOLATE SHROOMS AND THE BAMBOO SHOOTS THEN.
HM?
HELLO? ICHIKA, YOU STILL THERE?
SHIBA
HEEEY!
R...
RAGO ?!
YAAAWN

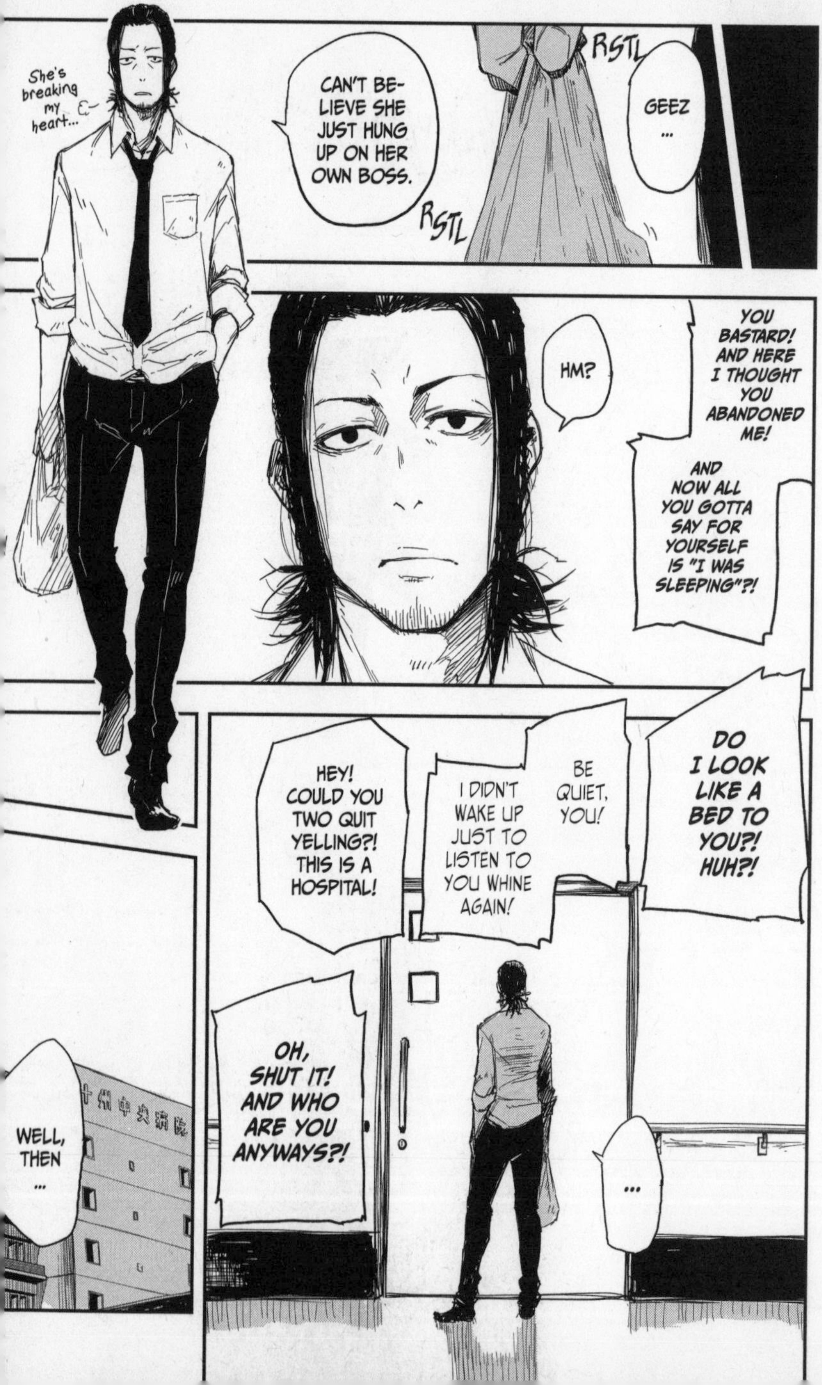
RSTL
GEEZ ...
CAN'T BE-LIEVE SHE JUST HUNG UP ON HER OWN BOSS.
RSTL
YOU BASTARD! AND HERE I THOUGHT YOU ABANDONED ME!
AND NOW ALL YOU GOTTA SAY FOR YOURSELF IS "I WAS SLEEPING"?!
HM?
She's breaking my heart...
DO I LOOK LIKE A BED TO YOU?! HUH?!
BE QUIET, YOU!
I DIDN'T WAKE UP JUST TO LISTEN TO YOU WHINE AGAIN!
HEY! COULD YOU TWO QUIT YELLING?! THIS IS A HOSPITAL!
...
OH, SHUT IT! AND WHO ARE YOU ANYWAYS?!
WELL, THEN ...

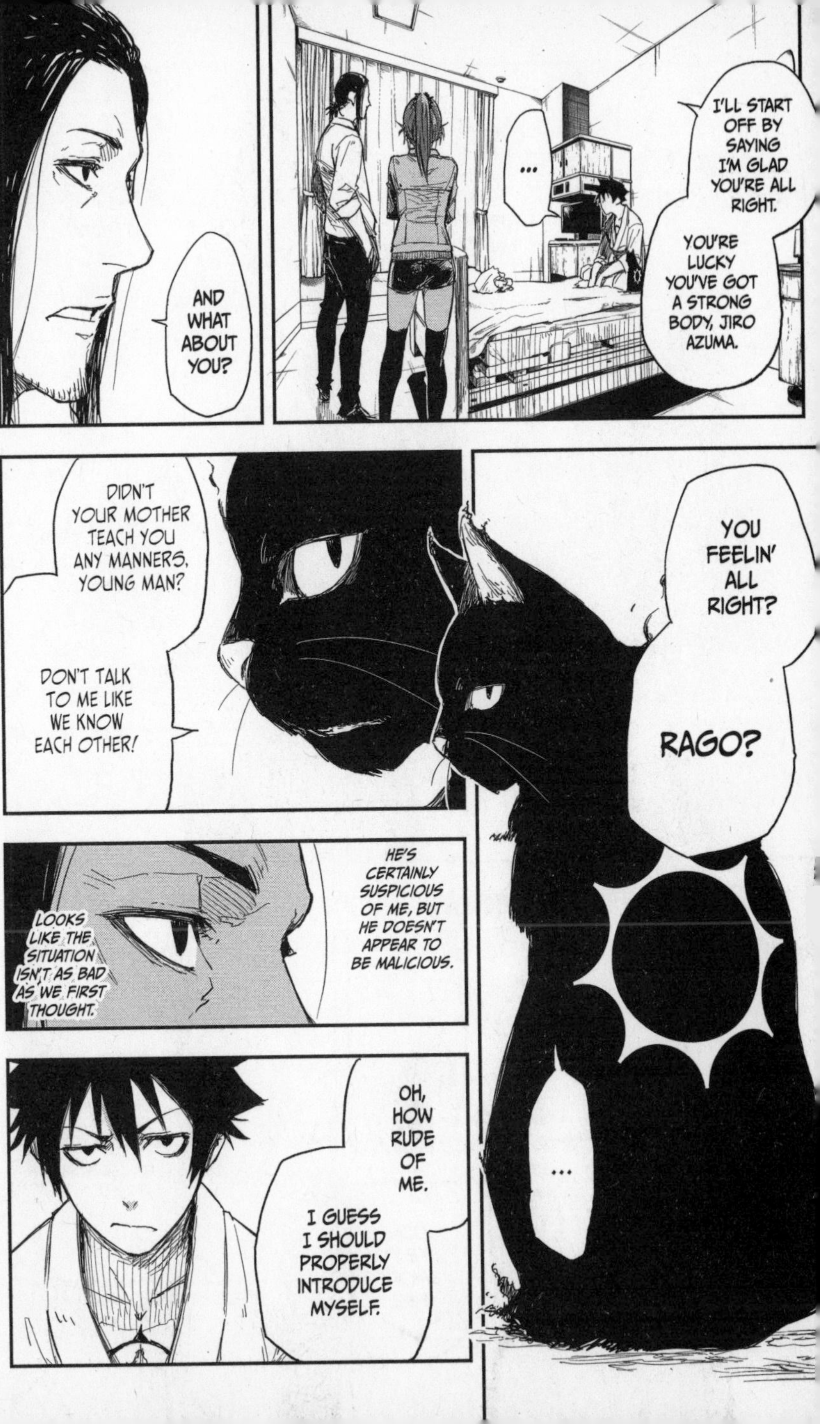
I'LL START OFF BY SAYING I'M GLAD YOU'RE ALL RIGHT.
YOU'RE LUCKY YOU'VE GOT A STRONG BODY, JIRO AZUMA.
...
AND WHAT ABOUT YOU?
YOU FEELIN' ALL RIGHT?
RAGO?
...
DIDN'T YOUR MOTHER TEACH YOU ANY MANNERS, YOUNG MAN?
DON'T TALK TO ME LIKE WE KNOW EACH OTHER!
HE'S CERTAINLY SUSPICIOUS OF ME, BUT HE DOESN'T APPEAR TO BE MALICIOUS.
LOOKS LIKE THE SITUATION ISN'T AS BAD AS WE FIRST THOUGHT.
OH, HOW RUDE OF ME.
I GUESS I SHOULD PROPERLY INTRODUCE MYSELF.

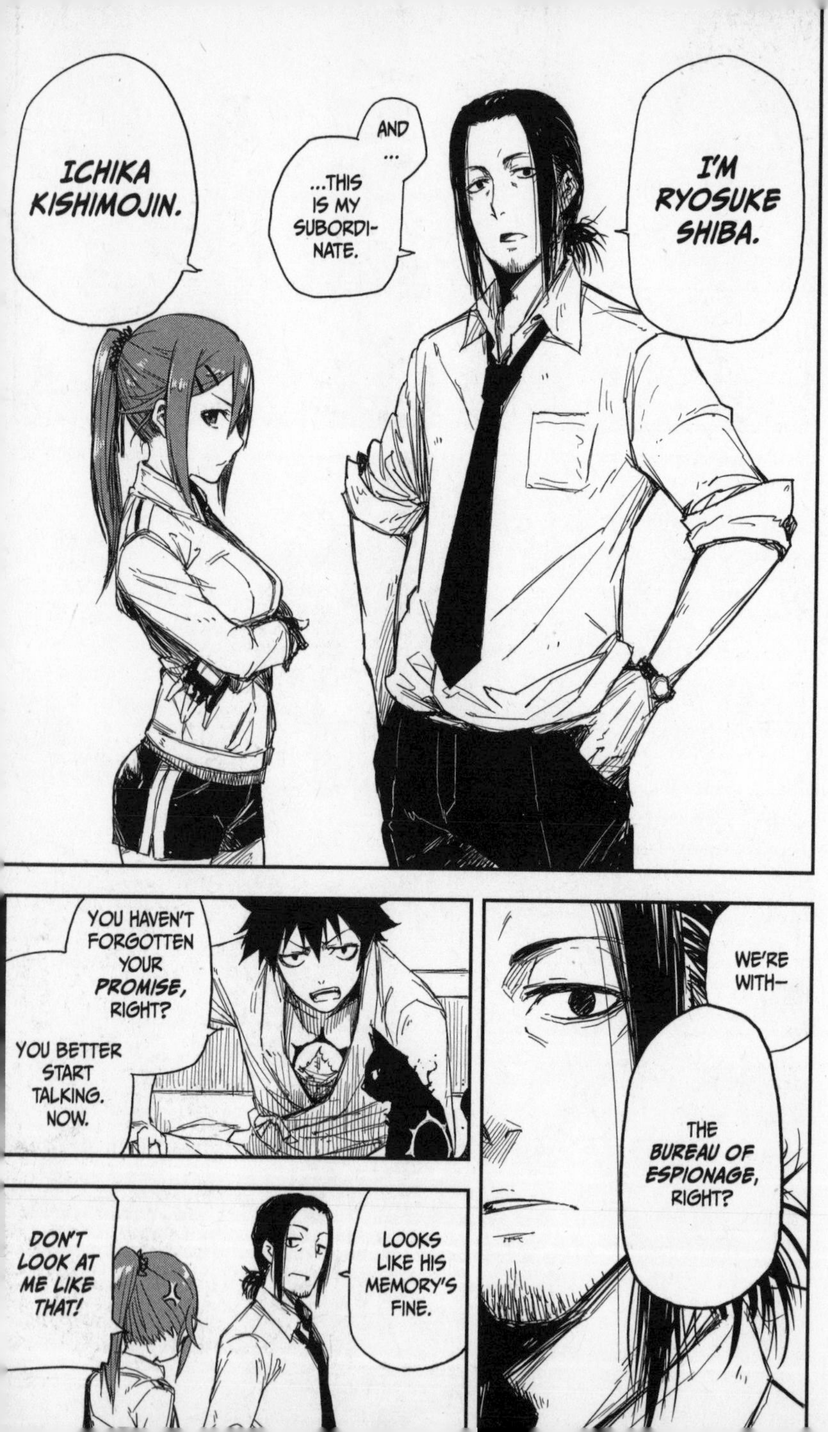
I'M RYOSUKE SHIBA.
AND ...
...THIS IS MY SUBORDI-NATE.
ICHIKA KISHIMOJIN.
WE'RE WITH—
THE BUREAU OF ESPIONAGE, RIGHT?
YOU HAVEN'T FORGOTTEN YOUR PROMISE, RIGHT?
YOU BETTER START TALKING. NOW.
LOOKS LIKE HIS MEMORY'S FINE.
DON'T LOOK AT ME LIKE THAT!

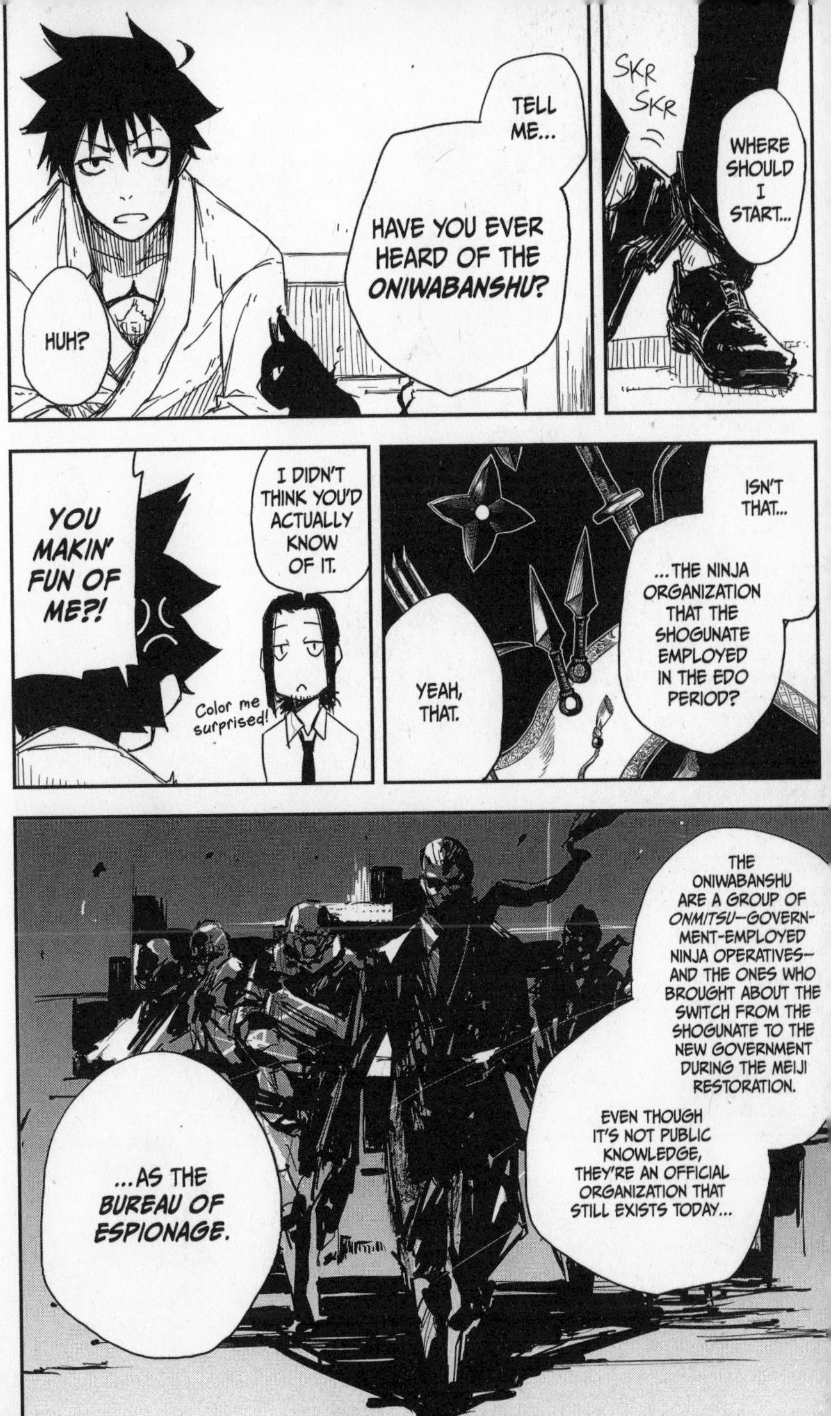
SKR SKR
WHERE SHOULD I START...
TELL ME...
HAVE YOU EVER HEARD OF THE *ONIWABANSHU*?
HUH?
ISN'T THAT...
...THE NINJA ORGANIZATION THAT THE SHOGUNATE EMPLOYED IN THE EDO PERIOD?
YEAH, THAT.
I DIDN'T THINK YOU'D ACTUALLY KNOW OF IT.
Color me surprised!
YOU MAKIN' FUN OF ME?!
THE ONIWABANSHU ARE A GROUP OF *ONMITSU*—GOVERNMENT-EMPLOYED NINJA OPERATIVES—AND THE ONES WHO BROUGHT ABOUT THE SWITCH FROM THE SHOGUNATE TO THE NEW GOVERNMENT DURING THE MEIJI RESTORATION.
EVEN THOUGH IT'S NOT PUBLIC KNOWLEDGE, THEY'RE AN OFFICIAL ORGANIZATION THAT STILL EXISTS TODAY...
...AS THE *BUREAU OF ESPIONAGE.*

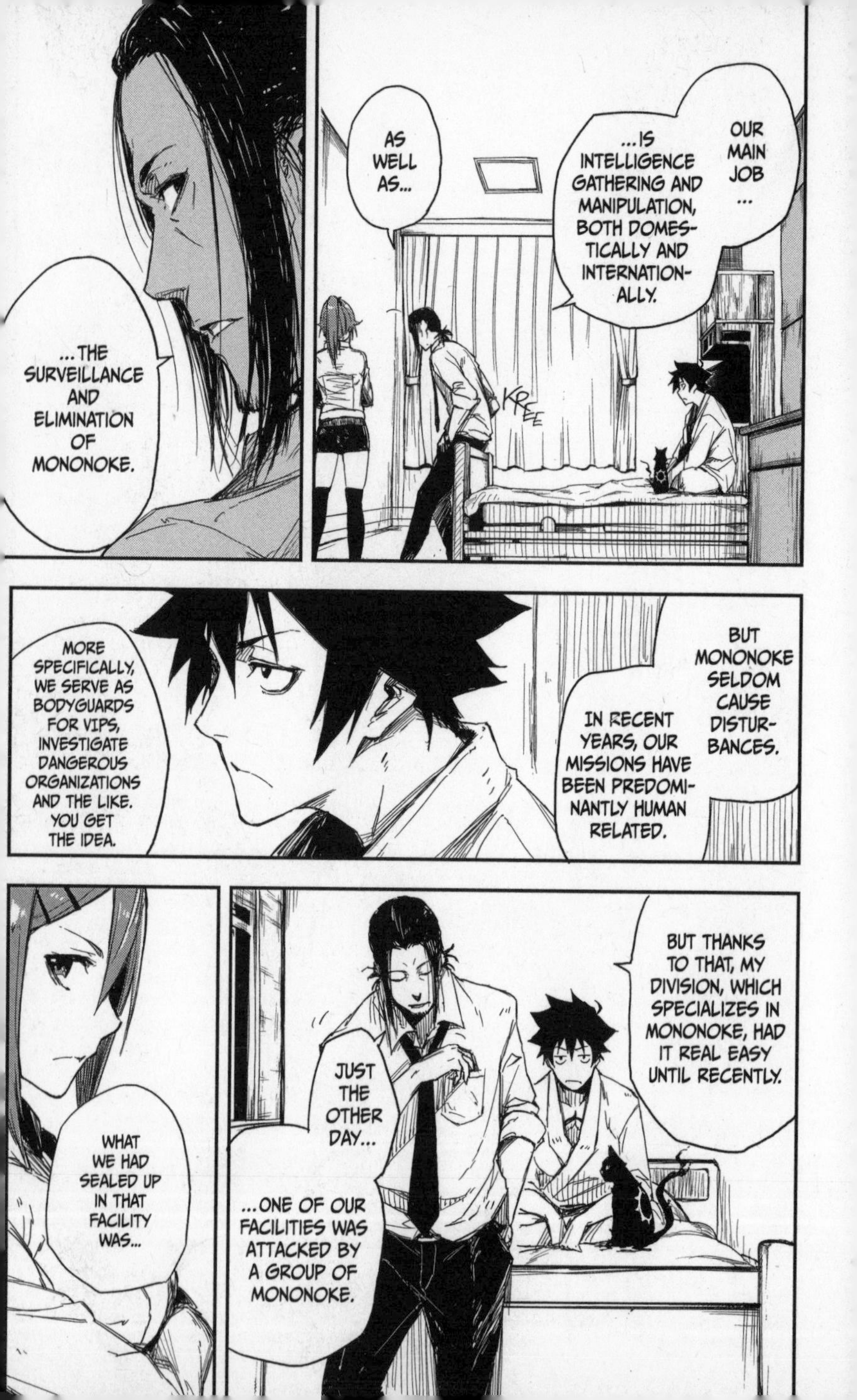
OUR MAIN JOB ...
...IS INTELLIGENCE GATHERING AND MANIPULATION, BOTH DOMESTICALLY AND INTERNATIONALLY.
AS WELL AS...
KREE
...THE SURVEILLANCE AND ELIMINATION OF MONONOKE.
BUT MONONOKE SELDOM CAUSE DISTURBANCES.
IN RECENT YEARS, OUR MISSIONS HAVE BEEN PREDOMINANTLY HUMAN RELATED.
MORE SPECIFICALLY, WE SERVE AS BODYGUARDS FOR VIPS, INVESTIGATE DANGEROUS ORGANIZATIONS AND THE LIKE. YOU GET THE IDEA.
BUT THANKS TO THAT, MY DIVISION, WHICH SPECIALIZES IN MONONOKE, HAD IT REAL EASY UNTIL RECENTLY.
JUST THE OTHER DAY...
...ONE OF OUR FACILITIES WAS ATTACKED BY A GROUP OF MONONOKE.
WHAT WE HAD SEALED UP IN THAT FACILITY WAS...

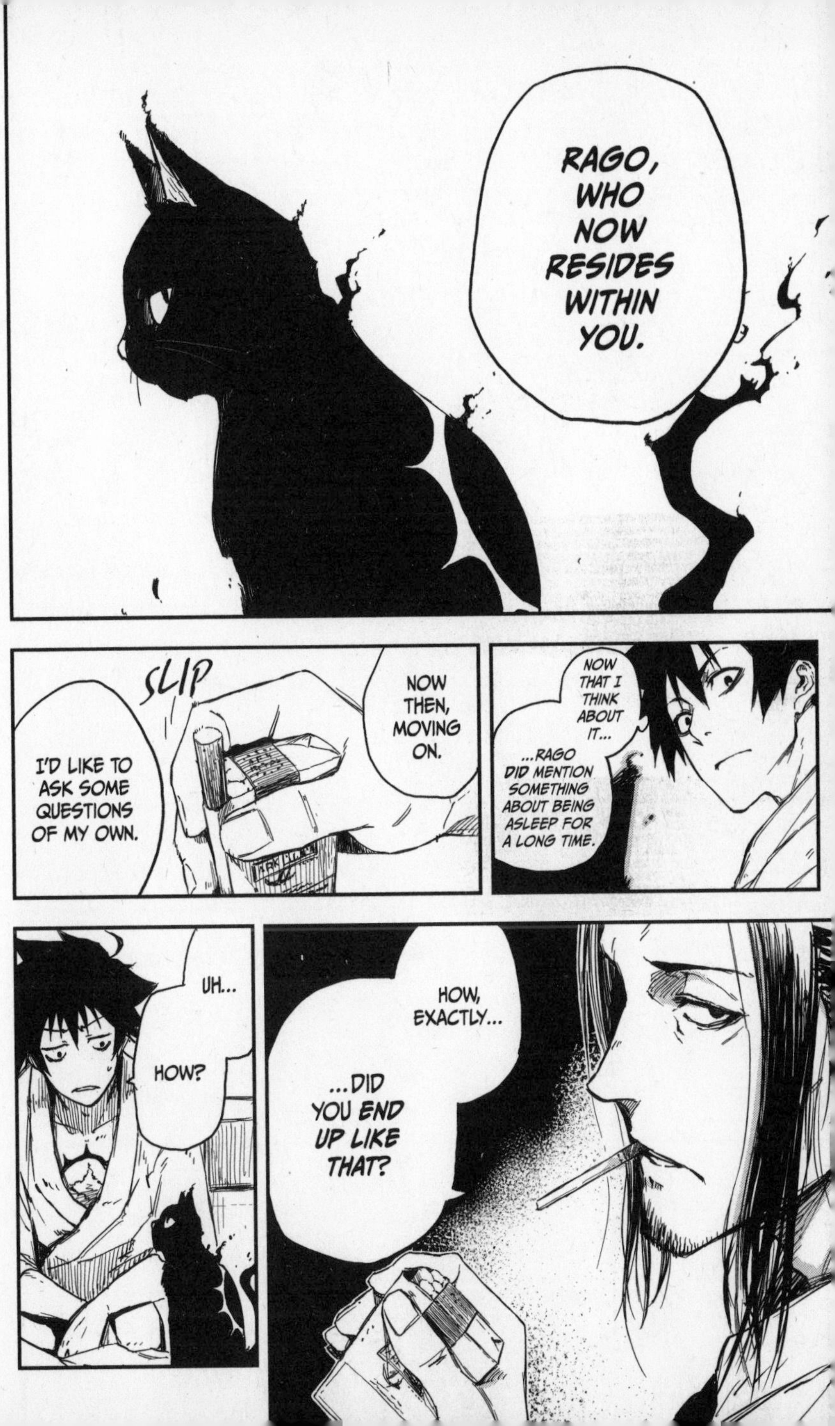
RAGO, WHO NOW RESIDES WITHIN YOU.
NOW THAT I THINK ABOUT IT...
...RAGO DID MENTION SOMETHING ABOUT BEING ASLEEP FOR A LONG TIME.
NOW THEN, MOVING ON.
SLIP
I'D LIKE TO ASK SOME QUESTIONS OF MY OWN.
HOW, EXACTLY...
...DID YOU END UP LIKE THAT?
UH...
HOW?

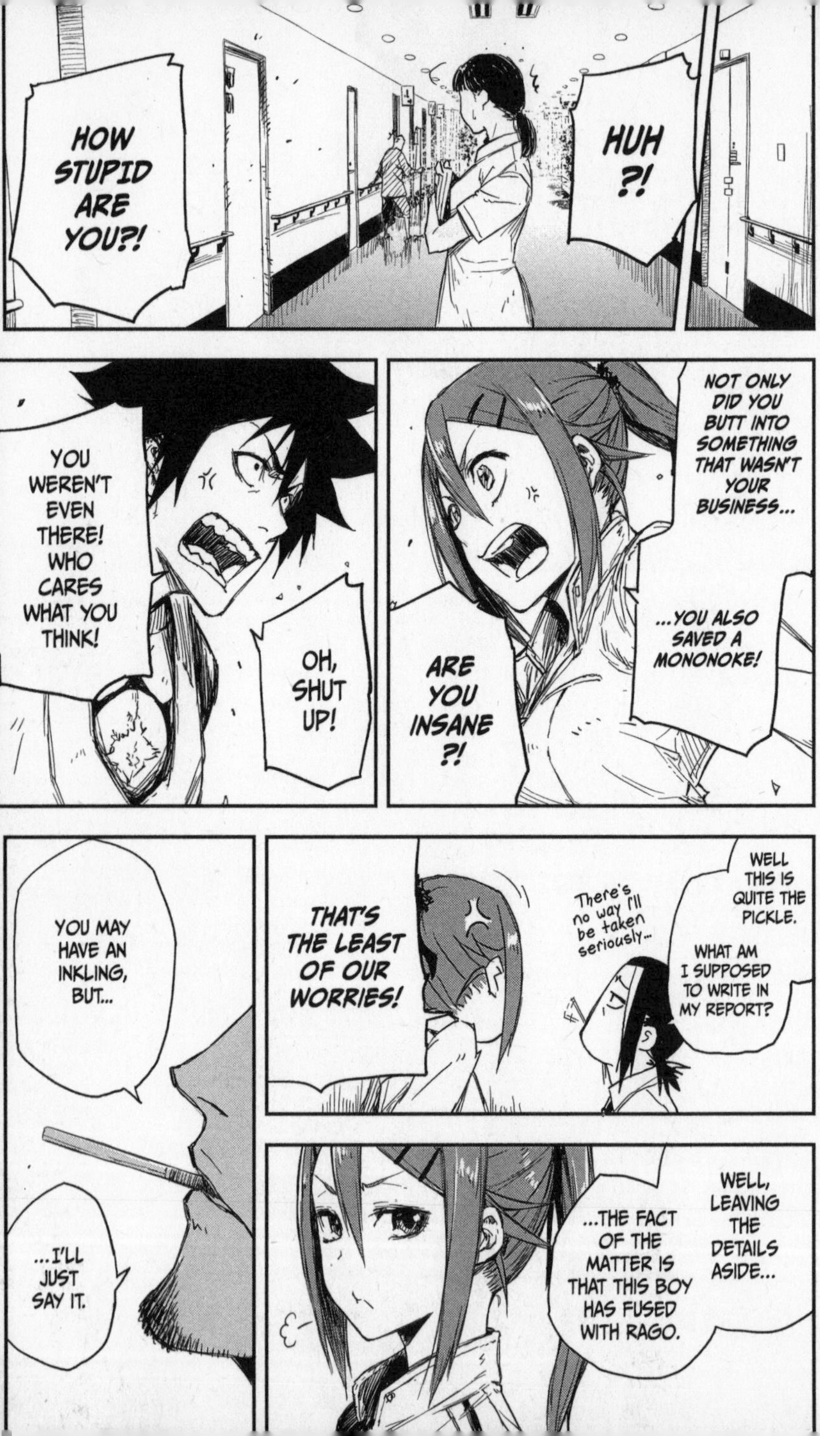
HUH ?!
HOW STUPID ARE YOU?!
NOT ONLY DID YOU BUTT INTO SOMETHING THAT WASN'T YOUR BUSINESS...
...YOU ALSO SAVED A MONONOKE!
ARE YOU INSANE ?!
OH, SHUT UP!
YOU WEREN'T EVEN THERE! WHO CARES WHAT YOU THINK!
WELL THIS IS QUITE THE PICKLE.
WHAT AM I SUPPOSED TO WRITE IN MY REPORT?
There's no way I'll be taken seriously...
THAT'S THE LEAST OF OUR WORRIES!
WELL, LEAVING THE DETAILS ASIDE...
...THE FACT OF THE MATTER IS THAT THIS BOY HAS FUSED WITH RAGO.
YOU MAY HAVE AN INKLING, BUT...
...I'LL JUST SAY IT.

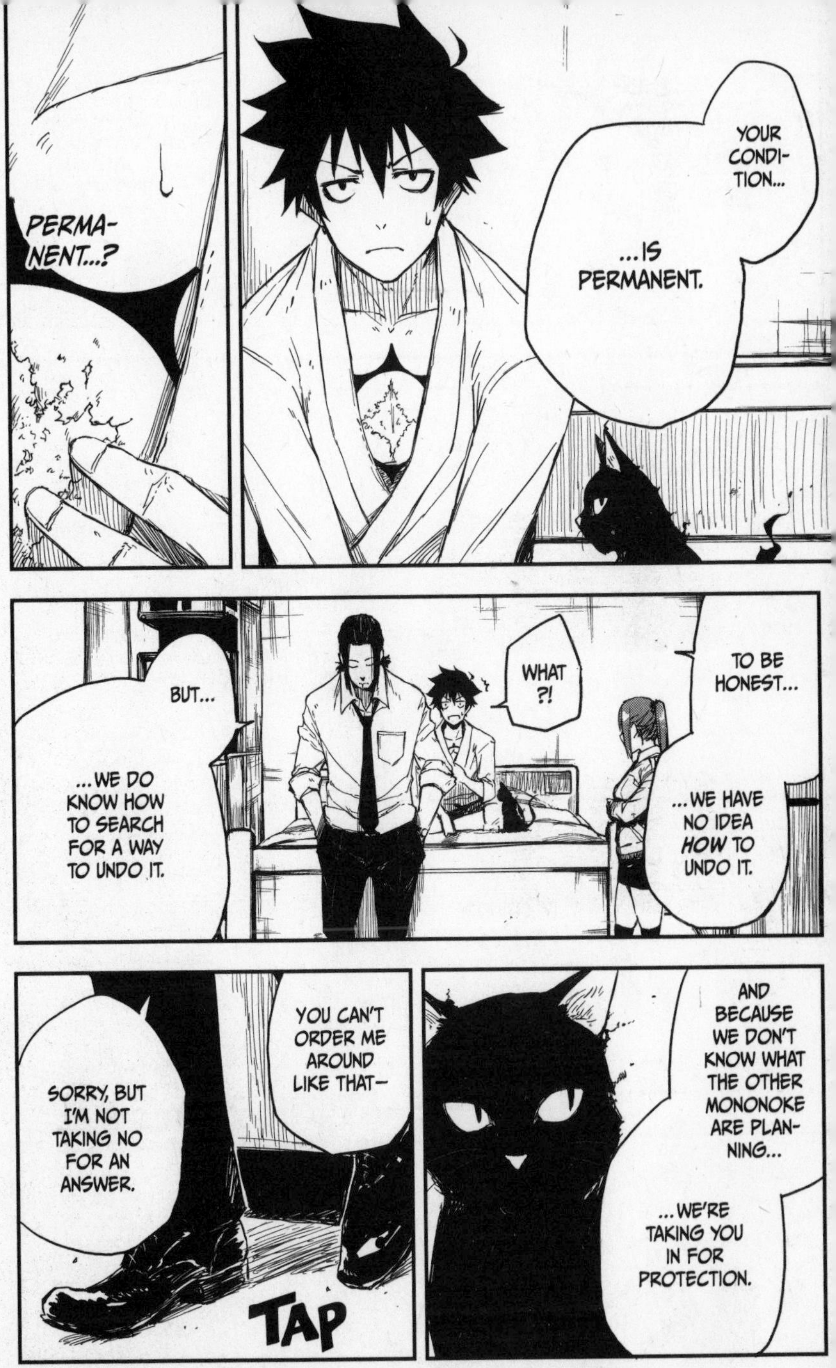
YOUR CONDI- TION...
...IS PERMANENT.
PERMA- NENT...?
TO BE HONEST...
...WE HAVE NO IDEA *HOW* TO UNDO IT.
WHAT ?!
BUT...
...WE DO KNOW HOW TO SEARCH FOR A WAY TO UNDO IT.
AND BECAUSE WE DON'T KNOW WHAT THE OTHER MONONOKE ARE PLAN- NING...
...WE'RE TAKING YOU IN FOR PROTECTION.
YOU CAN'T ORDER ME AROUND LIKE THAT—
SORRY, BUT I'M NOT TAKING NO FOR AN ANSWER.
TAP

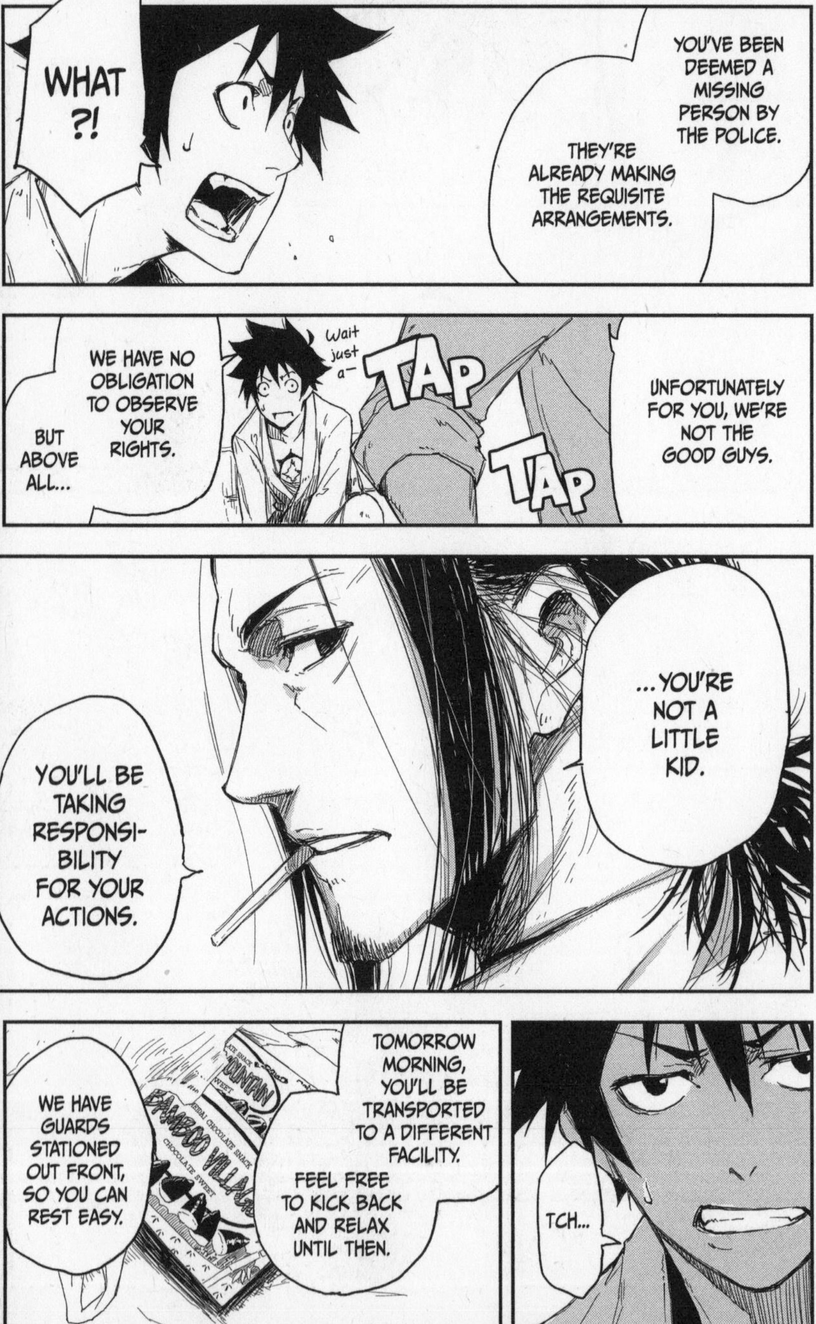
YOU'VE BEEN DEEMED A MISSING PERSON BY THE POLICE.
THEY'RE ALREADY MAKING THE REQUISITE ARRANGEMENTS.
WHAT ?!
UNFORTUNATELY FOR YOU, WE'RE NOT THE GOOD GUYS.
TAP
TAP
Wait just a—
WE HAVE NO OBLIGATION TO OBSERVE YOUR RIGHTS.
BUT ABOVE ALL...
...YOU'RE NOT A LITTLE KID.
YOU'LL BE TAKING RESPONSI-BILITY FOR YOUR ACTIONS.
TCH...
TOMORROW MORNING, YOU'LL BE TRANSPORTED TO A DIFFERENT FACILITY.
FEEL FREE TO KICK BACK AND RELAX UNTIL THEN.
WE HAVE GUARDS STATIONED OUT FRONT, SO YOU CAN REST EASY.

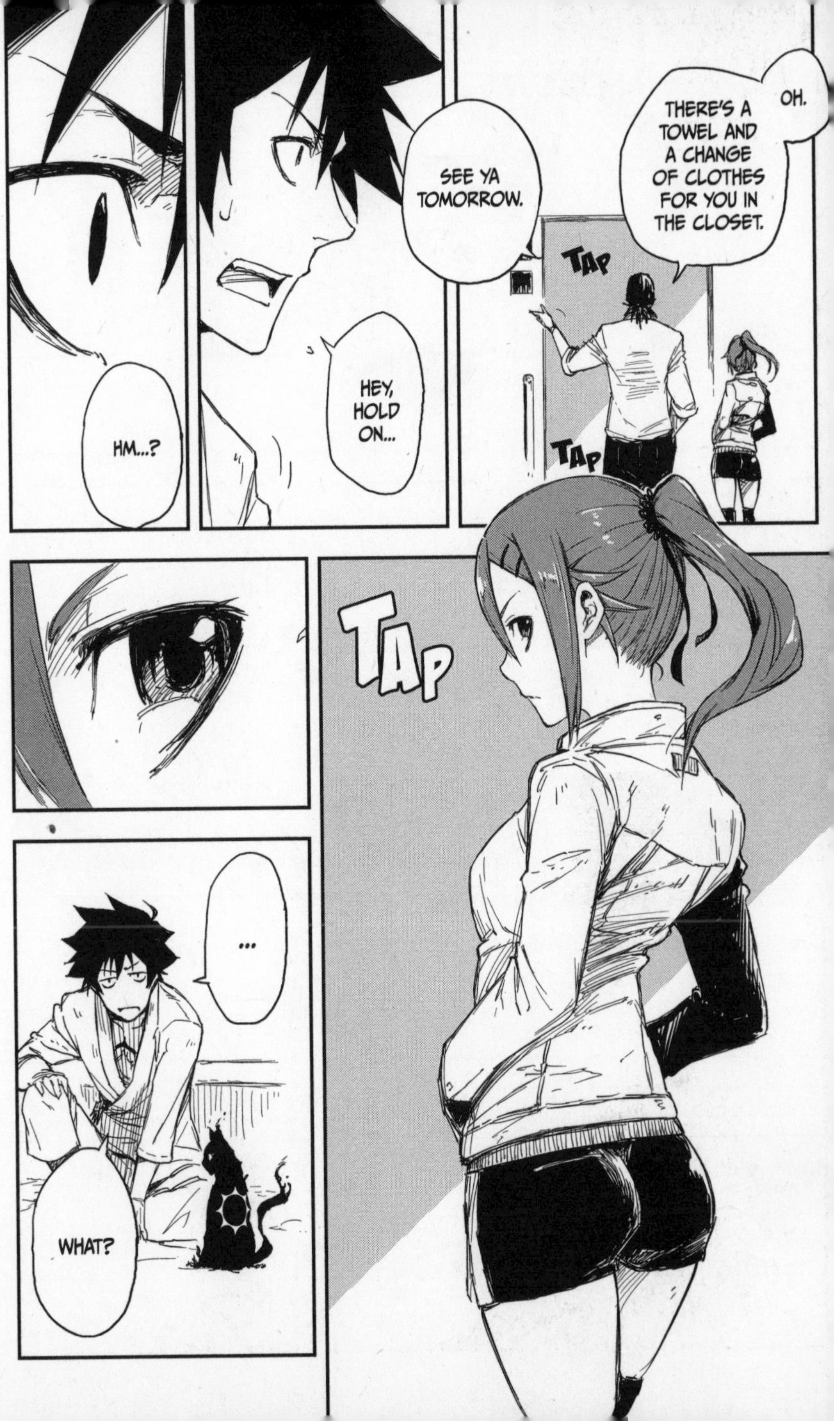
OH.
THERE'S A TOWEL AND A CHANGE OF CLOTHES FOR YOU IN THE CLOSET.
TAP
TAP
SEE YA TOMORROW.
HEY, HOLD ON...
HM...?
TAP
...
WHAT?

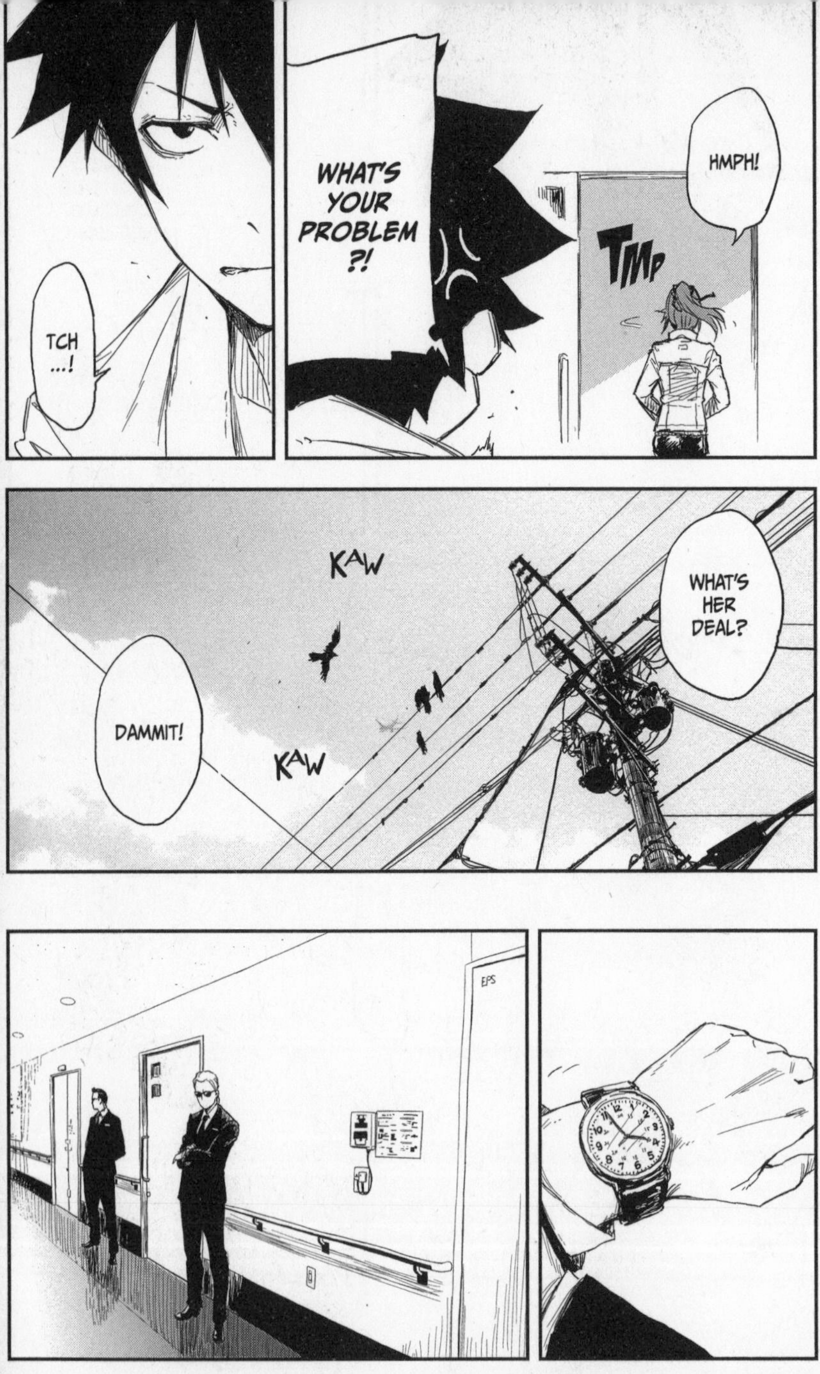
HMPH!
TMP
WHAT'S YOUR PROBLEM ?!
TCH ...!
WHAT'S HER DEAL?
KAW
DAMMIT!
KAW
EPS

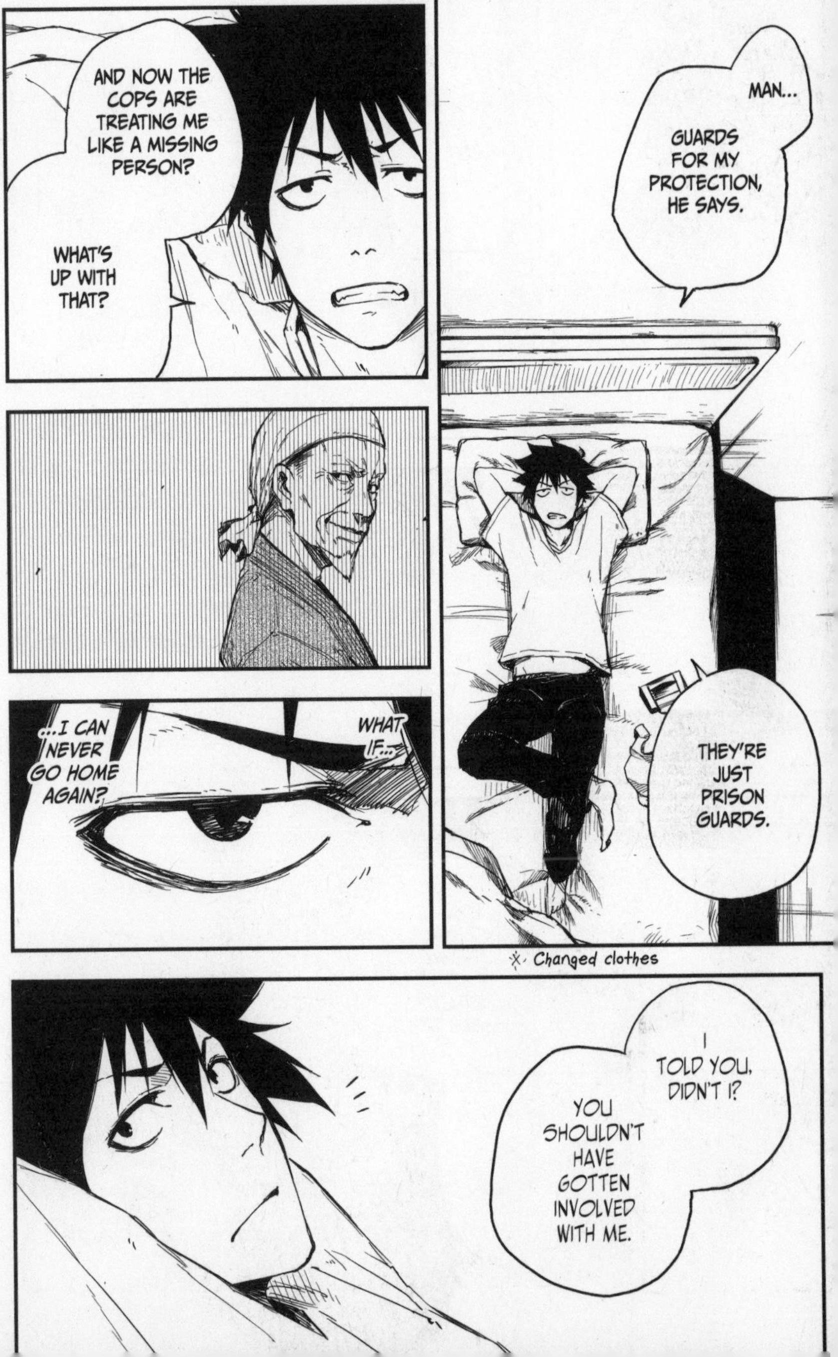
MAN...
GUARDS FOR MY PROTECTION, HE SAYS.
THEY'RE JUST PRISON GUARDS.
※ Changed clothes
AND NOW THE COPS ARE TREATING ME LIKE A MISSING PERSON?
WHAT'S UP WITH THAT?
WHAT IF...
...I CAN NEVER GO HOME AGAIN?
I TOLD YOU, DIDN'T I?
YOU SHOULDN'T HAVE GOTTEN INVOLVED WITH ME.

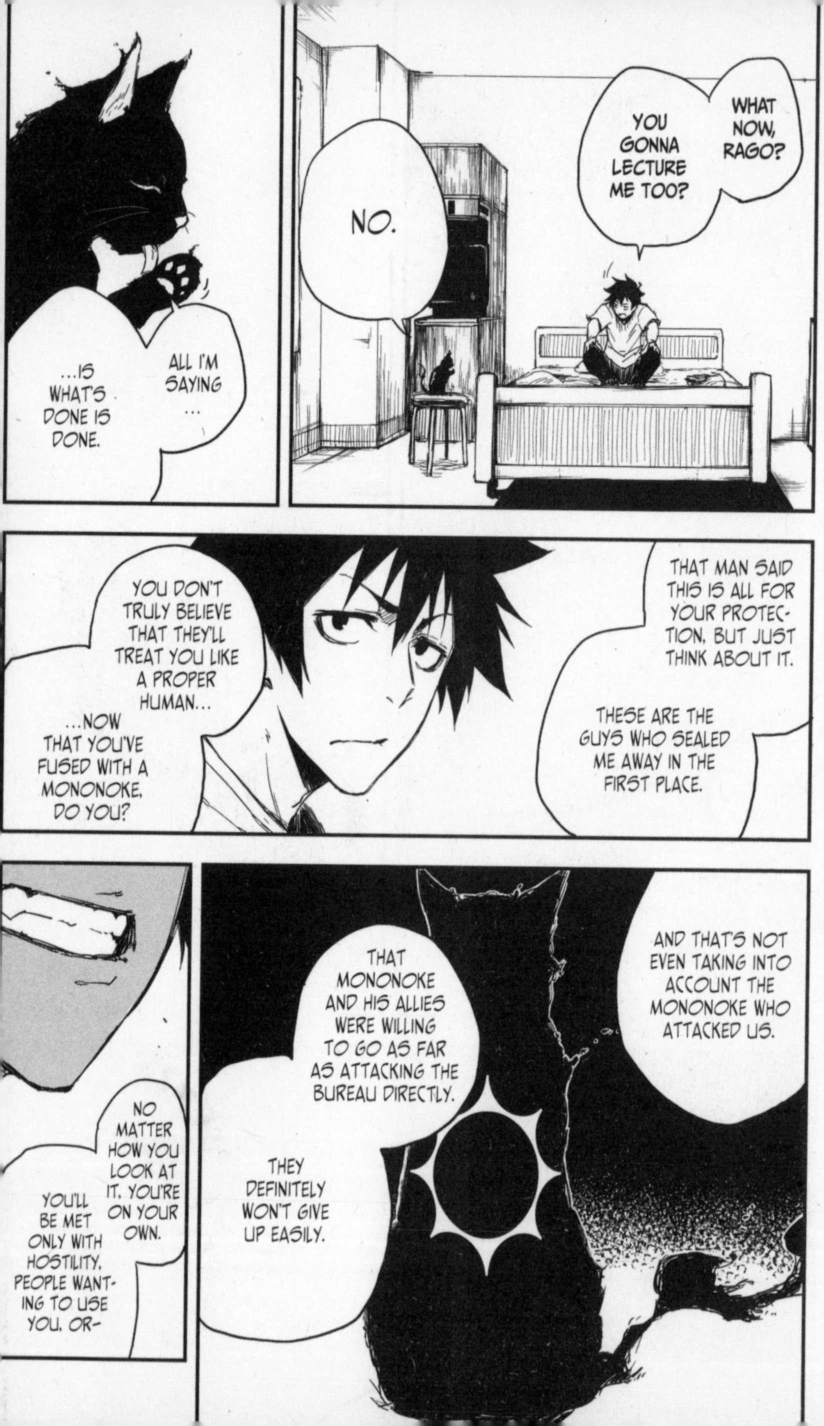
WHAT NOW, RAGO?
YOU GONNA LECTURE ME TOO?
NO.
ALL I'M SAYING ...
...IS WHAT'S DONE IS DONE.
THAT MAN SAID THIS IS ALL FOR YOUR PROTECTION, BUT JUST THINK ABOUT IT.
THESE ARE THE GUYS WHO SEALED ME AWAY IN THE FIRST PLACE.
YOU DON'T TRULY BELIEVE THAT THEY'LL TREAT YOU LIKE A PROPER HUMAN...
...NOW THAT YOU'VE FUSED WITH A MONONOKE, DO YOU?
AND THAT'S NOT EVEN TAKING INTO ACCOUNT THE MONONOKE WHO ATTACKED US.
THAT MONONOKE AND HIS ALLIES WERE WILLING TO GO AS FAR AS ATTACKING THE BUREAU DIRECTLY.
THEY DEFINITELY WON'T GIVE UP EASILY.
NO MATTER HOW YOU LOOK AT IT, YOU'RE ON YOUR OWN.
YOU'LL BE MET ONLY WITH HOSTILITY, PEOPLE WANTING TO USE YOU, OR-

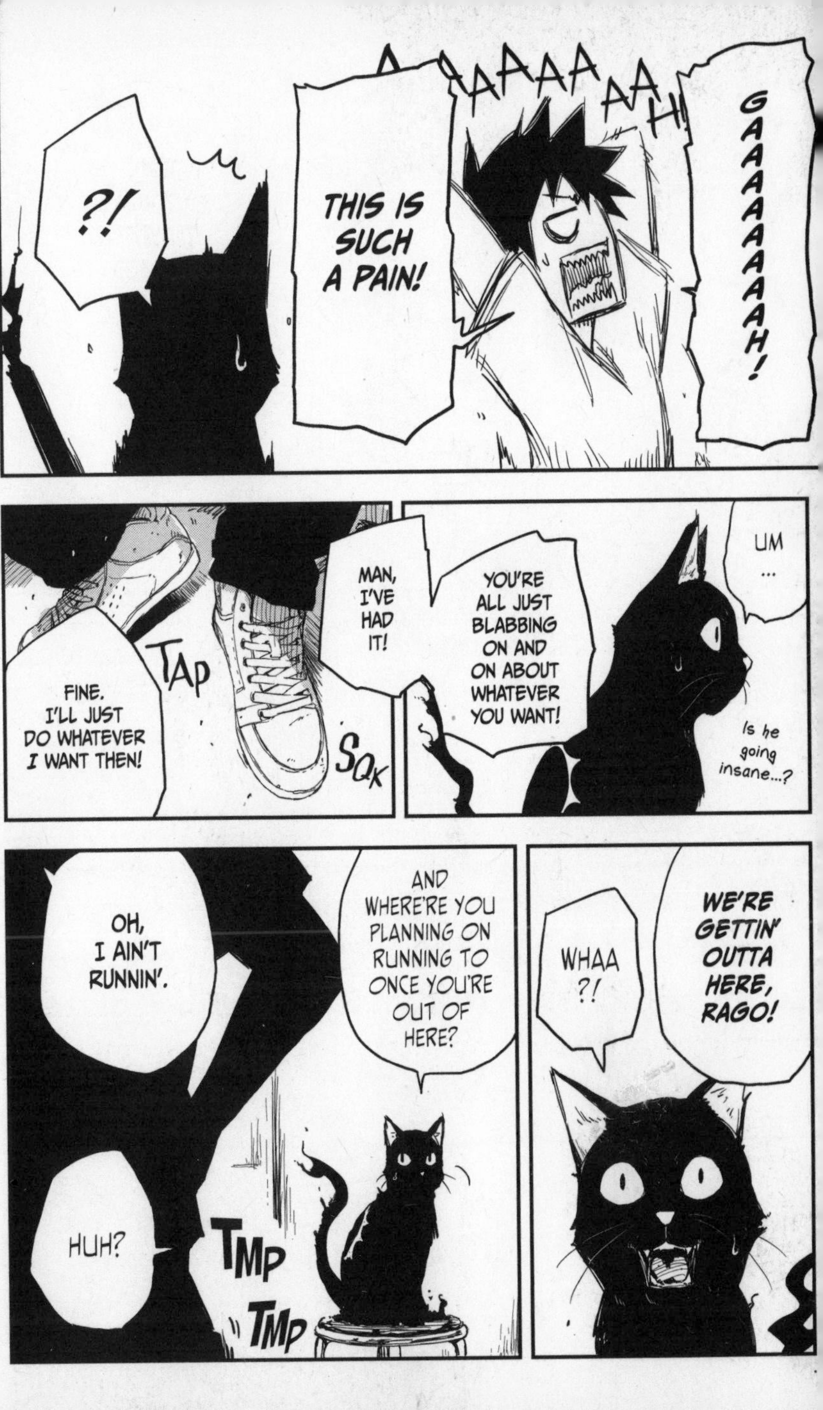
GAAAAAAAAAAAH!
AAAAAAAAH!
THIS IS SUCH A PAIN!
?!
UM ...
Is he going insane...?
YOU'RE ALL JUST BLABBING ON AND ON ABOUT WHATEVER YOU WANT!
MAN, I'VE HAD IT!
TAP
SQK
FINE. I'LL JUST DO WHATEVER I WANT THEN!
WE'RE GETTIN' OUTTA HERE, RAGO!
WHAA ?!
AND WHERE'RE YOU PLANNING ON RUNNING TO ONCE YOU'RE OUT OF HERE?
OH, I AIN'T RUNNIN'.
HUH?
TMP
TMP

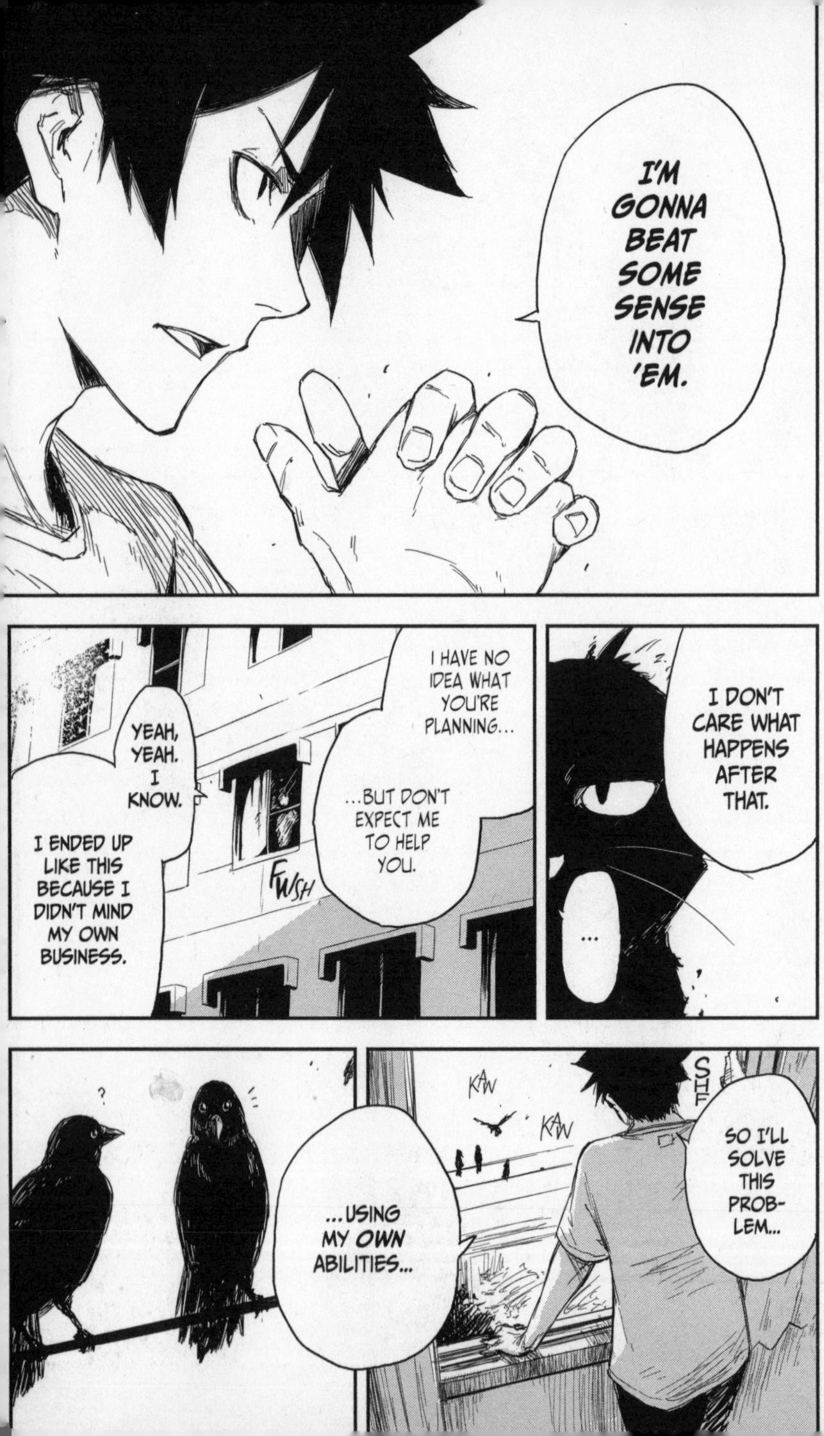
I'M GONNA BEAT SOME SENSE INTO 'EM.
I DON'T CARE WHAT HAPPENS AFTER THAT.
...
I HAVE NO IDEA WHAT YOU'RE PLANNING...
...BUT DON'T EXPECT ME TO HELP YOU.
FWISH
YEAH, YEAH. I KNOW.
I ENDED UP LIKE THIS BECAUSE I DIDN'T MIND MY OWN BUSINESS.
SHF
KAW
KAW
SO I'LL SOLVE THIS PROB-LEM...
?
...USING MY OWN ABILITIES...

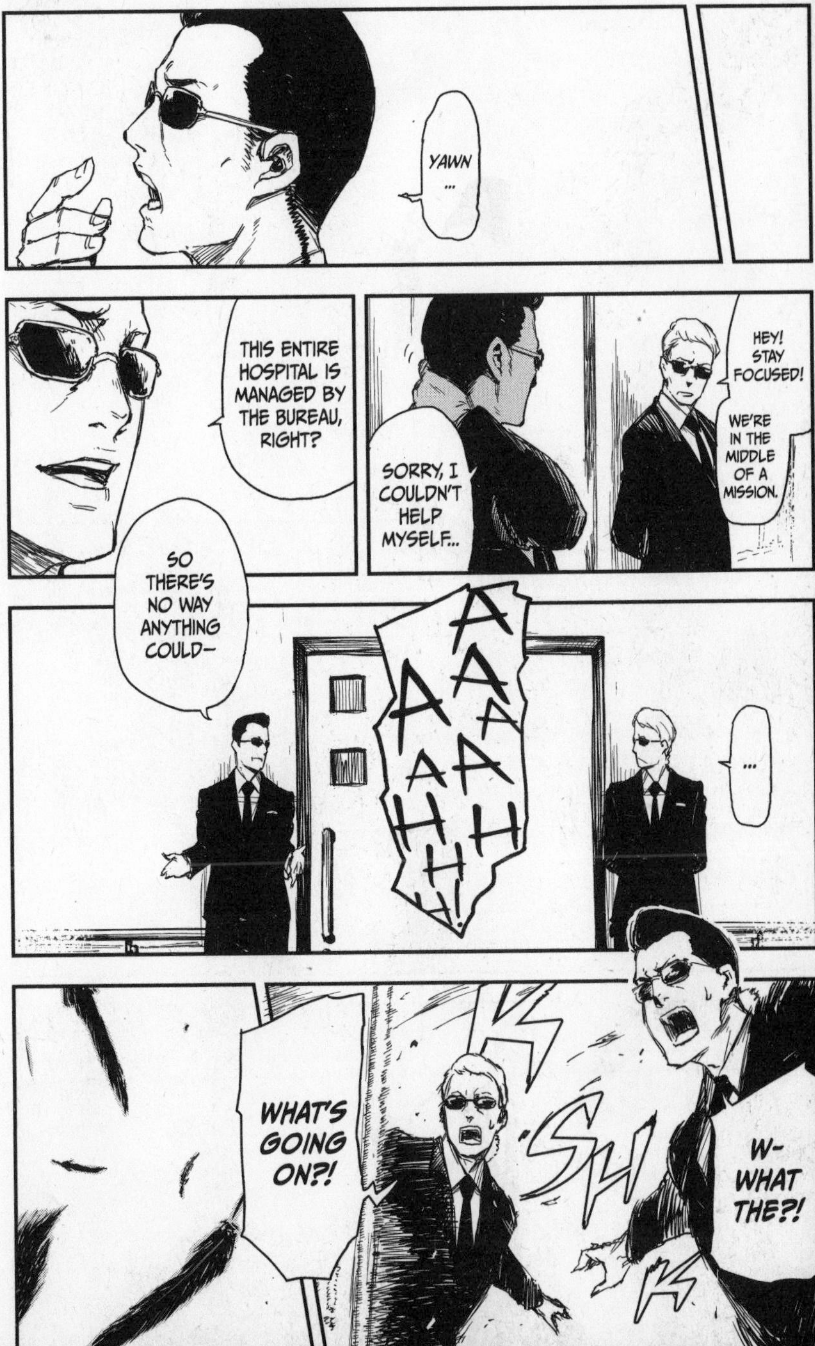
YAWN ...
HEY! STAY FOCUSED!
WE'RE IN THE MIDDLE OF A MISSION.
SORRY, I COULDN'T HELP MYSELF...
THIS ENTIRE HOSPITAL IS MANAGED BY THE BUREAU, RIGHT?
SO THERE'S NO WAY ANYTHING COULD–
AAAAAAHHHH!
...
W-WHAT THE?!
SHK
WHAT'S GOING ON?!

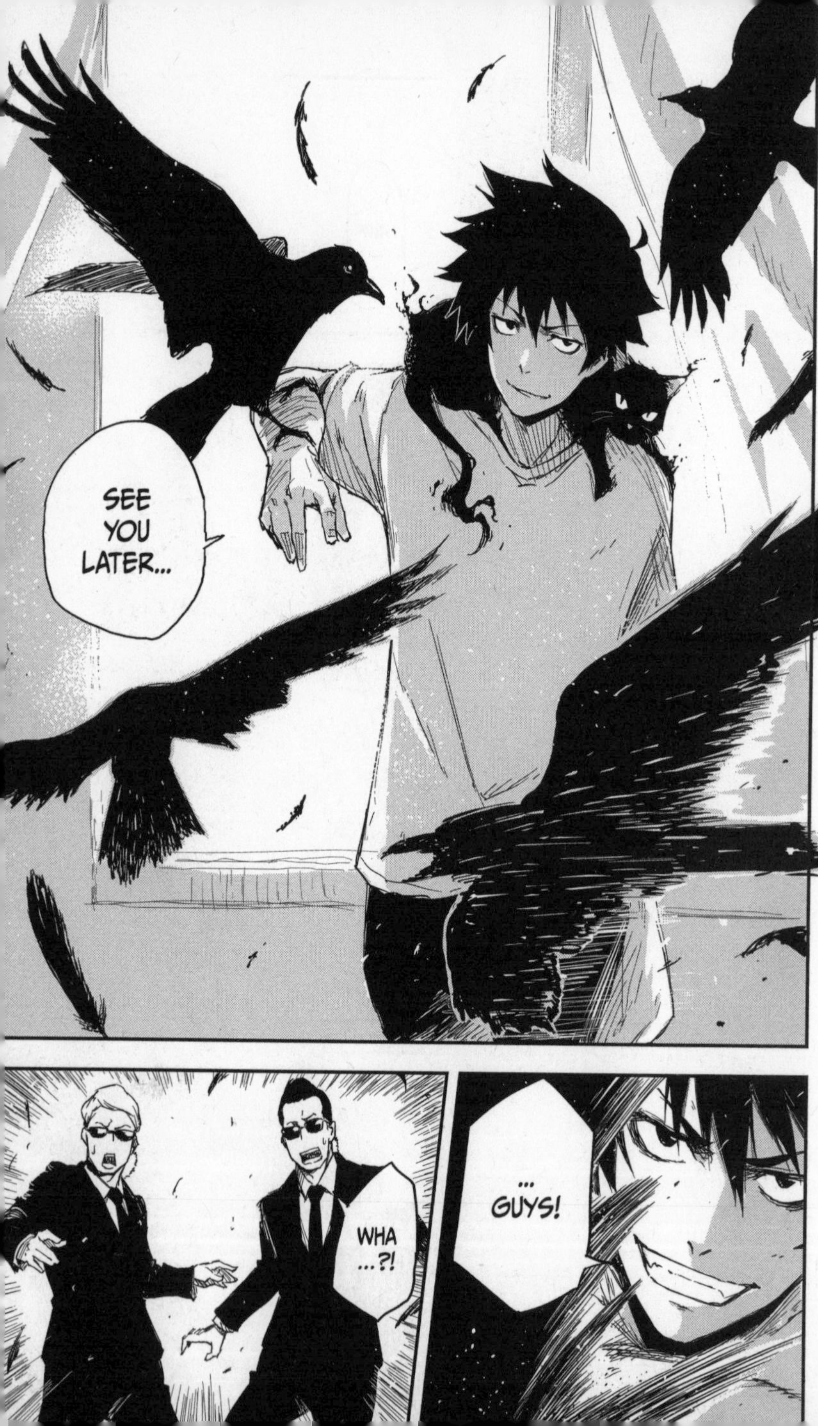
SEE YOU LATER...
... GUYS!
WHA ...?!

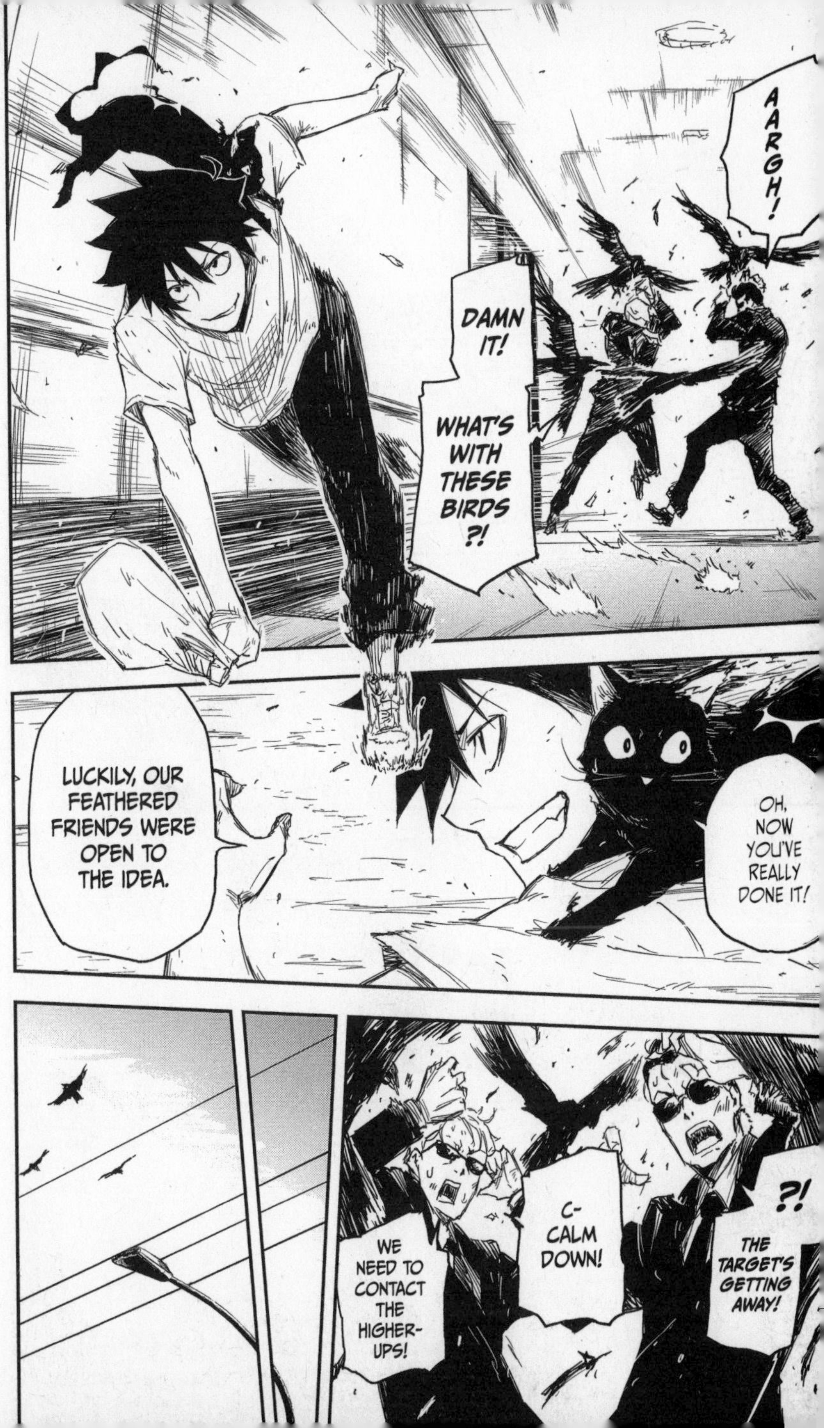
AARGH!
DAMN IT!
WHAT'S WITH THESE BIRDS?!
OH, NOW YOU'VE REALLY DONE IT!
LUCKILY, OUR FEATHERED FRIENDS WERE OPEN TO THE IDEA.
?!
THE TARGET'S GETTING AWAY!
C-CALM DOWN!
WE NEED TO CONTACT THE HIGHER-UPS!

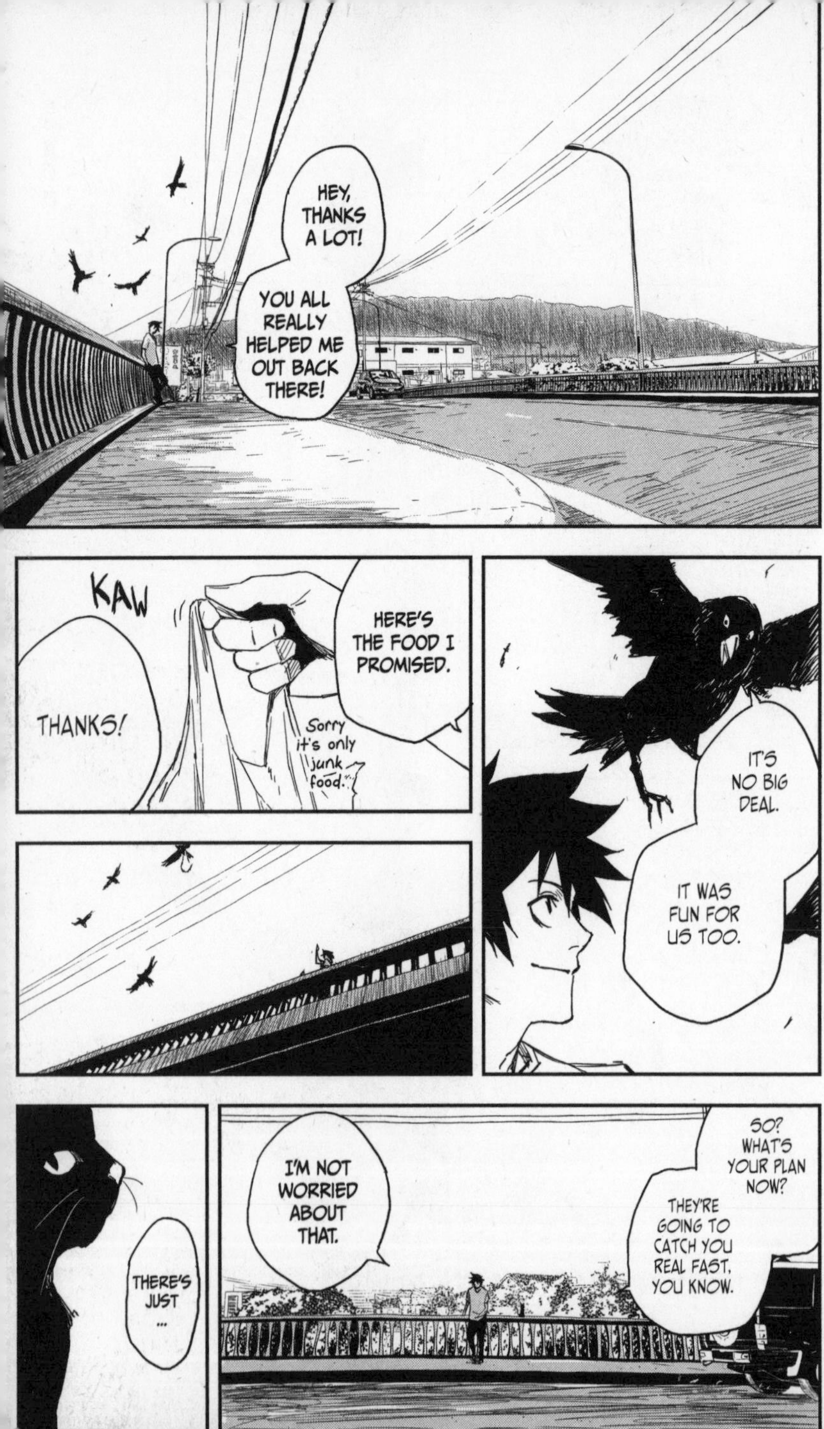
HEY, THANKS A LOT!
YOU ALL REALLY HELPED ME OUT BACK THERE!
IT'S NO BIG DEAL.
IT WAS FUN FOR US TOO.
HERE'S THE FOOD I PROMISED.
Sorry it's only junk food.
KAW
THANKS!
SO? WHAT'S YOUR PLAN NOW?
THEY'RE GOING TO CATCH YOU REAL FAST, YOU KNOW.
I'M NOT WORRIED ABOUT THAT.
THERE'S JUST ...

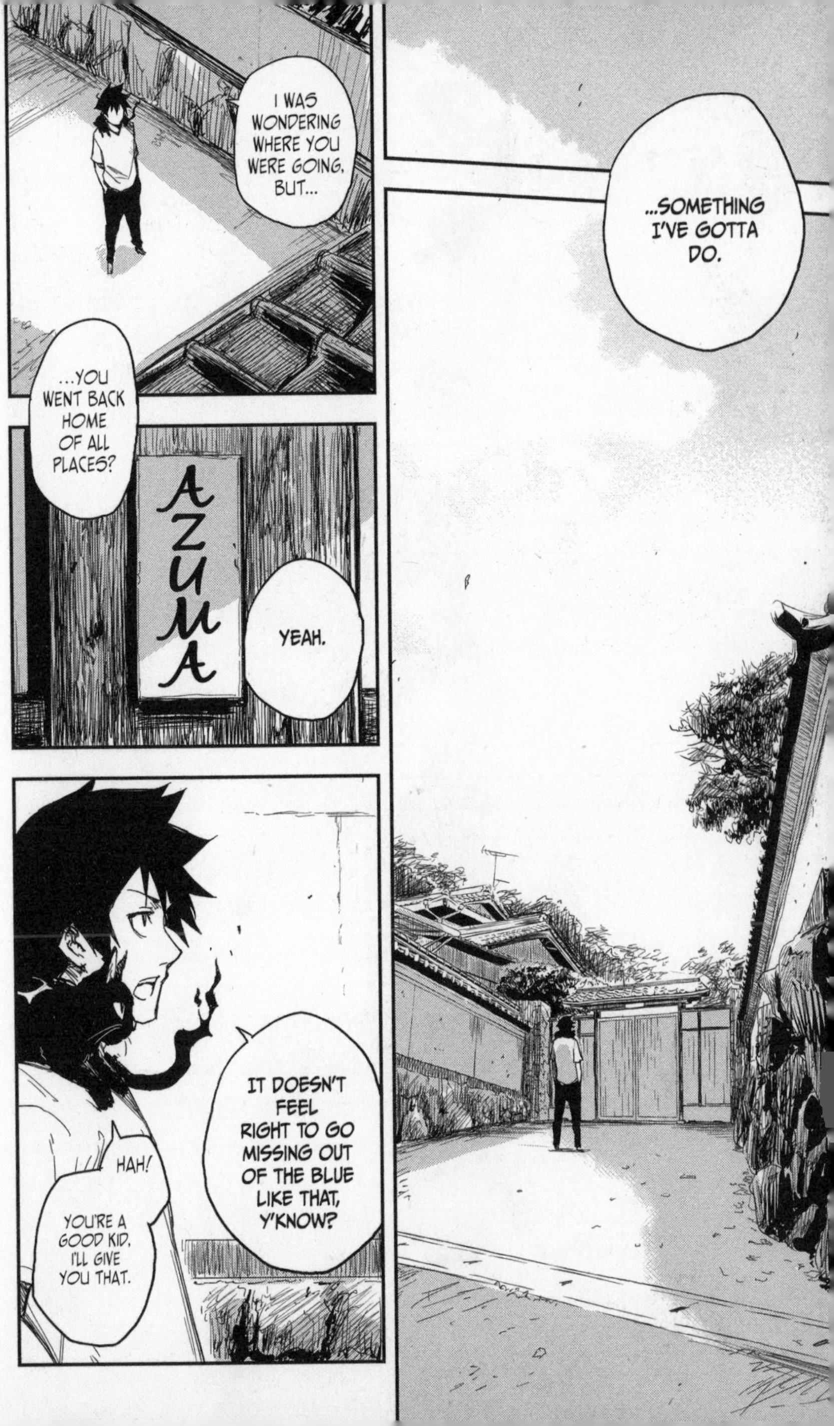
...SOMETHING I'VE GOTTA DO.
I WAS WONDERING WHERE YOU WERE GOING, BUT...
...YOU WENT BACK HOME OF ALL PLACES?
AZUMA
YEAH.
IT DOESN'T FEEL RIGHT TO GO MISSING OUT OF THE BLUE LIKE THAT, Y'KNOW?
HAH!
YOU'RE A GOOD KID, I'LL GIVE YOU THAT.

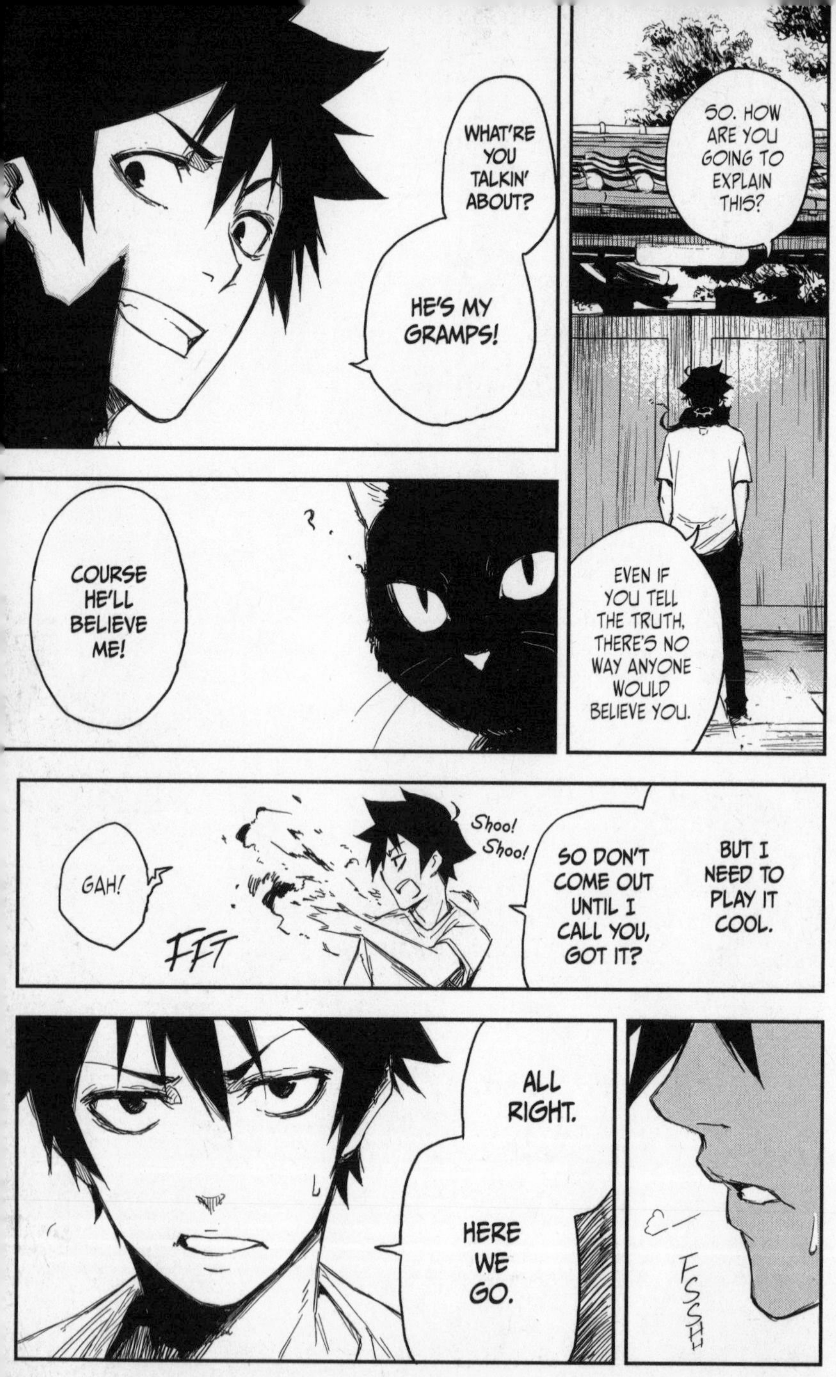
SO. HOW ARE YOU GOING TO EXPLAIN THIS?
EVEN IF YOU TELL THE TRUTH, THERE'S NO WAY ANYONE WOULD BELIEVE YOU.
WHAT'RE YOU TALKIN' ABOUT?
HE'S MY GRAMPS!
COURSE HE'LL BELIEVE ME!
BUT I NEED TO PLAY IT COOL.
SO DON'T COME OUT UNTIL I CALL YOU, GOT IT?
Shoo! Shoo!
GAH!
FFT
FSSH
ALL RIGHT.
HERE WE GO.

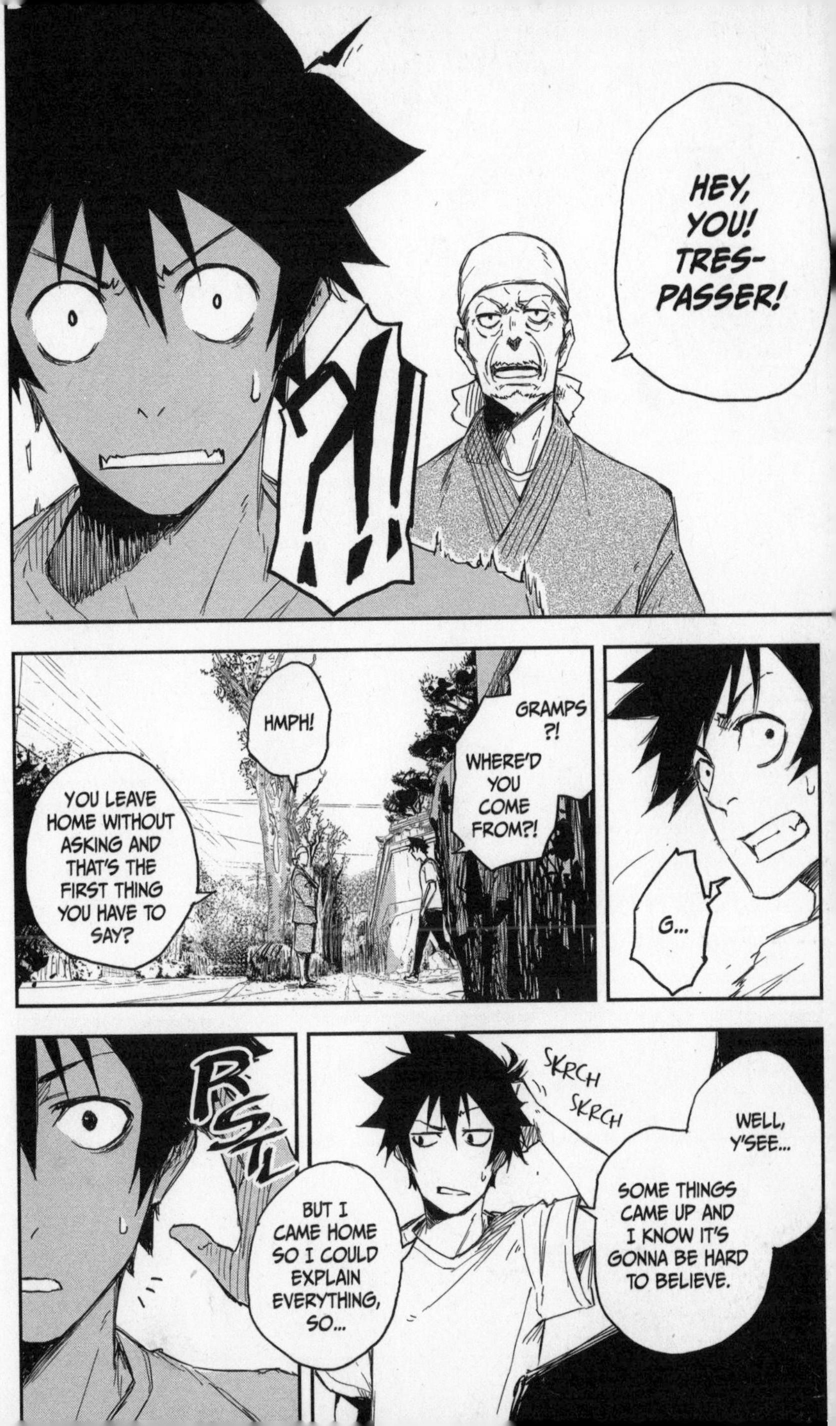
HEY, YOU! TRES-PASSER!
?!
G...
GRAMPS?!
WHERE'D YOU COME FROM?!
HMPH!
YOU LEAVE HOME WITHOUT ASKING AND THAT'S THE FIRST THING YOU HAVE TO SAY?
SKRCH SKRCH
WELL, Y'SEE...
SOME THINGS CAME UP AND I KNOW IT'S GONNA BE HARD TO BELIEVE.
BUT I CAME HOME SO I COULD EXPLAIN EVERYTHING, SO...
RSTL

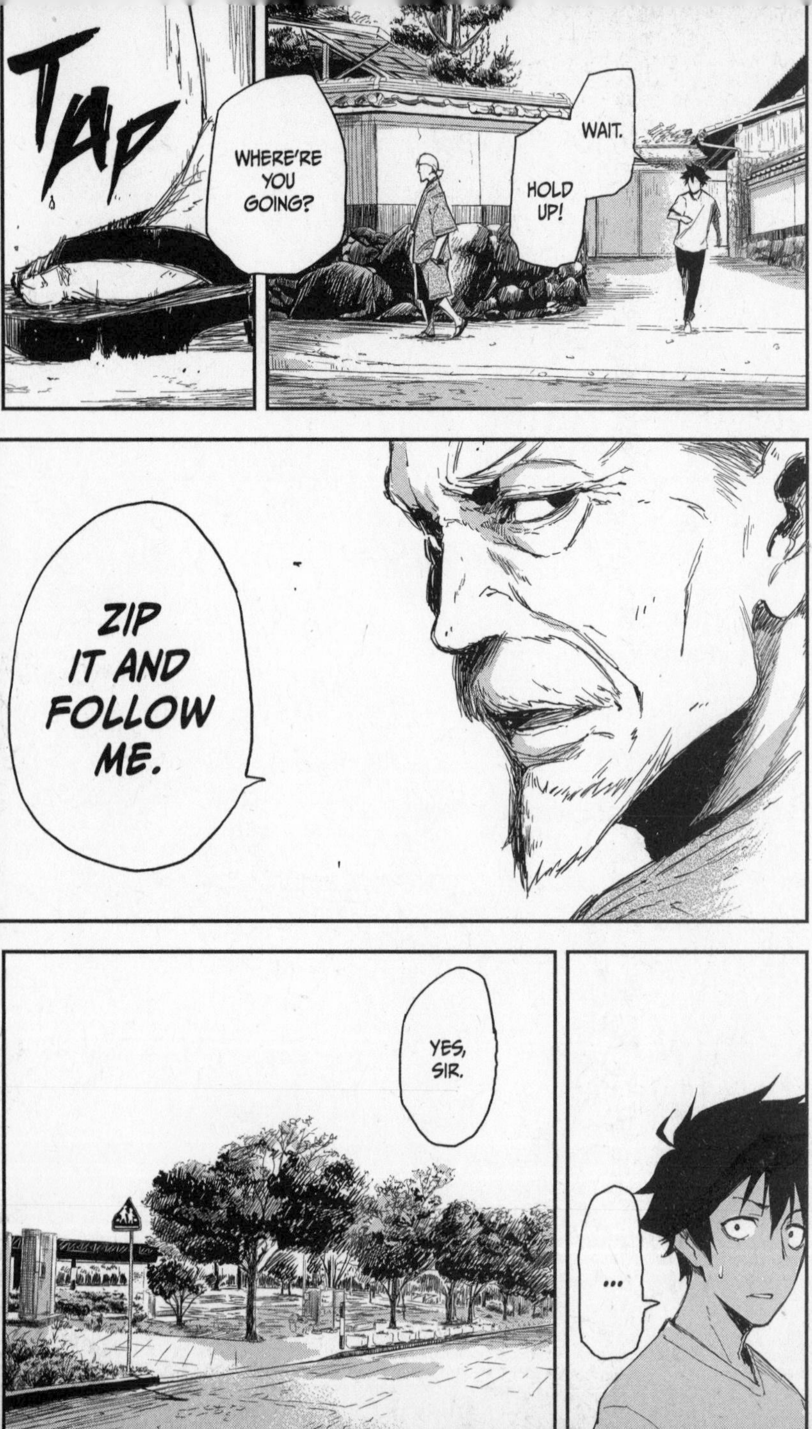
WAIT.
HOLD UP!
WHERE'RE YOU GOING?
TAP
ZIP IT AND FOLLOW ME.
...
YES, SIR.

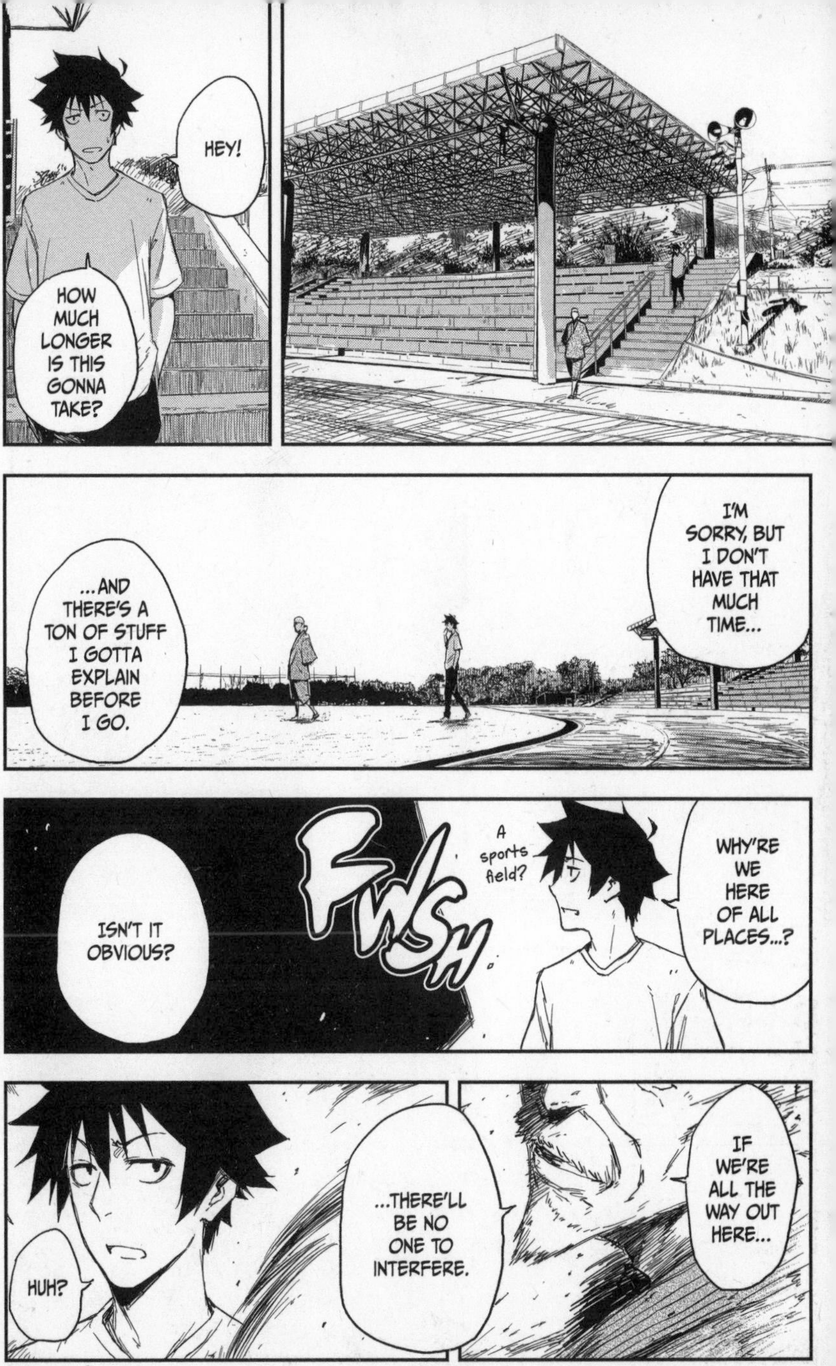
HEY!
HOW MUCH LONGER IS THIS GONNA TAKE?
I'M SORRY, BUT I DON'T HAVE THAT MUCH TIME...
...AND THERE'S A TON OF STUFF I GOTTA EXPLAIN BEFORE I GO.
WHY'RE WE HERE OF ALL PLACES...?
A sports field?
FWSH
ISN'T IT OBVIOUS?
IF WE'RE ALL THE WAY OUT HERE...
...THERE'LL BE NO ONE TO INTERFERE.
HUH?

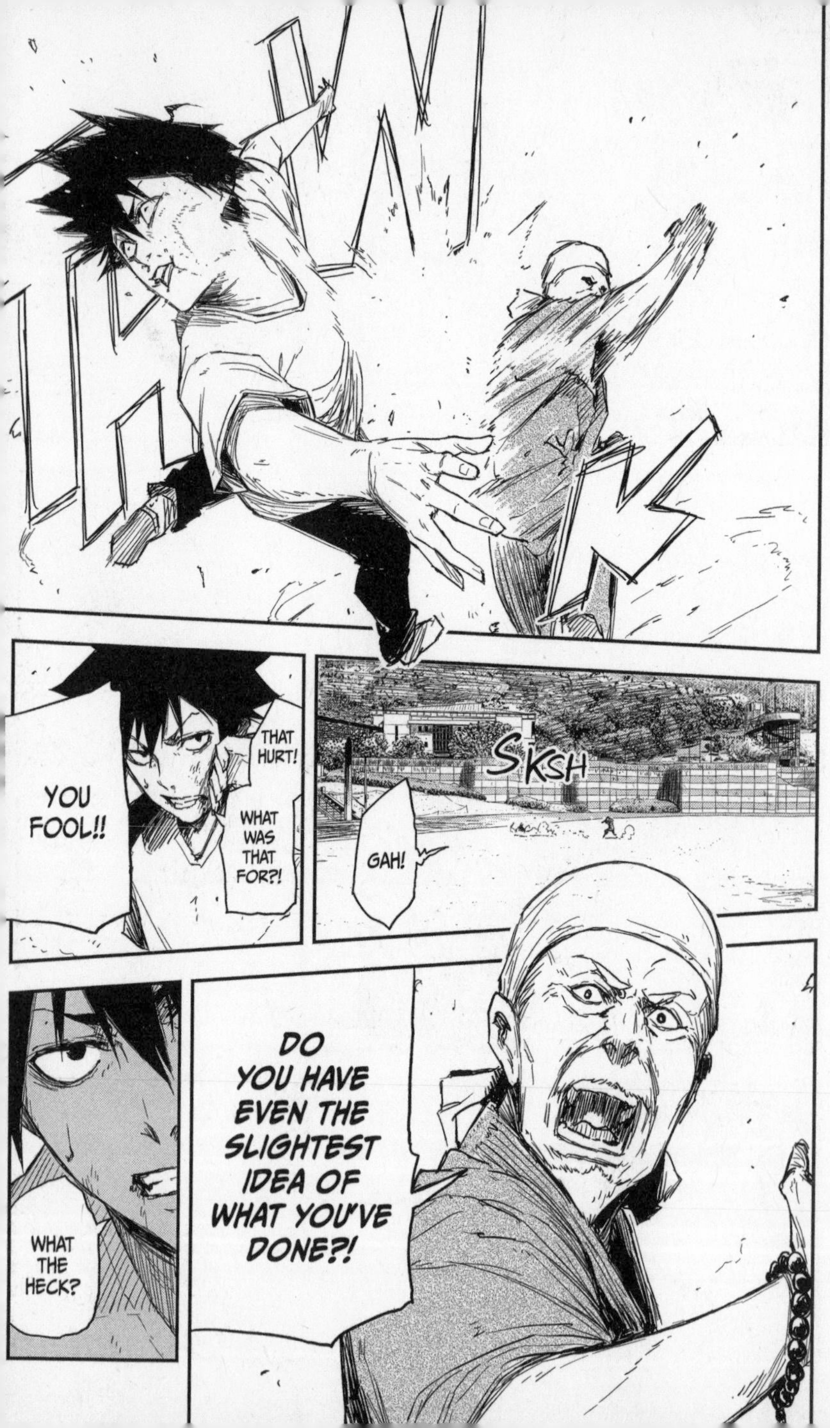
SKSH
GAH!
THAT HURT!
WHAT WAS THAT FOR?!
YOU FOOL!!
DO YOU HAVE EVEN THE SLIGHTEST IDEA OF WHAT YOU'VE DONE?!
WHAT THE HECK?

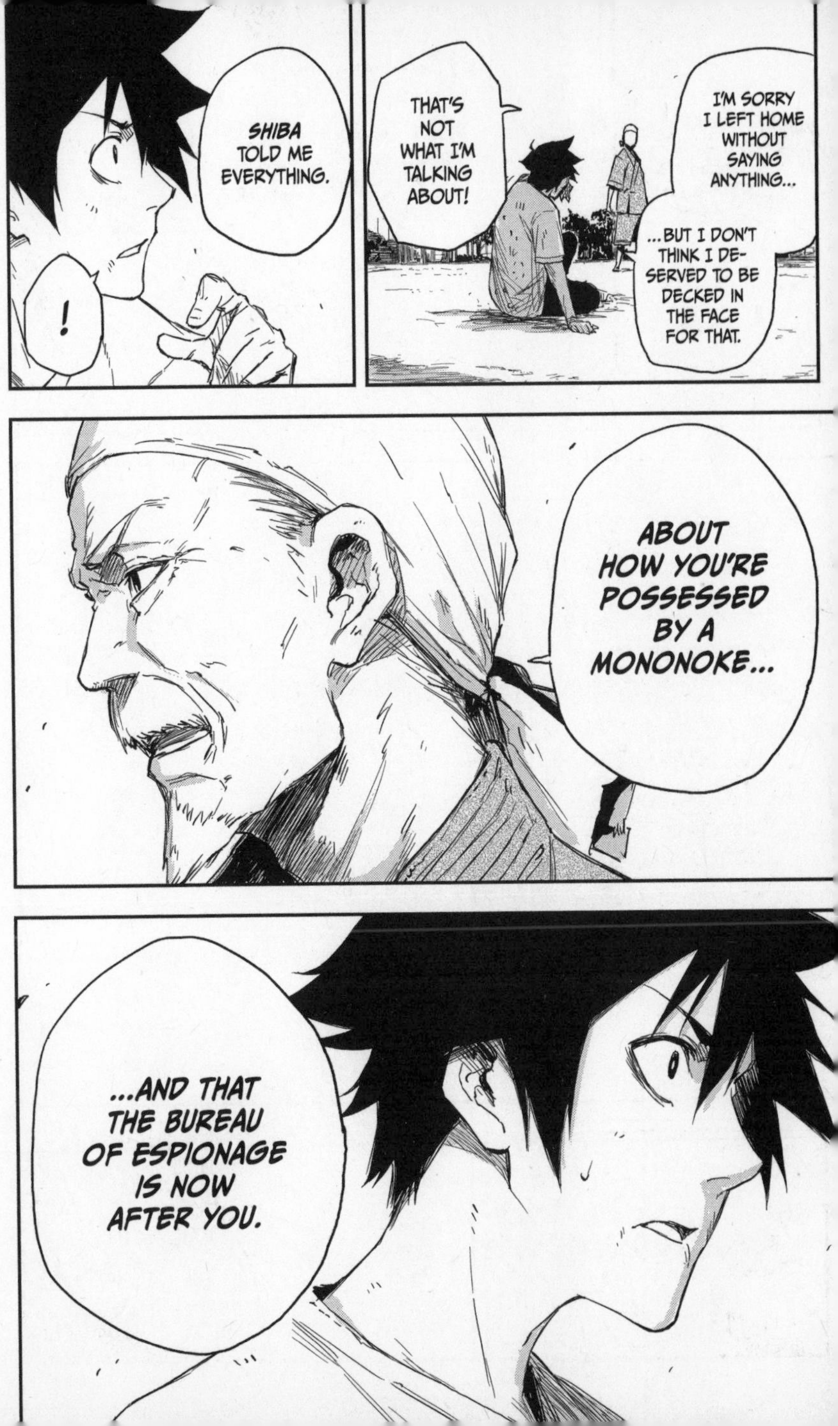
I'M SORRY I LEFT HOME WITHOUT SAYING ANYTHING...
...BUT I DON'T THINK I DE-SERVED TO BE DECKED IN THE FACE FOR THAT.
THAT'S NOT WHAT I'M TALKING ABOUT!
SHIBA TOLD ME EVERYTHING.
!
ABOUT HOW YOU'RE POSSESSED BY A MONONOKE...
...AND THAT THE BUREAU OF ESPIONAGE IS NOW AFTER YOU.

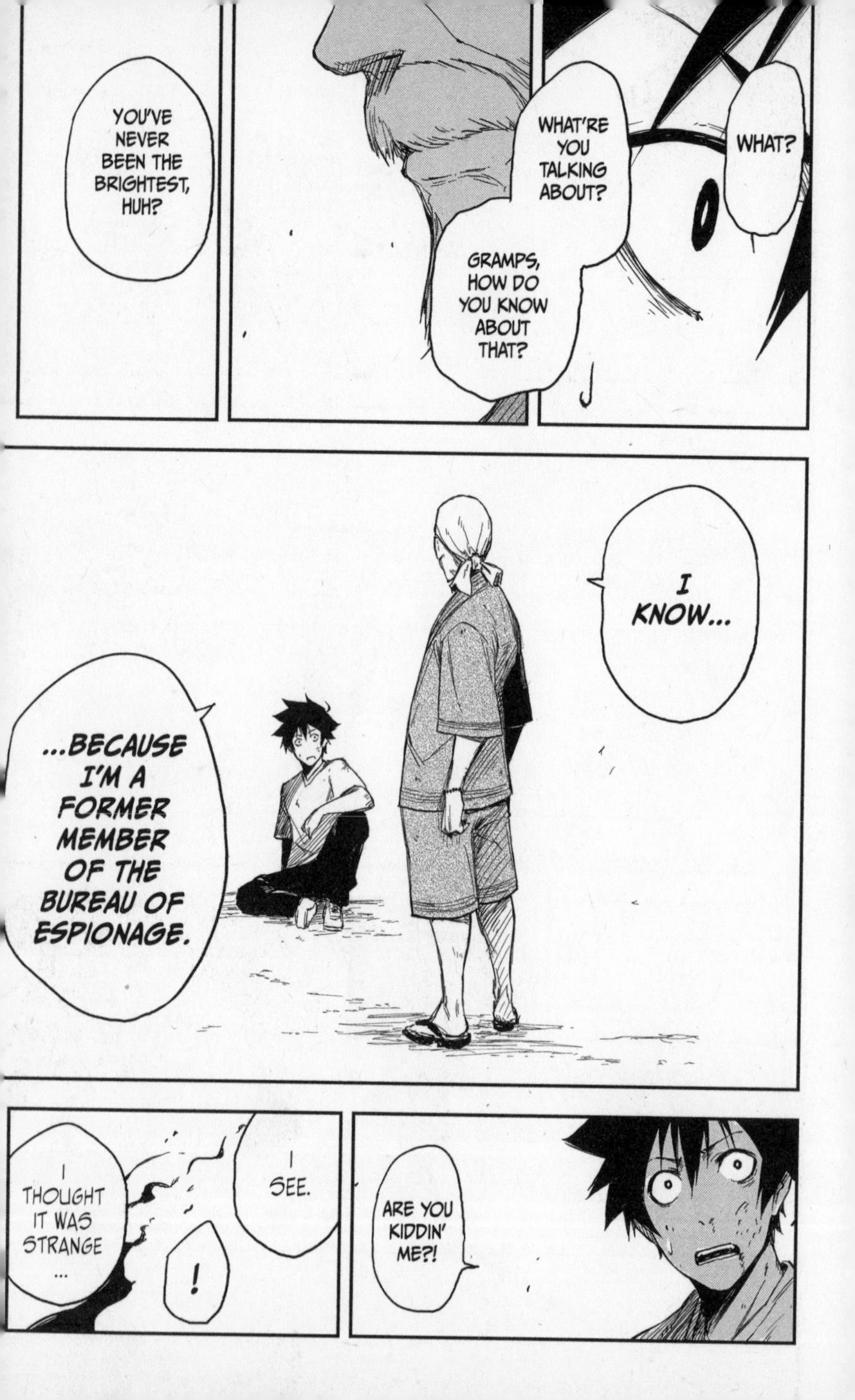
WHAT?
WHAT'RE YOU TALKING ABOUT?
GRAMPS, HOW DO YOU KNOW ABOUT THAT?
YOU'VE NEVER BEEN THE BRIGHTEST, HUH?
I KNOW...
...BECAUSE I'M A FORMER MEMBER OF THE BUREAU OF ESPIONAGE.
ARE YOU KIDDIN' ME?!
I SEE.
!
I THOUGHT IT WAS STRANGE...

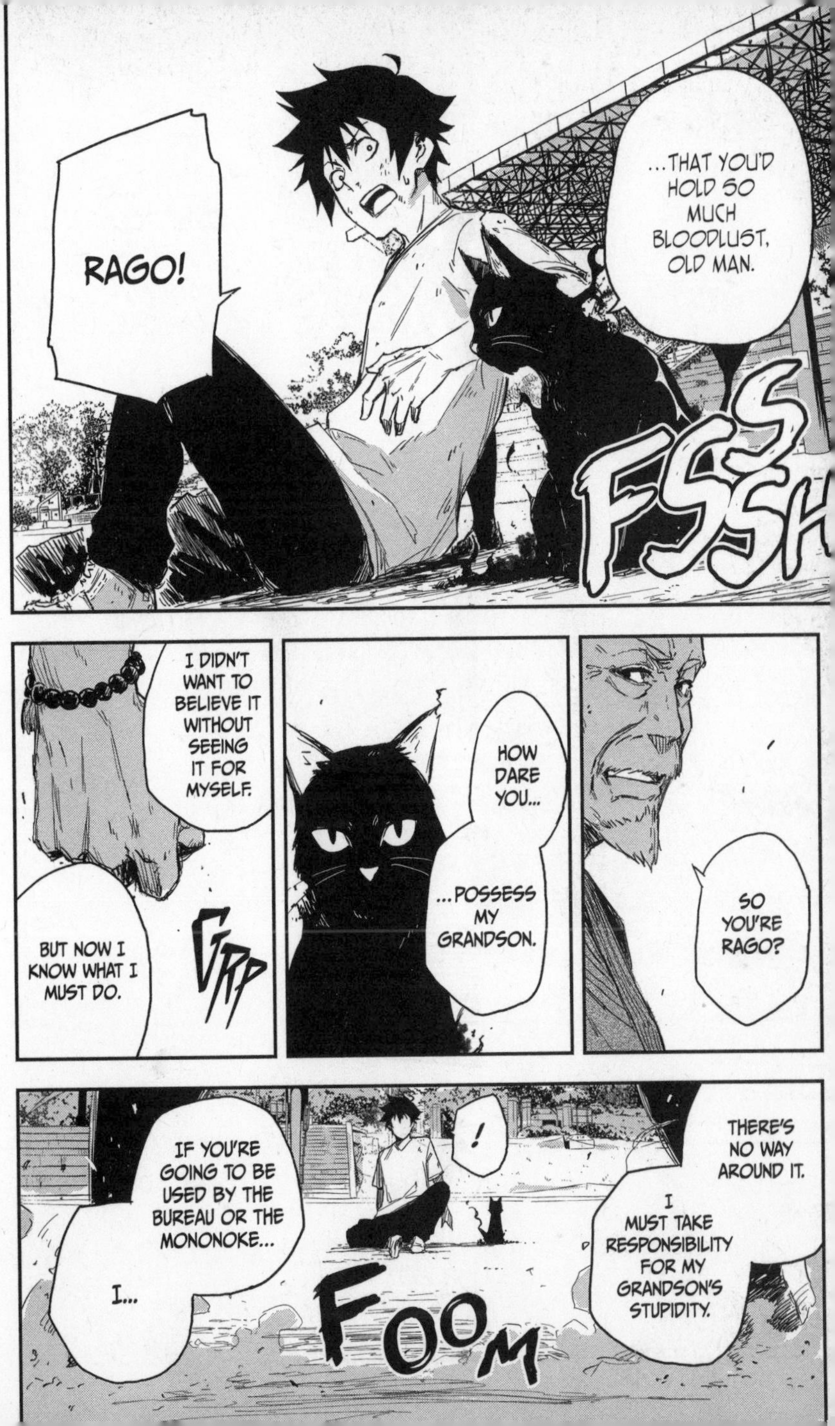
...THAT YOU'D HOLD SO MUCH BLOODLUST, OLD MAN.
RAGO!
FSSSH
SO YOU'RE RAGO?
HOW DARE YOU...
...POSSESS MY GRANDSON.
I DIDN'T WANT TO BELIEVE IT WITHOUT SEEING IT FOR MYSELF.
GRP
BUT NOW I KNOW WHAT I MUST DO.
THERE'S NO WAY AROUND IT.
I MUST TAKE RESPONSIBILITY FOR MY GRANDSON'S STUPIDITY.
!
IF YOU'RE GOING TO BE USED BY THE BUREAU OR THE MONONOKE...
I...
FOOM

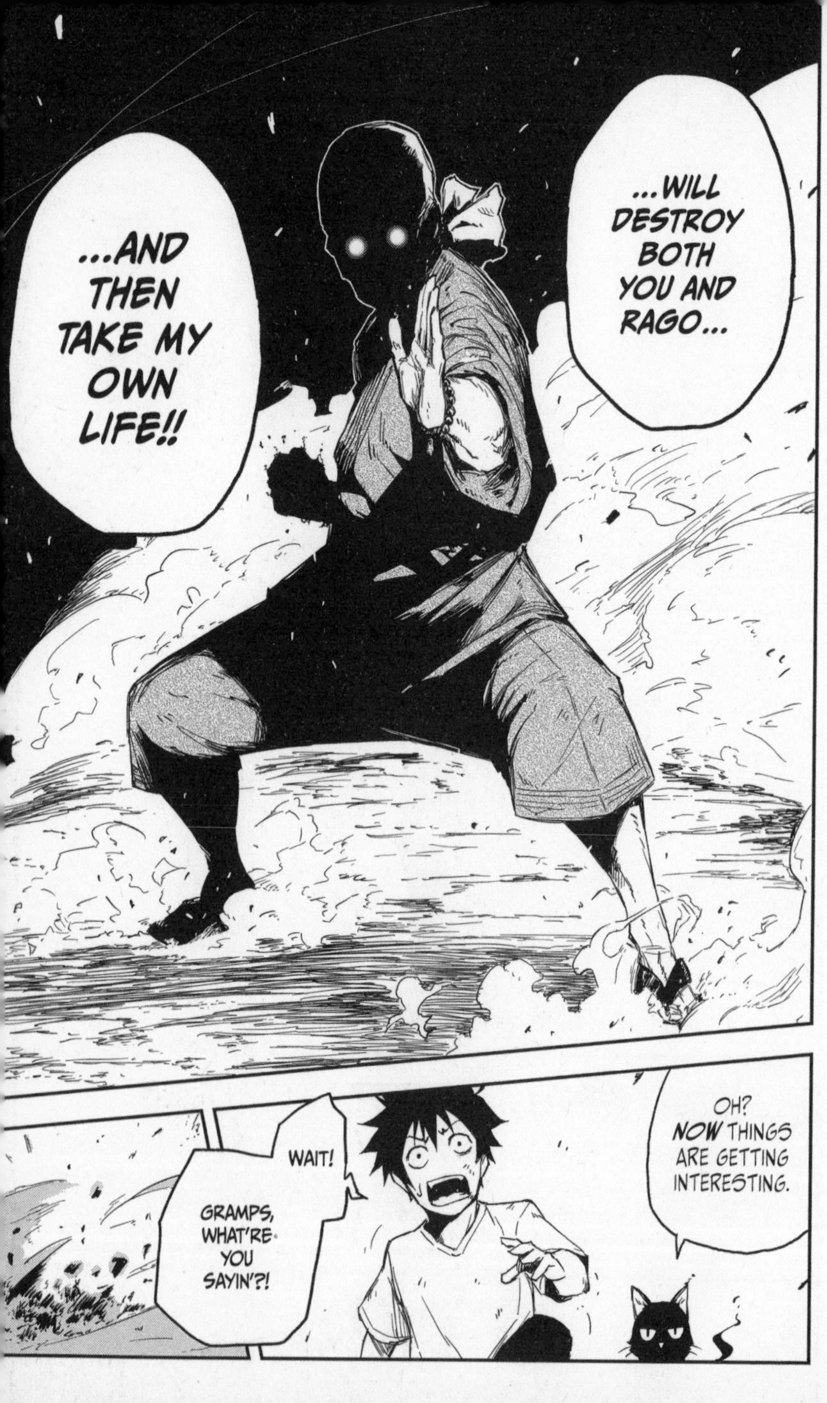
...WILL DESTROY BOTH YOU AND RAGO...
...AND THEN TAKE MY OWN LIFE!!
OH? NOW THINGS ARE GETTING INTERESTING.
WAIT!
GRAMPS, WHAT'RE YOU SAYIN'?!

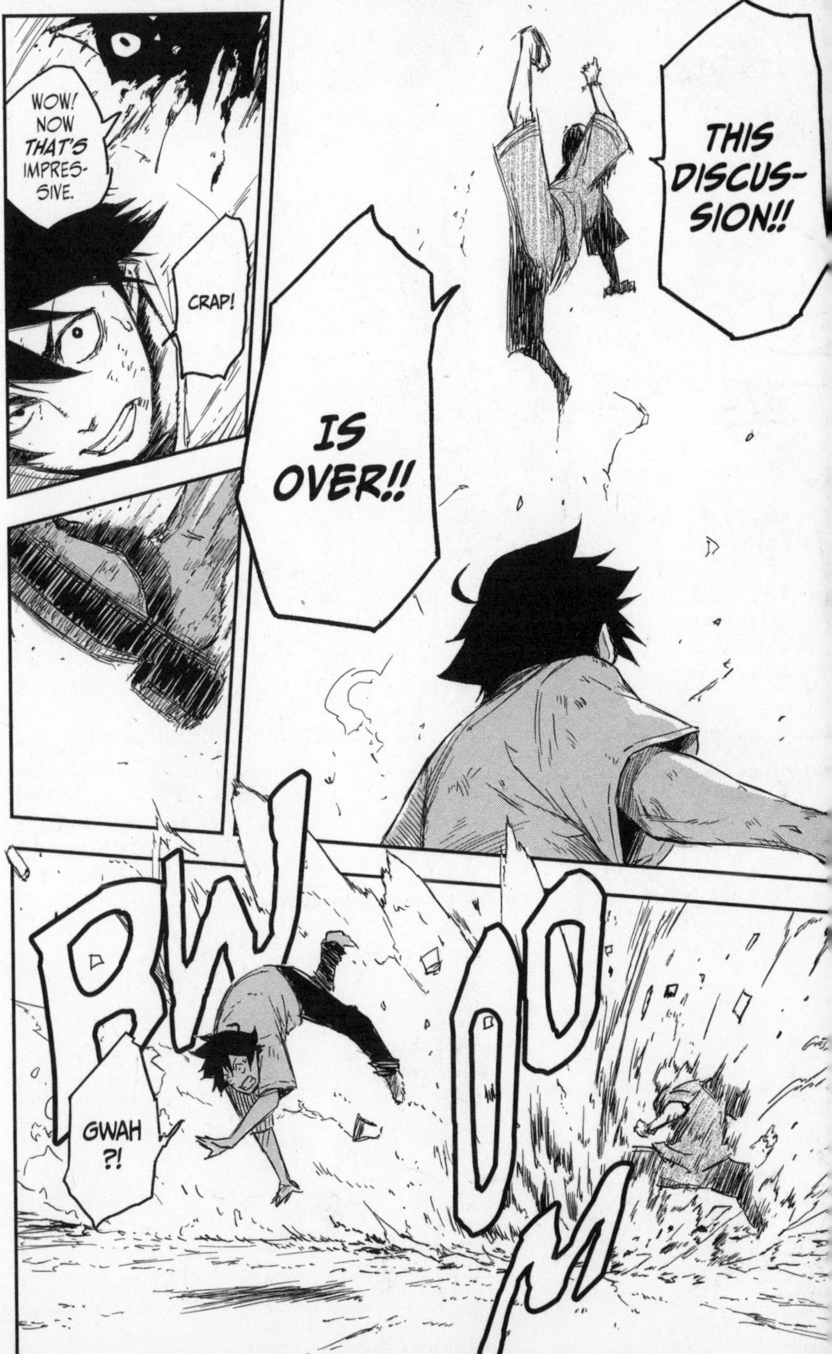
THIS DISCUSSION!!
IS OVER!!
WOW! NOW THAT'S IMPRESSIVE.
CRAP!
BWOOM
GWAH ?!

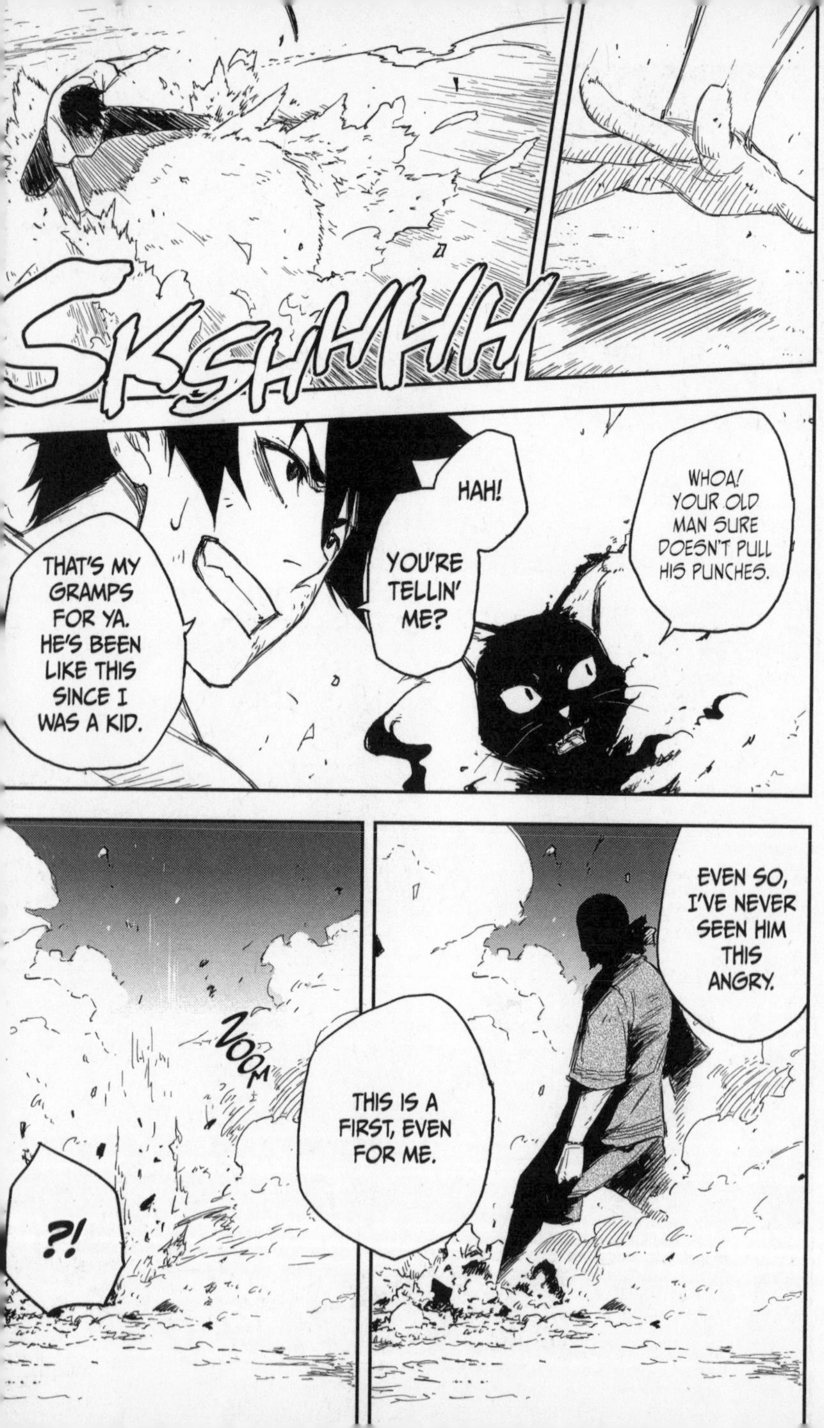
SKSHHHH
WHOA! YOUR OLD MAN SURE DOESN'T PULL HIS PUNCHES.
HAH!
YOU'RE TELLIN' ME?
THAT'S MY GRAMPS FOR YA. HE'S BEEN LIKE THIS SINCE I WAS A KID.
EVEN SO, I'VE NEVER SEEN HIM THIS ANGRY.
THIS IS A FIRST, EVEN FOR ME.
VOOOM
?!

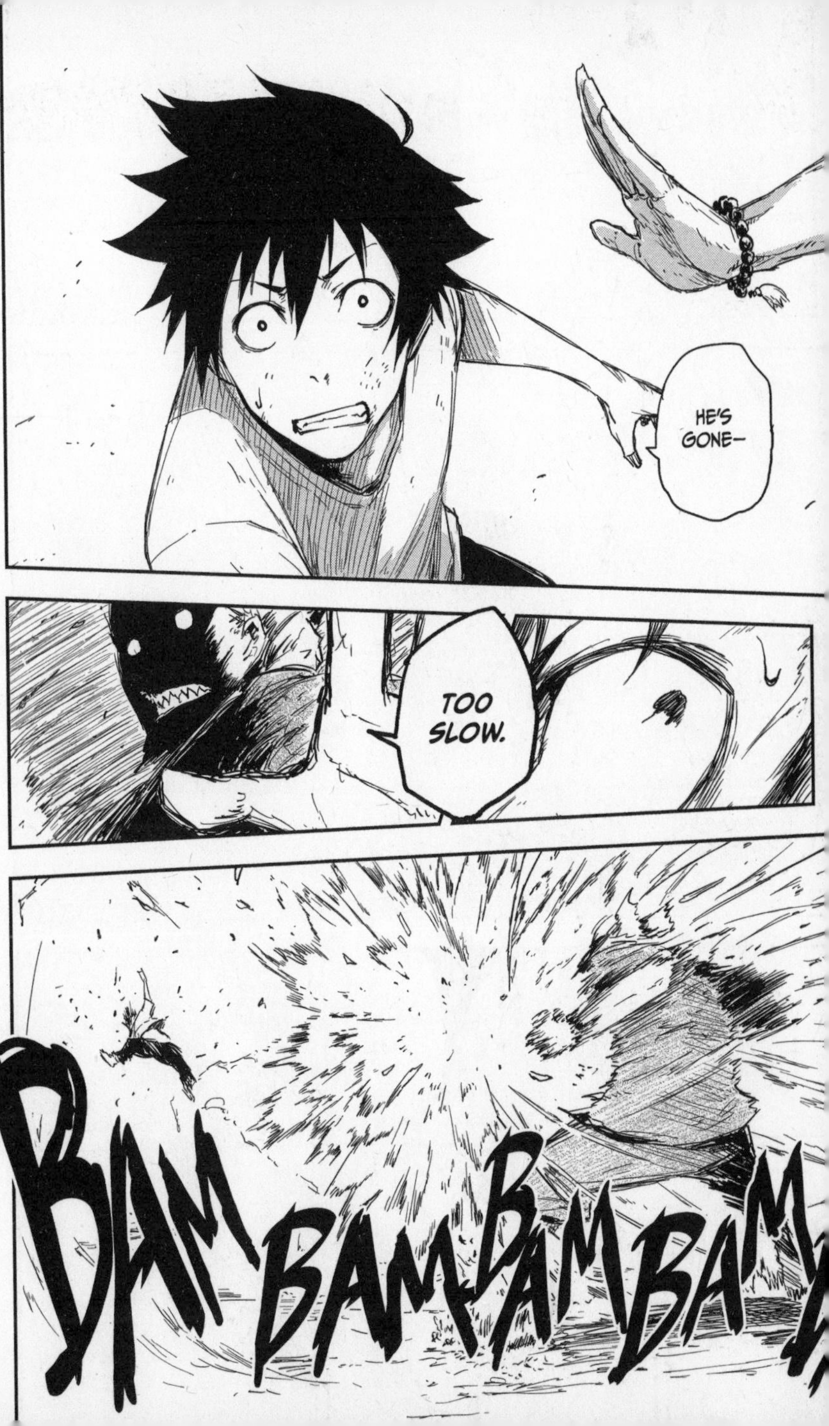
HE'S GONE—
TOO SLOW.
BAM BAM BAM BAM BAM

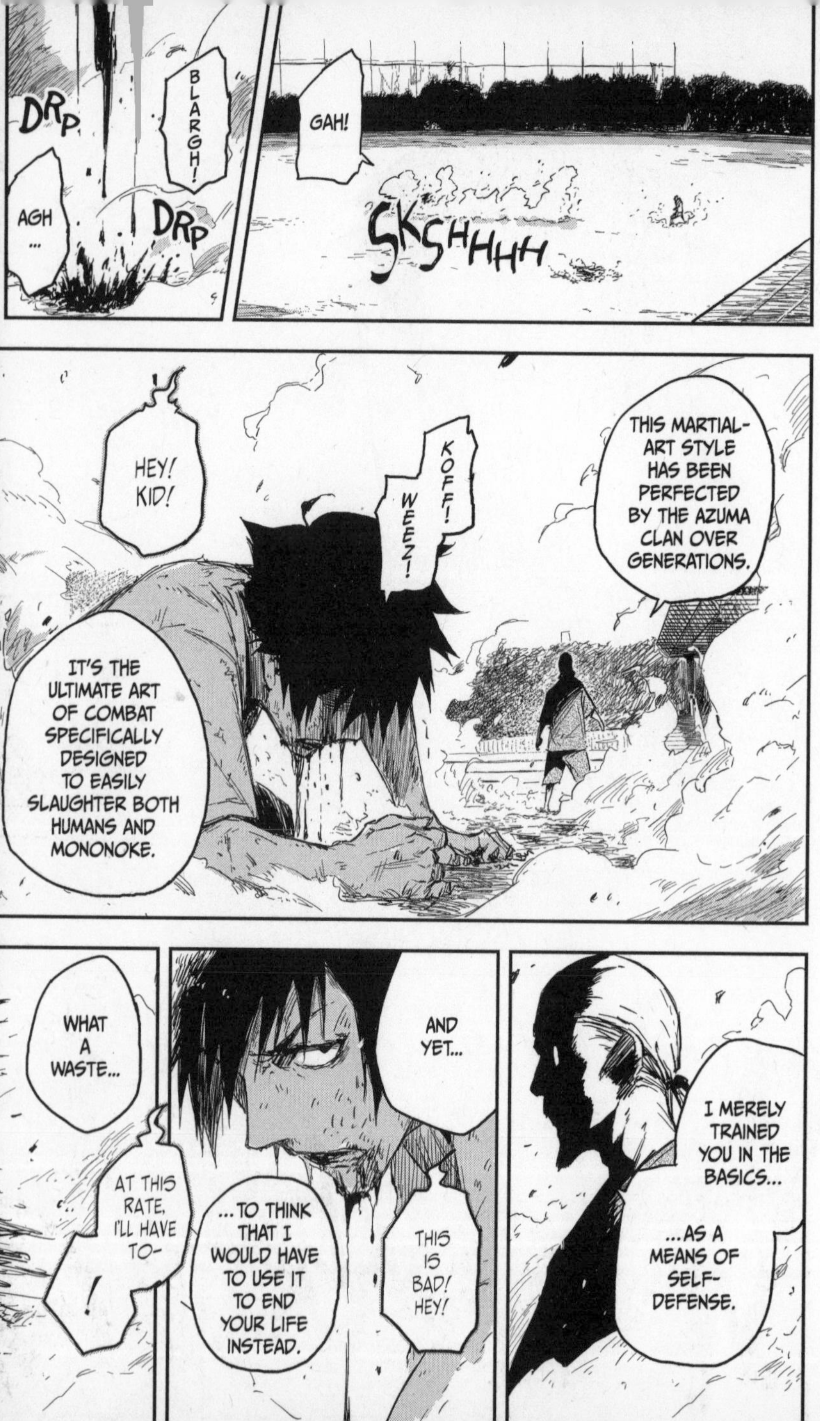
GAH!
SKSHHHH
BLARGH!
DRP
DRP
AGH...
THIS MARTIAL-ART STYLE HAS BEEN PERFECTED BY THE AZUMA CLAN OVER GENERATIONS.
KOFF! WEEZ!
HEY! KID!
IT'S THE ULTIMATE ART OF COMBAT SPECIFICALLY DESIGNED TO EASILY SLAUGHTER BOTH HUMANS AND MONONOKE.
I MERELY TRAINED YOU IN THE BASICS...
...AS A MEANS OF SELF-DEFENSE.
AND YET...
THIS IS BAD! HEY!
...TO THINK THAT I WOULD HAVE TO USE IT TO END YOUR LIFE INSTEAD.
WHAT A WASTE...
AT THIS RATE, I'LL HAVE TO-
!

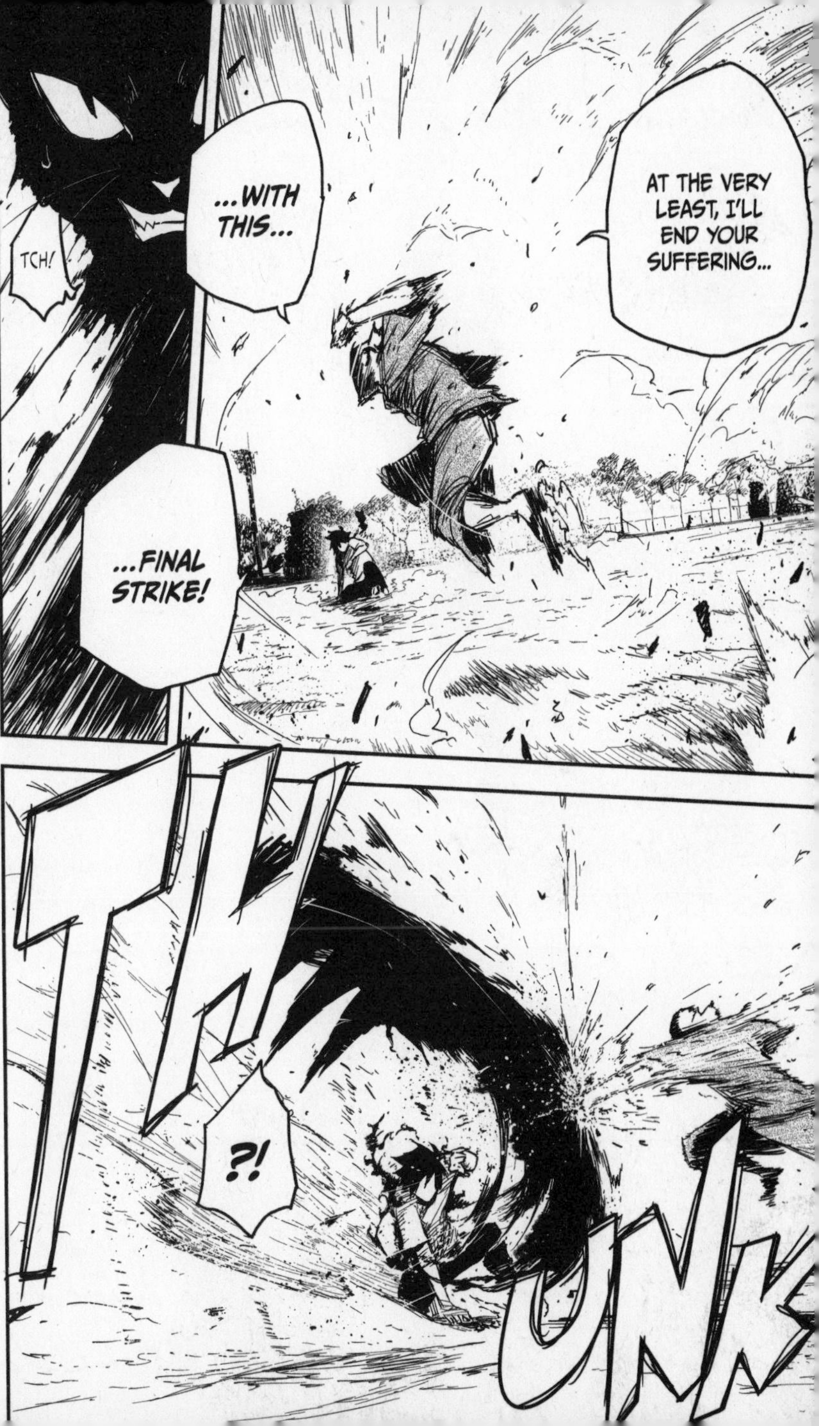
AT THE VERY LEAST, I'LL END YOUR SUFFERING...
...WITH THIS...
...FINAL STRIKE!
TCH!
TH
?!
UNK

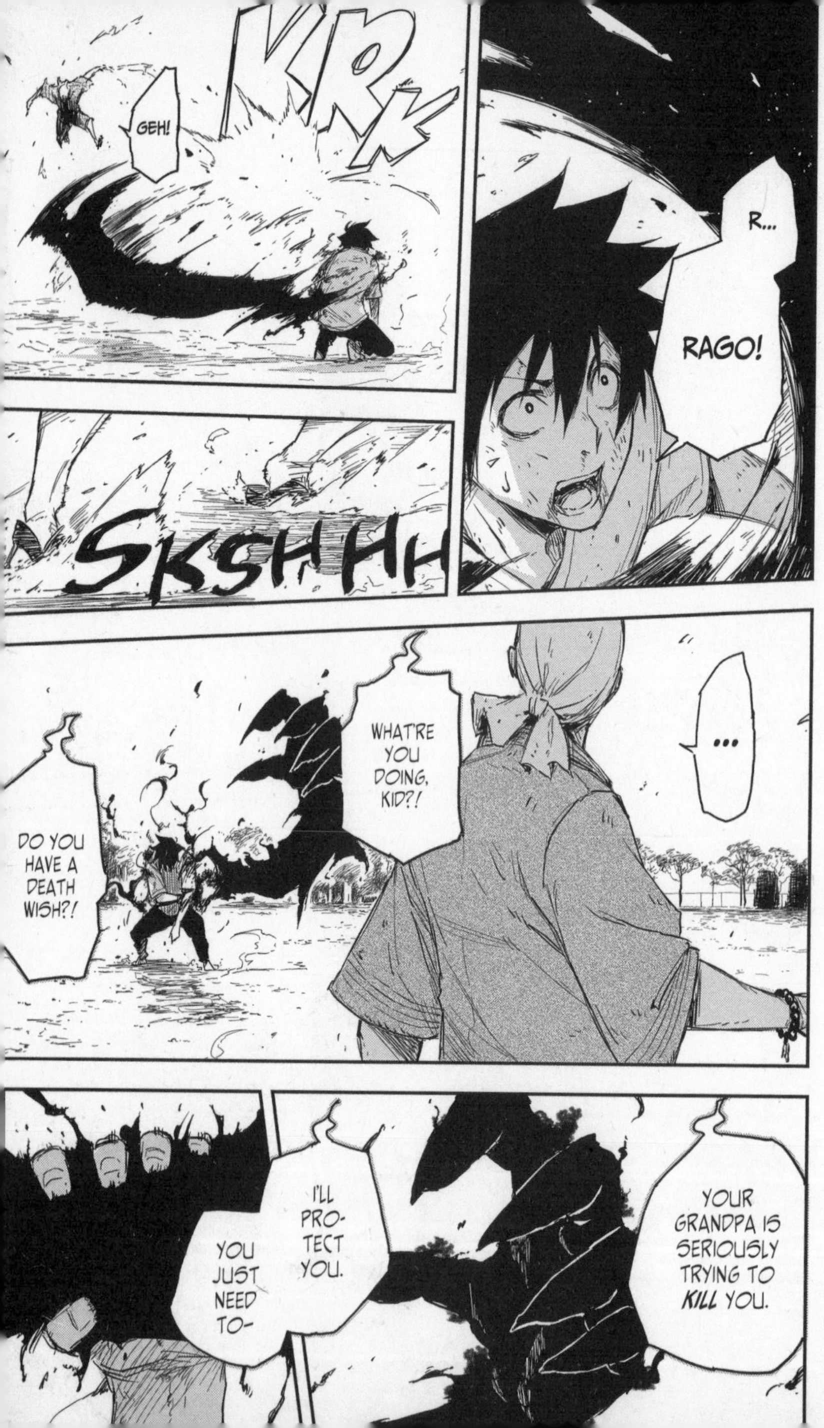
R...
RAGO!
KRAK
GEH!
SKSHHH
...
WHAT'RE YOU DOING, KID?!
DO YOU HAVE A DEATH WISH?!
YOUR GRANDPA IS SERIOUSLY TRYING TO *KILL* YOU.
I'LL PRO-TECT YOU.
YOU JUST NEED TO-

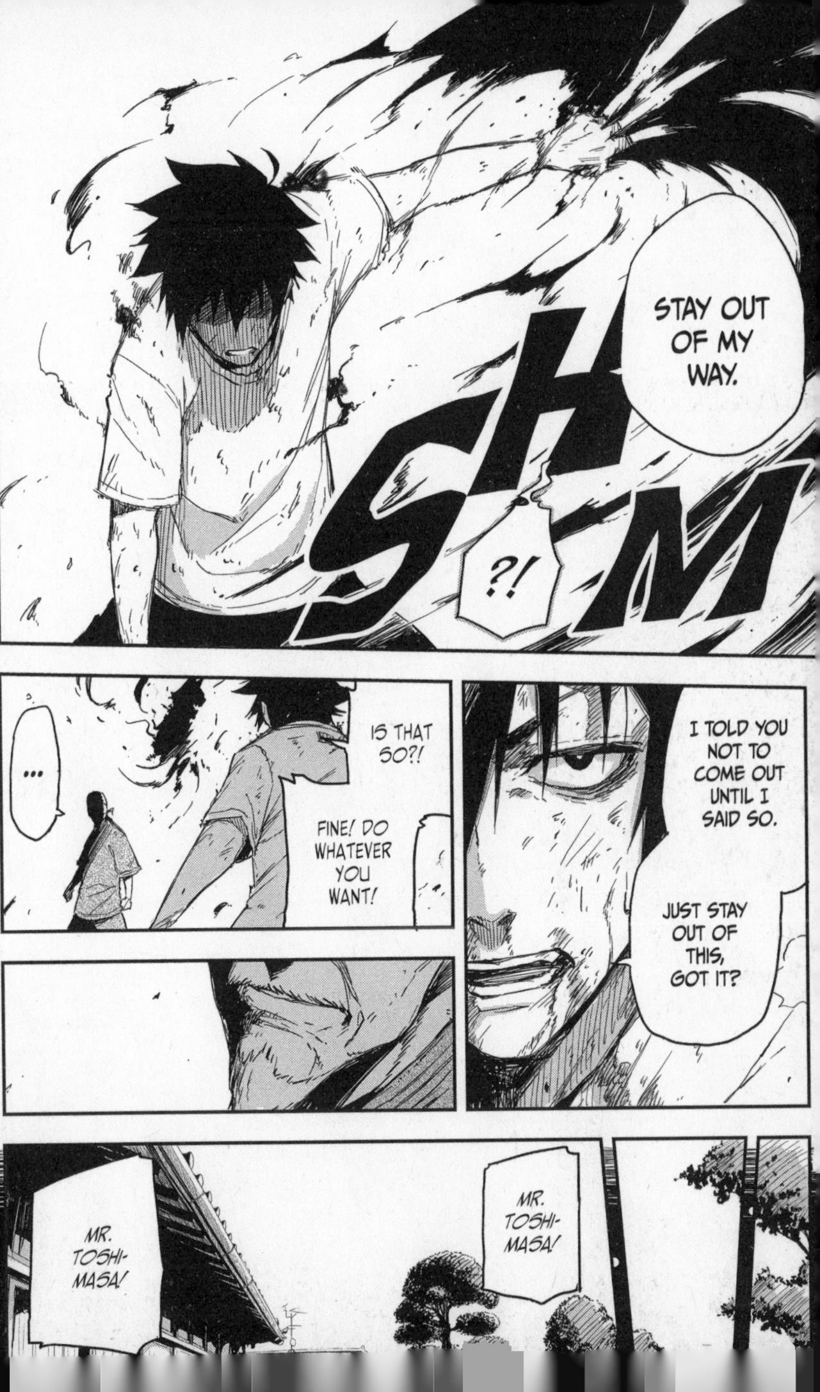
STAY OUT OF MY WAY.
?!
I TOLD YOU NOT TO COME OUT UNTIL I SAID SO.
JUST STAY OUT OF THIS, GOT IT?
IS THAT SO?!
FINE! DO WHATEVER YOU WANT!
...
MR. TOSHI-MASA!
MR. TOSHI-MASA!

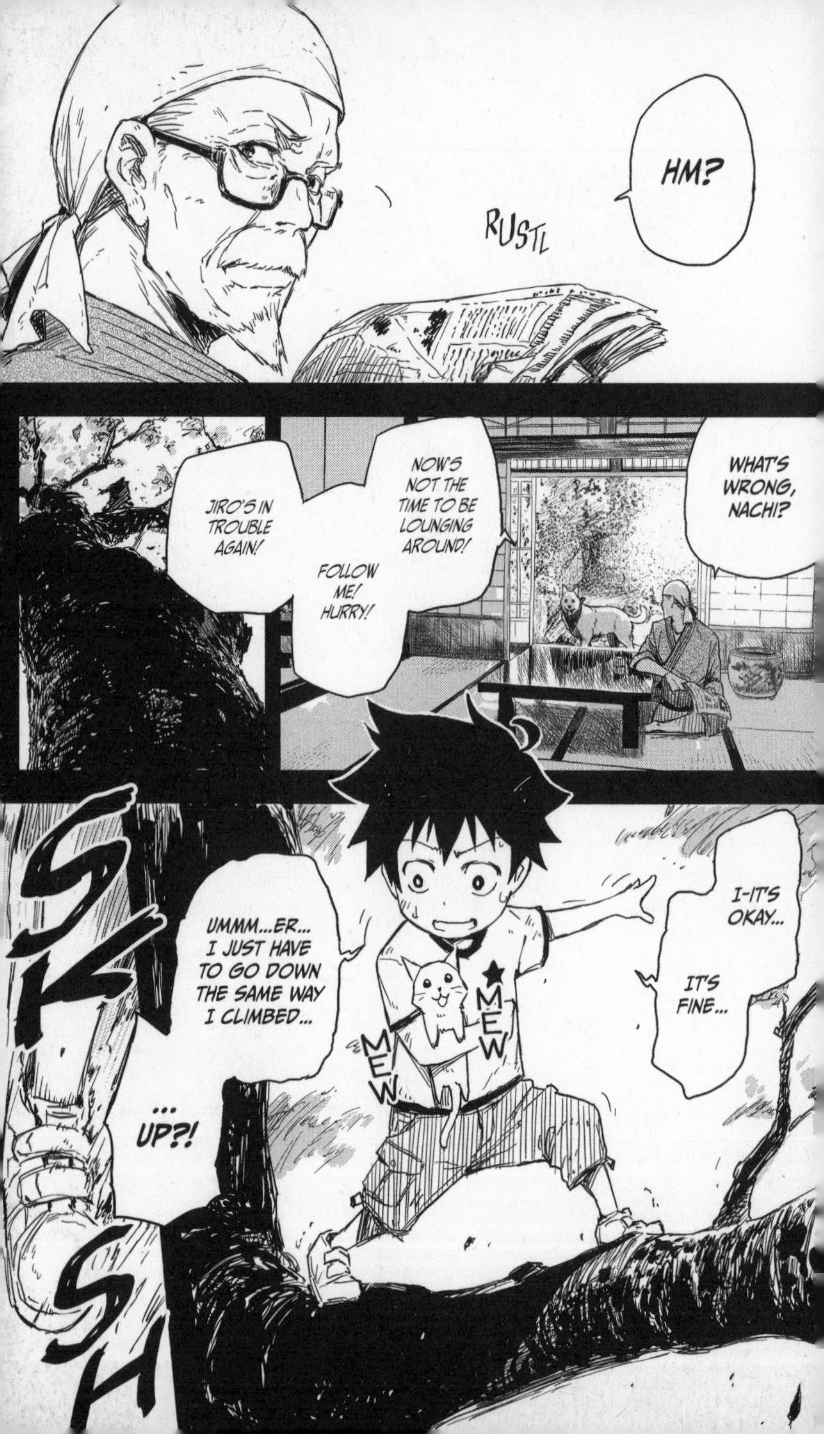
HM?
RUSTL
WHAT'S WRONG, NACHI?
NOW'S NOT THE TIME TO BE LOUNGING AROUND!
JIRO'S IN TROUBLE AGAIN!
FOLLOW ME! HURRY!
I-IT'S OKAY...
IT'S FINE...
MEW
MEW
UMMM...ER... I JUST HAVE TO GO DOWN THE SAME WAY I CLIMBED...
... UP?!
SHK
SH

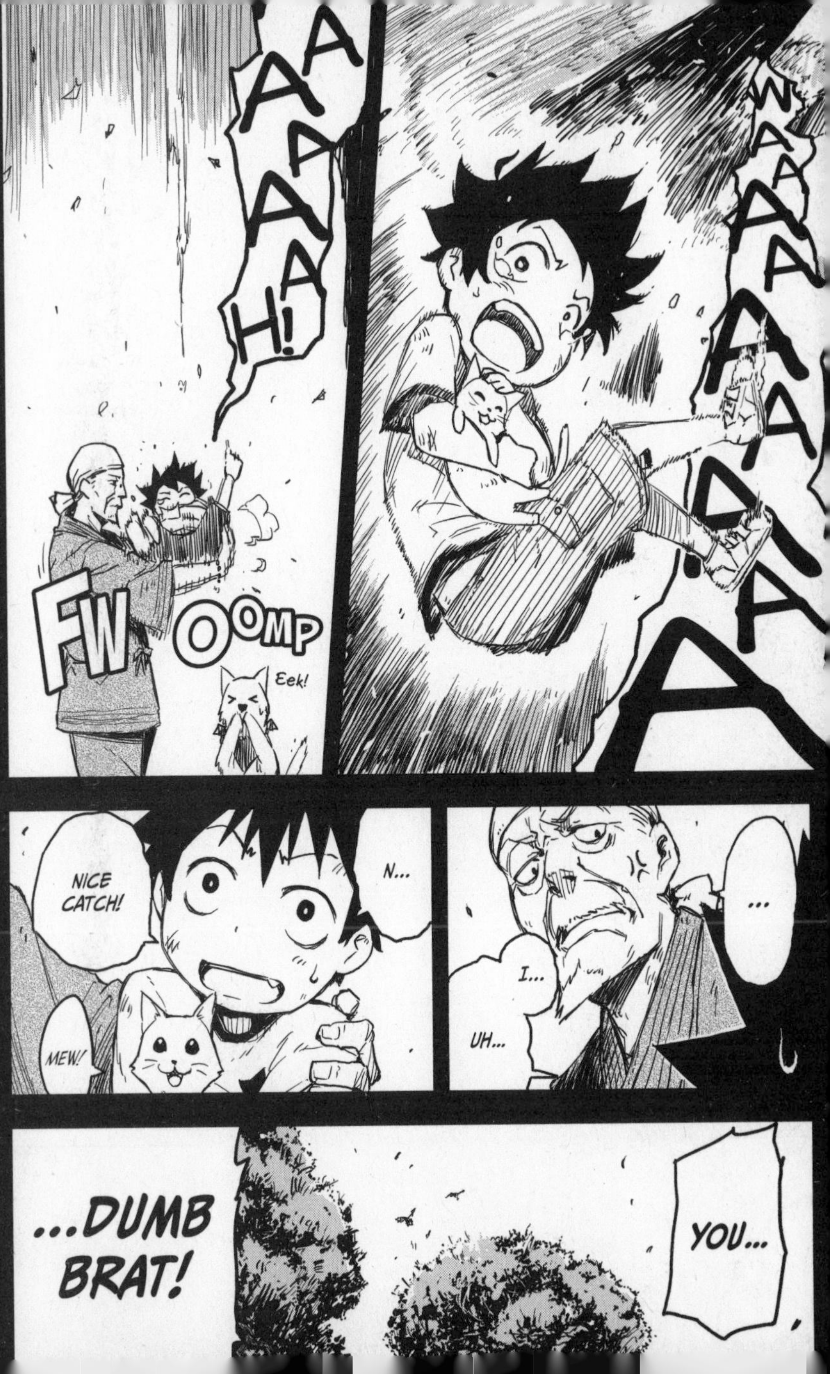
WAAAAAAAAAA
AAAAAH!
FWOOMP
Eek!
...
I...
UH...
N...
NICE CATCH!
MEW!
YOU...
...DUMB BRAT!

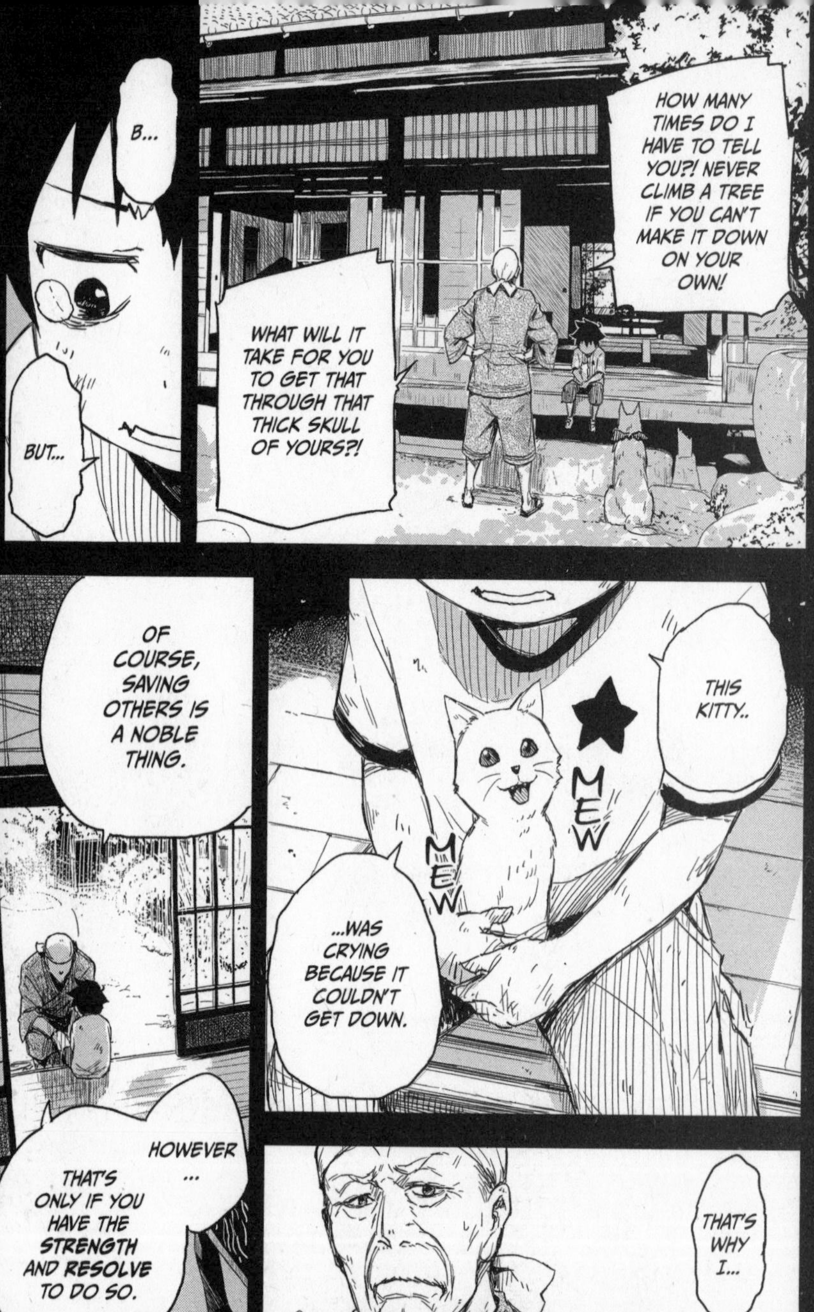
HOW MANY TIMES DO I HAVE TO TELL YOU?! NEVER CLIMB A TREE IF YOU CAN'T MAKE IT DOWN ON YOUR OWN!
WHAT WILL IT TAKE FOR YOU TO GET THAT THROUGH THAT THICK SKULL OF YOURS?!
B...
BUT...
THIS KITTY..
MEW
MEW
...WAS CRYING BECAUSE IT COULDN'T GET DOWN.
THAT'S WHY I...
OF COURSE, SAVING OTHERS IS A NOBLE THING.
HOWEVER ...
THAT'S ONLY IF YOU HAVE THE STRENGTH AND RESOLVE TO DO SO.

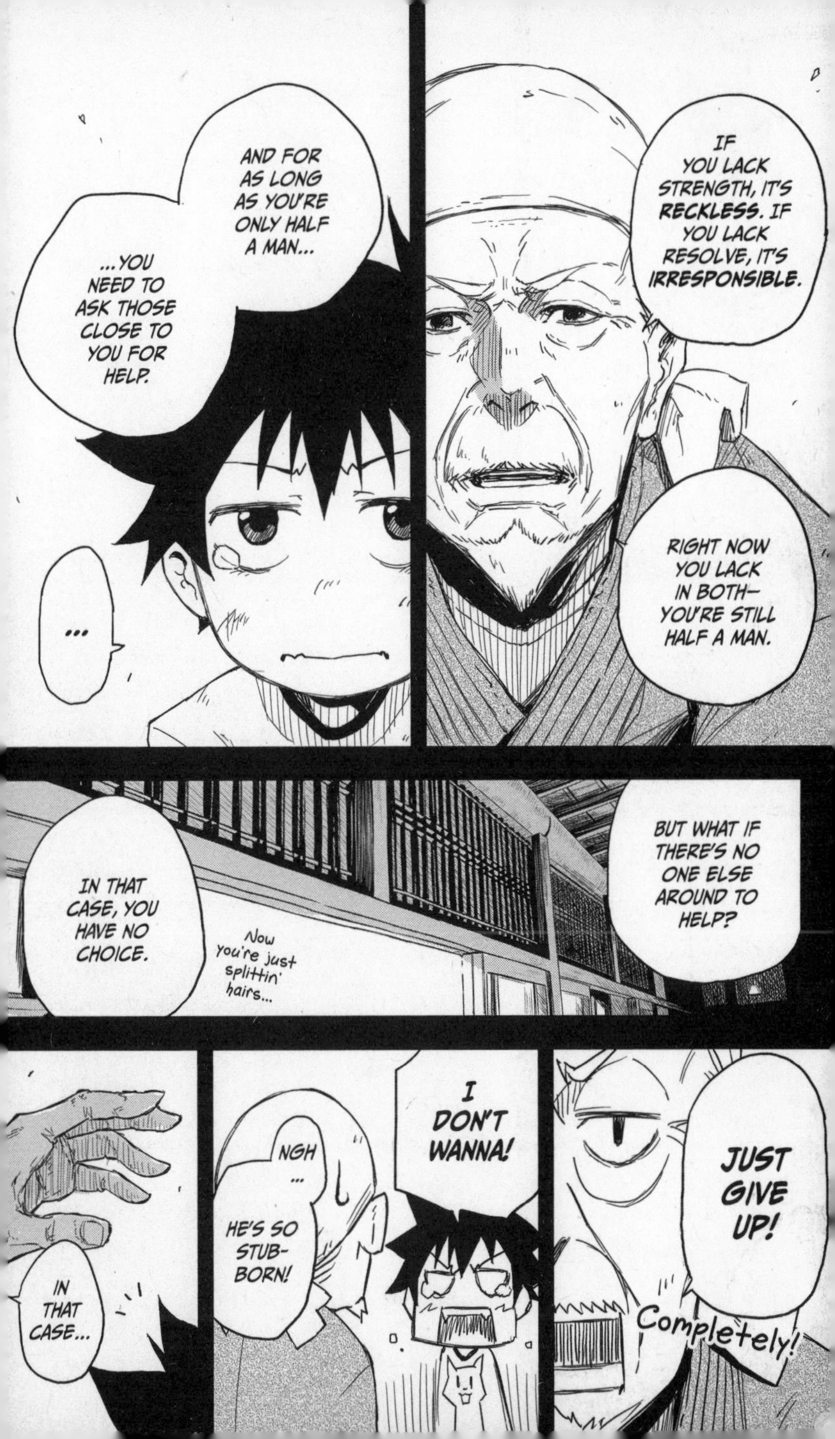
IF YOU LACK STRENGTH, IT'S **RECKLESS**. IF YOU LACK RESOLVE, IT'S **IRRESPONSIBLE**.
RIGHT NOW YOU LACK IN BOTH— YOU'RE STILL HALF A MAN.
AND FOR AS LONG AS YOU'RE ONLY HALF A MAN...
...YOU NEED TO ASK THOSE CLOSE TO YOU FOR HELP.
...
BUT WHAT IF THERE'S NO ONE ELSE AROUND TO HELP?
IN THAT CASE, YOU HAVE NO CHOICE.
Now you're just splittin' hairs...
JUST GIVE UP!
Completely!
I DON'T WANNA!
NGH...
HE'S SO STUB-BORN!
IN THAT CASE...

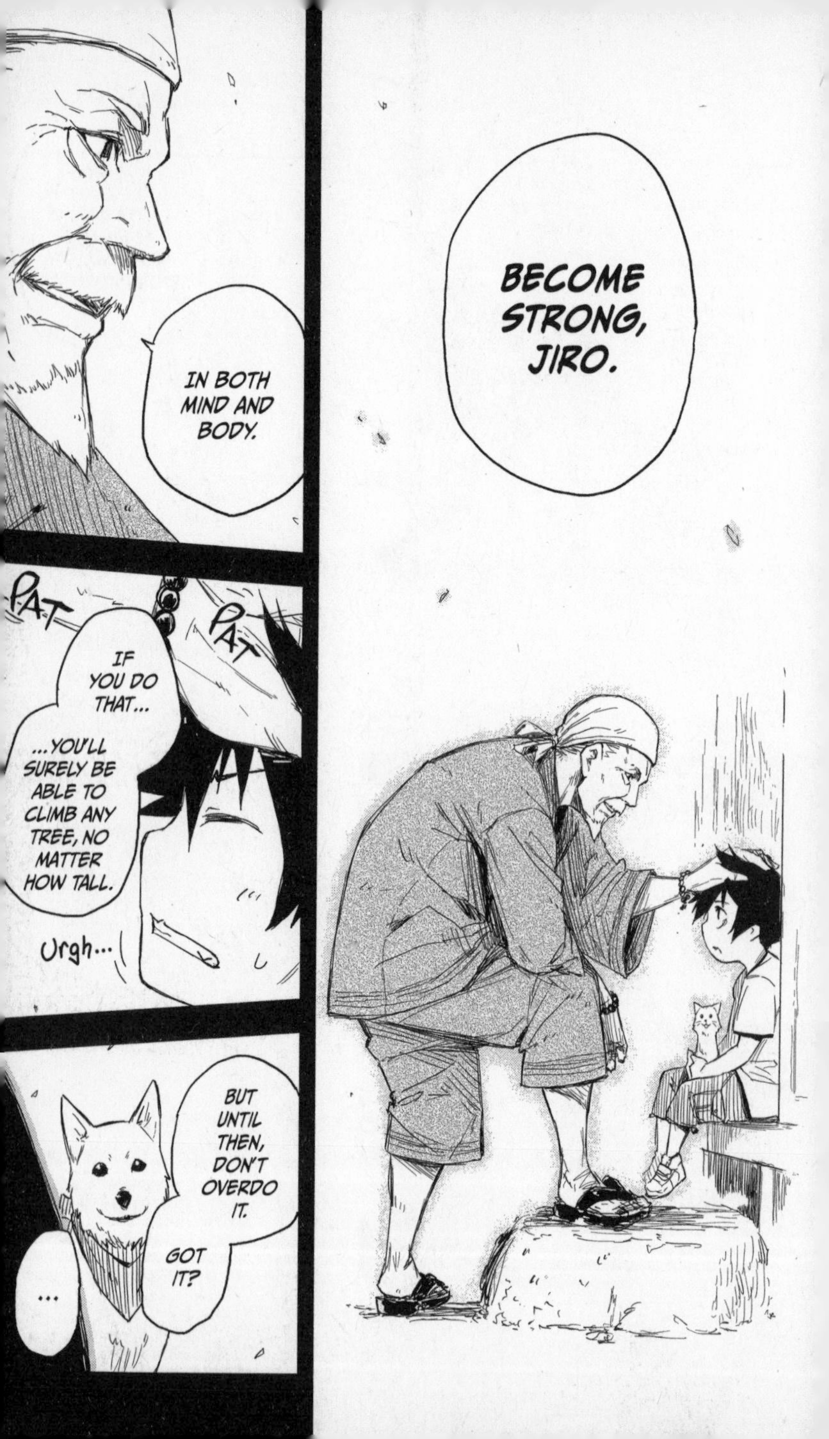
BECOME STRONG, JIRO.
IN BOTH MIND AND BODY.
PAT
PAT
IF YOU DO THAT...
...YOU'LL SURELY BE ABLE TO CLIMB ANY TREE, NO MATTER HOW TALL.
Urgh...
BUT UNTIL THEN, DON'T OVERDO IT.
GOT IT?
...

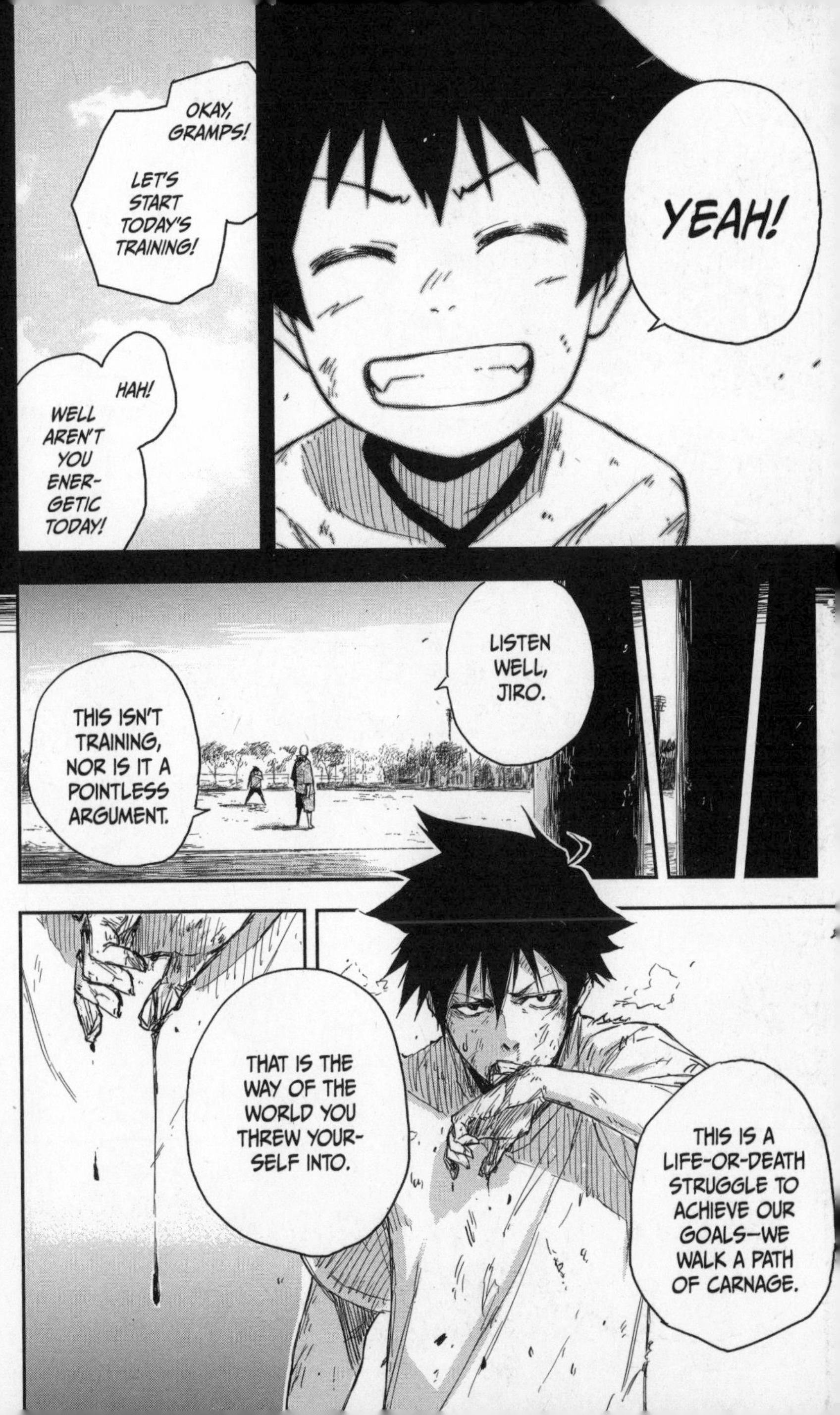
YEAH!
OKAY, GRAMPS! LET'S START TODAY'S TRAINING!
HAH! WELL AREN'T YOU ENER-GETIC TODAY!
LISTEN WELL, JIRO.
THIS ISN'T TRAINING, NOR IS IT A POINTLESS ARGUMENT.
THIS IS A LIFE-OR-DEATH STRUGGLE TO ACHIEVE OUR GOALS—WE WALK A PATH OF CARNAGE.
THAT IS THE WAY OF THE WORLD YOU THREW YOUR-SELF INTO.

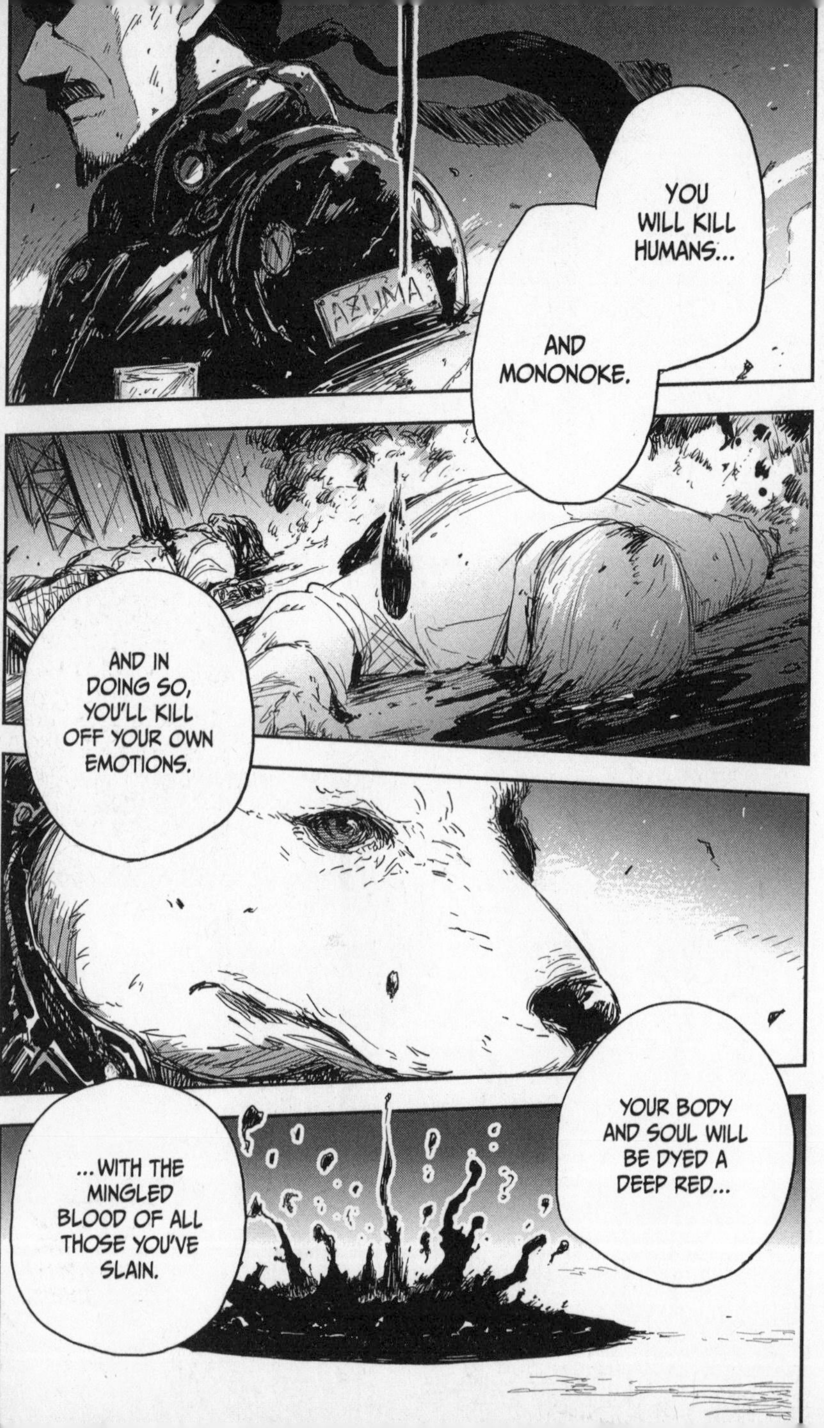
YOU WILL KILL HUMANS...
AND MONONOKE.
AZUMA
AND IN DOING SO, YOU'LL KILL OFF YOUR OWN EMOTIONS.
YOUR BODY AND SOUL WILL BE DYED A DEEP RED...
...WITH THE MINGLED BLOOD OF ALL THOSE YOU'VE SLAIN.

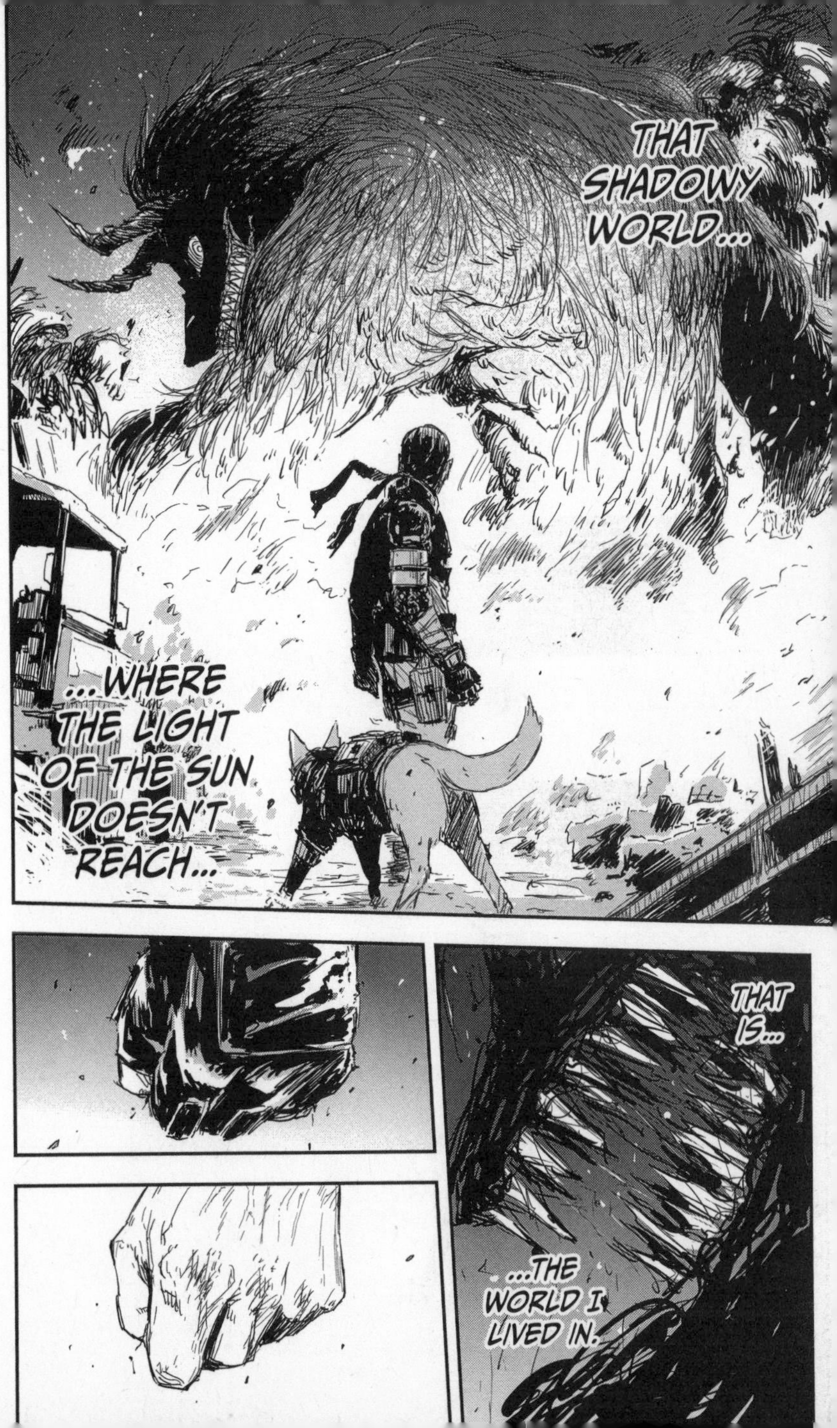
THAT SHADOWY WORLD...
...WHERE THE LIGHT OF THE SUN DOESN'T REACH...
THAT IS...
...THE WORLD I LIVED IN.

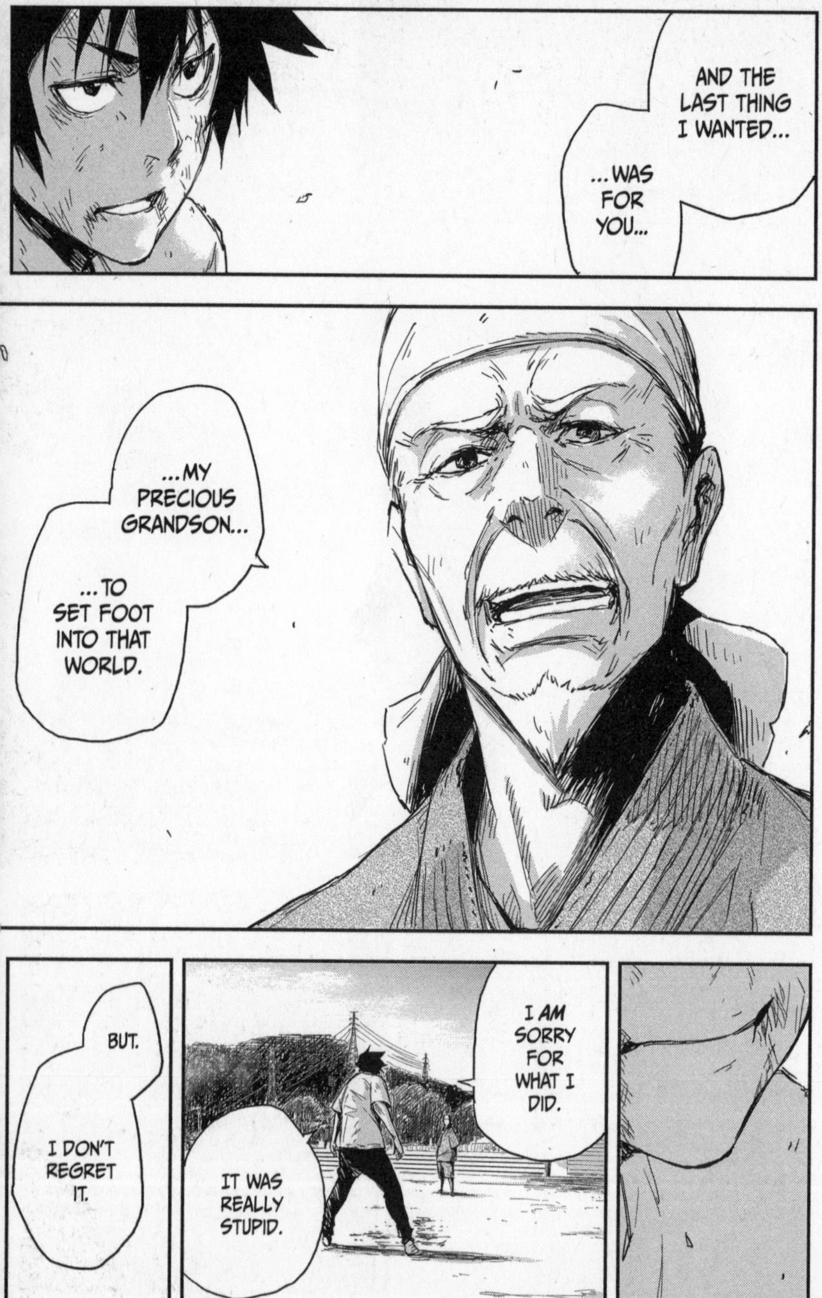
AND THE LAST THING I WANTED...
...WAS FOR YOU...
...MY PRECIOUS GRANDSON...
...TO SET FOOT INTO THAT WORLD.
I AM SORRY FOR WHAT I DID.
IT WAS REALLY STUPID.
BUT.
I DON'T REGRET IT.

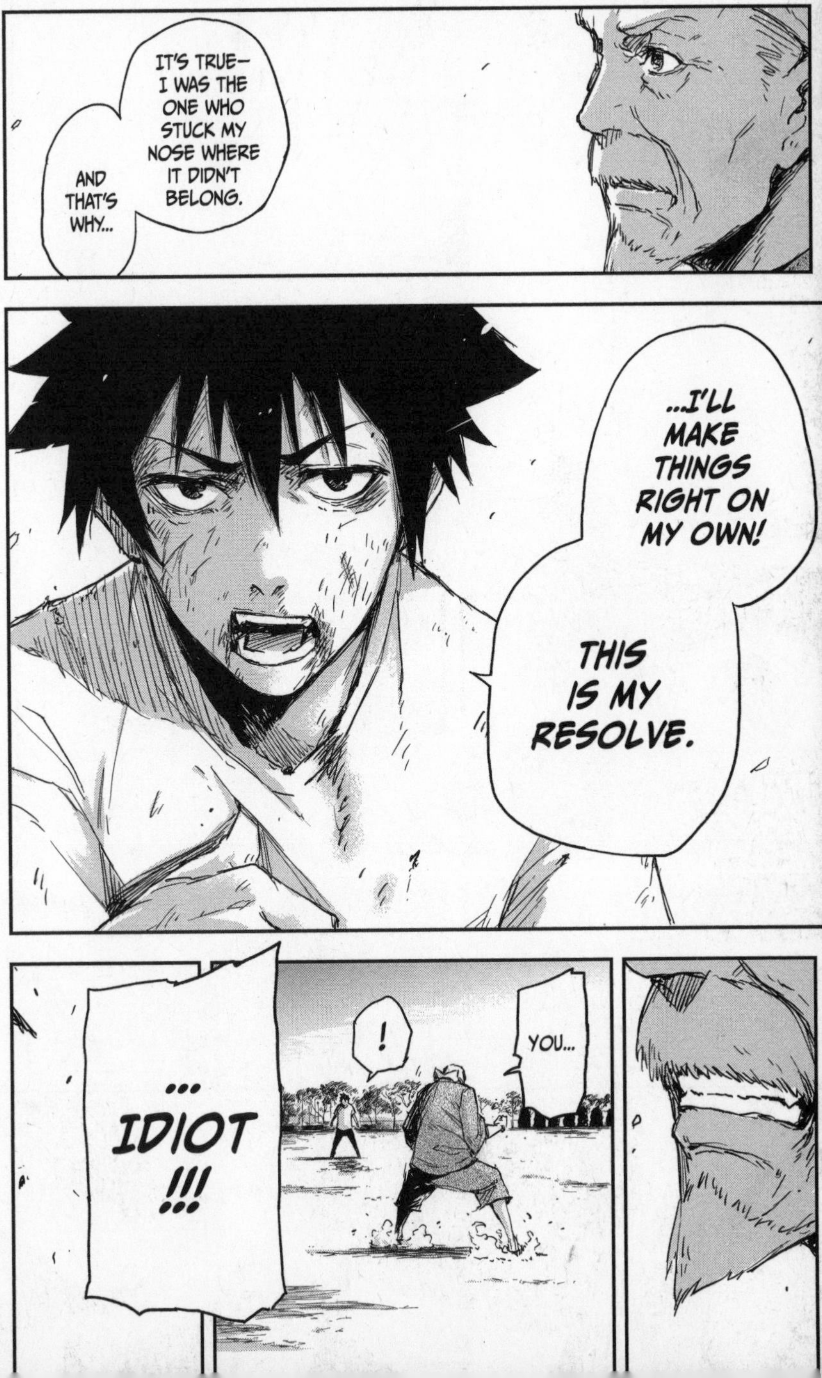
IT'S TRUE— I WAS THE ONE WHO STUCK MY NOSE WHERE IT DIDN'T BELONG.
AND THAT'S WHY...
...I'LL MAKE THINGS RIGHT ON MY OWN!
THIS IS MY RESOLVE.
YOU...
!
...IDIOT!!!

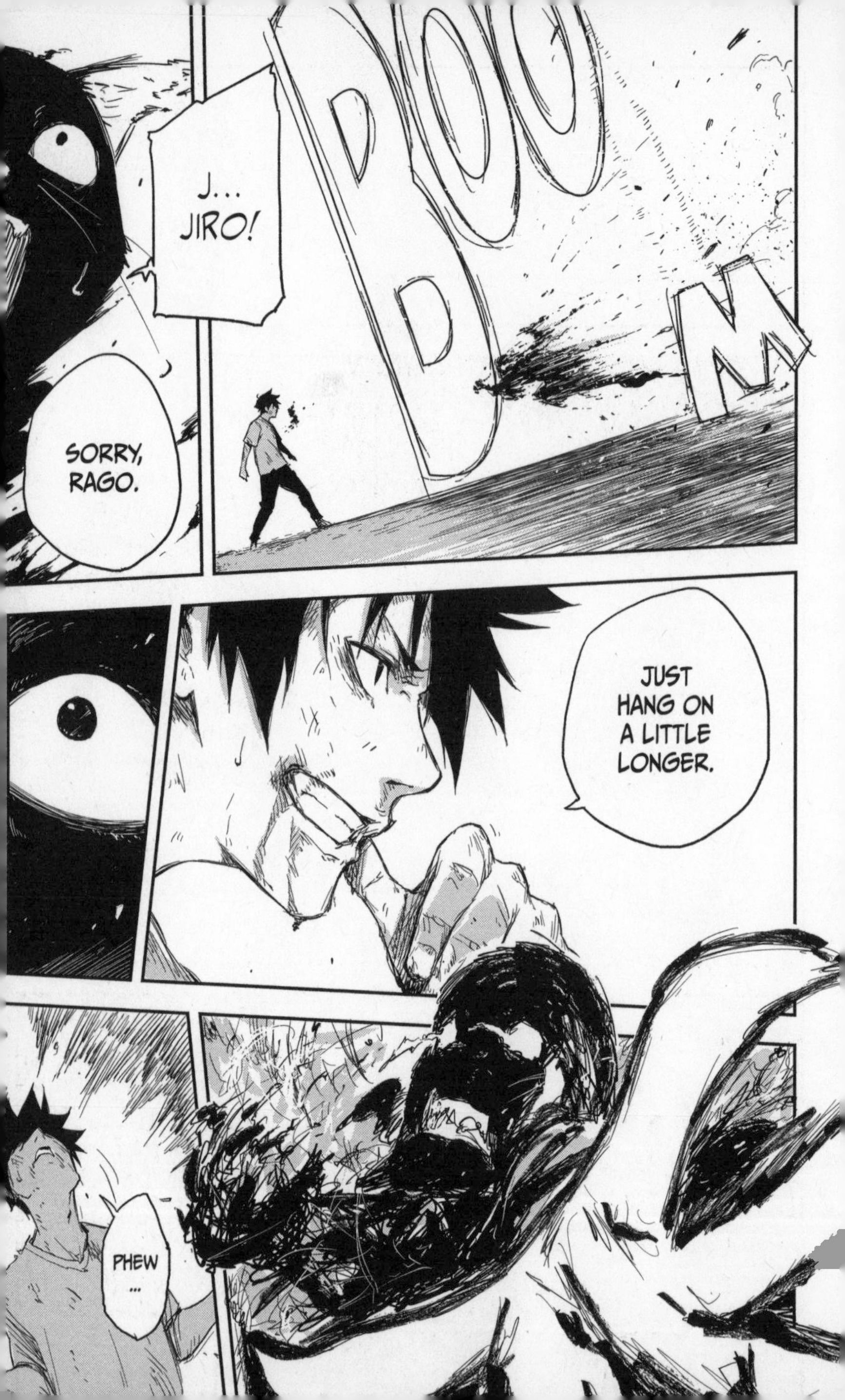

J... JIRO!
SORRY, RAGO.
JUST HANG ON A LITTLE LONGER.
PHEW ...

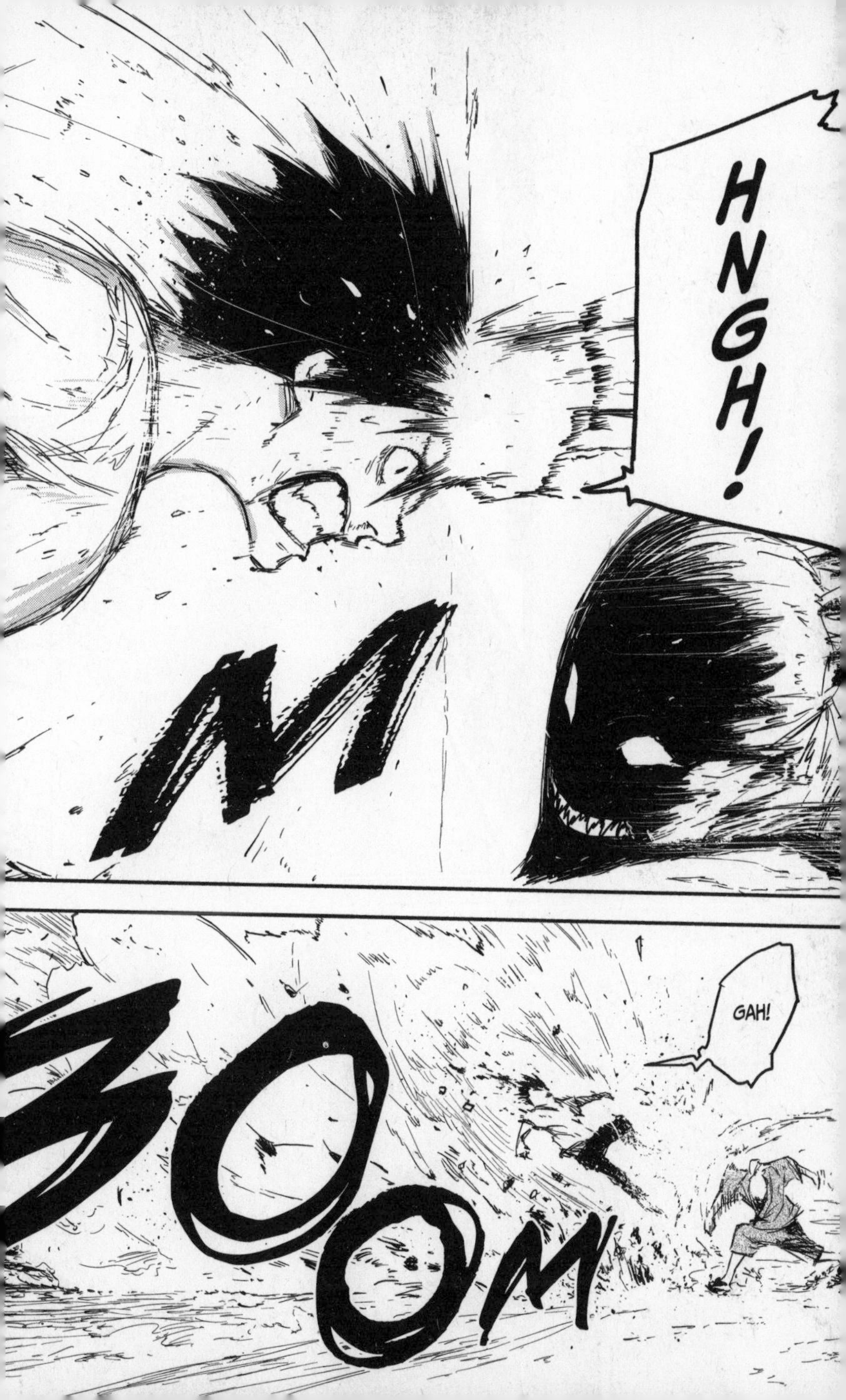
HNGH!
GAH!
BOOM

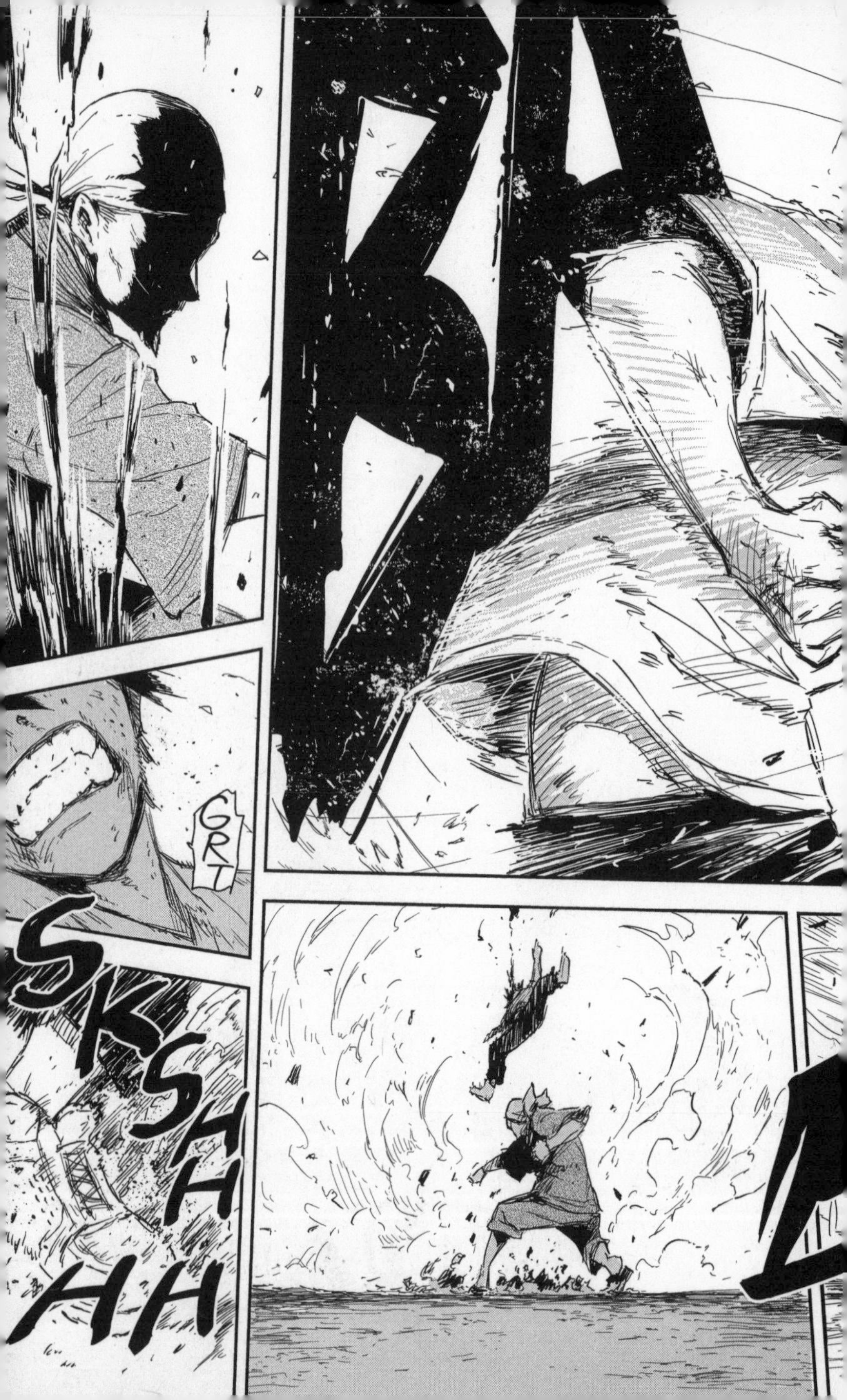
GRT
SKSHHHH

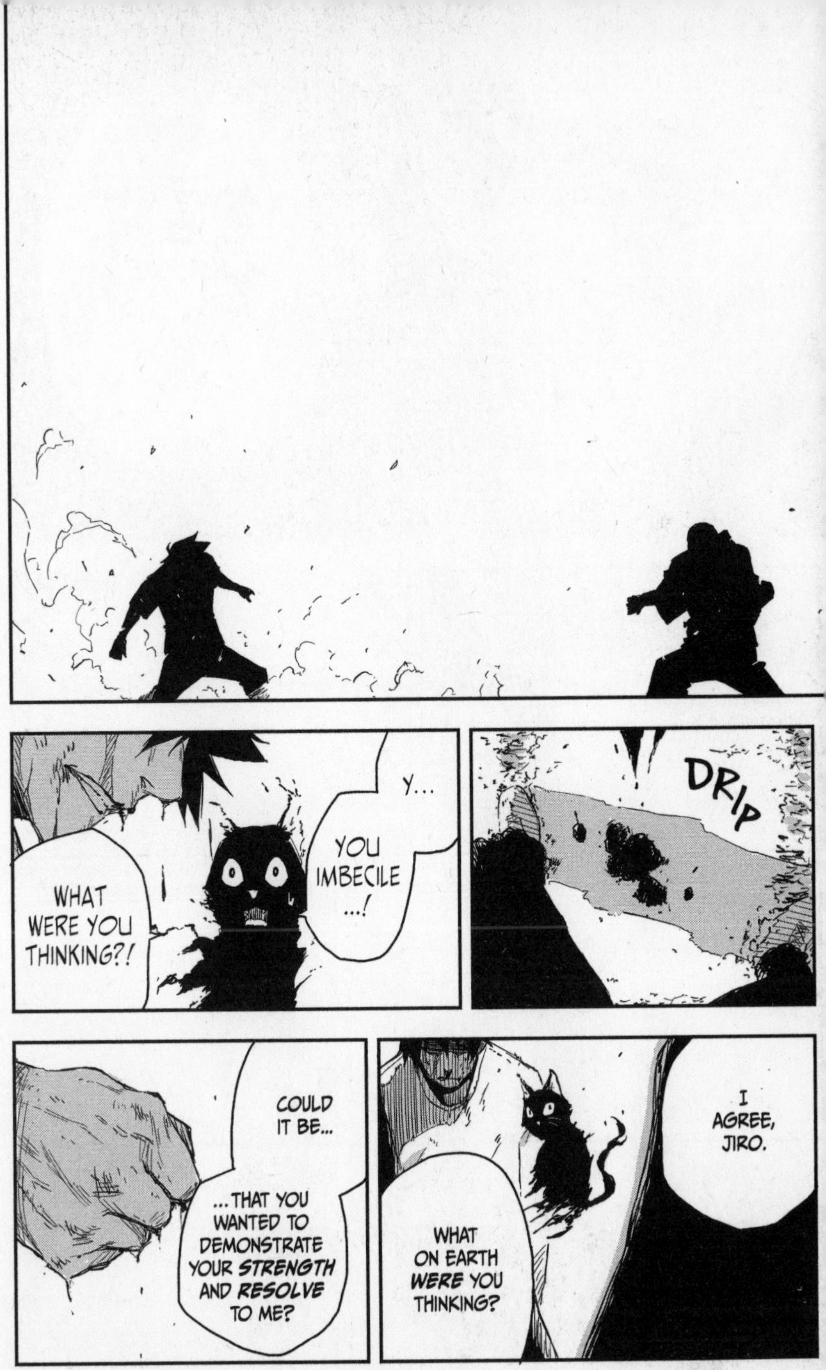
DRIP
Y...
YOU IMBECILE ...!
WHAT WERE YOU THINKING?!
I AGREE, JIRO.
WHAT ON EARTH *WERE* YOU THINKING?
COULD IT BE...
...THAT YOU WANTED TO DEMONSTRATE YOUR *STRENGTH* AND *RESOLVE* TO ME?

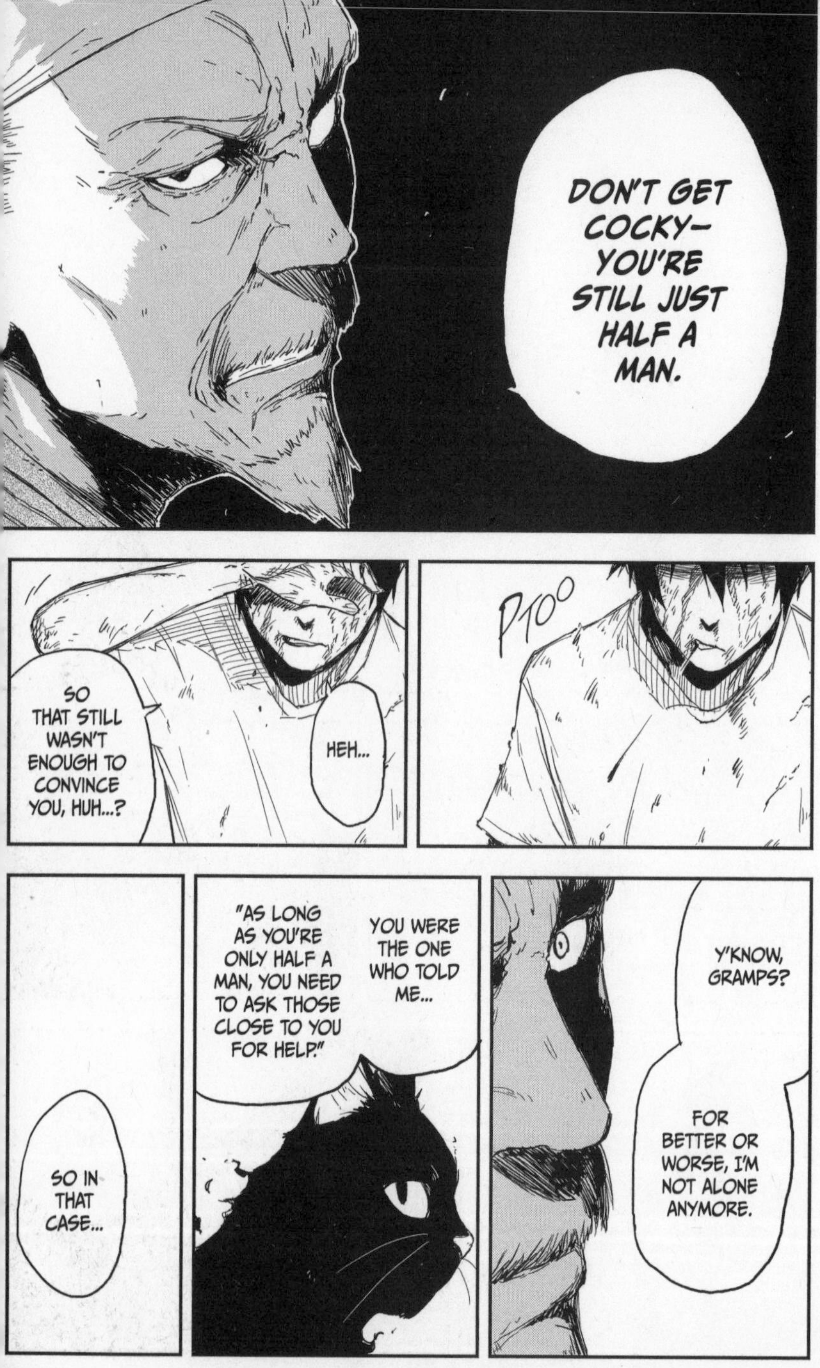
DON'T GET COCKY— YOU'RE STILL JUST HALF A MAN.
PTOO
HEH...
SO THAT STILL WASN'T ENOUGH TO CONVINCE YOU, HUH...?
Y'KNOW, GRAMPS?
FOR BETTER OR WORSE, I'M NOT ALONE ANYMORE.
YOU WERE THE ONE WHO TOLD ME...
"AS LONG AS YOU'RE ONLY HALF A MAN, YOU NEED TO ASK THOSE CLOSE TO YOU FOR HELP."
SO IN THAT CASE...

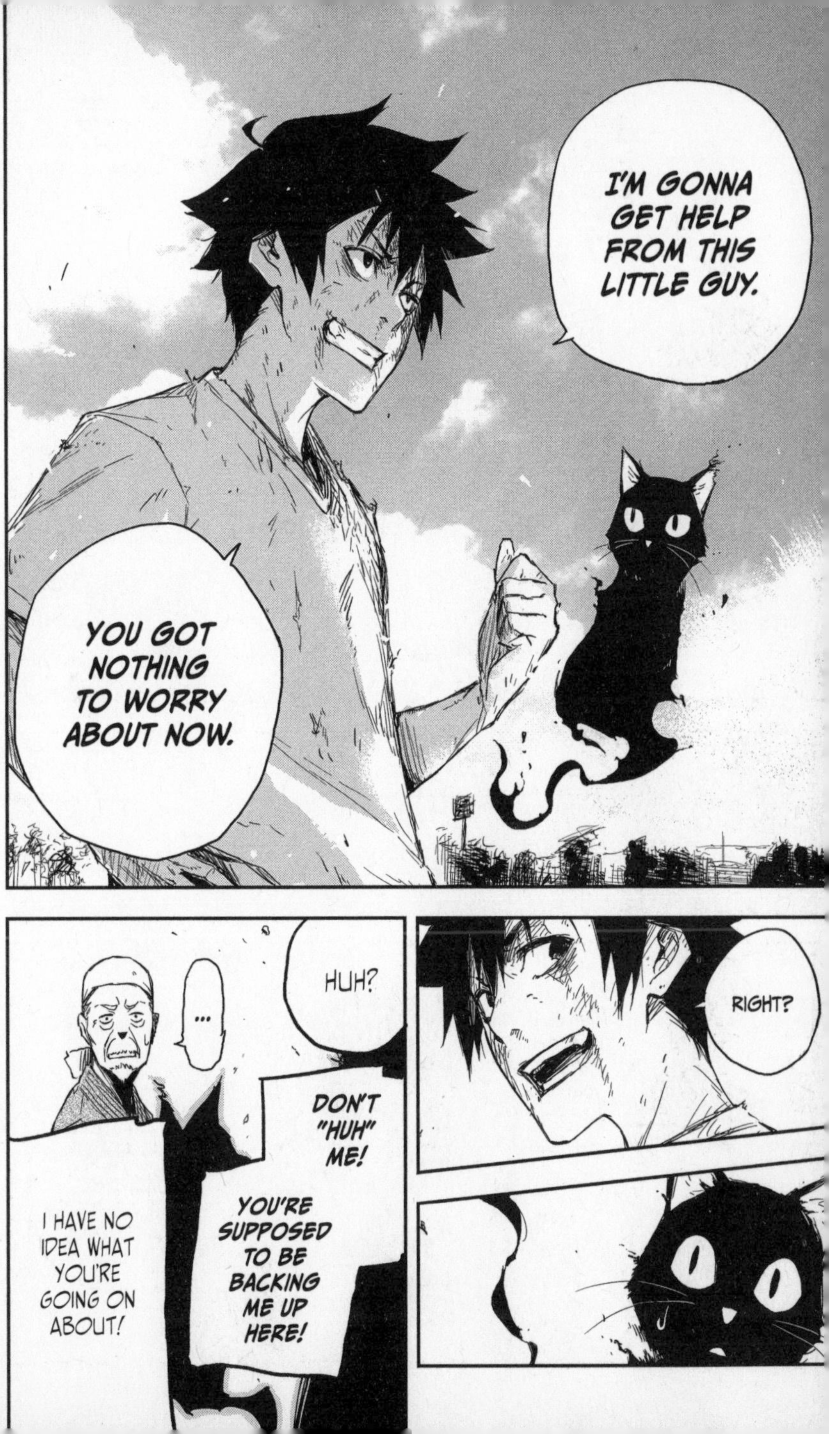

I'M GONNA GET HELP FROM THIS LITTLE GUY.
YOU GOT NOTHING TO WORRY ABOUT NOW.
RIGHT?
HUH?
...
DON'T "HUH" ME!
YOU'RE SUPPOSED TO BE BACKING ME UP HERE!
I HAVE NO IDEA WHAT YOU'RE GOING ON ABOUT!

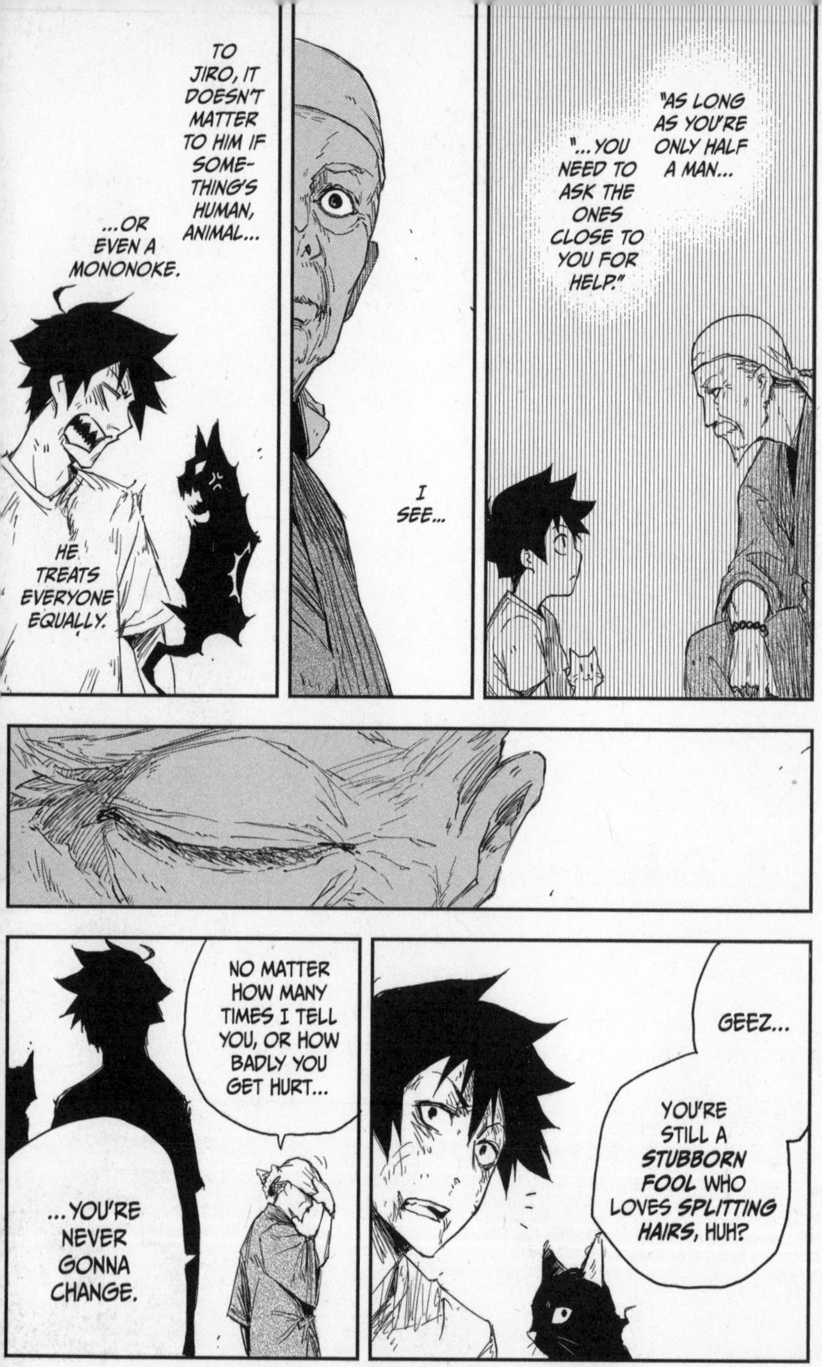
"AS LONG AS YOU'RE ONLY HALF A MAN...
"...YOU NEED TO ASK THE ONES CLOSE TO YOU FOR HELP."
I SEE...
TO JIRO, IT DOESN'T MATTER TO HIM IF SOMETHING'S HUMAN, ANIMAL...
...OR EVEN A MONONOKE.
HE TREATS EVERYONE EQUALLY.
GEEZ...
YOU'RE STILL A STUBBORN FOOL WHO LOVES SPLITTING HAIRS, HUH?
NO MATTER HOW MANY TIMES I TELL YOU, OR HOW BADLY YOU GET HURT...
...YOU'RE NEVER GONNA CHANGE.

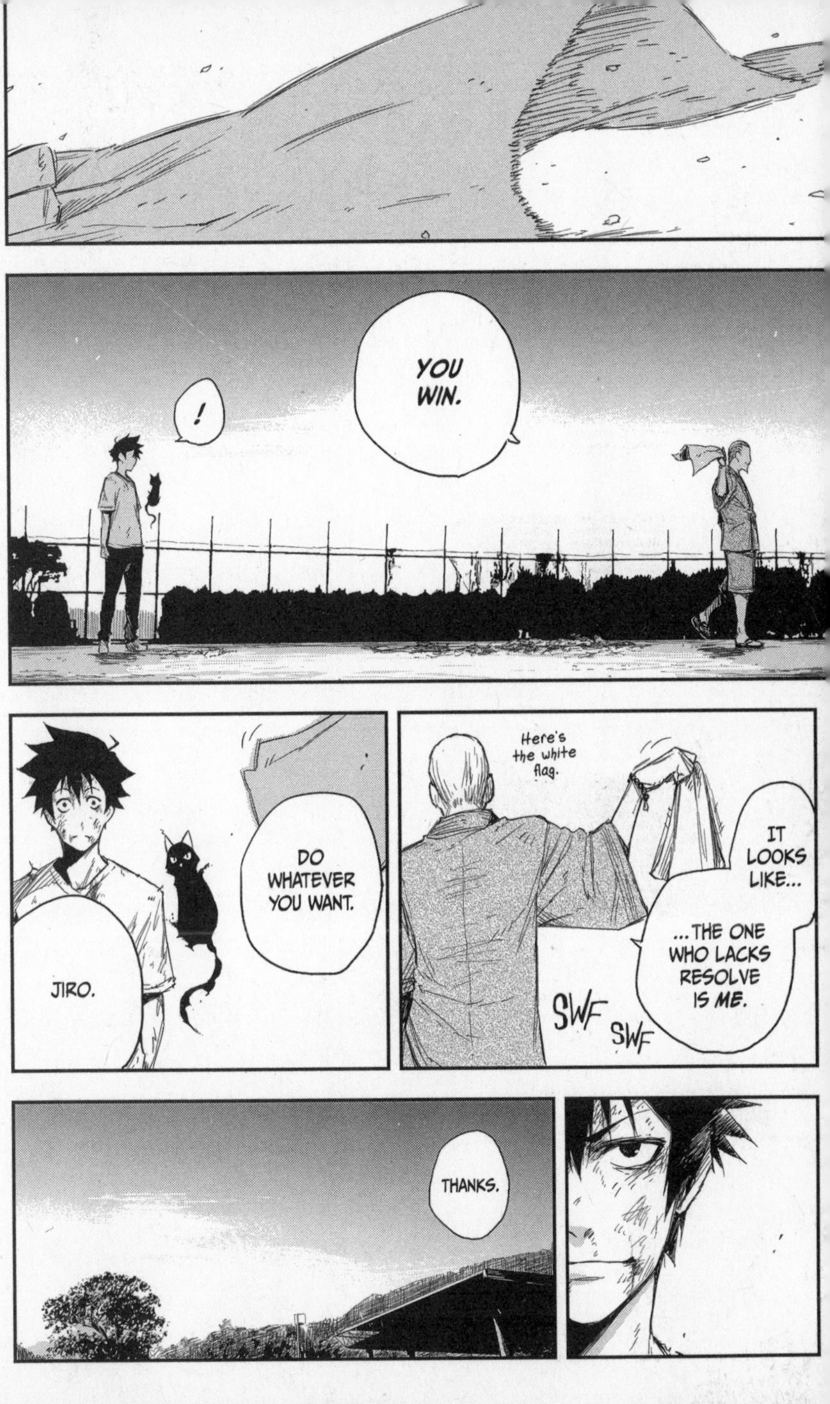
YOU WIN.
!
Here's the white flag.
IT LOOKS LIKE...
...THE ONE WHO LACKS RESOLVE IS ME.
SWF SWF
DO WHATEVER YOU WANT.
JIRO.
THANKS.

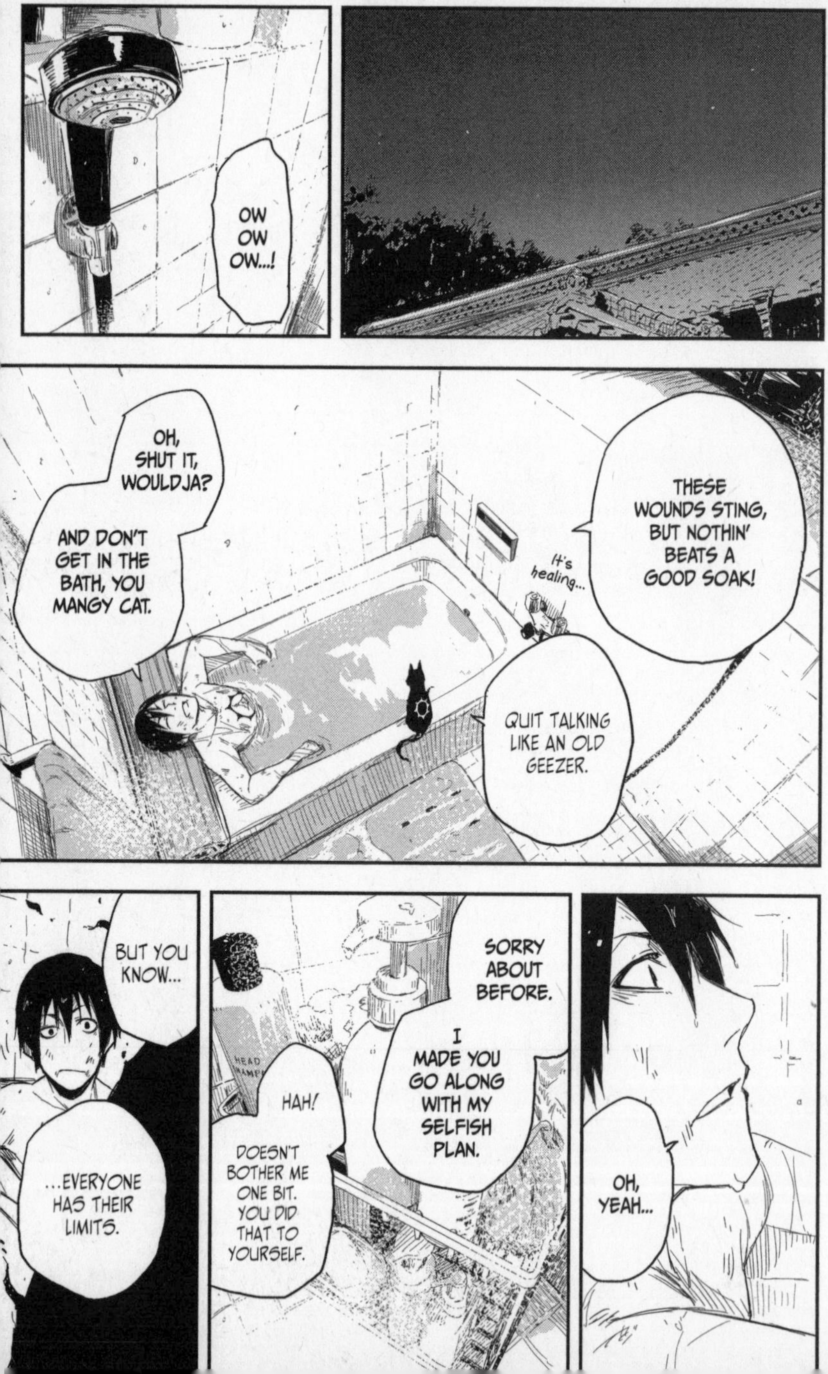
OW OW OW...!
THESE WOUNDS STING, BUT NOTHIN' BEATS A GOOD SOAK!
It's healing...
QUIT TALKING LIKE AN OLD GEEZER.
OH, SHUT IT, WOULDJA?
AND DON'T GET IN THE BATH, YOU MANGY CAT.
OH, YEAH...
SORRY ABOUT BEFORE.
I MADE YOU GO ALONG WITH MY SELFISH PLAN.
HAH!
DOESN'T BOTHER ME ONE BIT. YOU DID THAT TO YOURSELF.
BUT YOU KNOW...
...EVERYONE HAS THEIR LIMITS.

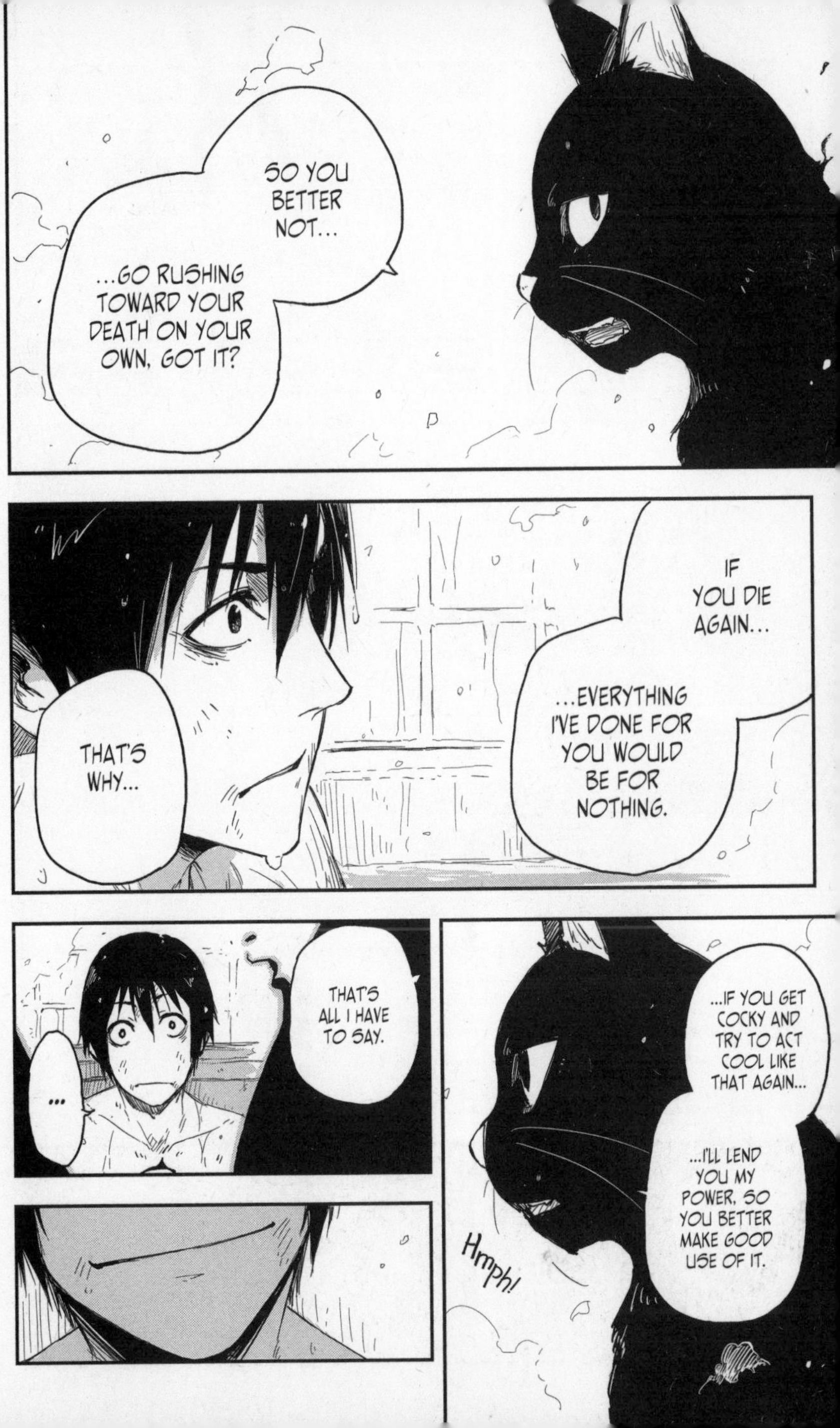
SO YOU BETTER NOT...
...GO RUSHING TOWARD YOUR DEATH ON YOUR OWN, GOT IT?
IF YOU DIE AGAIN...
...EVERYTHING I'VE DONE FOR YOU WOULD BE FOR NOTHING.
THAT'S WHY...
...IF YOU GET COCKY AND TRY TO ACT COOL LIKE THAT AGAIN...
...I'LL LEND YOU MY POWER, SO YOU BETTER MAKE GOOD USE OF IT.
Hmph!
THAT'S ALL I HAVE TO SAY.
...

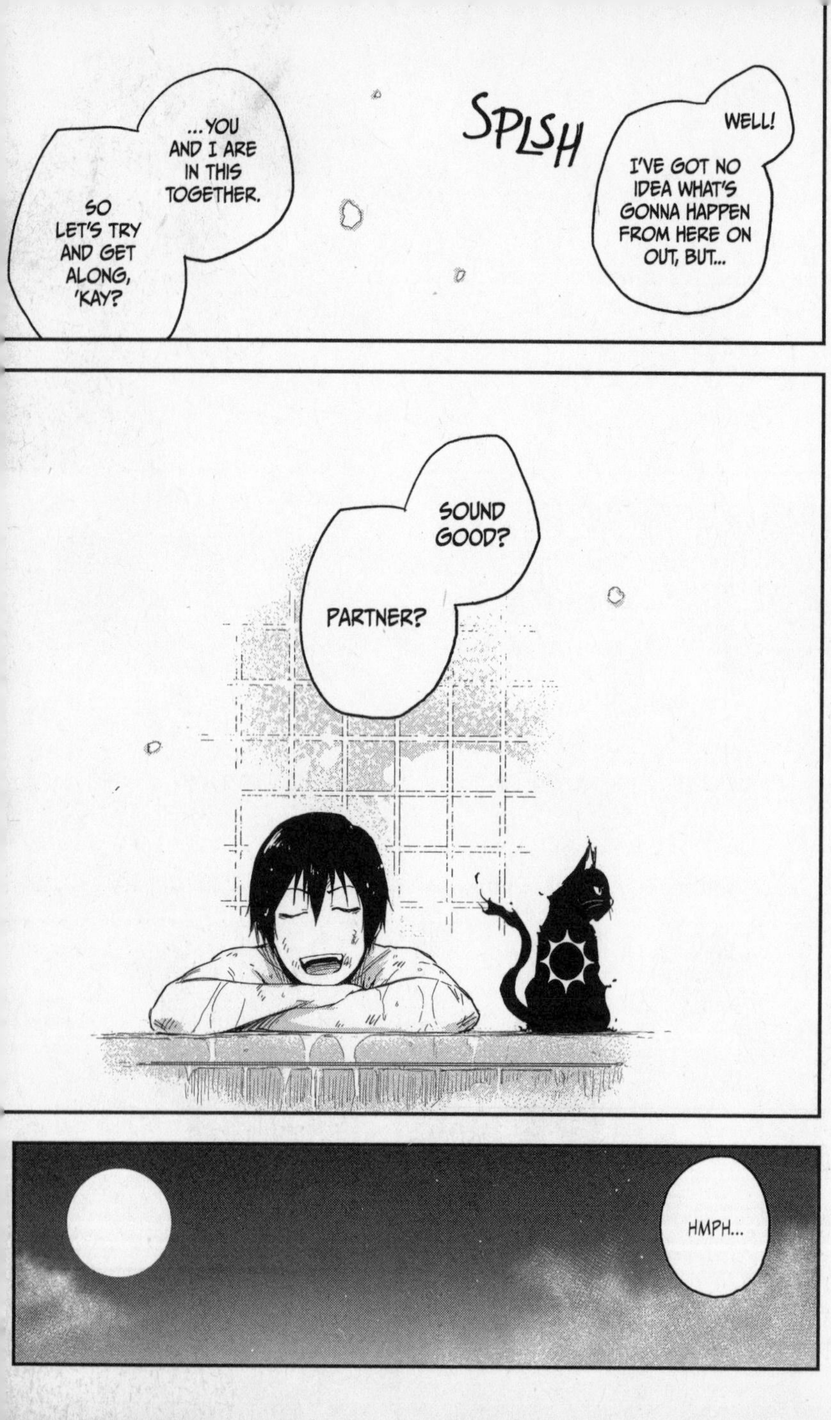
WELL!
I'VE GOT NO IDEA WHAT'S GONNA HAPPEN FROM HERE ON OUT, BUT...
SPLSH
...YOU AND I ARE IN THIS TOGETHER.
SO LET'S TRY AND GET ALONG, 'KAY?
SOUND GOOD?
PARTNER?
HMPH...

BLACK TORCH

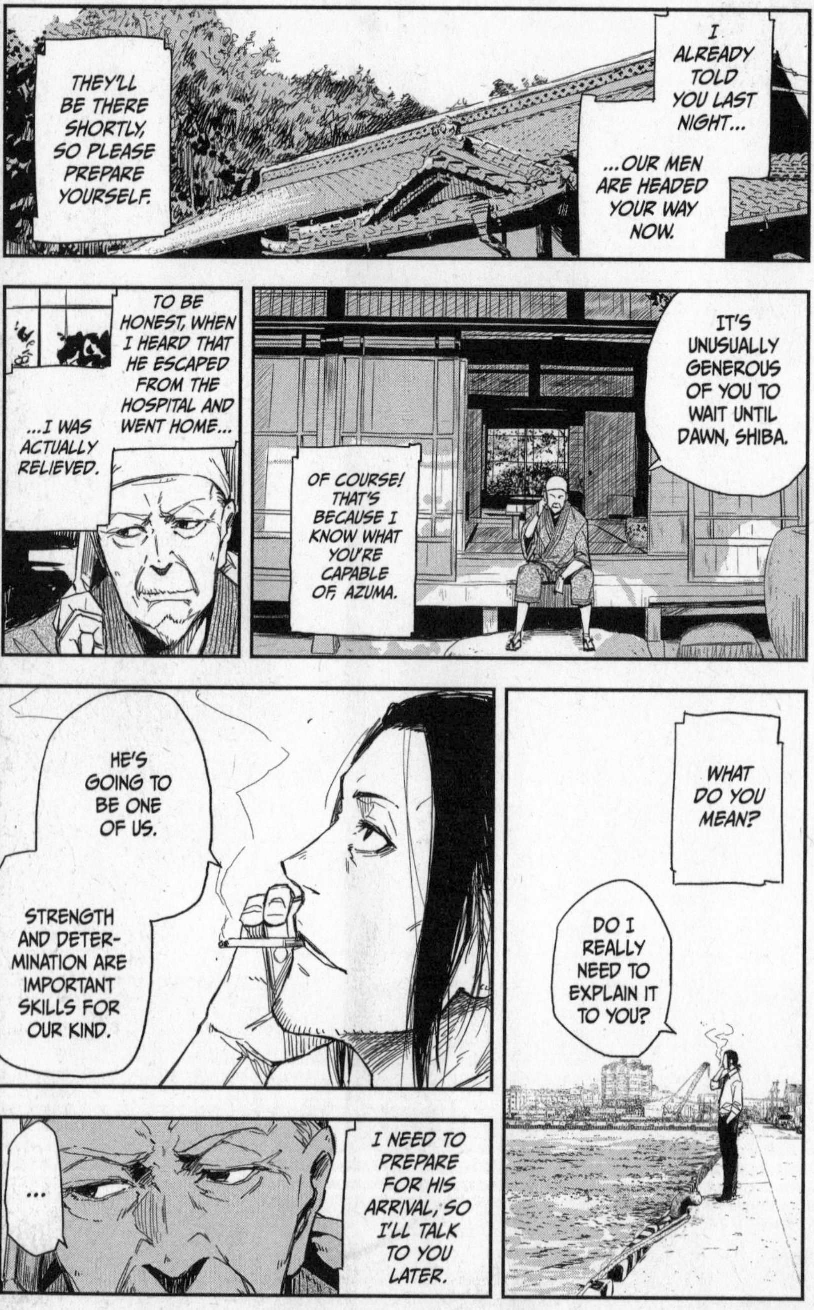
I ALREADY TOLD YOU LAST NIGHT...
...OUR MEN ARE HEADED YOUR WAY NOW.
THEY'LL BE THERE SHORTLY, SO PLEASE PREPARE YOURSELF.
IT'S UNUSUALLY GENEROUS OF YOU TO WAIT UNTIL DAWN, SHIBA.
OF COURSE! THAT'S BECAUSE I KNOW WHAT YOU'RE CAPABLE OF, AZUMA.
TO BE HONEST, WHEN I HEARD THAT HE ESCAPED FROM THE HOSPITAL AND WENT HOME...
...I WAS ACTUALLY RELIEVED.
WHAT DO YOU MEAN?
DO I REALLY NEED TO EXPLAIN IT TO YOU?
HE'S GOING TO BE ONE OF US.
STRENGTH AND DETERMINATION ARE IMPORTANT SKILLS FOR OUR KIND.
I NEED TO PREPARE FOR HIS ARRIVAL, SO I'LL TALK TO YOU LATER.
...

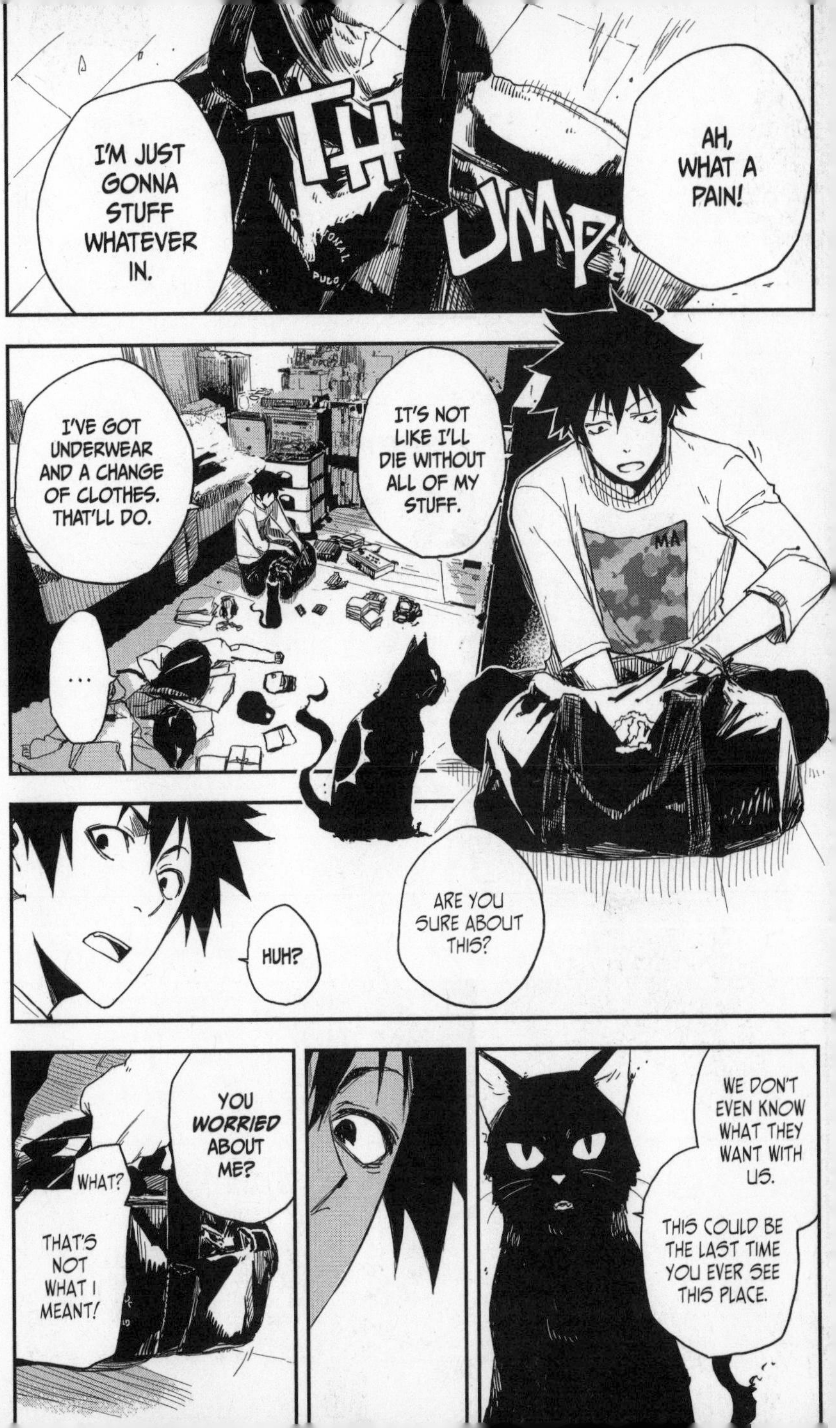
AH, WHAT A PAIN!
THUMP
I'M JUST GONNA STUFF WHATEVER IN.
IT'S NOT LIKE I'LL DIE WITHOUT ALL OF MY STUFF.
I'VE GOT UNDERWEAR AND A CHANGE OF CLOTHES. THAT'LL DO.
...
ARE YOU SURE ABOUT THIS?
HUH?
WE DON'T EVEN KNOW WHAT THEY WANT WITH US.
THIS COULD BE THE LAST TIME YOU EVER SEE THIS PLACE.
YOU *WORRIED* ABOUT ME?
WHAT?
THAT'S NOT WHAT I MEANT!

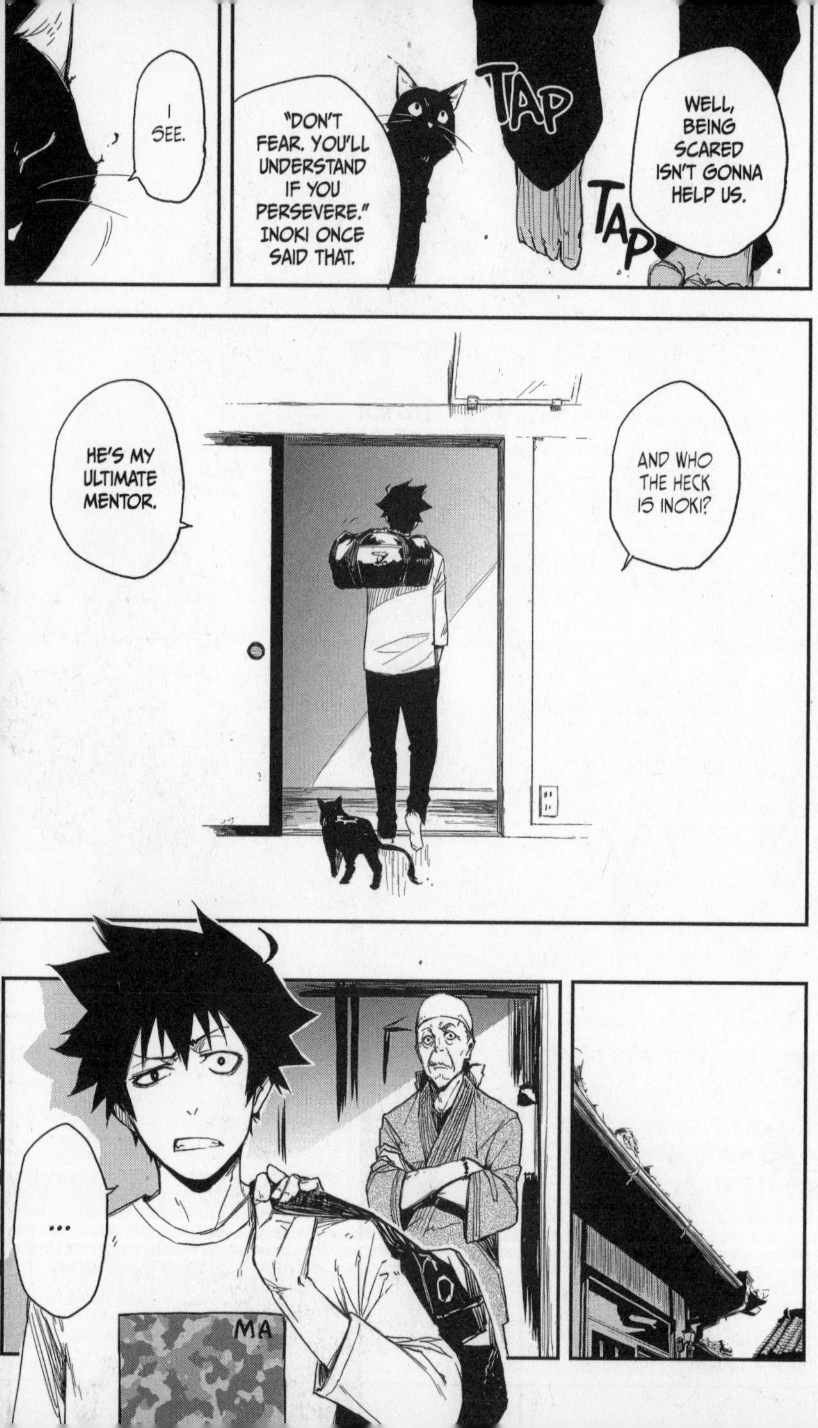
WELL, BEING SCARED ISN'T GONNA HELP US.
TAP
TAP
"DON'T FEAR. YOU'LL UNDERSTAND IF YOU PERSEVERE." INOKI ONCE SAID THAT.
I SEE.
AND WHO THE HECK IS INOKI?
HE'S MY ULTIMATE MENTOR.
...
MA

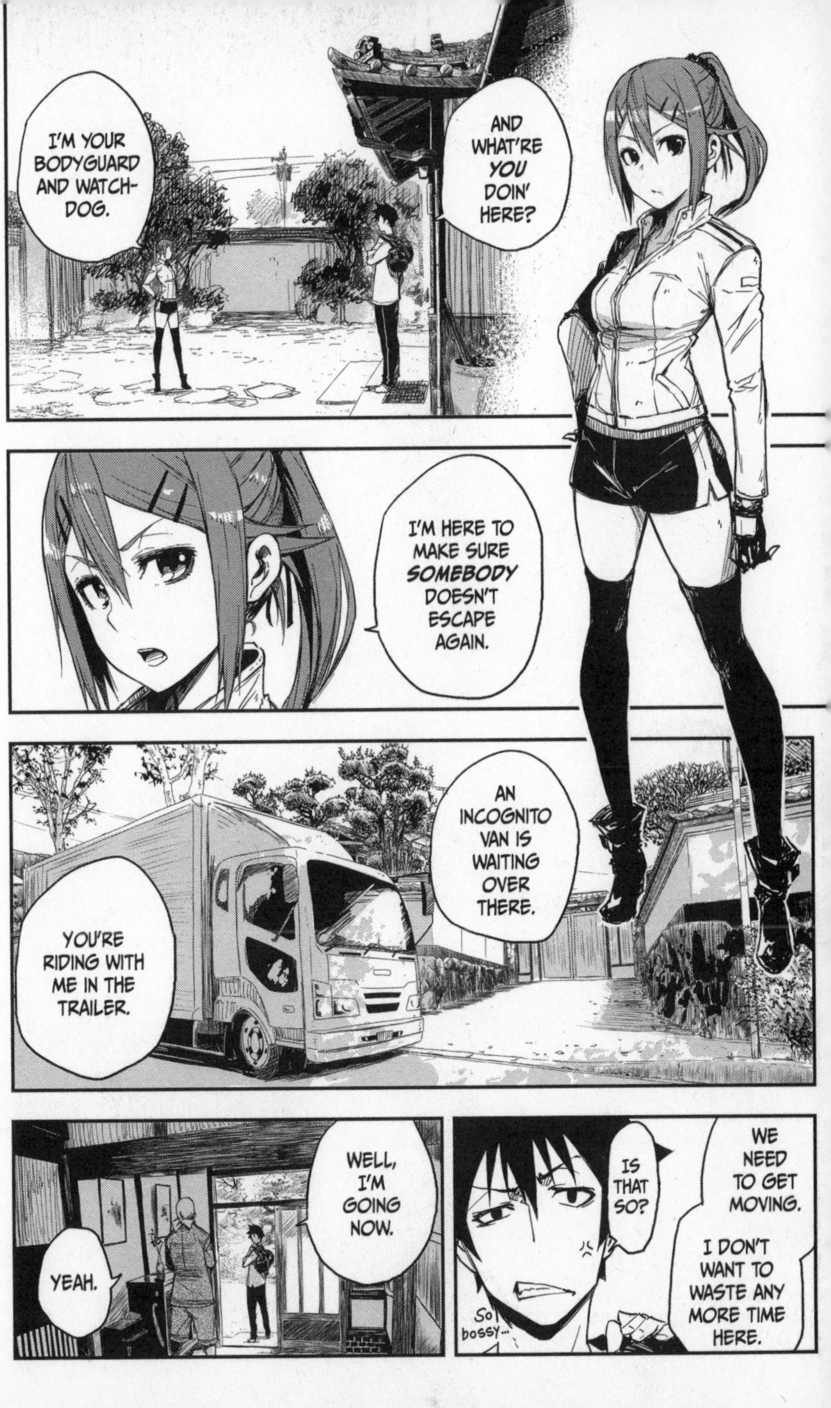
AND WHAT'RE *YOU* DOIN' HERE?
I'M YOUR BODYGUARD AND WATCH-DOG.
I'M HERE TO MAKE SURE *SOMEBODY* DOESN'T ESCAPE AGAIN.
AN INCOGNITO VAN IS WAITING OVER THERE.
YOU'RE RIDING WITH ME IN THE TRAILER.
WE NEED TO GET MOVING.
I DON'T WANT TO WASTE ANY MORE TIME HERE.
IS THAT SO?
So bossy...
WELL, I'M GOING NOW.
YEAH.

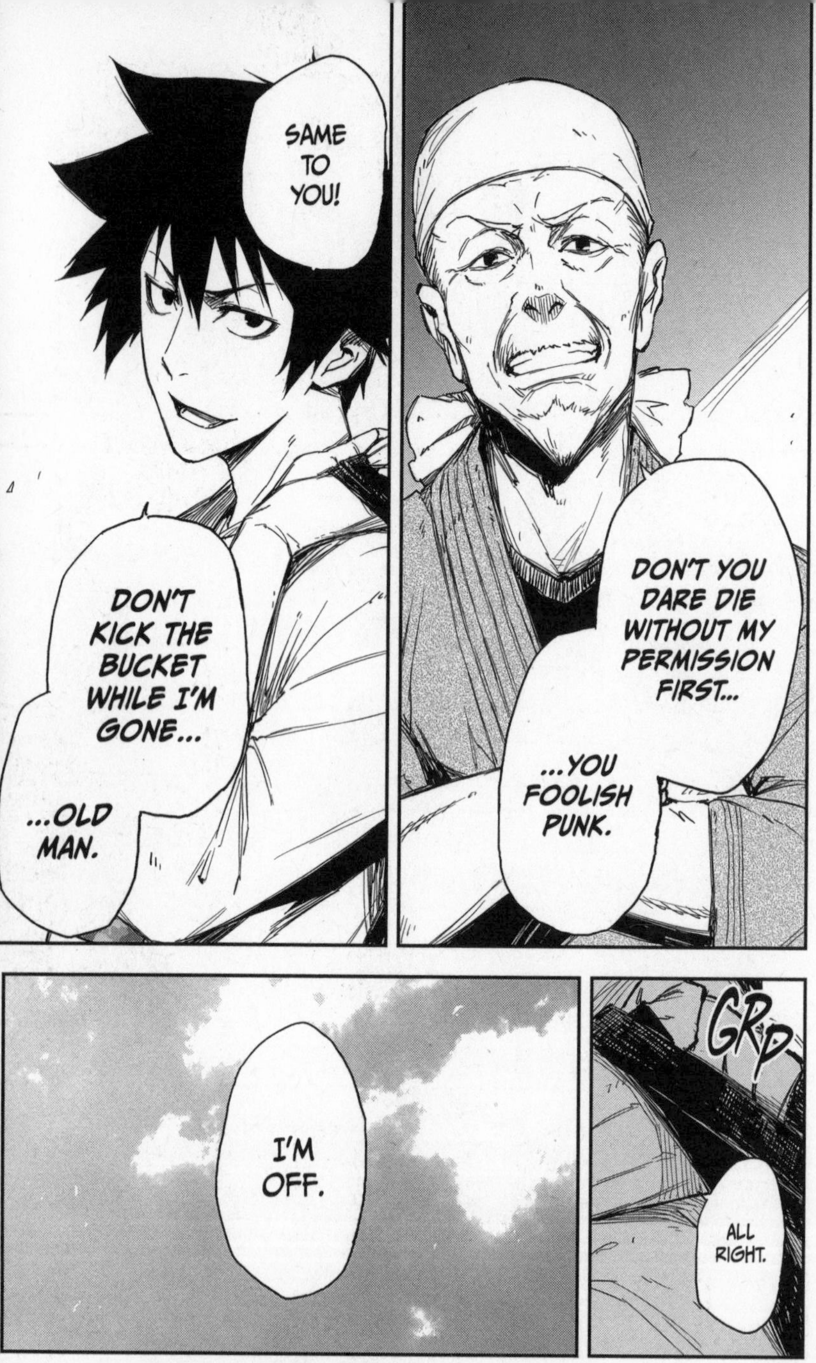
DON'T YOU DARE DIE WITHOUT MY PERMISSION FIRST...
...YOU FOOLISH PUNK.
SAME TO YOU!
DON'T KICK THE BUCKET WHILE I'M GONE...
...OLD MAN.
GRP
ALL RIGHT.
I'M OFF.

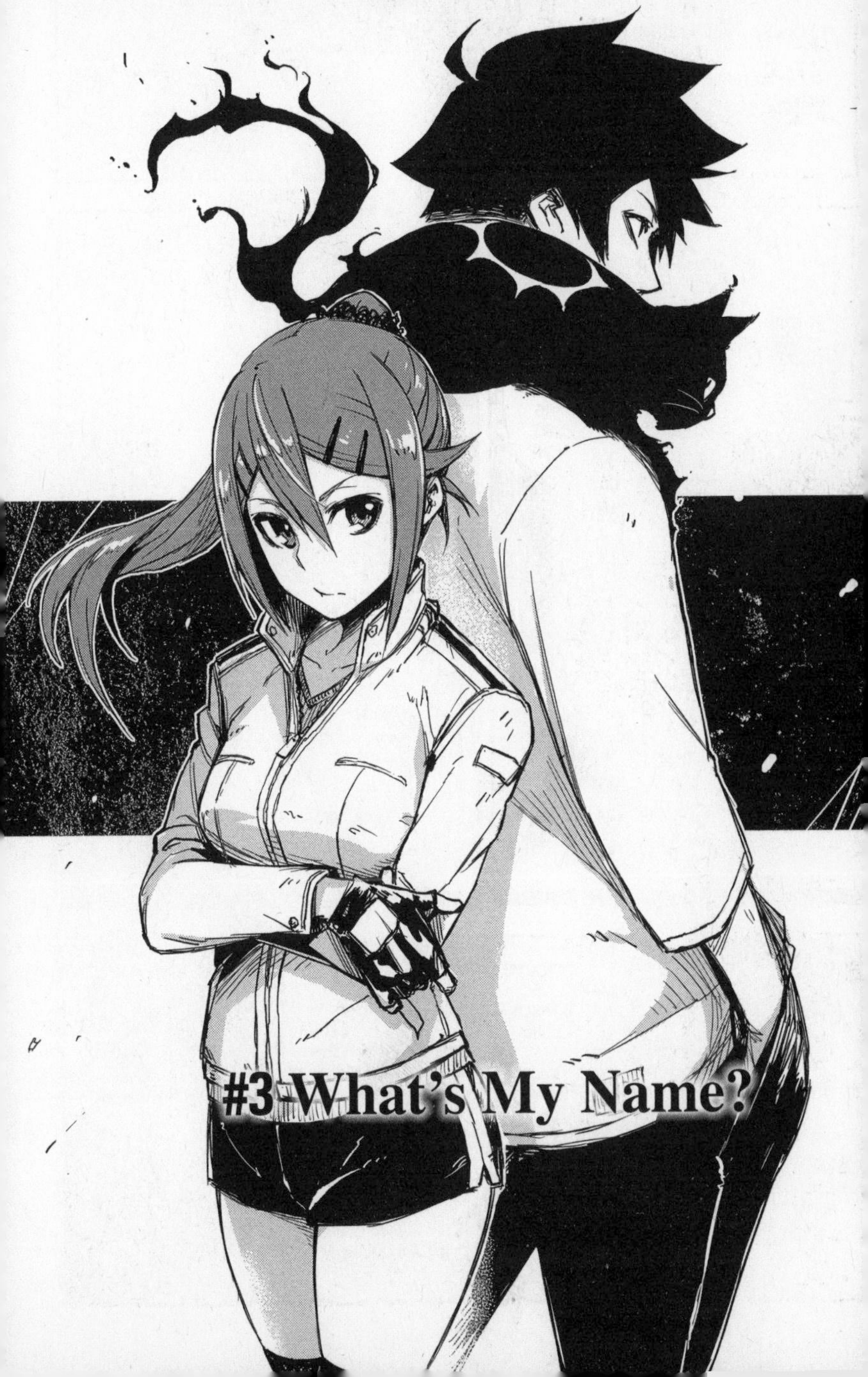
#3 What's My Name?

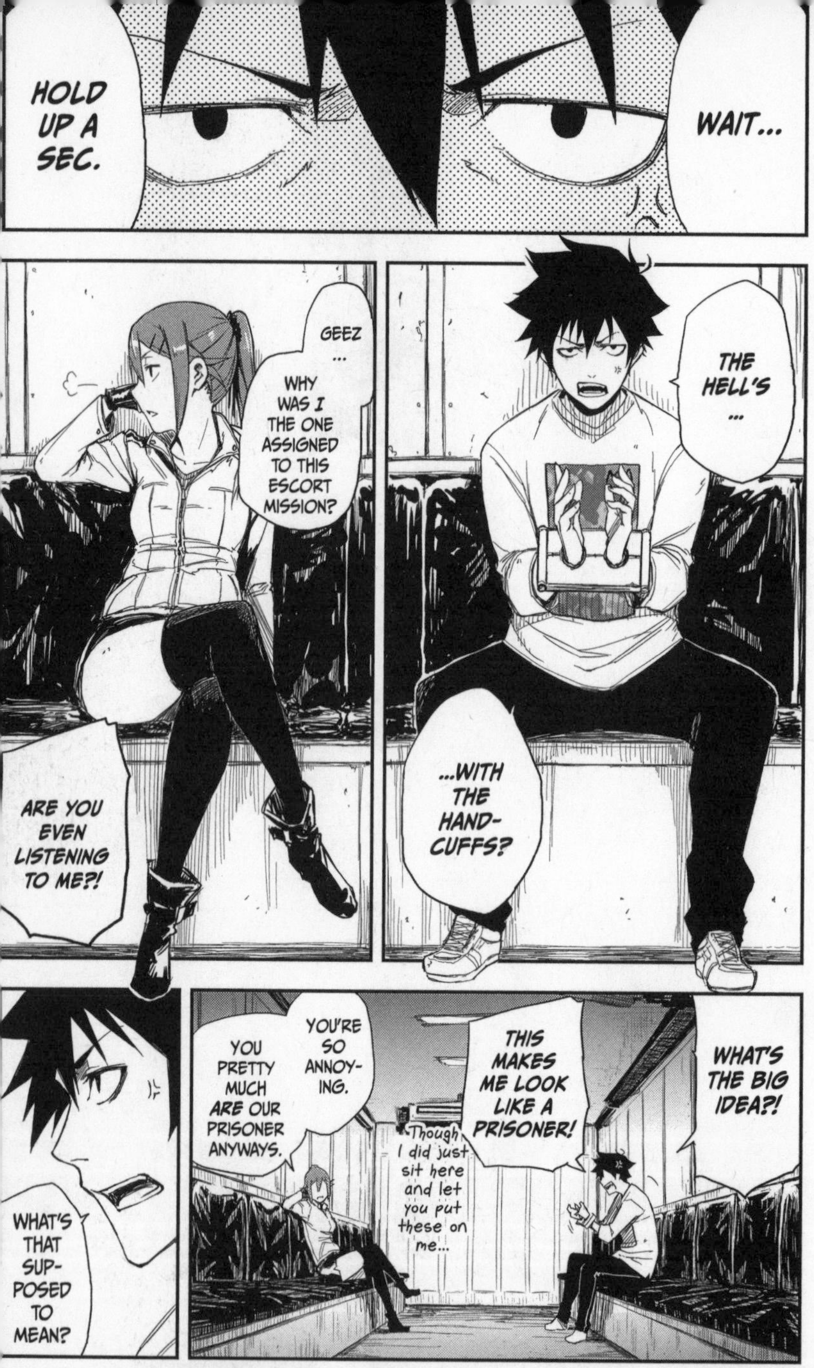
WAIT...
HOLD UP A SEC.
THE HELL'S ...
...WITH THE HAND-CUFFS?
GEEZ ... WHY WAS I THE ONE ASSIGNED TO THIS ESCORT MISSION?
ARE YOU EVEN LISTENING TO ME?!
WHAT'S THE BIG IDEA?!
THIS MAKES ME LOOK LIKE A PRISONER!
Though I did just sit here and let you put these on me...
YOU'RE SO ANNOY-ING.
YOU PRETTY MUCH ARE OUR PRISONER ANYWAYS.
WHAT'S THAT SUP-POSED TO MEAN?

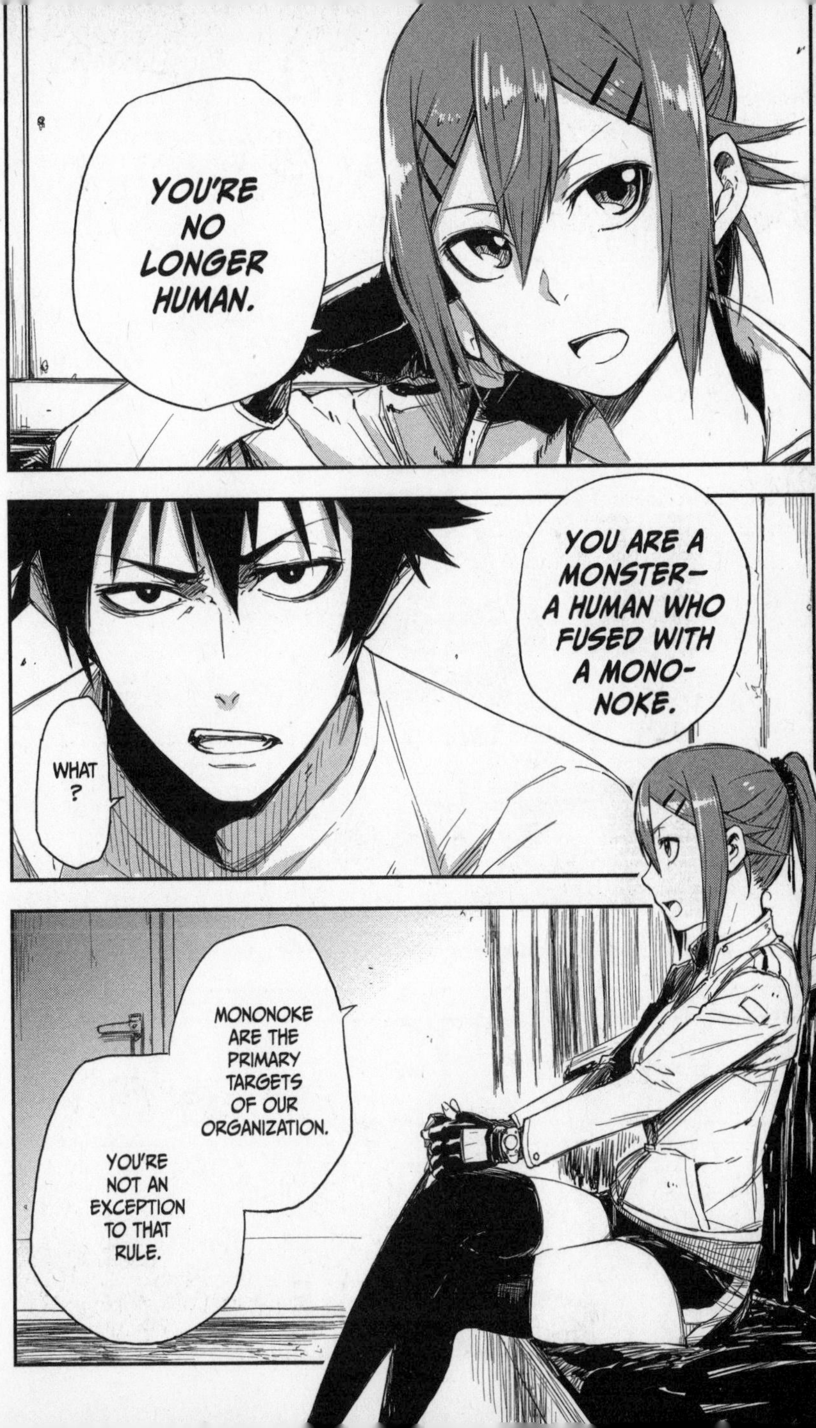
YOU'RE NO LONGER HUMAN.
YOU ARE A MONSTER— A HUMAN WHO FUSED WITH A MONO-NOKE.
WHAT?
MONONOKE ARE THE PRIMARY TARGETS OF OUR ORGANIZATION.
YOU'RE NOT AN EXCEPTION TO THAT RULE.

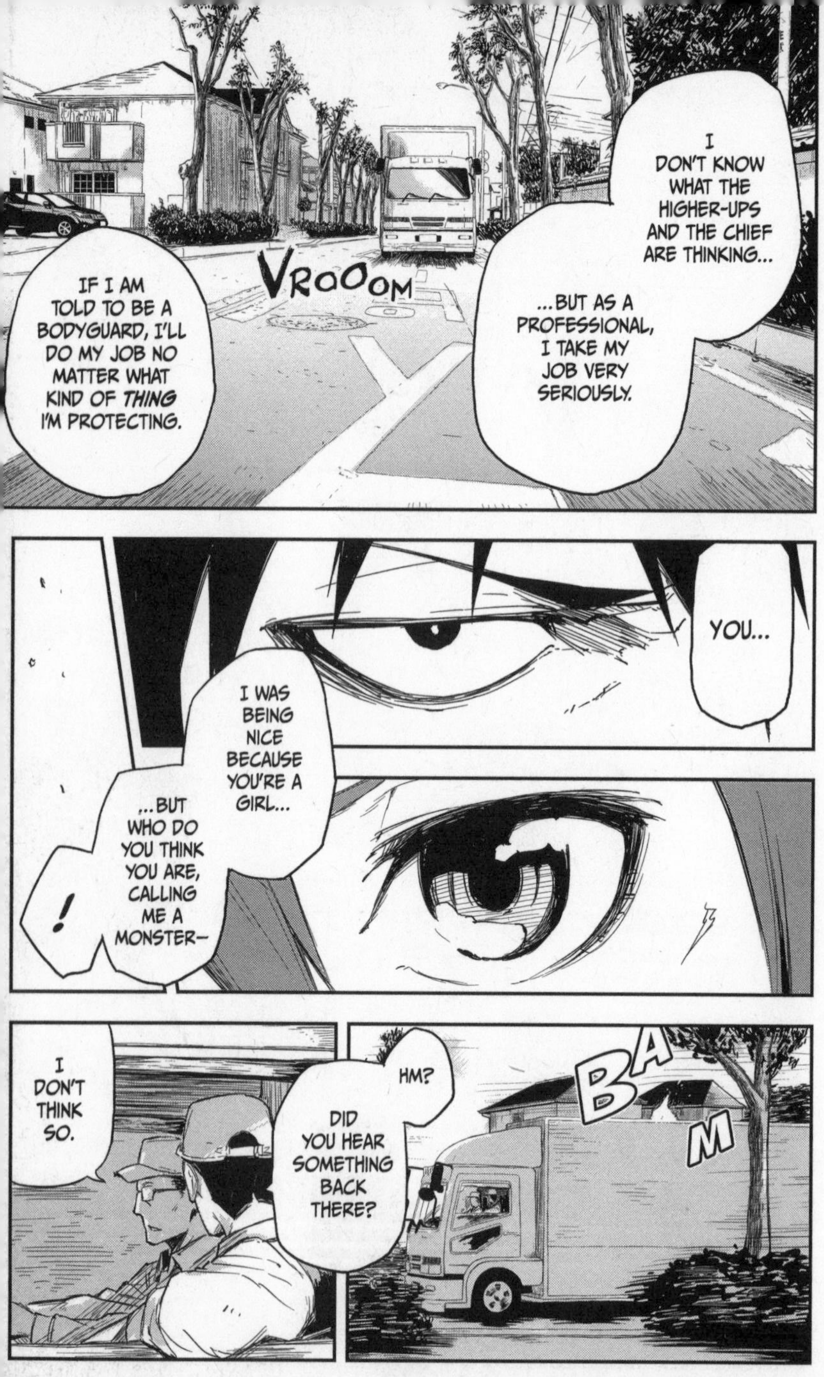
I DON'T KNOW WHAT THE HIGHER-UPS AND THE CHIEF ARE THINKING...
...BUT AS A PROFESSIONAL, I TAKE MY JOB VERY SERIOUSLY.
VROOOM
IF I AM TOLD TO BE A BODYGUARD, I'LL DO MY JOB NO MATTER WHAT KIND OF *THING* I'M PROTECTING.
YOU...
I WAS BEING NICE BECAUSE YOU'RE A GIRL...
...BUT WHO DO YOU THINK YOU ARE, CALLING ME A MONSTER–
!
BAM
HM?
DID YOU HEAR SOMETHING BACK THERE?
I DON'T THINK SO.

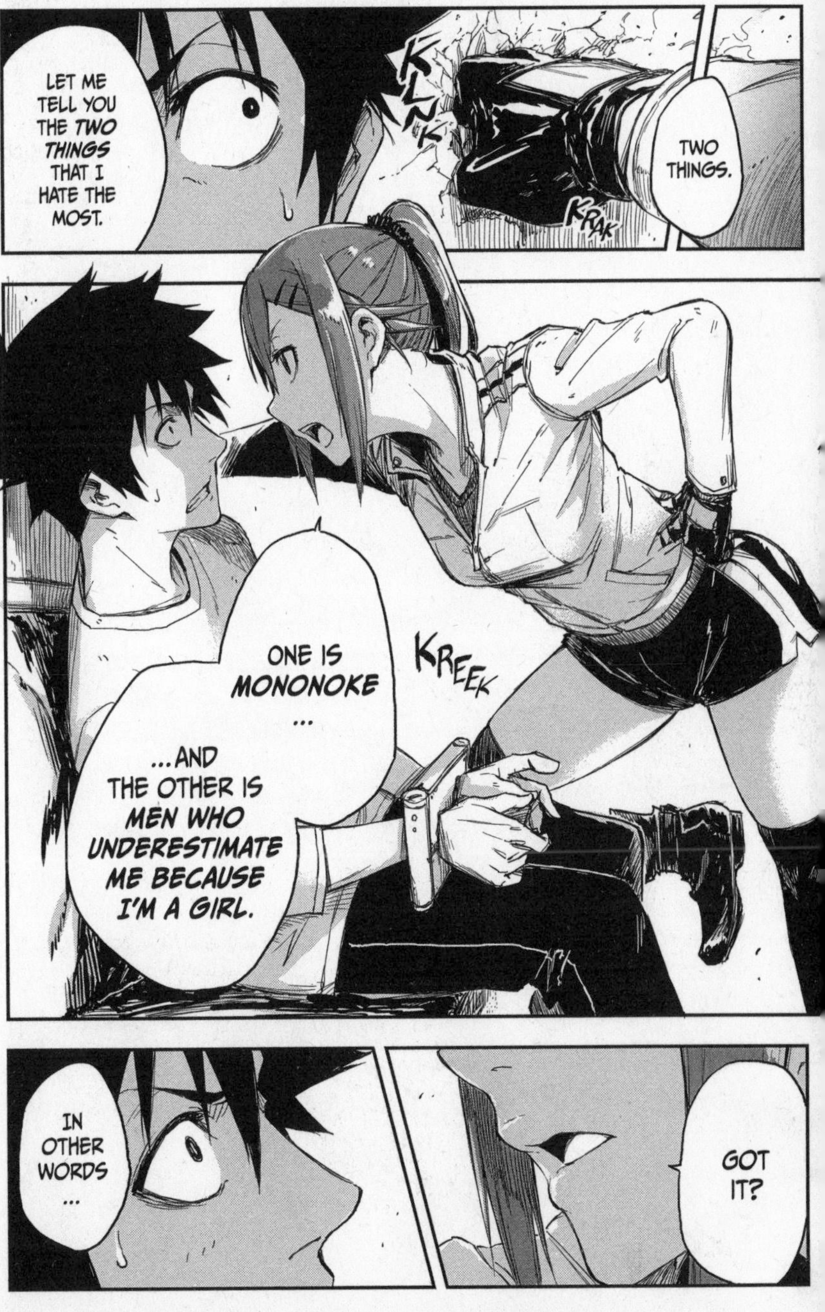
LET ME TELL YOU THE *TWO THINGS* THAT I HATE THE MOST.
KLNK
KRAK
TWO THINGS.
ONE IS *MONONOKE* ...
...AND THE OTHER IS *MEN WHO UNDERESTIMATE ME BECAUSE I'M A GIRL.*
KREEK
IN OTHER WORDS ...
GOT IT?

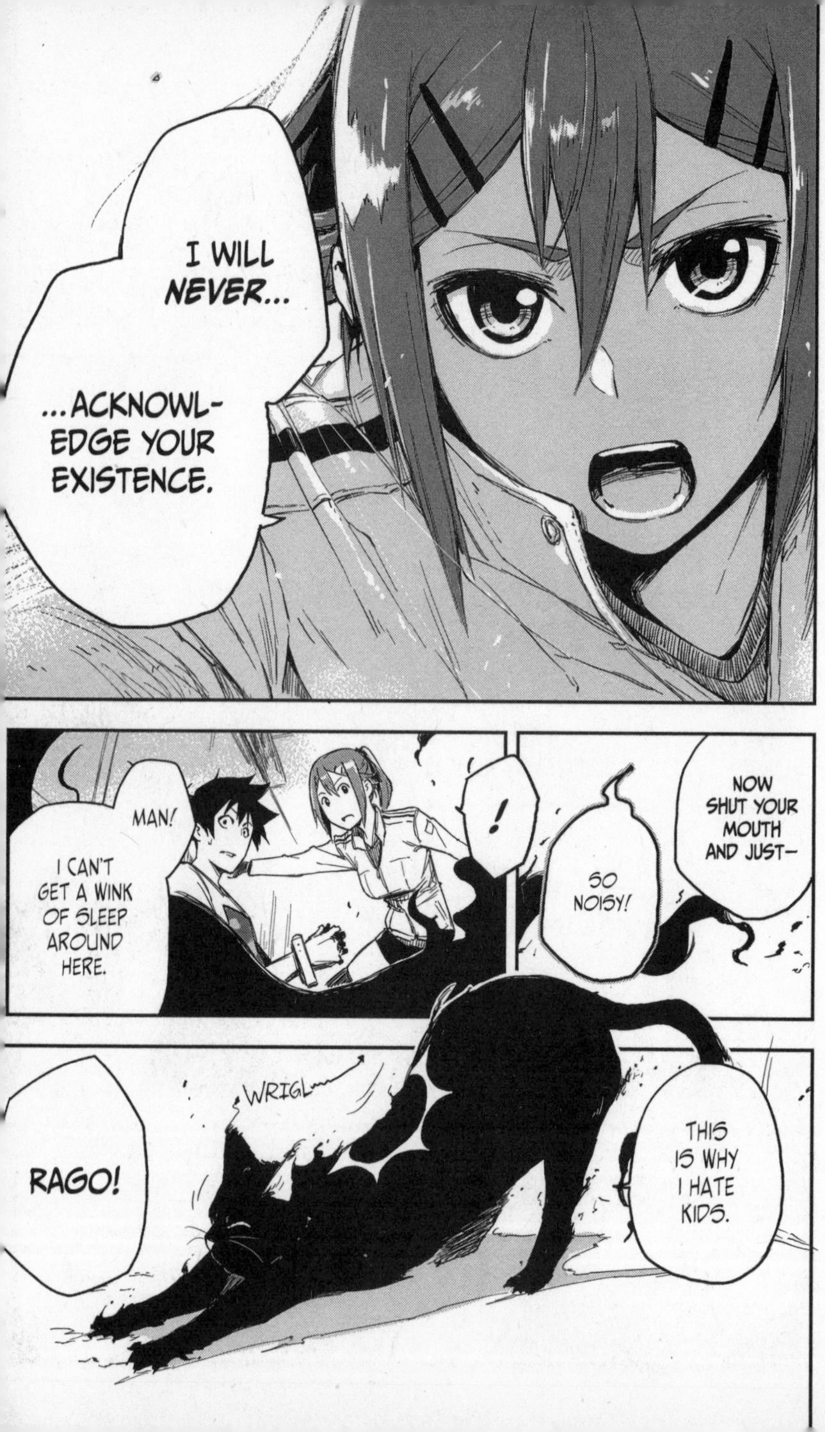
I WILL NEVER...
...ACKNOWL-EDGE YOUR EXISTENCE.
NOW SHUT YOUR MOUTH AND JUST—
SO NOISY!
!
MAN!
I CAN'T GET A WINK OF SLEEP AROUND HERE.
THIS IS WHY I HATE KIDS.
WRIGL
RAGO!

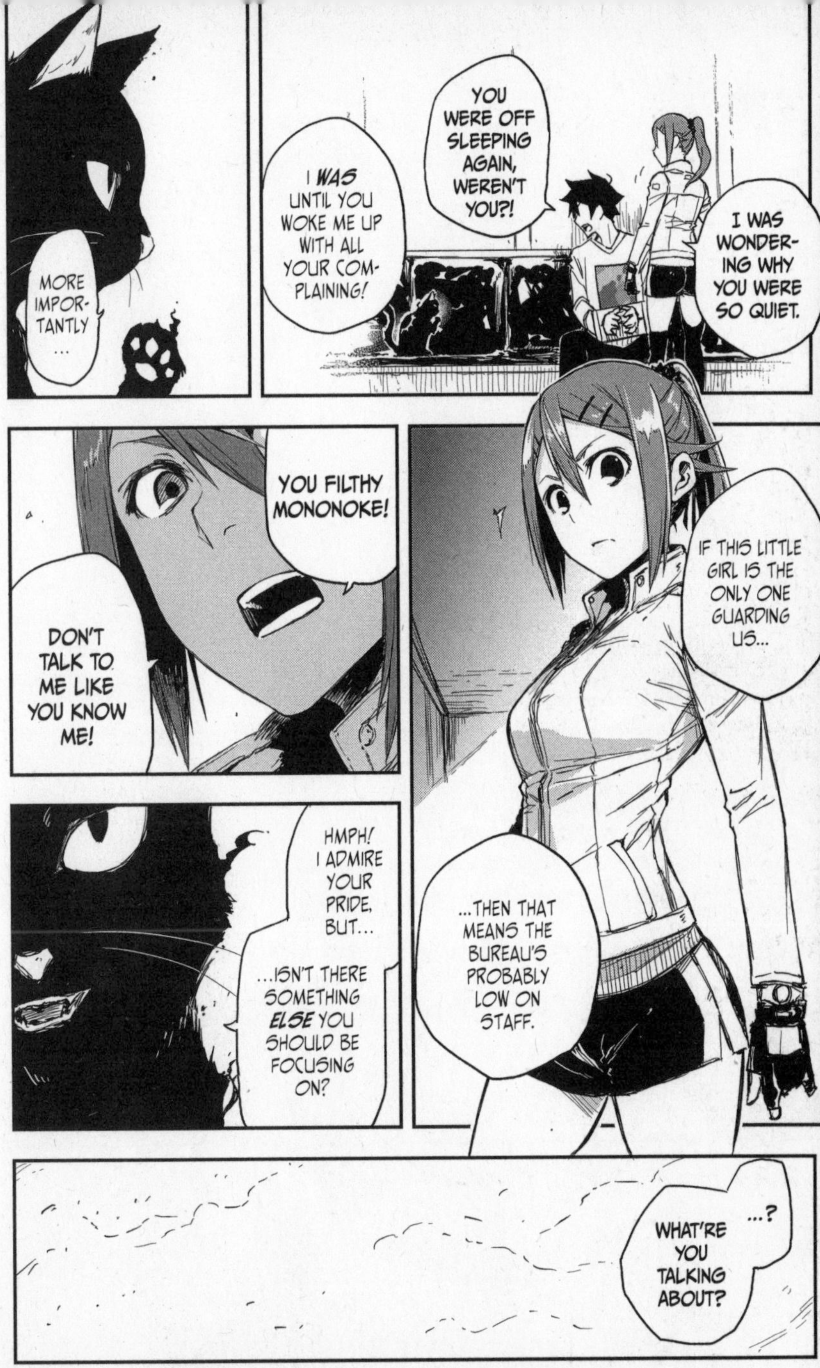
I WAS WONDERING WHY YOU WERE SO QUIET.
YOU WERE OFF SLEEPING AGAIN, WEREN'T YOU?!
I *WAS* UNTIL YOU WOKE ME UP WITH ALL YOUR COMPLAINING!
MORE IMPORTANTLY...
IF THIS LITTLE GIRL IS THE ONLY ONE GUARDING US...
...THEN THAT MEANS THE BUREAU'S PROBABLY LOW ON STAFF.
YOU FILTHY MONONOKE!
DON'T TALK TO ME LIKE YOU KNOW ME!
HMPH! I ADMIRE YOUR PRIDE, BUT...
...ISN'T THERE SOMETHING *ELSE* YOU SHOULD BE FOCUSING ON?
...?
WHAT'RE YOU TALKING ABOUT?

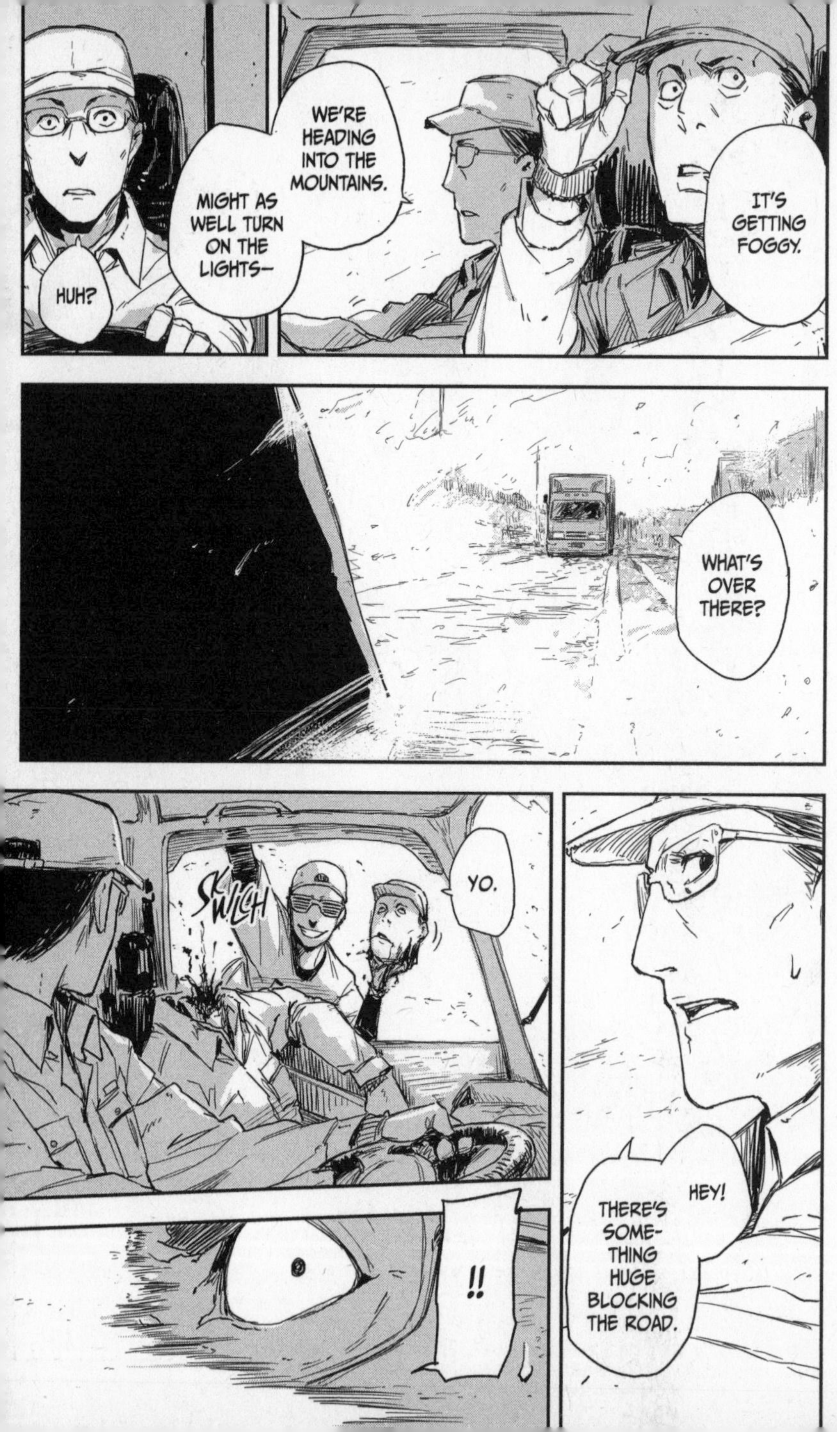
IT'S GETTING FOGGY.
WE'RE HEADING INTO THE MOUNTAINS.
MIGHT AS WELL TURN ON THE LIGHTS—
HUH?
WHAT'S OVER THERE?
HEY!
THERE'S SOME-THING HUGE BLOCKING THE ROAD.
YO.
SKWLCH
!!

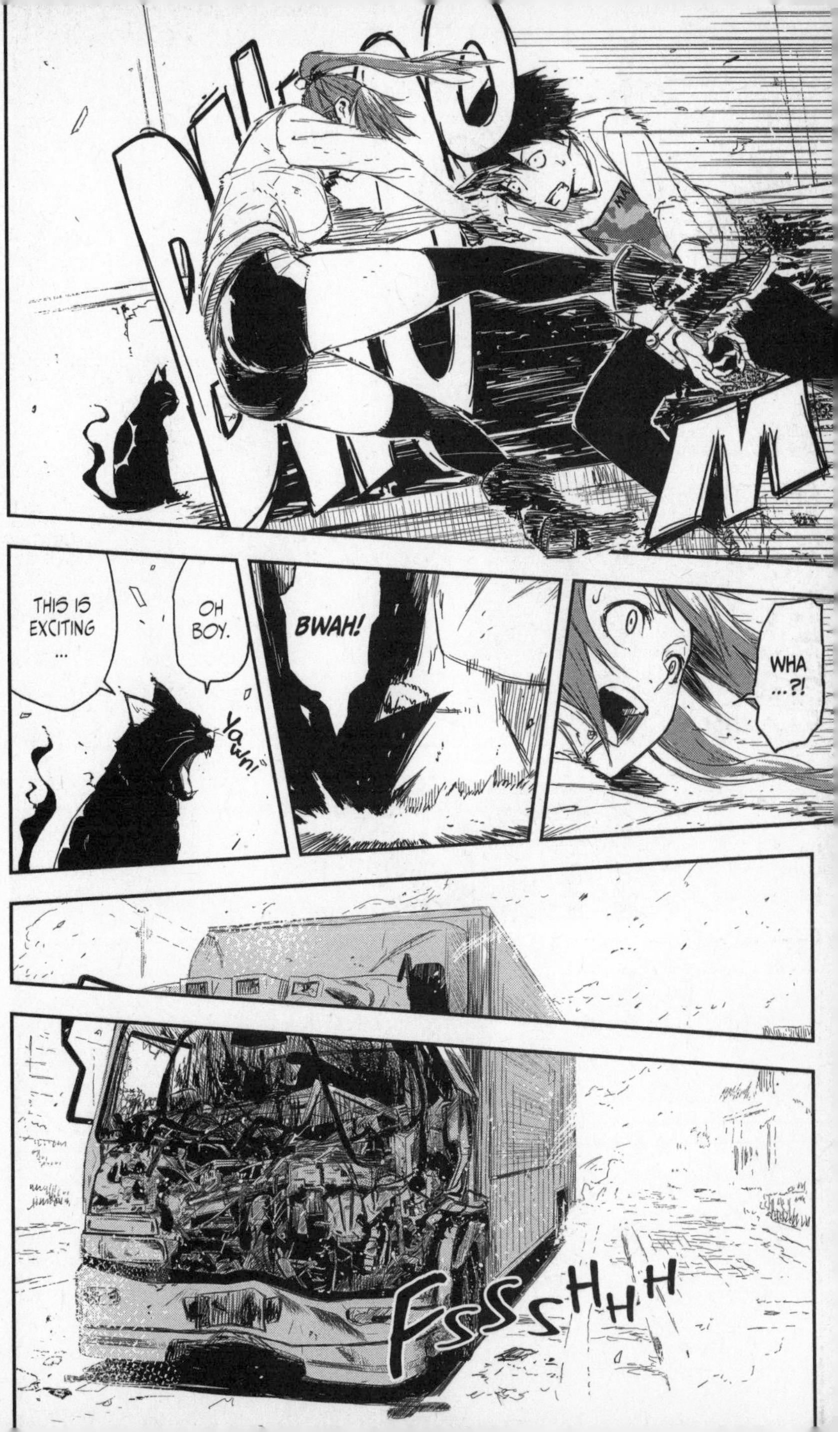
WHA ...?!
BWAH!
OH BOY.
THIS IS EXCITING ...
Yawn!
FSSSHHH

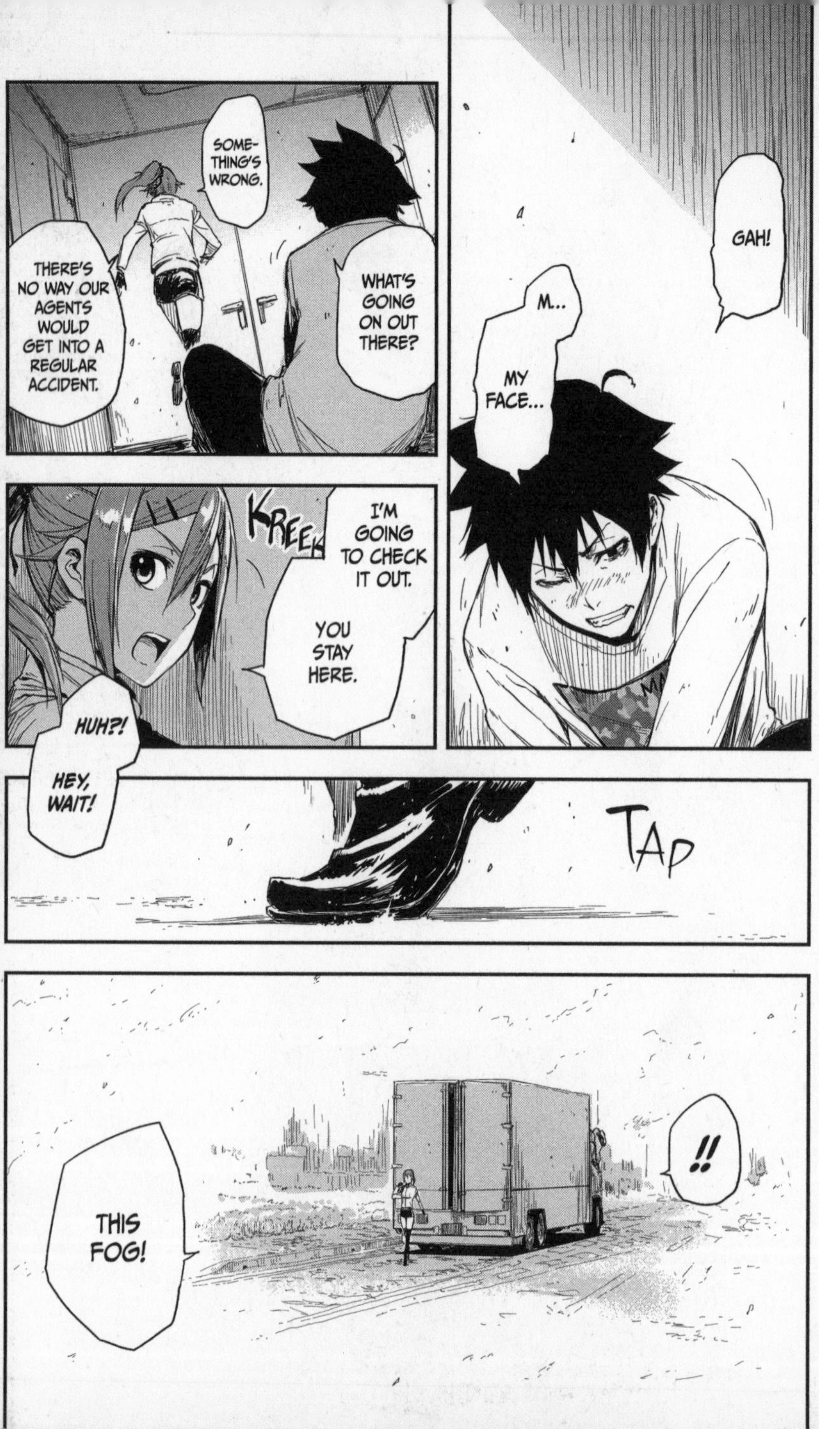
GAH!
M...
MY FACE...
WHAT'S GOING ON OUT THERE?
SOME-THING'S WRONG.
THERE'S NO WAY OUR AGENTS WOULD GET INTO A REGULAR ACCIDENT.
I'M GOING TO CHECK IT OUT.
KREEK
YOU STAY HERE.
HUH?!
HEY, WAIT!
TAP
!!
THIS FOG!

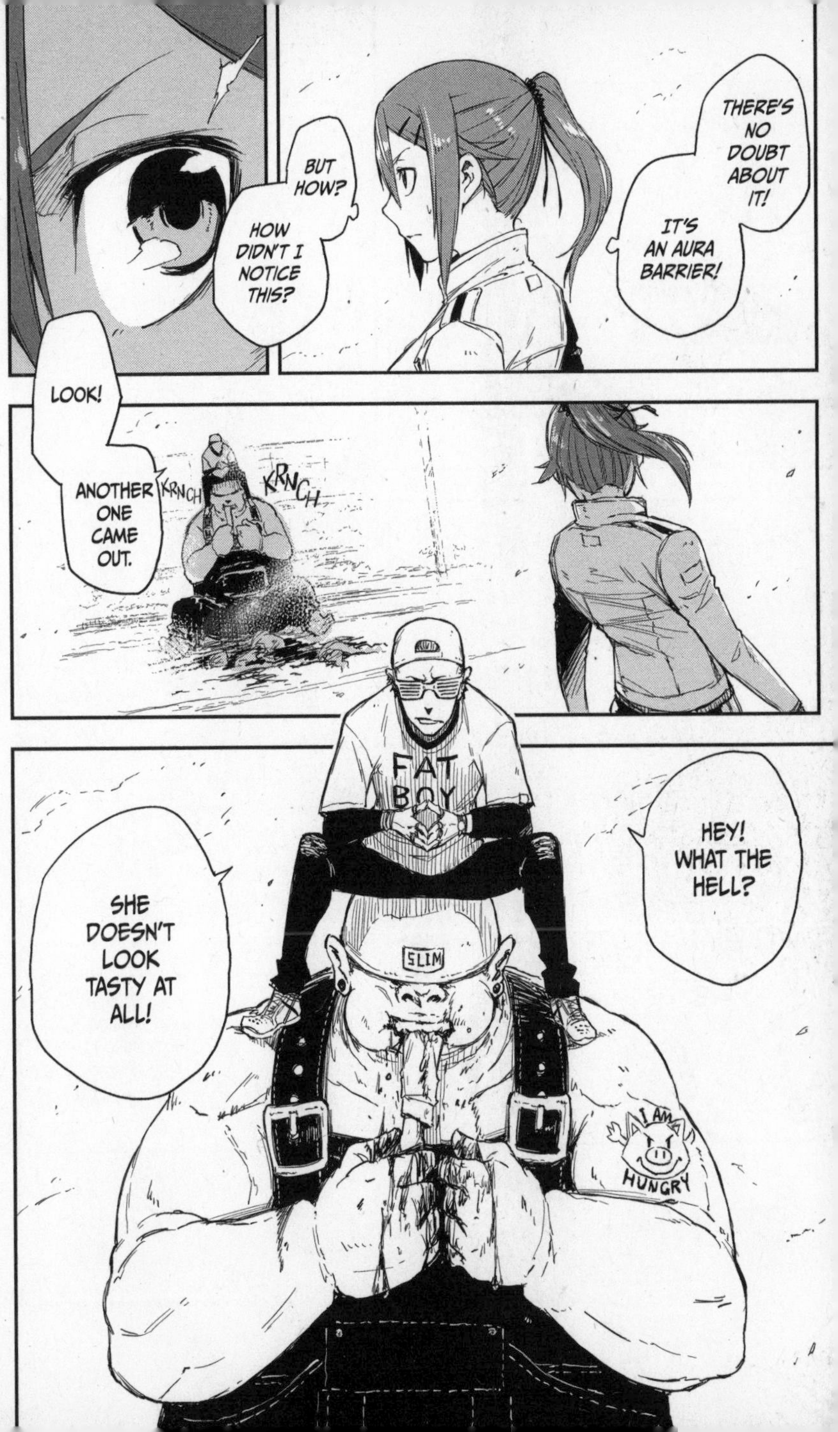
THERE'S NO DOUBT ABOUT IT!
IT'S AN AURA BARRIER!
BUT HOW?
HOW DIDN'T I NOTICE THIS?
LOOK!
KRNCH
KRNCH
ANOTHER ONE CAME OUT.
FAT BOY
HEY! WHAT THE HELL?
SLIM
SHE DOESN'T LOOK TASTY AT ALL!
I AM HUNGRY

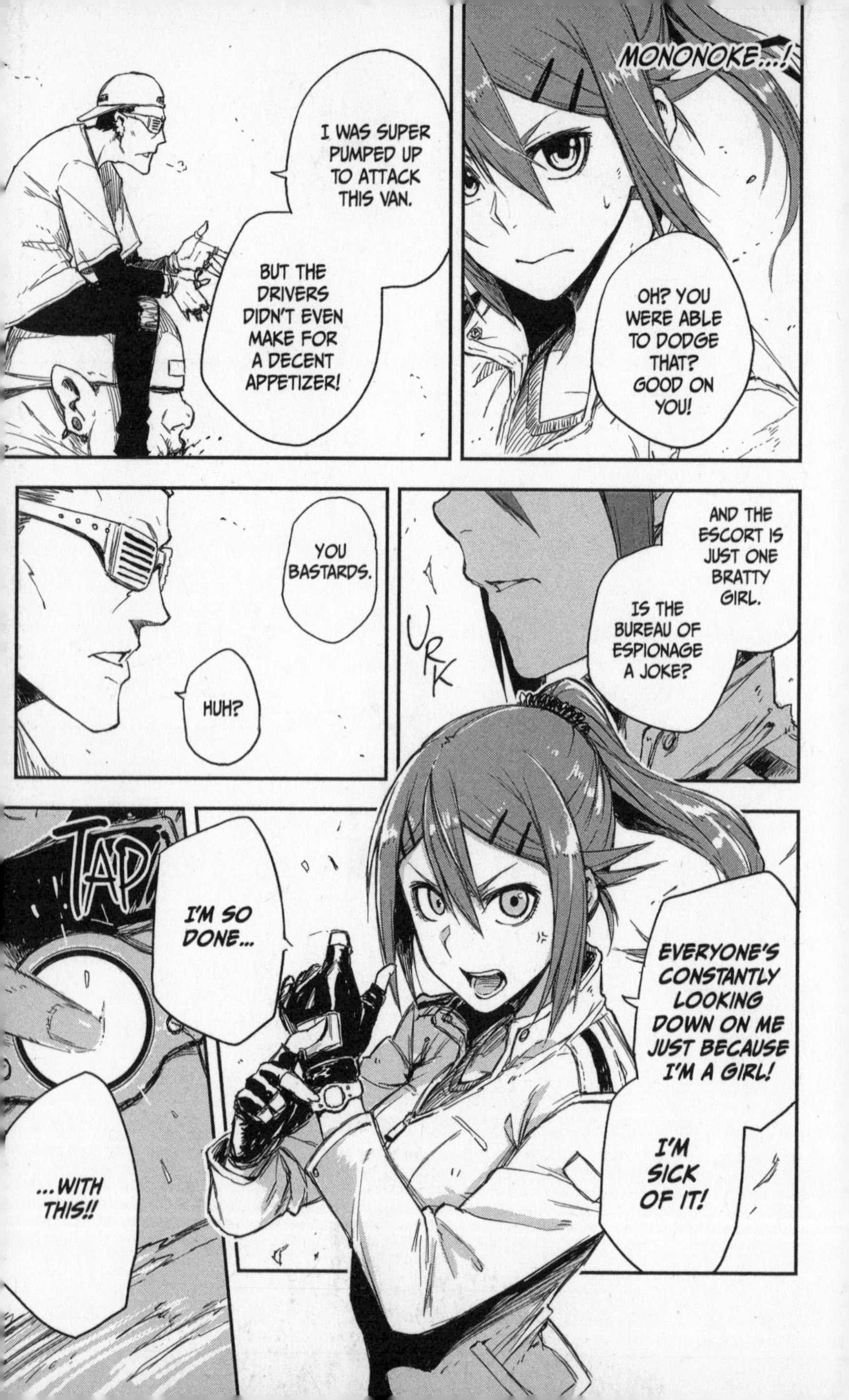
MONONOKE...!
OH? YOU WERE ABLE TO DODGE THAT? GOOD ON YOU!
I WAS SUPER PUMPED UP TO ATTACK THIS VAN.
BUT THE DRIVERS DIDN'T EVEN MAKE FOR A DECENT APPETIZER!
AND THE ESCORT IS JUST ONE BRATTY GIRL.
IS THE BUREAU OF ESPIONAGE A JOKE?
URK
YOU BASTARDS.
HUH?
EVERYONE'S CONSTANTLY LOOKING DOWN ON ME JUST BECAUSE I'M A GIRL!
I'M SICK OF IT!
I'M SO DONE...
TAP
...WITH THIS!!

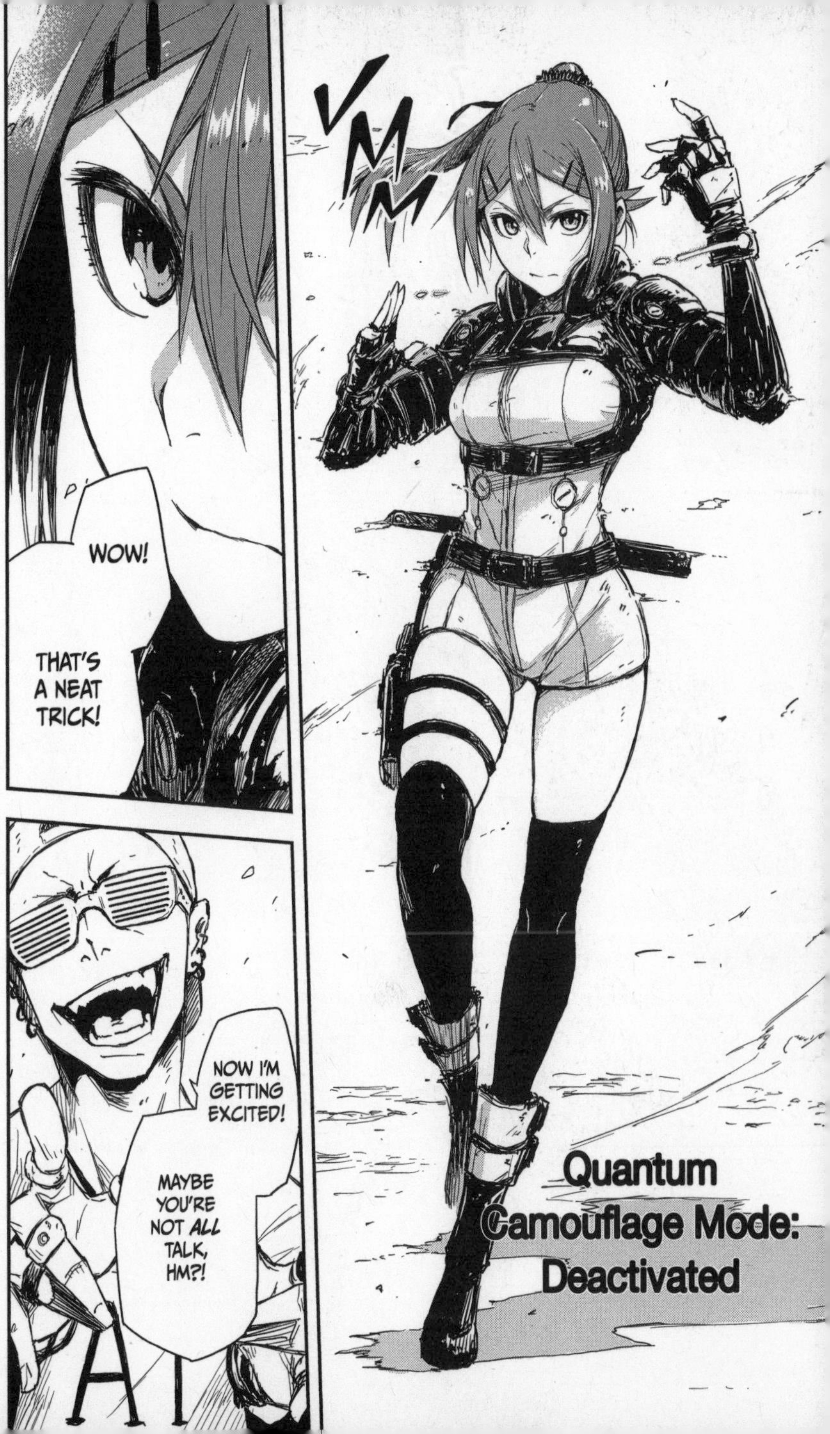
VMM
Quantum Camouflage Mode: Deactivated
WOW!
THAT'S A NEAT TRICK!
NOW I'M GETTING EXCITED!
MAYBE YOU'RE NOT *ALL* TALK, HM?!

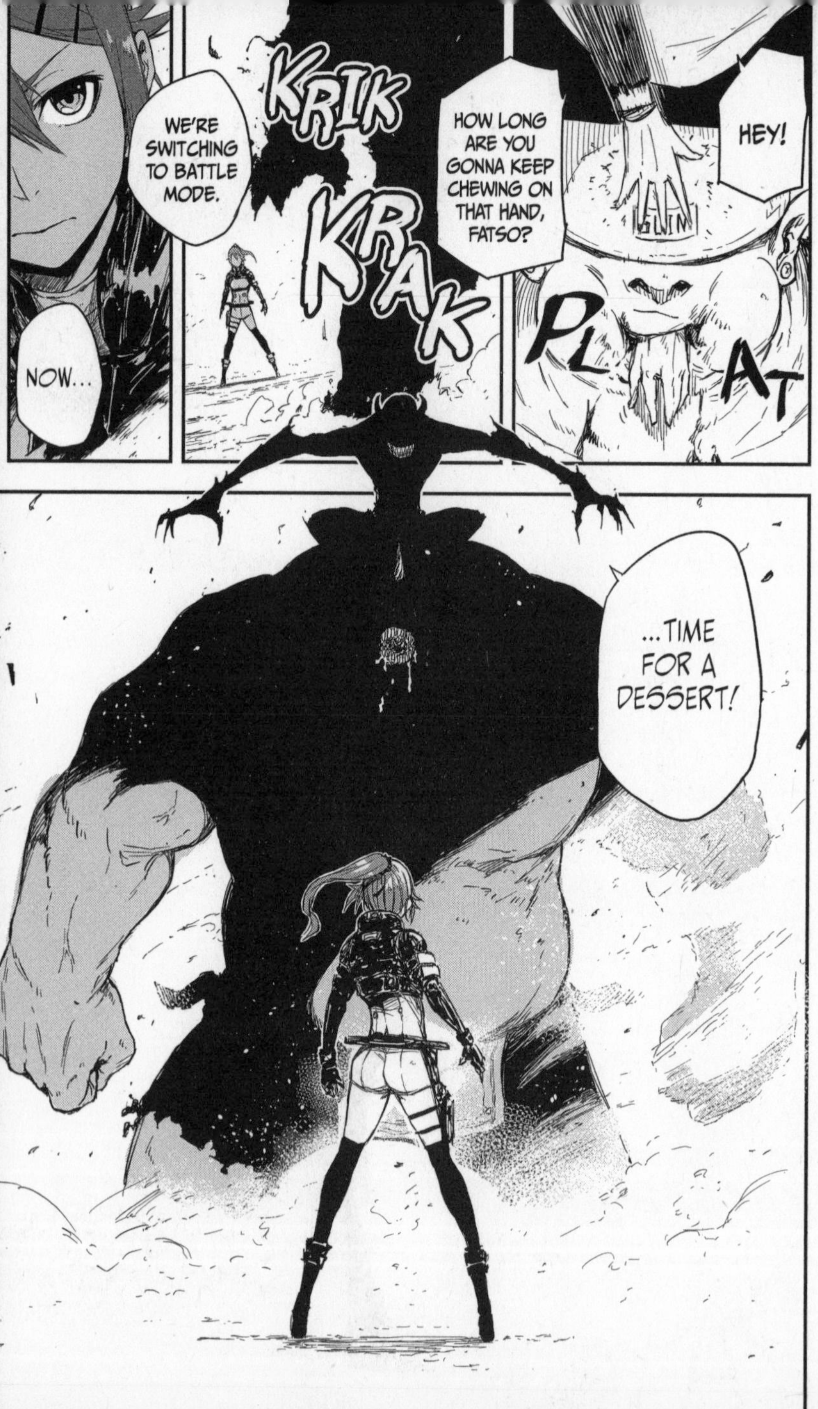
HEY!
HOW LONG ARE YOU GONNA KEEP CHEWING ON THAT HAND, FATSO?
PLAT
KRIK
KRAK
WE'RE SWITCHING TO BATTLE MODE.
NOW...
...TIME FOR A DESSERT!

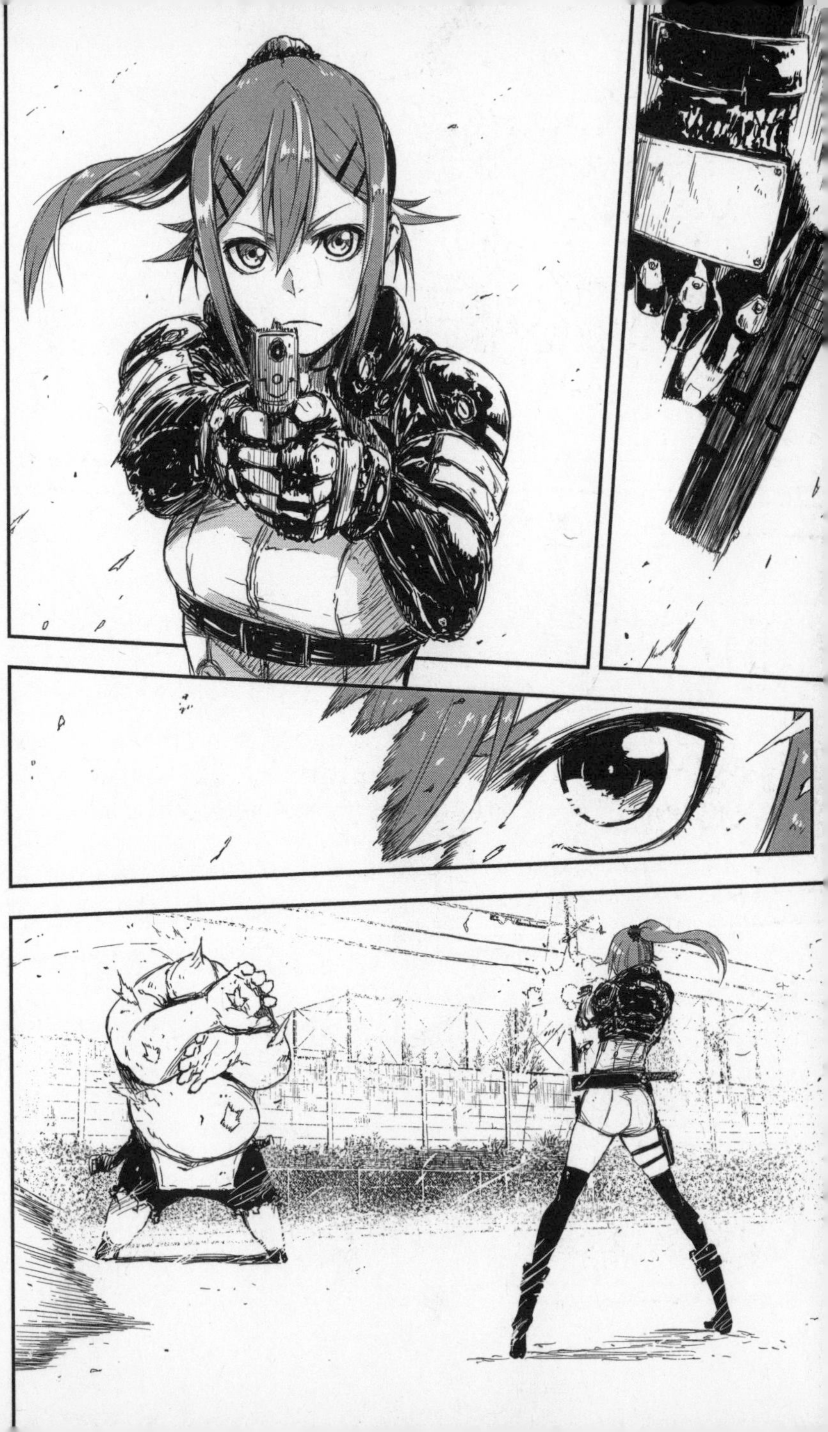

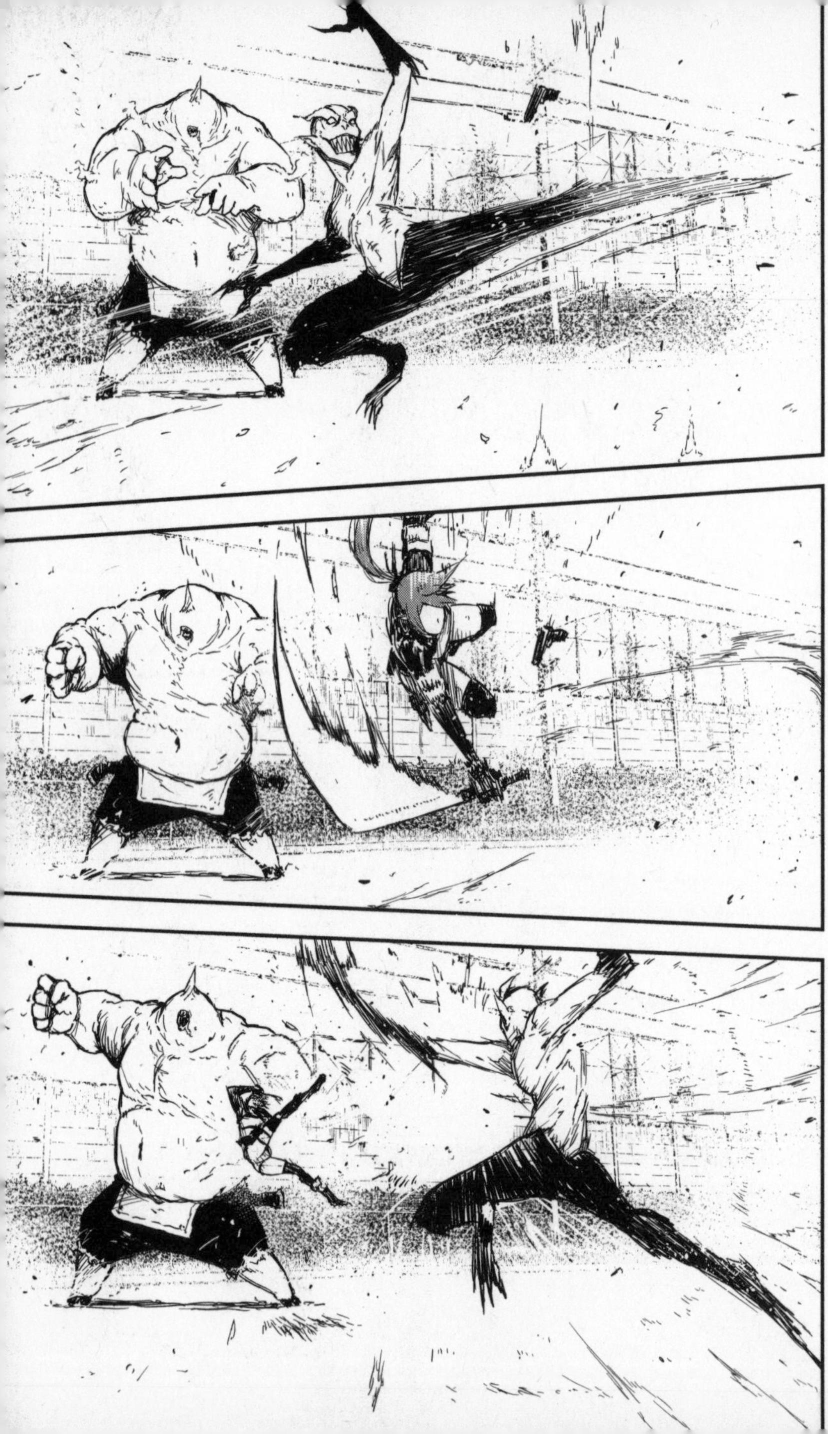

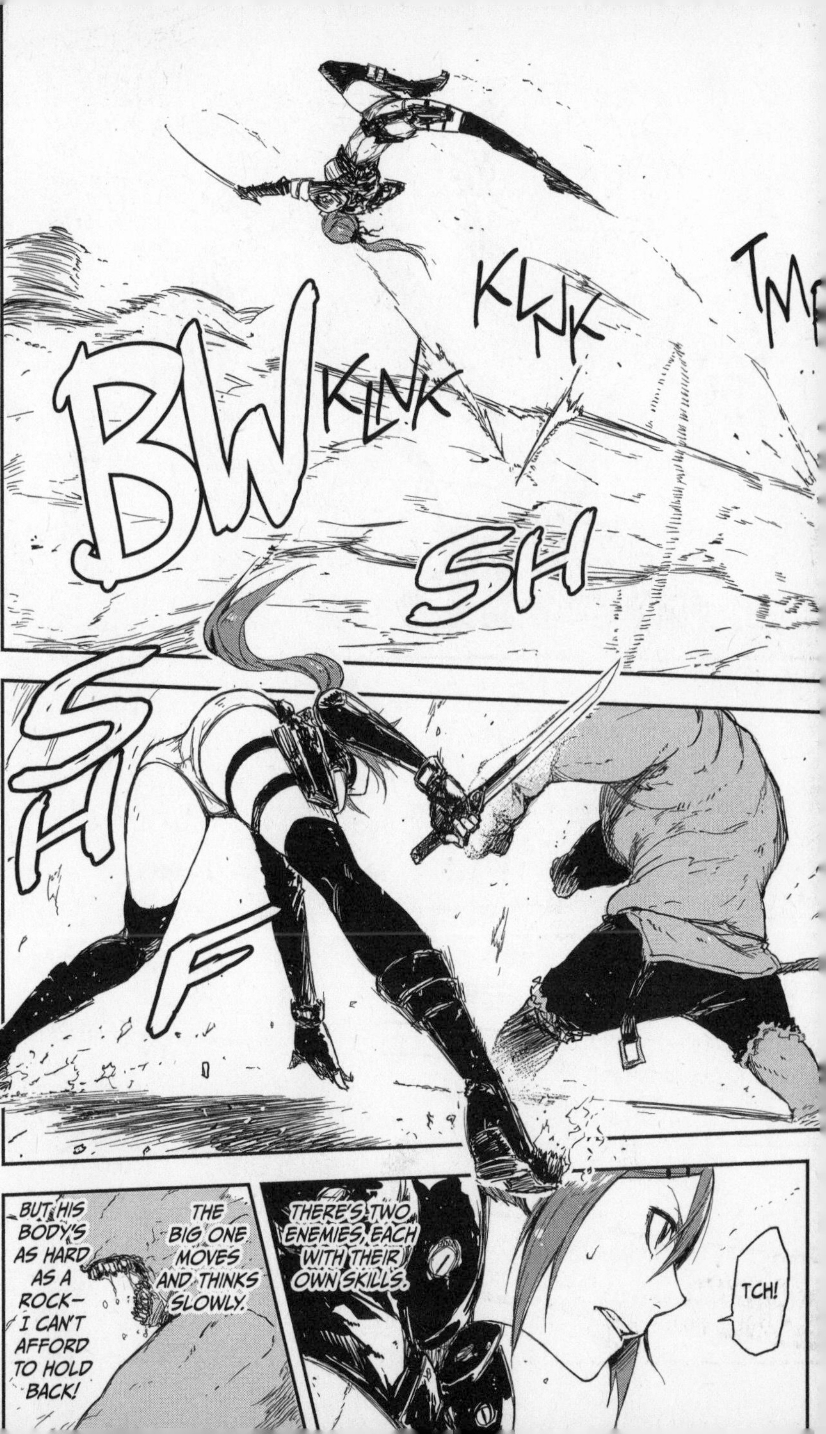
TMP
KLNK
KLNK
BW
SH
SH
F
TCH!
THERE'S TWO ENEMIES, EACH WITH THEIR OWN SKILLS.
THE BIG ONE MOVES AND THINKS SLOWLY.
BUT HIS BODY'S AS HARD AS A ROCK— I CAN'T AFFORD TO HOLD BACK!

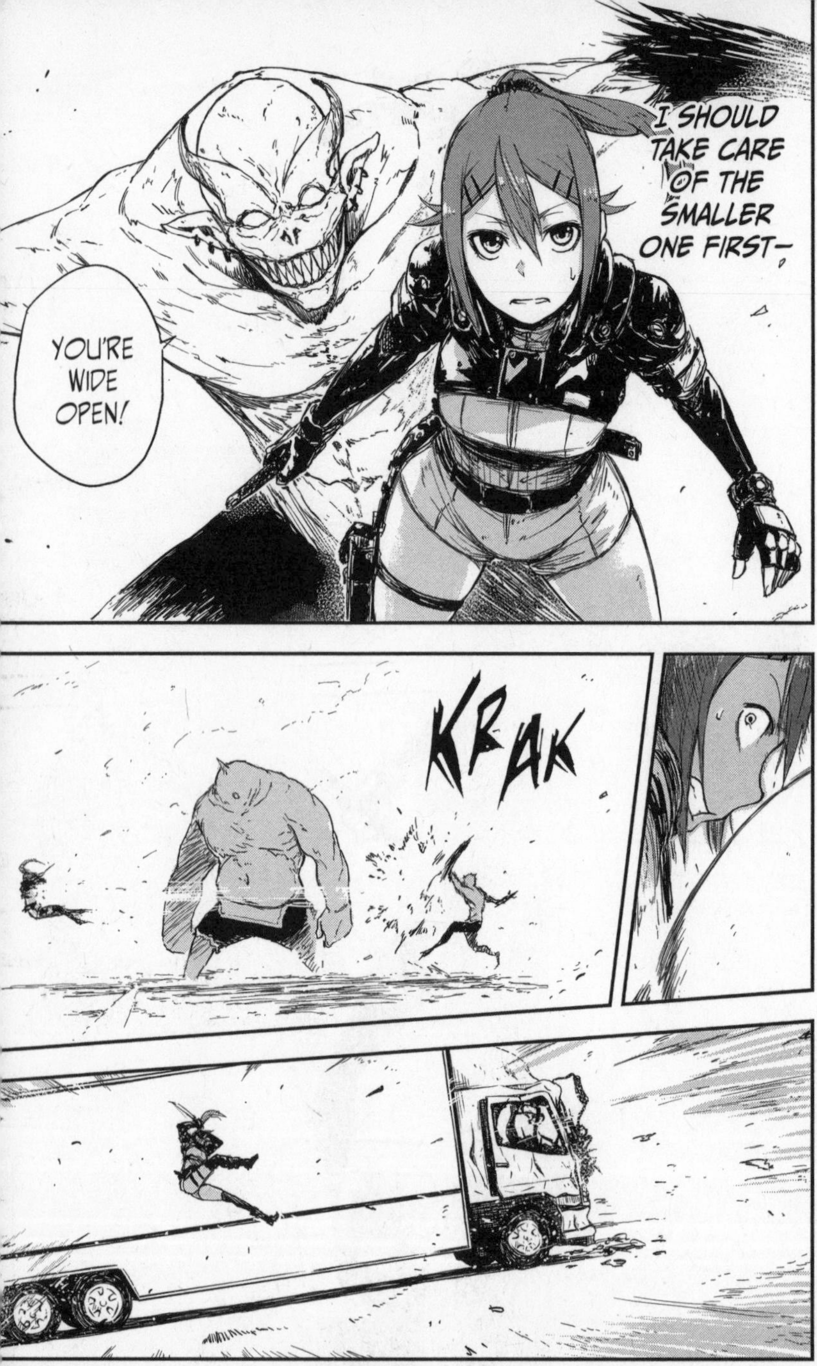
I SHOULD TAKE CARE OF THE SMALLER ONE FIRST–
YOU'RE WIDE OPEN!
KRAK

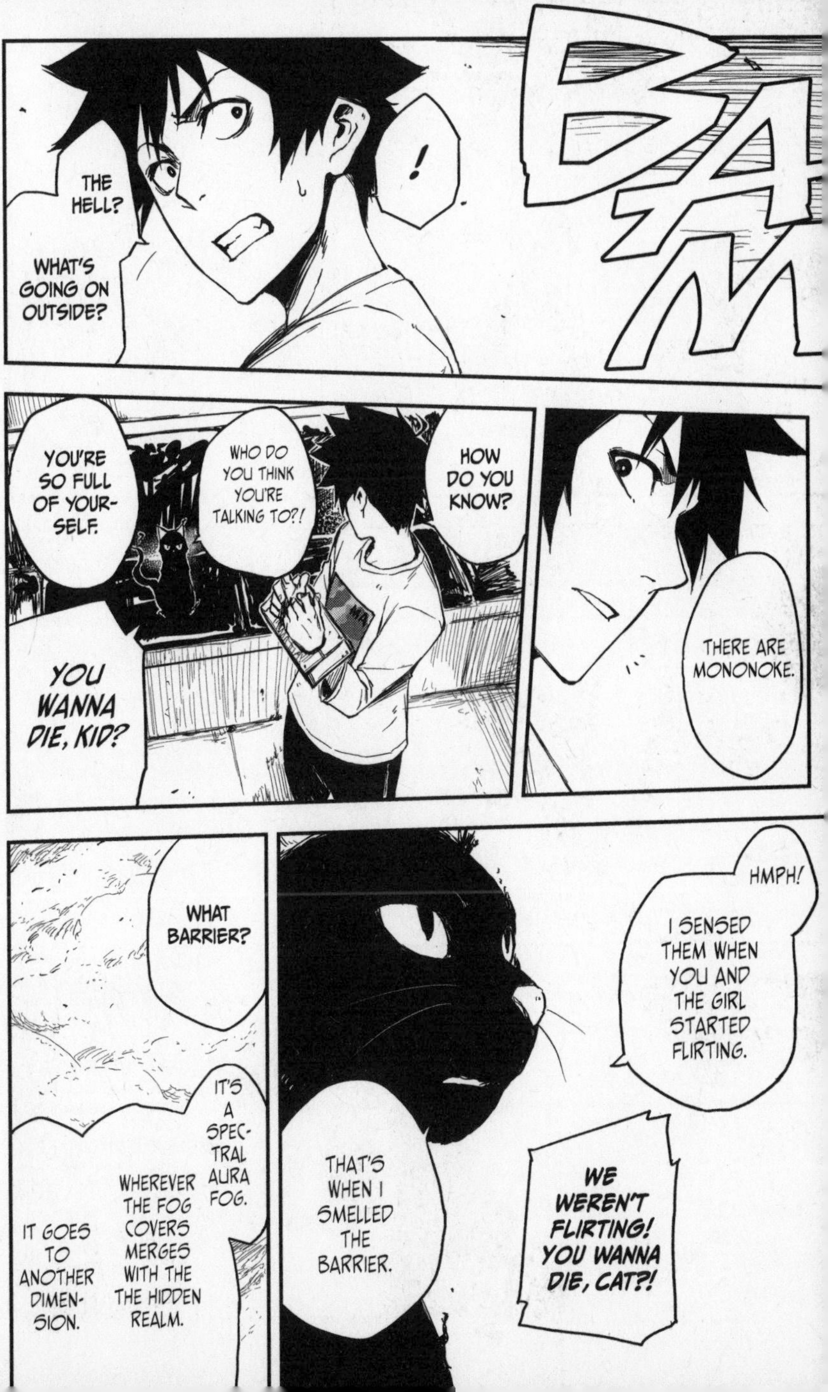

BAM
!
THE HELL?
WHAT'S GOING ON OUTSIDE?
THERE ARE MONONOKE.
HOW DO YOU KNOW?
WHO DO YOU THINK YOU'RE TALKING TO?!
YOU'RE SO FULL OF YOUR-SELF.
YOU WANNA DIE, KID?
HMPH!
I SENSED THEM WHEN YOU AND THE GIRL STARTED FLIRTING.
WE WEREN'T FLIRTING! YOU WANNA DIE, CAT?!
THAT'S WHEN I SMELLED THE BARRIER.
WHAT BARRIER?
IT'S A SPEC-TRAL AURA FOG.
WHEREVER THE FOG COVERS MERGES WITH THE HIDDEN REALM.
IT GOES TO ANOTHER DIMEN-SION.

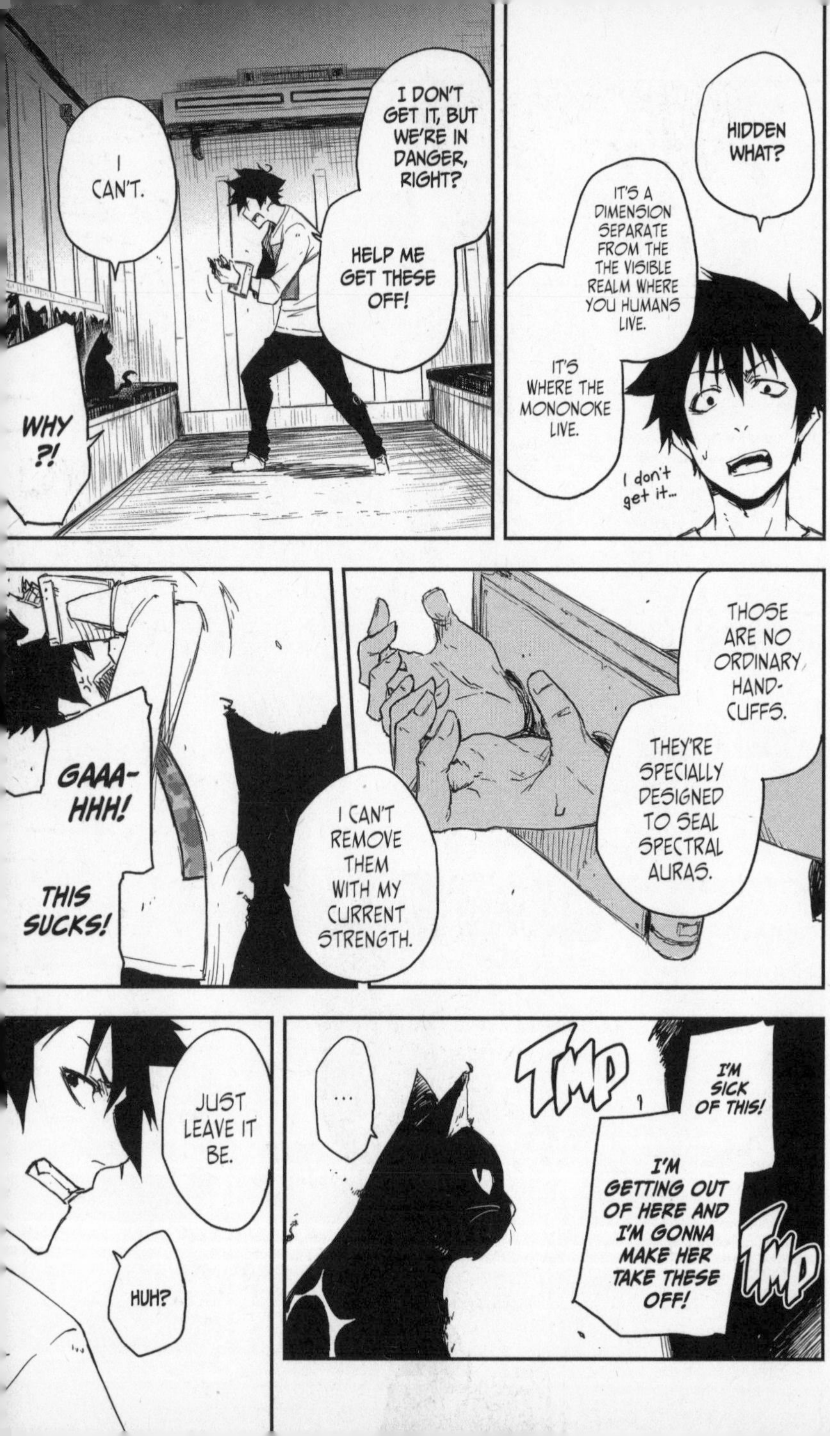
HIDDEN WHAT?
IT'S A DIMENSION SEPARATE FROM THE THE VISIBLE REALM WHERE YOU HUMANS LIVE.
IT'S WHERE THE MONONOKE LIVE.
I don't get it...
I DON'T GET IT, BUT WE'RE IN DANGER, RIGHT?
HELP ME GET THESE OFF!
I CAN'T.
WHY?!
THOSE ARE NO ORDINARY HAND-CUFFS.
THEY'RE SPECIALLY DESIGNED TO SEAL SPECTRAL AURAS.
I CAN'T REMOVE THEM WITH MY CURRENT STRENGTH.
GAAA-HHH!
THIS SUCKS!
TMP
I'M SICK OF THIS!
I'M GETTING OUT OF HERE AND I'M GONNA MAKE HER TAKE THESE OFF!
TMP
...
JUST LEAVE IT BE.
HUH?

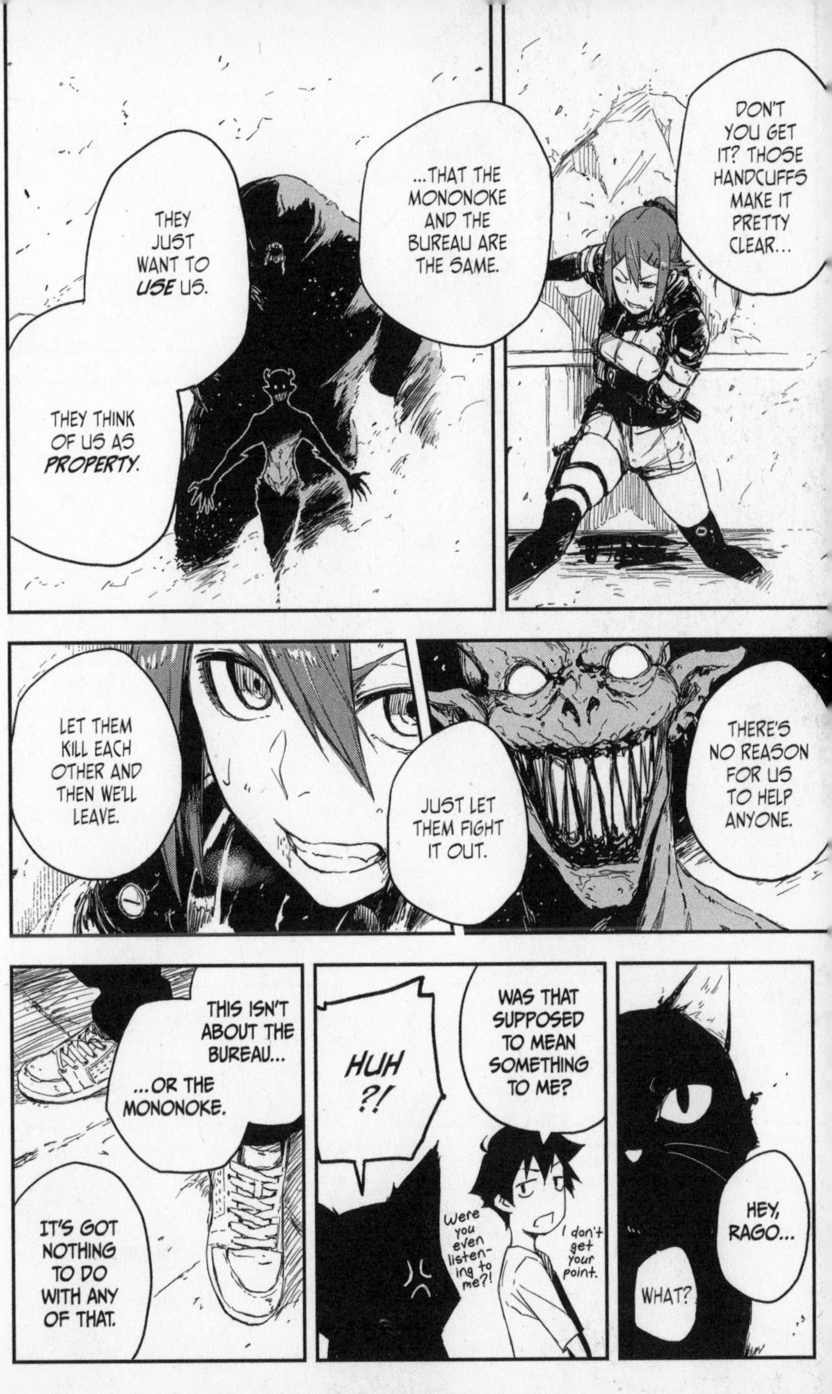
DON'T YOU GET IT? THOSE HANDCUFFS MAKE IT PRETTY CLEAR...
...THAT THE MONONOKE AND THE BUREAU ARE THE SAME.
THEY JUST WANT TO *USE* US.
THEY THINK OF US AS *PROPERTY*.
THERE'S NO REASON FOR US TO HELP ANYONE.
JUST LET THEM FIGHT IT OUT.
LET THEM KILL EACH OTHER AND THEN WE'LL LEAVE.
HEY, RAGO...
WHAT?
WAS THAT SUPPOSED TO MEAN SOMETHING TO ME?
HUH ?!
I don't get your point.
Were you even listen-ing to me?!
THIS ISN'T ABOUT THE BUREAU...
...OR THE MONONOKE.
IT'S GOT NOTHING TO DO WITH ANY OF THAT.

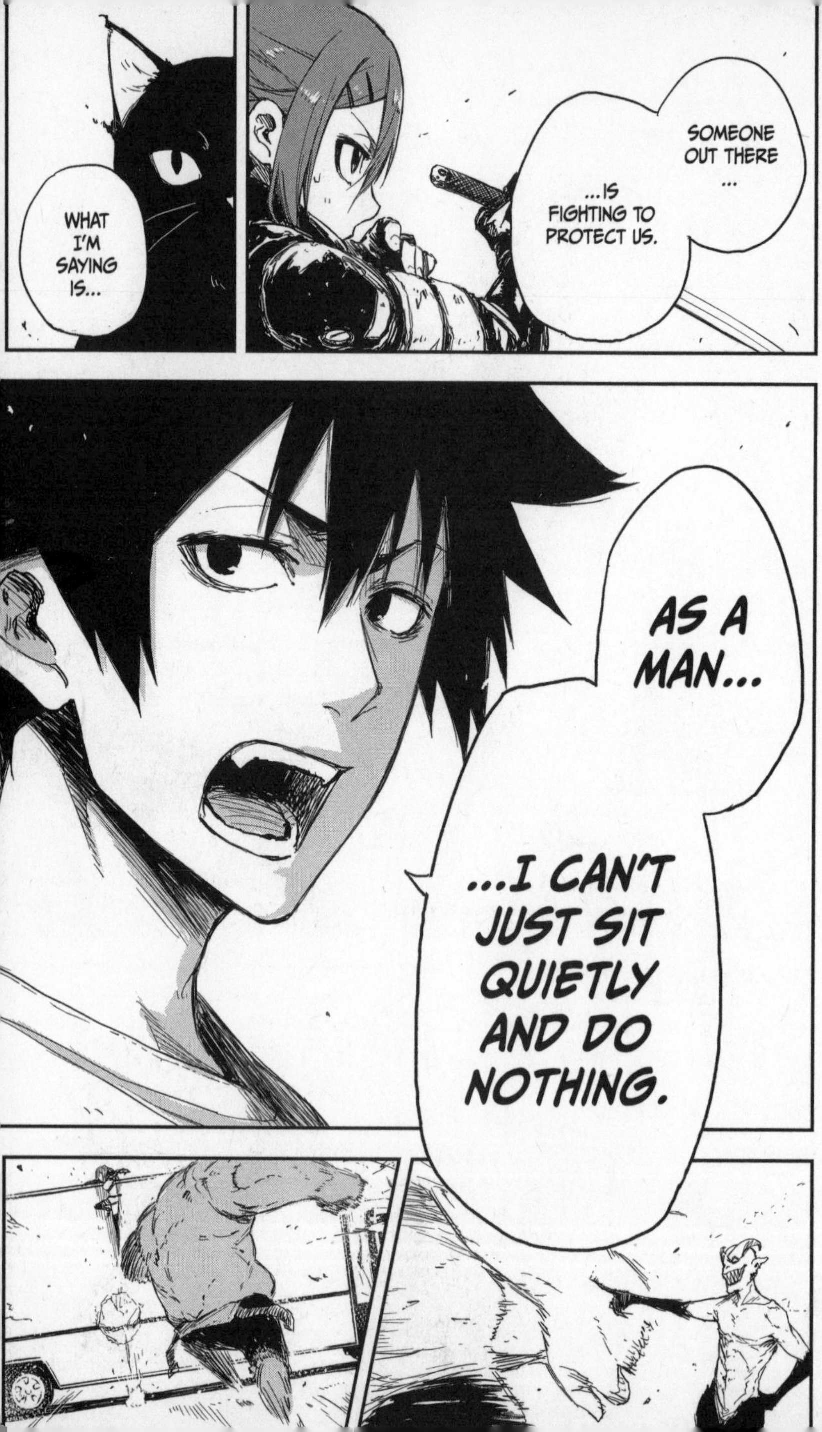
SOMEONE OUT THERE ...
...IS FIGHTING TO PROTECT US.
WHAT I'M SAYING IS...
AS A MAN...
...I CAN'T JUST SIT QUIETLY AND DO NOTHING.

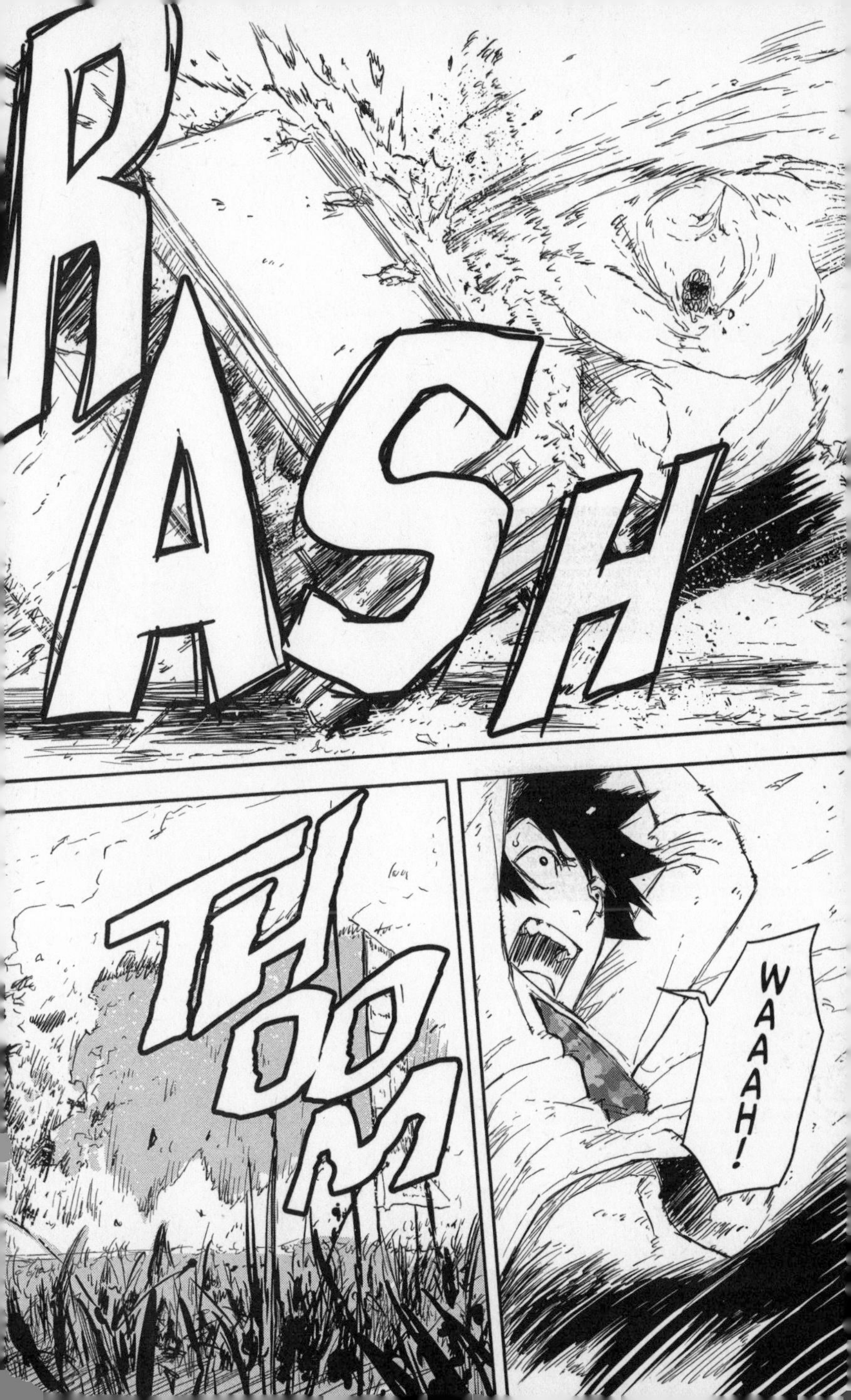
RASH
WAAAH!
THOOM

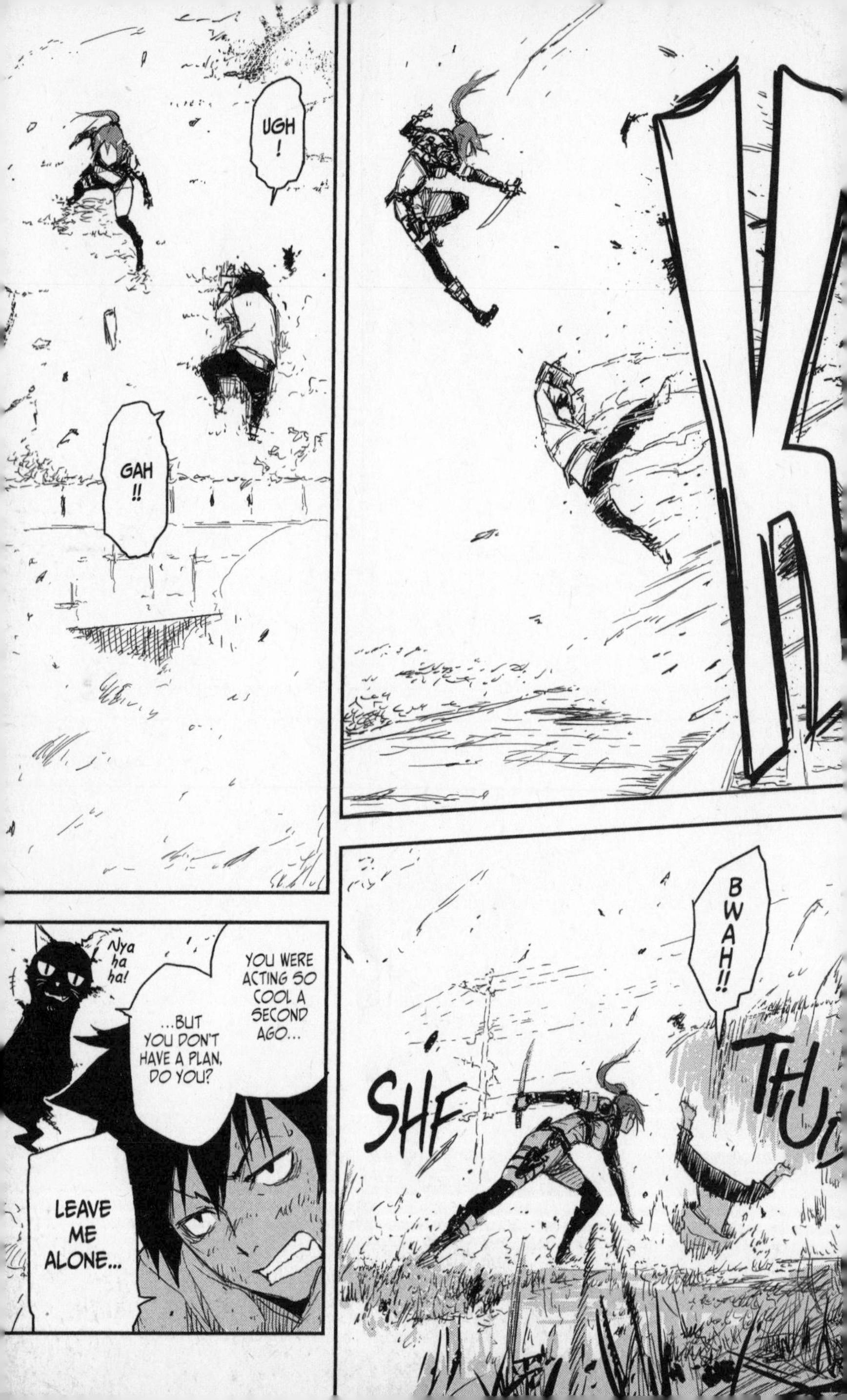
UGH!
GAH!!
BWAH!!
SHF
THU
Nya ha ha!
YOU WERE ACTING SO COOL A SECOND AGO...
...BUT YOU DON'T HAVE A PLAN, DO YOU?
LEAVE ME ALONE...

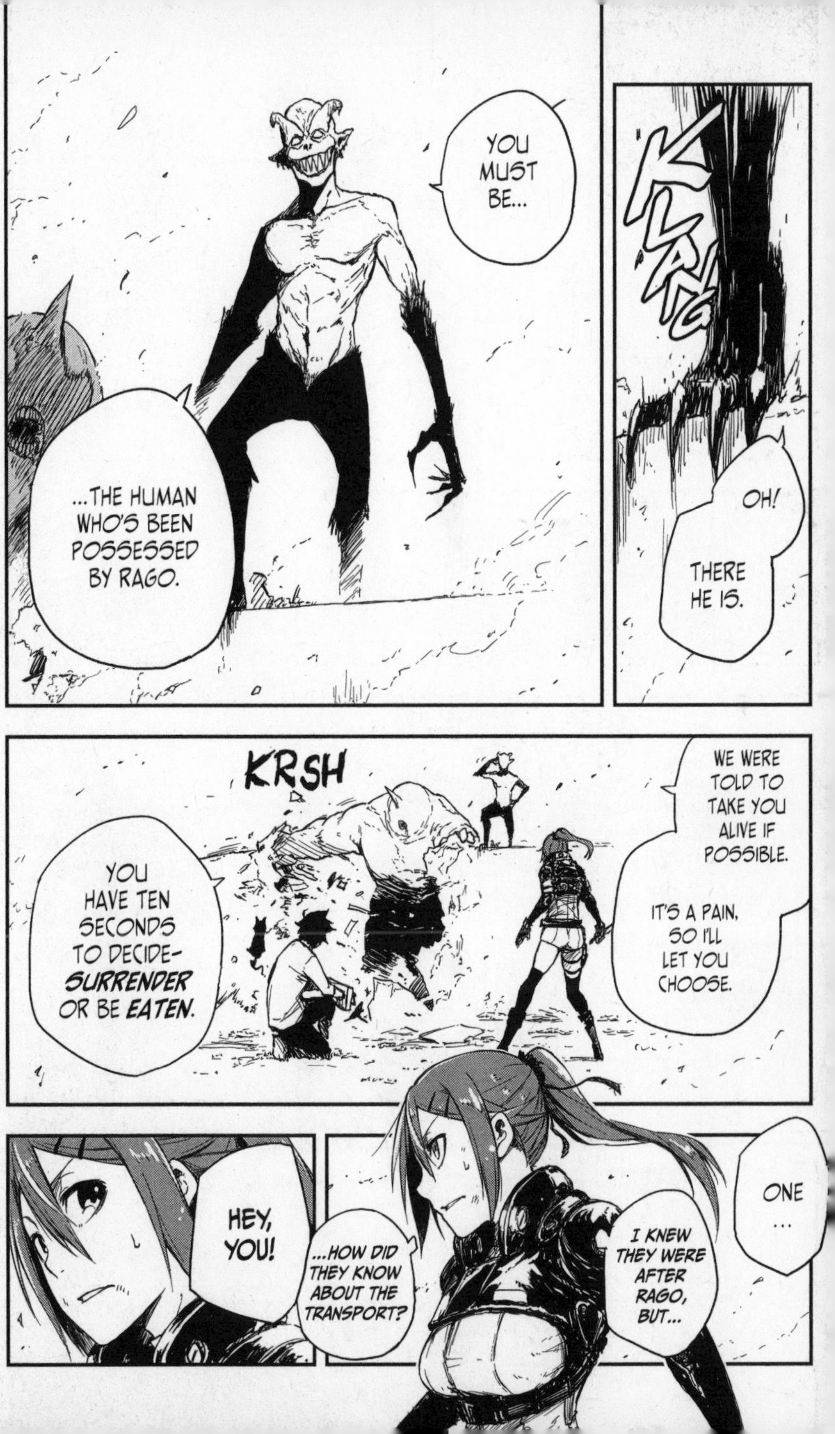
KVRAG
OH!
THERE HE IS.
YOU MUST BE...
...THE HUMAN WHO'S BEEN POSSESSED BY RAGO.
WE WERE TOLD TO TAKE YOU ALIVE IF POSSIBLE.
KRSH
IT'S A PAIN, SO I'LL LET YOU CHOOSE.
YOU HAVE TEN SECONDS TO DECIDE- SURRENDER OR BE EATEN.
ONE ...
I KNEW THEY WERE AFTER RAGO, BUT...
...HOW DID THEY KNOW ABOUT THE TRANSPORT?
HEY, YOU!

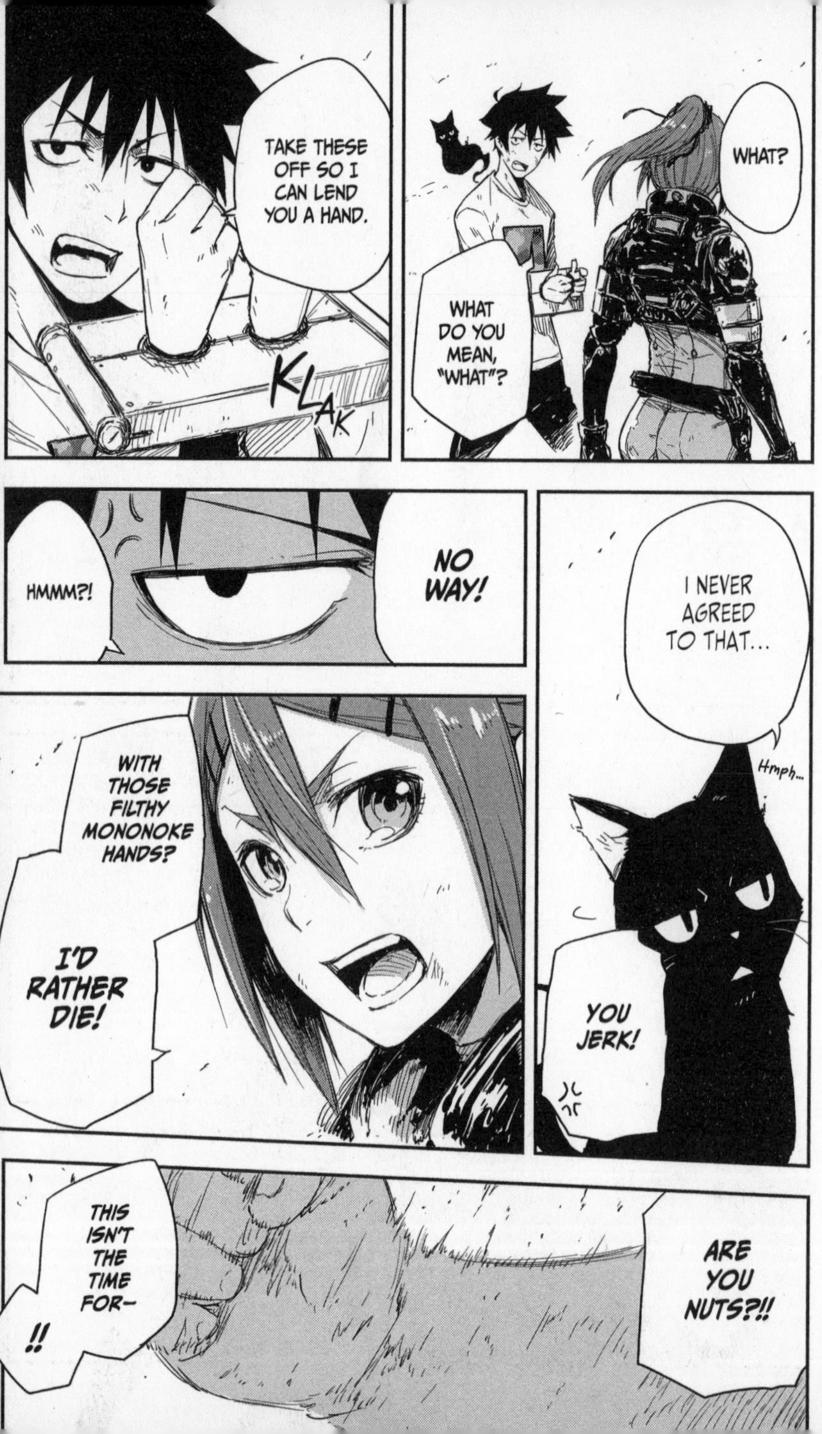

WHAT?
WHAT DO YOU MEAN, "WHAT"?
TAKE THESE OFF SO I CAN LEND YOU A HAND.
KLAK
I NEVER AGREED TO THAT...
Hmph...
YOU JERK!
NO WAY!
HMMM?!
WITH THOSE FILTHY MONONOKE HANDS?
I'D RATHER DIE!
ARE YOU NUTS?!!
THIS ISN'T THE TIME FOR-
!!

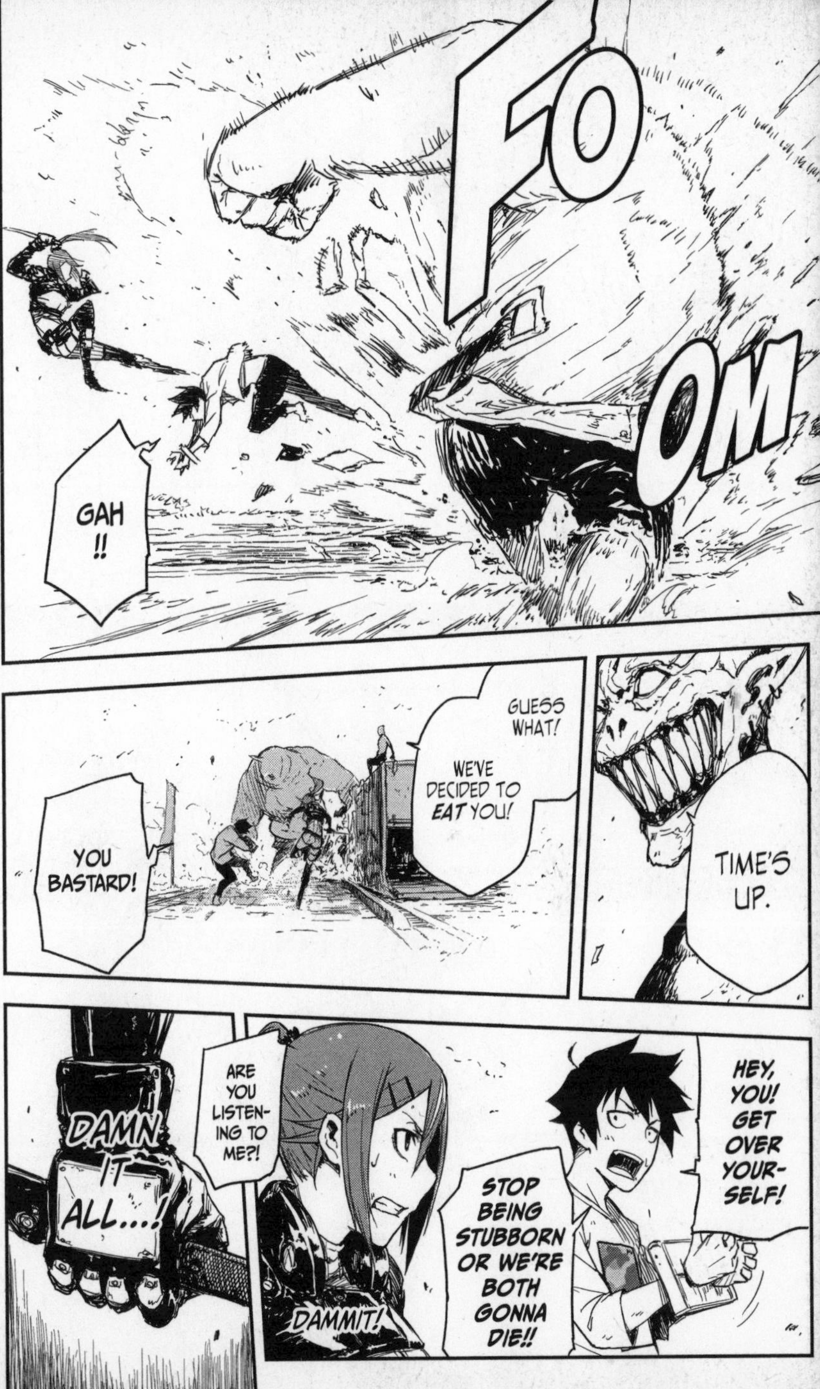
FOOM
GAH!!
TIME'S UP.
GUESS WHAT!
WE'VE DECIDED TO EAT YOU!
YOU BASTARD!
HEY, YOU! GET OVER YOURSELF!
STOP BEING STUBBORN OR WE'RE BOTH GONNA DIE!!
ARE YOU LISTENING TO ME?!
DAMMIT!
DAMN IT ALL...!

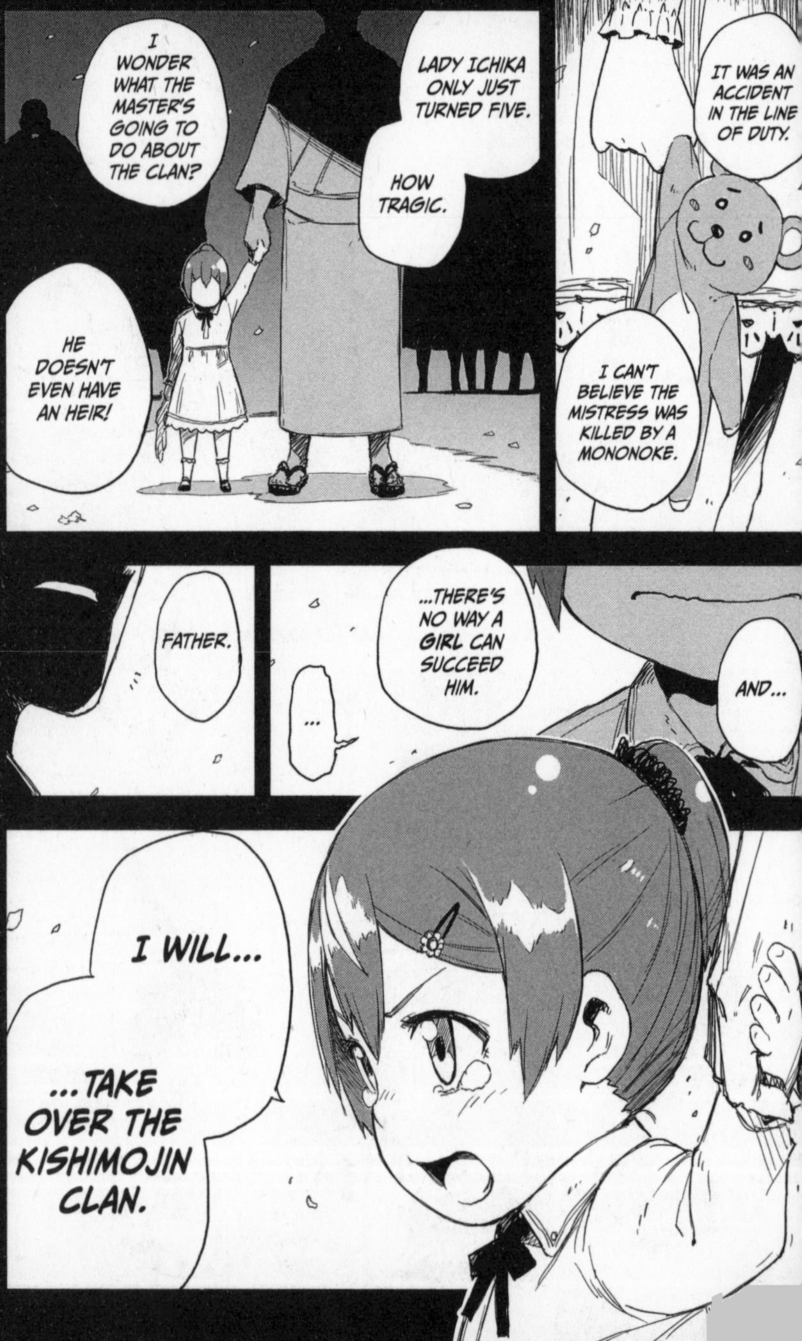
IT WAS AN ACCIDENT IN THE LINE OF DUTY.
I CAN'T BELIEVE THE MISTRESS WAS KILLED BY A MONONOKE.
LADY ICHIKA ONLY JUST TURNED FIVE.
HOW TRAGIC.
I WONDER WHAT THE MASTER'S GOING TO DO ABOUT THE CLAN?
HE DOESN'T EVEN HAVE AN HEIR!
AND...
...THERE'S NO WAY A GIRL CAN SUCCEED HIM.
...
FATHER.
I WILL...
...TAKE OVER THE KISHIMOJIN CLAN.

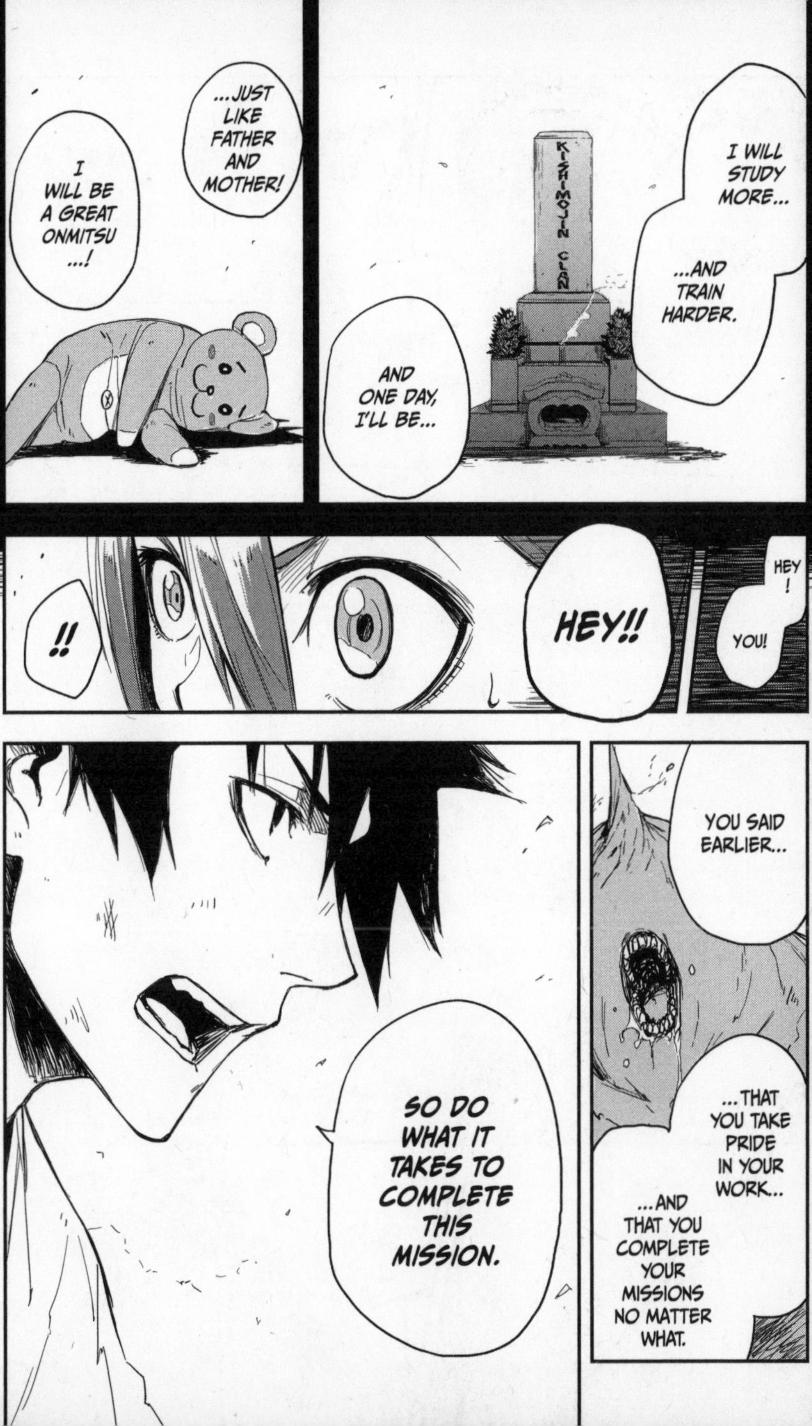
I WILL STUDY MORE...
...AND TRAIN HARDER.
KISHIMOJIN CLAN
AND ONE DAY, I'LL BE...
...JUST LIKE FATHER AND MOTHER!
I WILL BE A GREAT ONMITSU ...!
HEY! YOU!
HEY!!
!!
YOU SAID EARLIER...
...THAT YOU TAKE PRIDE IN YOUR WORK...
...AND THAT YOU COMPLETE YOUR MISSIONS NO MATTER WHAT.
SO DO WHAT IT TAKES TO COMPLETE THIS MISSION.

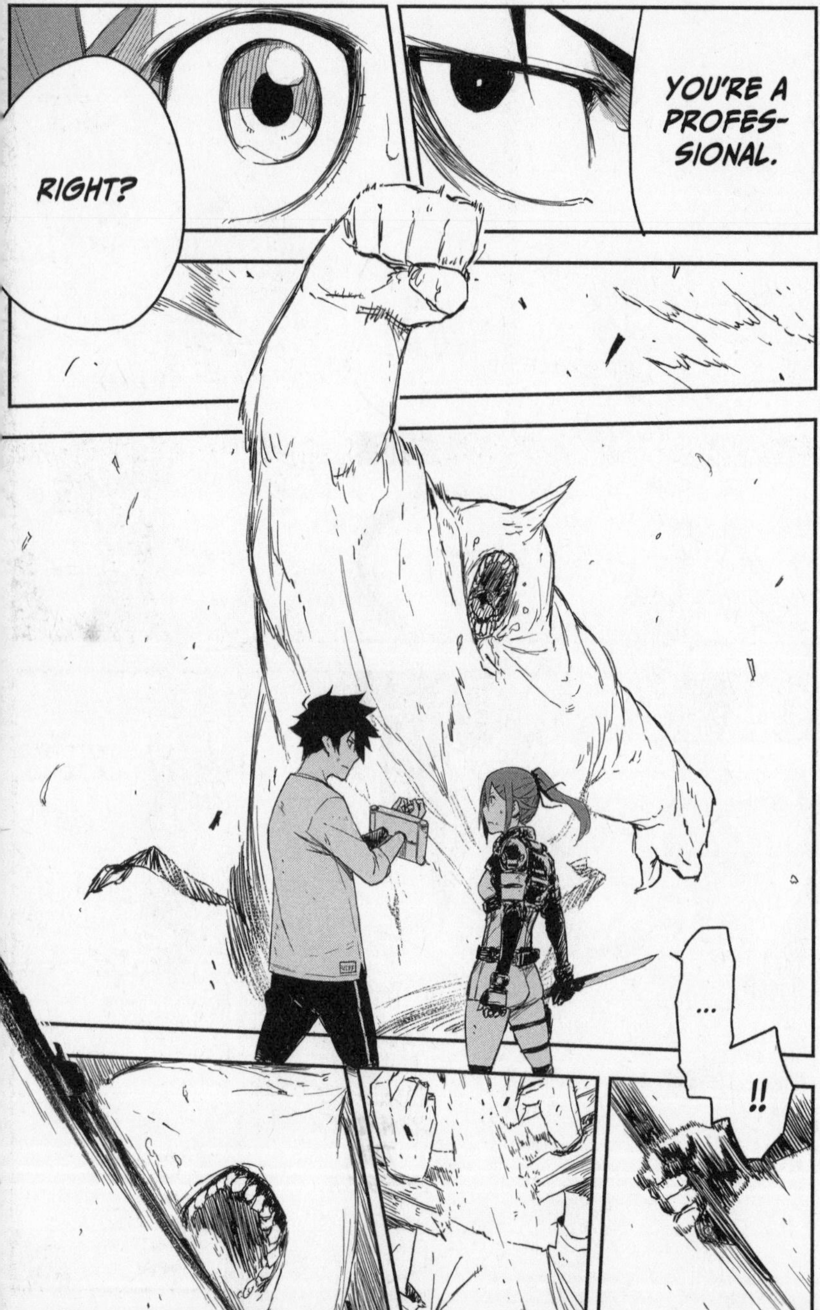
YOU'RE A PROFES-SIONAL.
RIGHT?
...
!!

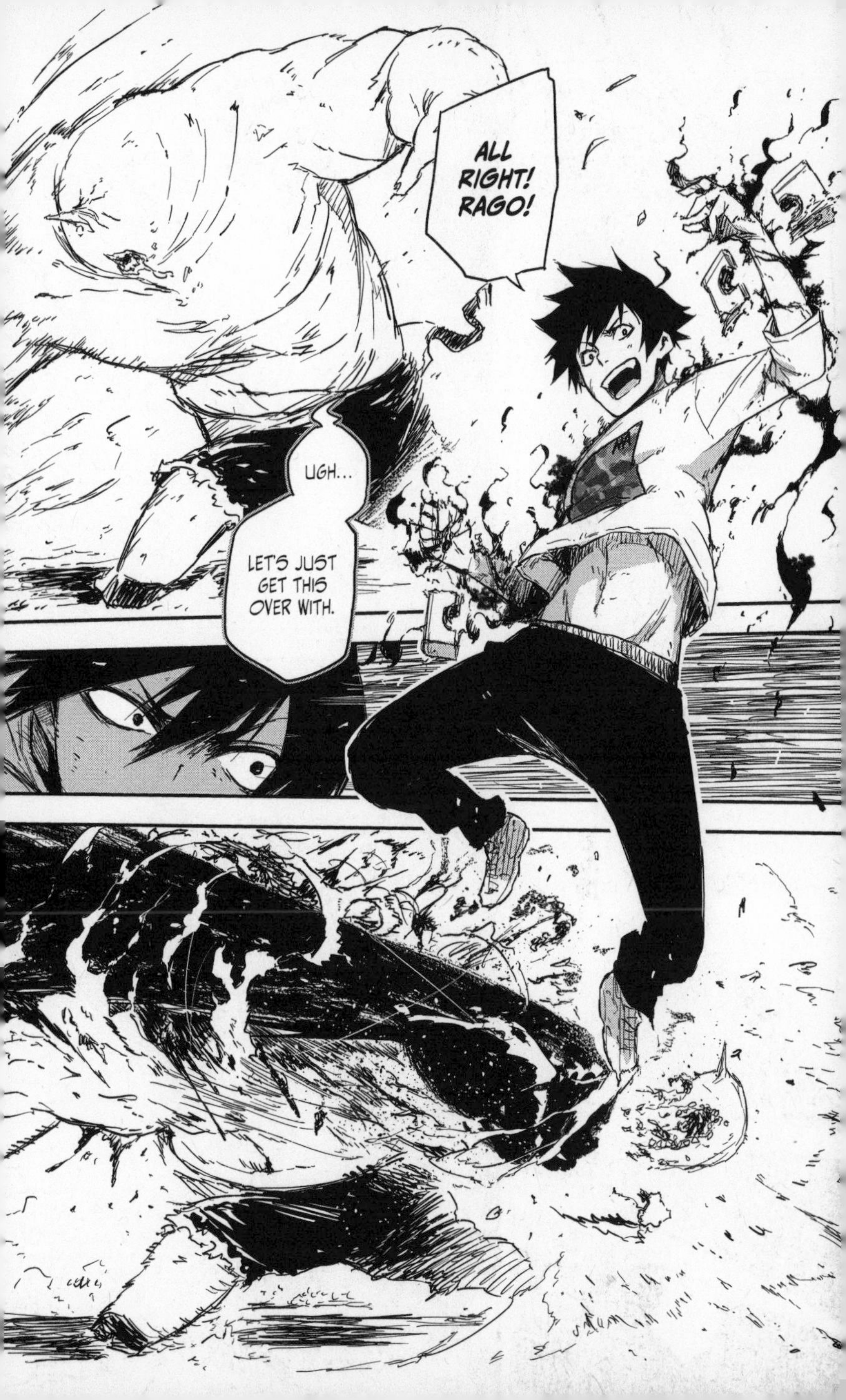
ALL RIGHT! RAGO!
UGH...
LET'S JUST GET THIS OVER WITH.

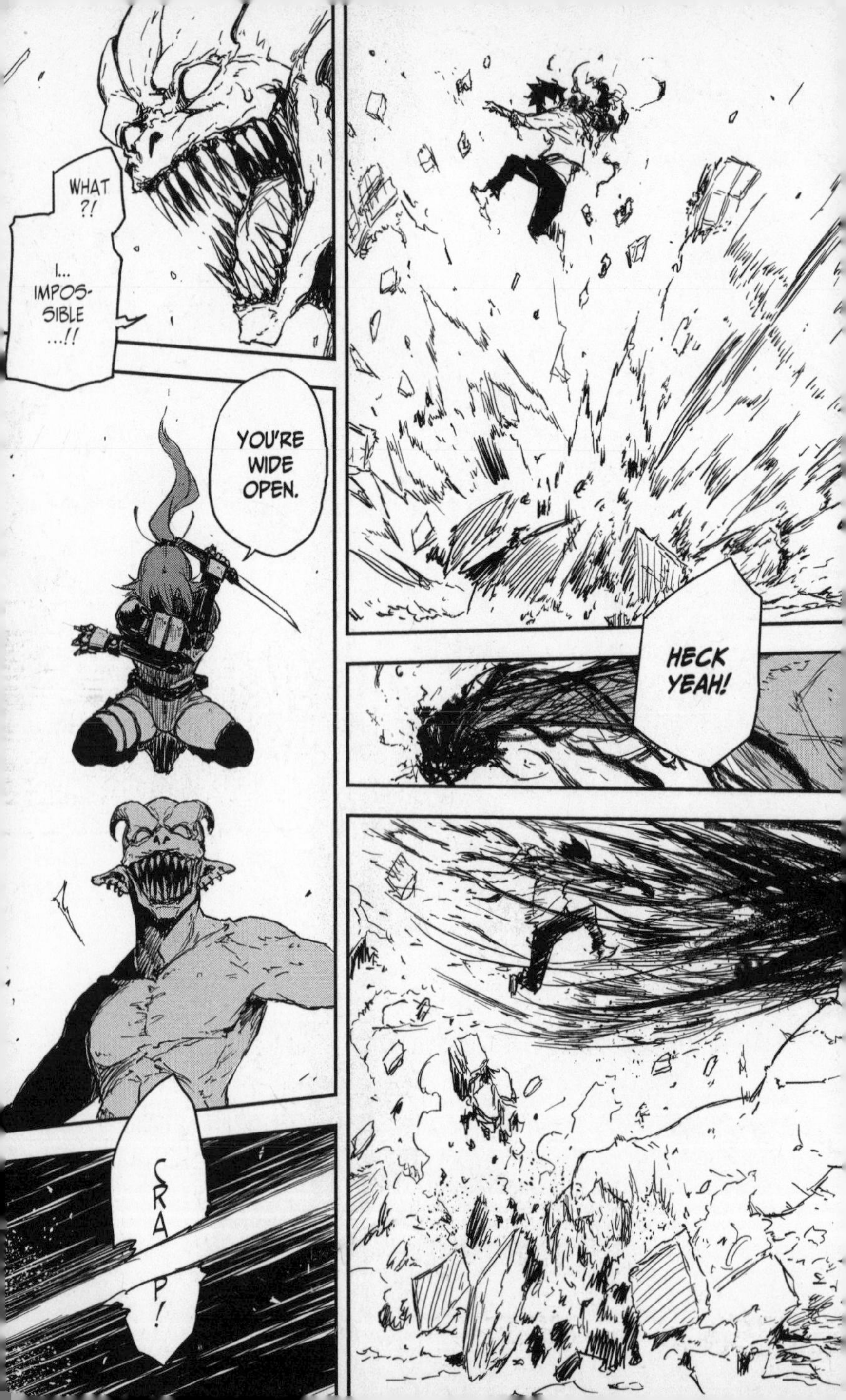
HECK YEAH!
WHAT ?!
I... IMPOS-SIBLE ...!!
YOU'RE WIDE OPEN.
CRAP!

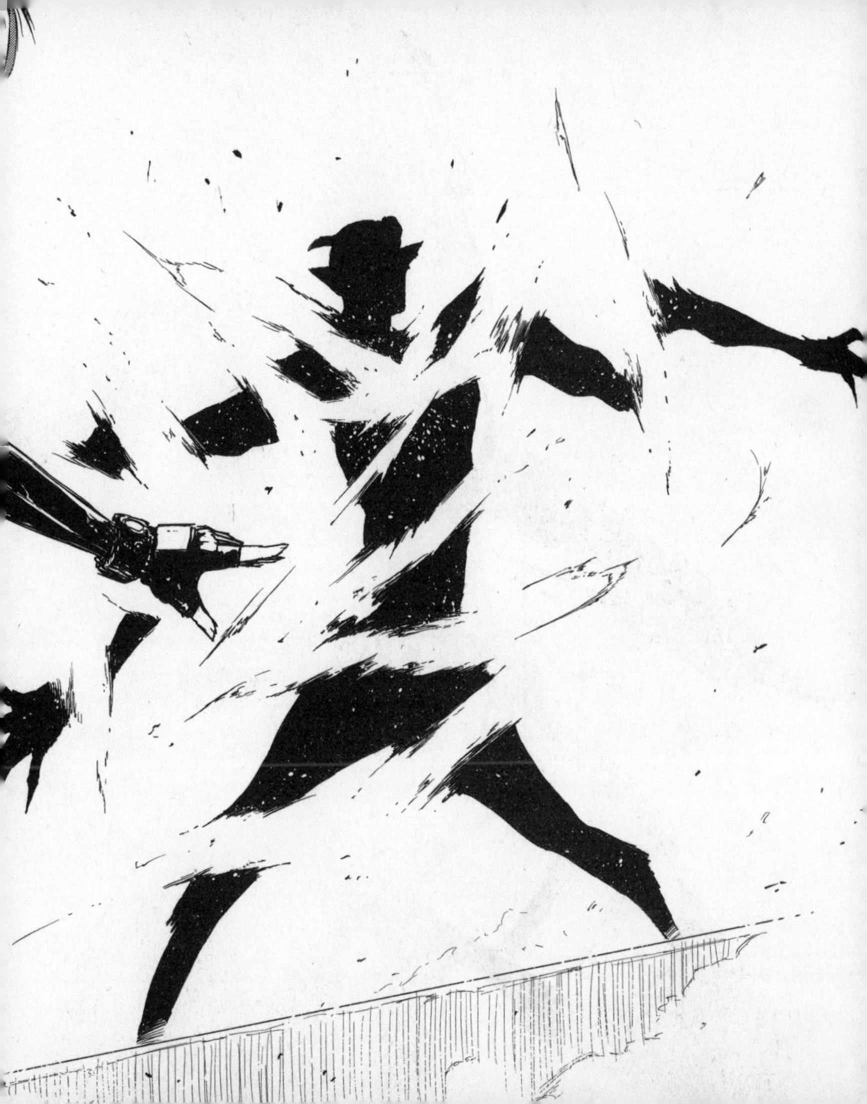

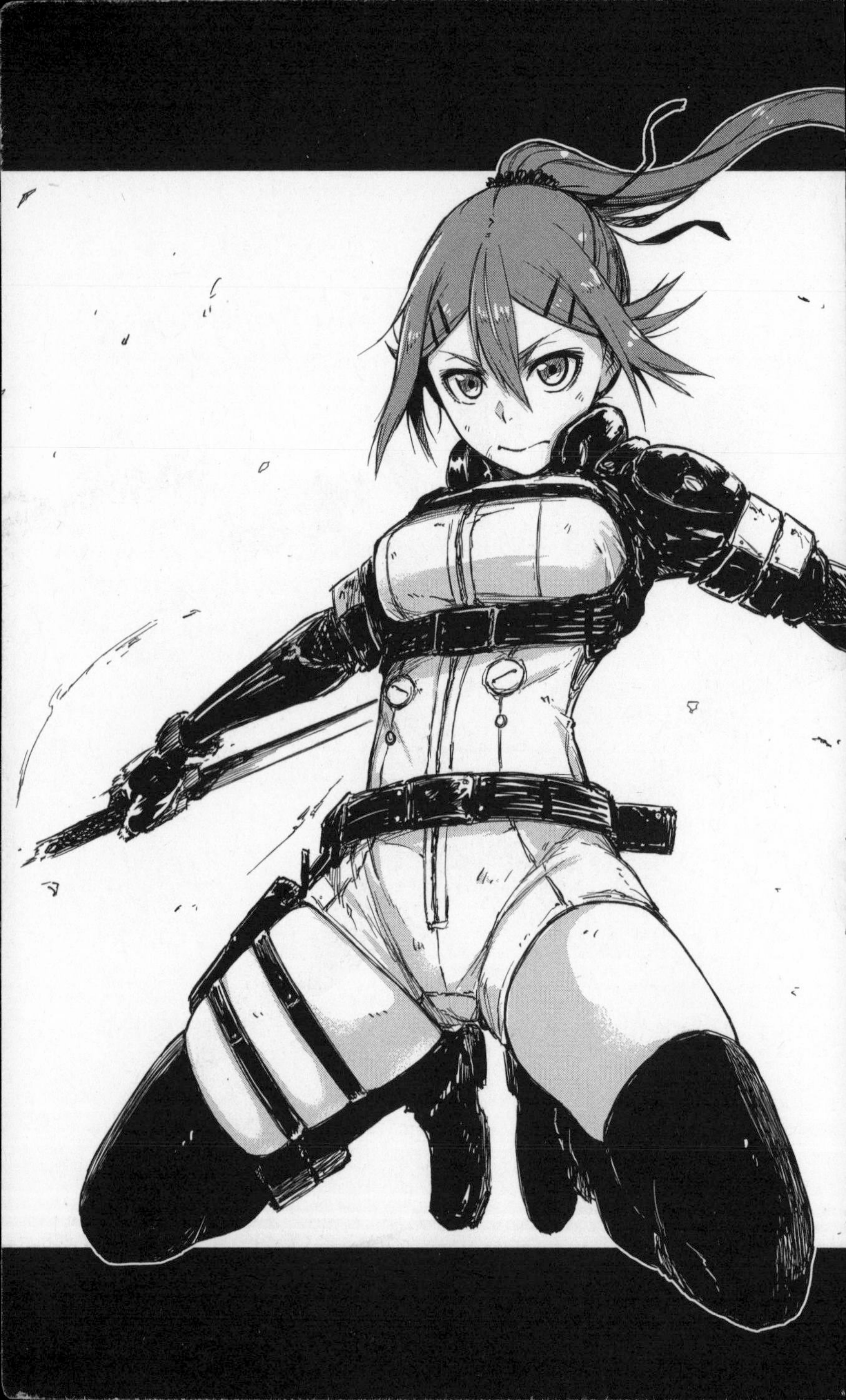

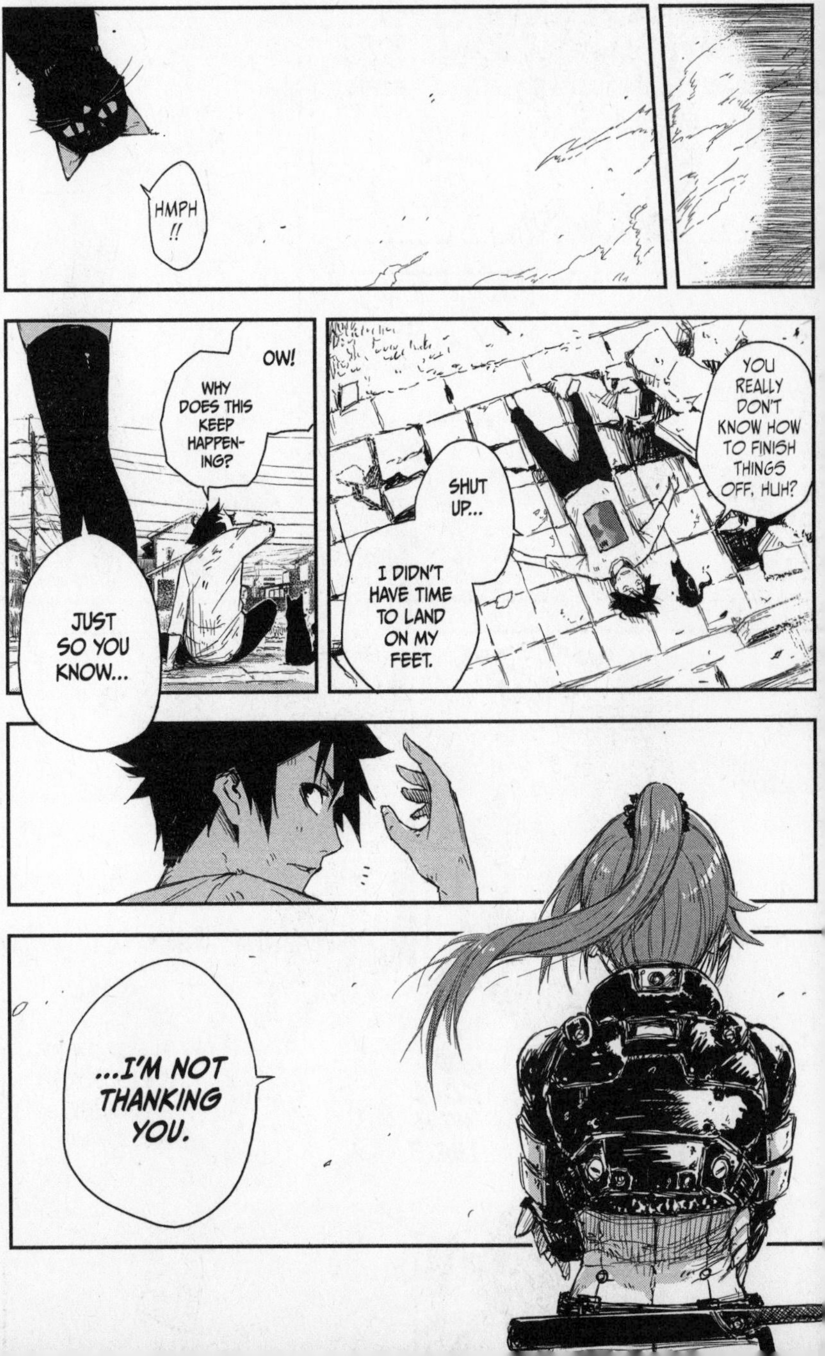
HMPH !!
YOU REALLY DON'T KNOW HOW TO FINISH THINGS OFF, HUH?
SHUT UP...
I DIDN'T HAVE TIME TO LAND ON MY FEET.
OW!
WHY DOES THIS KEEP HAPPEN-ING?
JUST SO YOU KNOW...
...I'M NOT THANKING YOU.

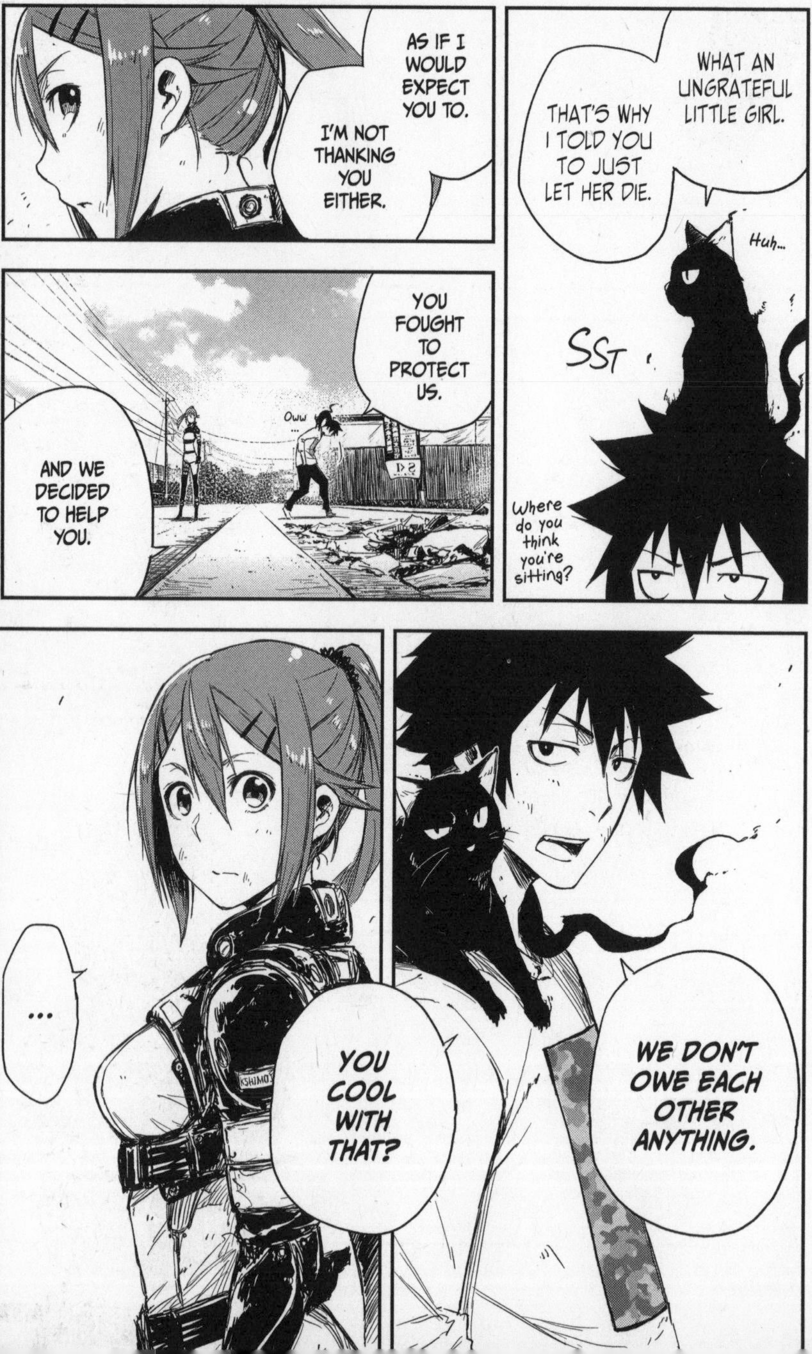
WHAT AN UNGRATEFUL LITTLE GIRL.
THAT'S WHY I TOLD YOU TO JUST LET HER DIE.
Huh...
SST
Where do you think you're sitting?
AS IF I WOULD EXPECT YOU TO.
I'M NOT THANKING YOU EITHER.
YOU FOUGHT TO PROTECT US.
Oww...
AND WE DECIDED TO HELP YOU.
WE DON'T OWE EACH OTHER ANYTHING.
YOU COOL WITH THAT?
...

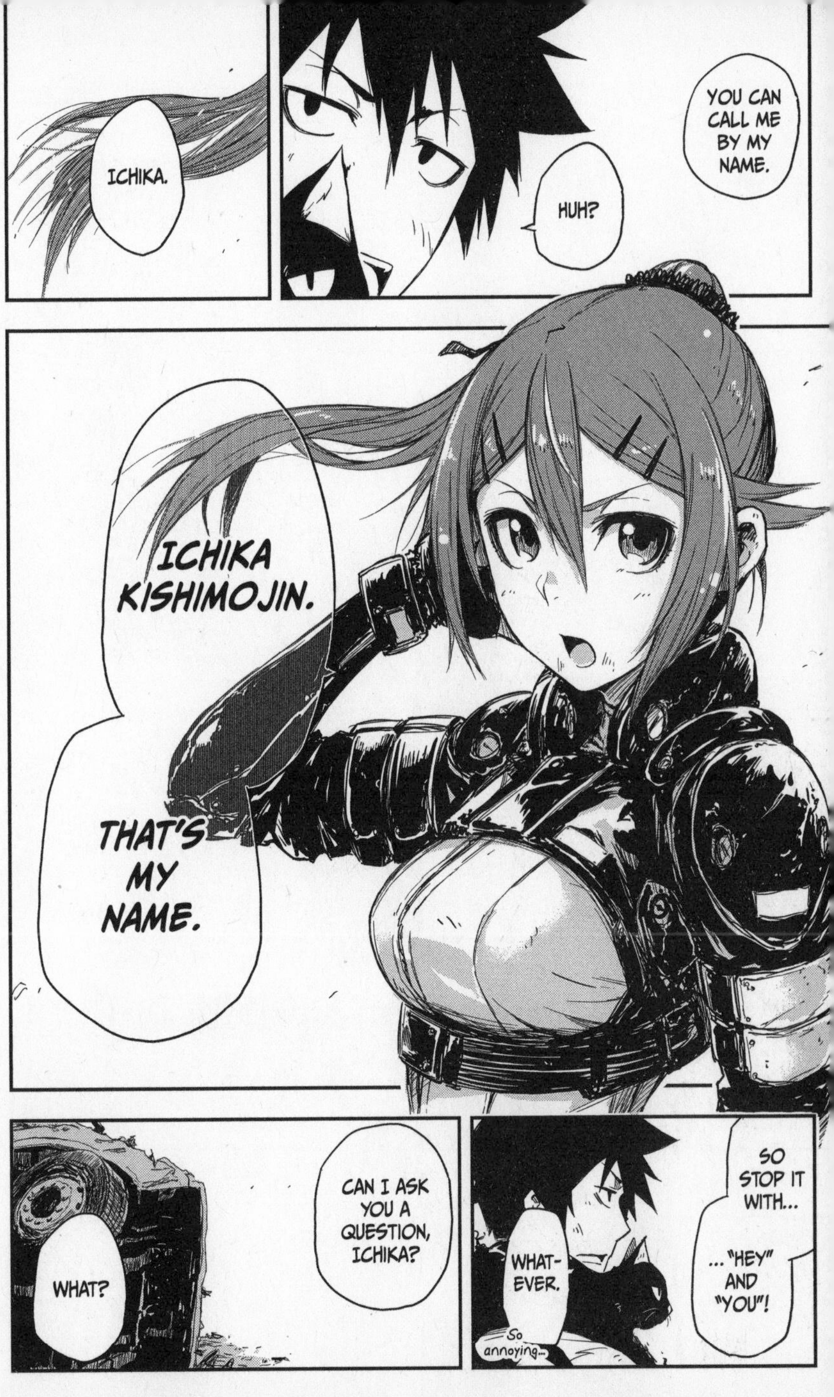
YOU CAN CALL ME BY MY NAME.
HUH?
ICHIKA.
ICHIKA KISHIMOJIN.
THAT'S MY NAME.
SO STOP IT WITH...
... "HEY" AND "YOU"!
WHAT-EVER.
So annoying...
CAN I ASK YOU A QUESTION, ICHIKA?
WHAT?

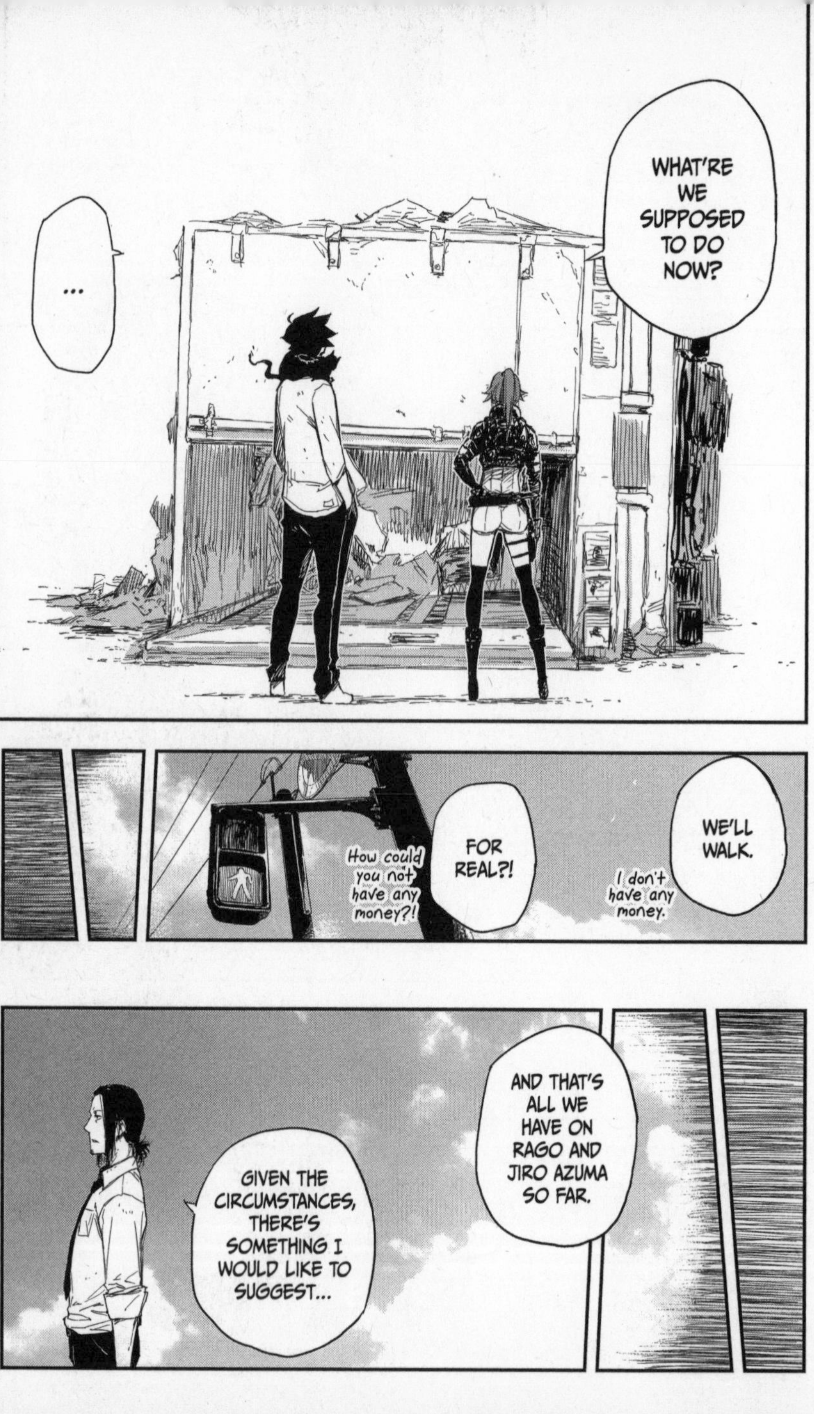
WHAT'RE WE SUPPOSED TO DO NOW?
...
WE'LL WALK.
I don't have any money.
FOR REAL?!
How could you not have any money?!
AND THAT'S ALL WE HAVE ON RAGO AND JIRO AZUMA SO FAR.
GIVEN THE CIRCUMSTANCES, THERE'S SOMETHING I WOULD LIKE TO SUGGEST...

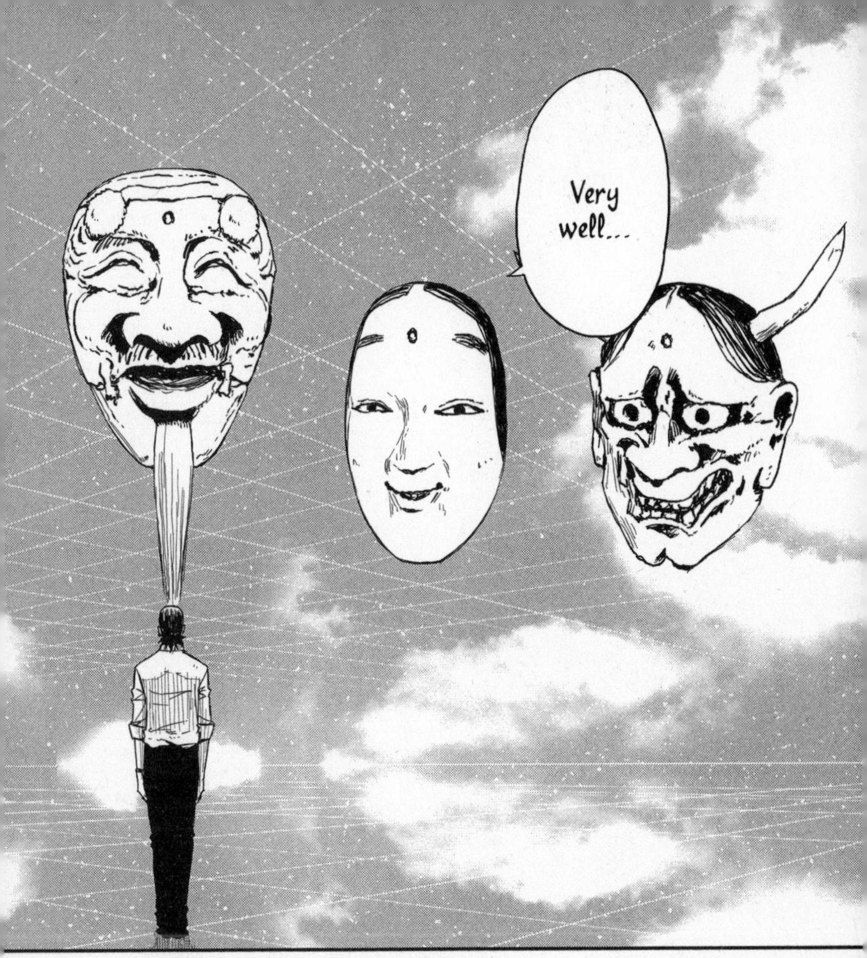
Very well...

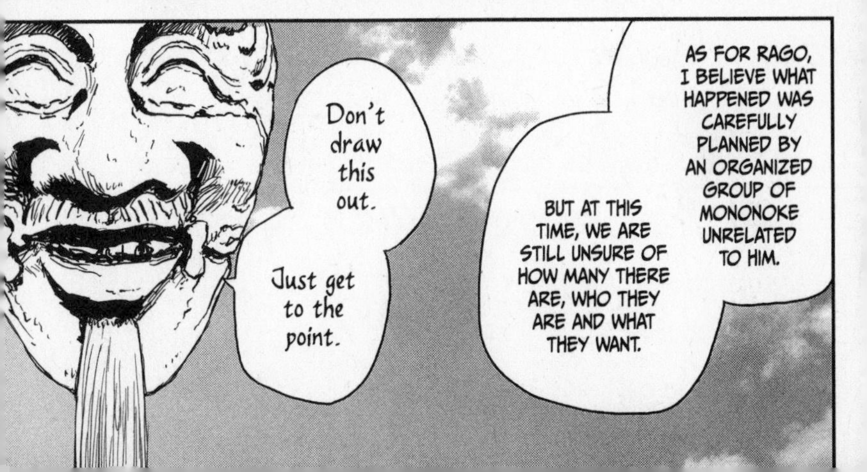
AS FOR RAGO, I BELIEVE WHAT HAPPENED WAS CAREFULLY PLANNED BY AN ORGANIZED GROUP OF MONONOKE UNRELATED TO HIM.
BUT AT THIS TIME, WE ARE STILL UNSURE OF HOW MANY THERE ARE, WHO THEY ARE AND WHAT THEY WANT.
Don't draw this out.
Just get to the point.

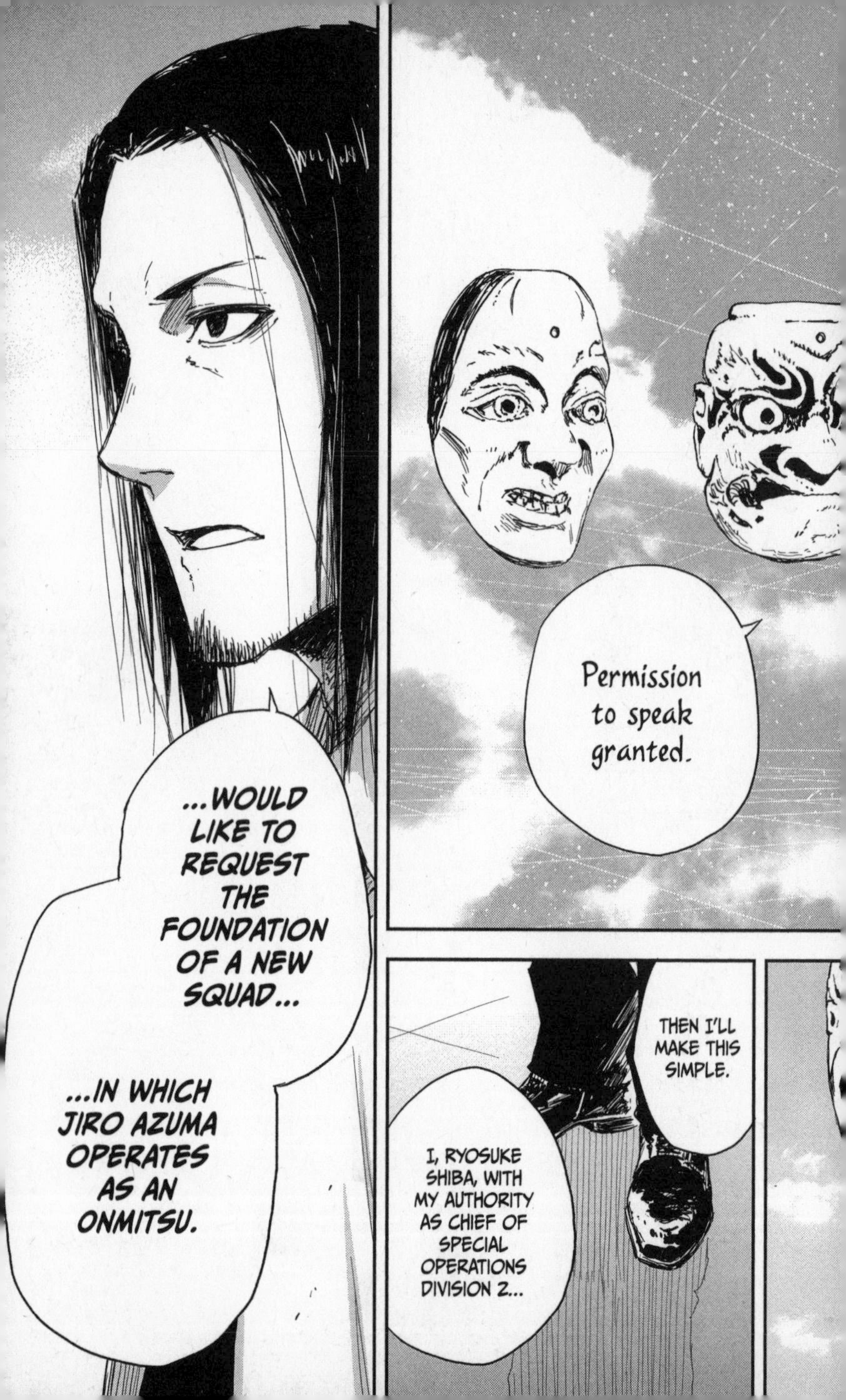
Permission to speak granted.
THEN I'LL MAKE THIS SIMPLE.
I, RYOSUKE SHIBA, WITH MY AUTHORITY AS CHIEF OF SPECIAL OPERATIONS DIVISION 2...
...WOULD LIKE TO REQUEST THE FOUNDATION OF A NEW SQUAD...
...IN WHICH JIRO AZUMA OPERATES AS AN ONMITSU.

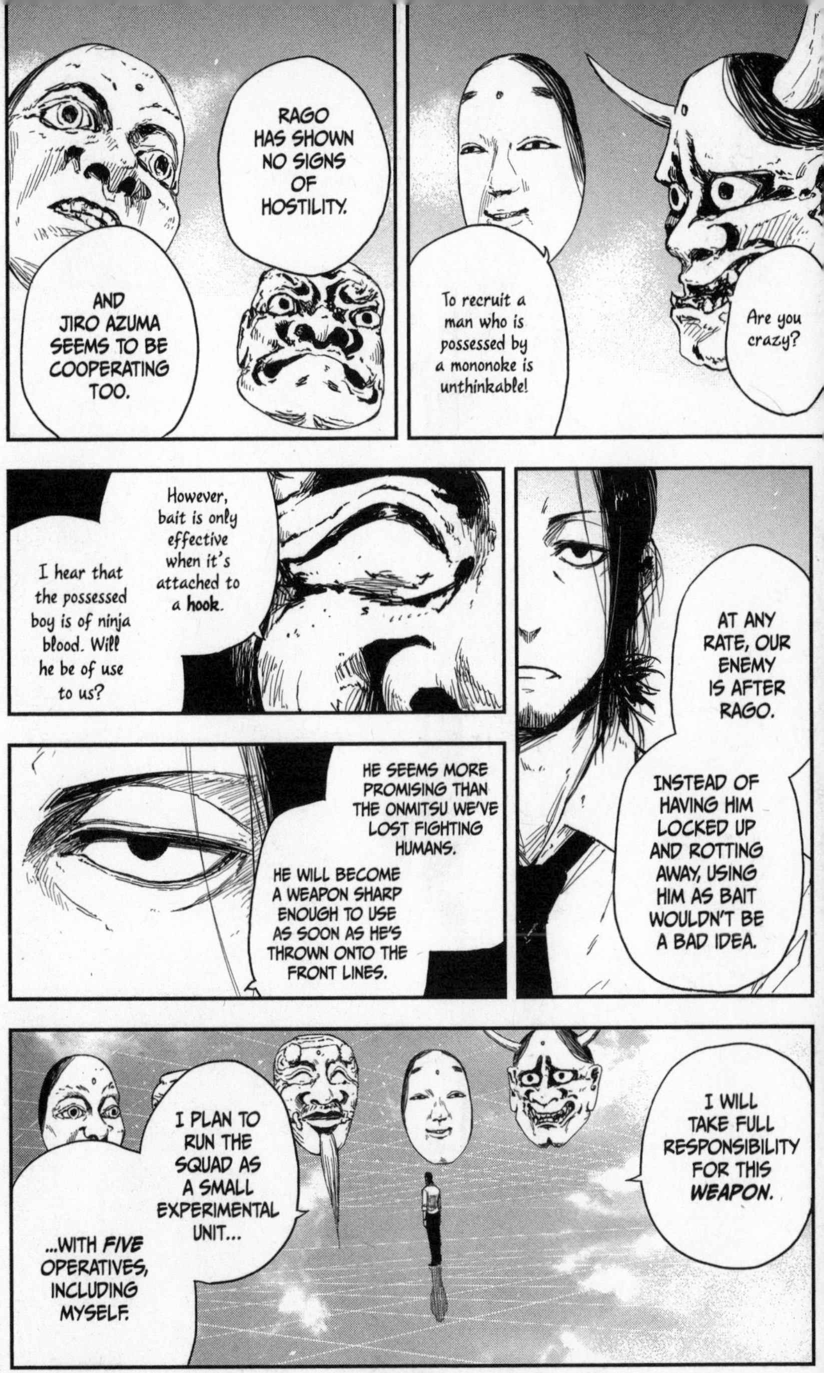

To recruit a man who is possessed by a mononoke is unthinkable!
Are you crazy?
RAGO HAS SHOWN NO SIGNS OF HOSTILITY.
AND JIRO AZUMA SEEMS TO BE COOPERATING TOO.
AT ANY RATE, OUR ENEMY IS AFTER RAGO.
INSTEAD OF HAVING HIM LOCKED UP AND ROTTING AWAY, USING HIM AS BAIT WOULDN'T BE A BAD IDEA.
However, bait is only effective when it's attached to a **hook**.
I hear that the possessed boy is of ninja blood. Will he be of use to us?
HE SEEMS MORE PROMISING THAN THE ONMITSU WE'VE LOST FIGHTING HUMANS.
HE WILL BECOME A WEAPON SHARP ENOUGH TO USE AS SOON AS HE'S THROWN ONTO THE FRONT LINES.
I WILL TAKE FULL RESPONSIBILITY FOR THIS *WEAPON*.
I PLAN TO RUN THE SQUAD AS A SMALL EXPERIMENTAL UNIT...
...WITH *FIVE* OPERATIVES, INCLUDING MYSELF.

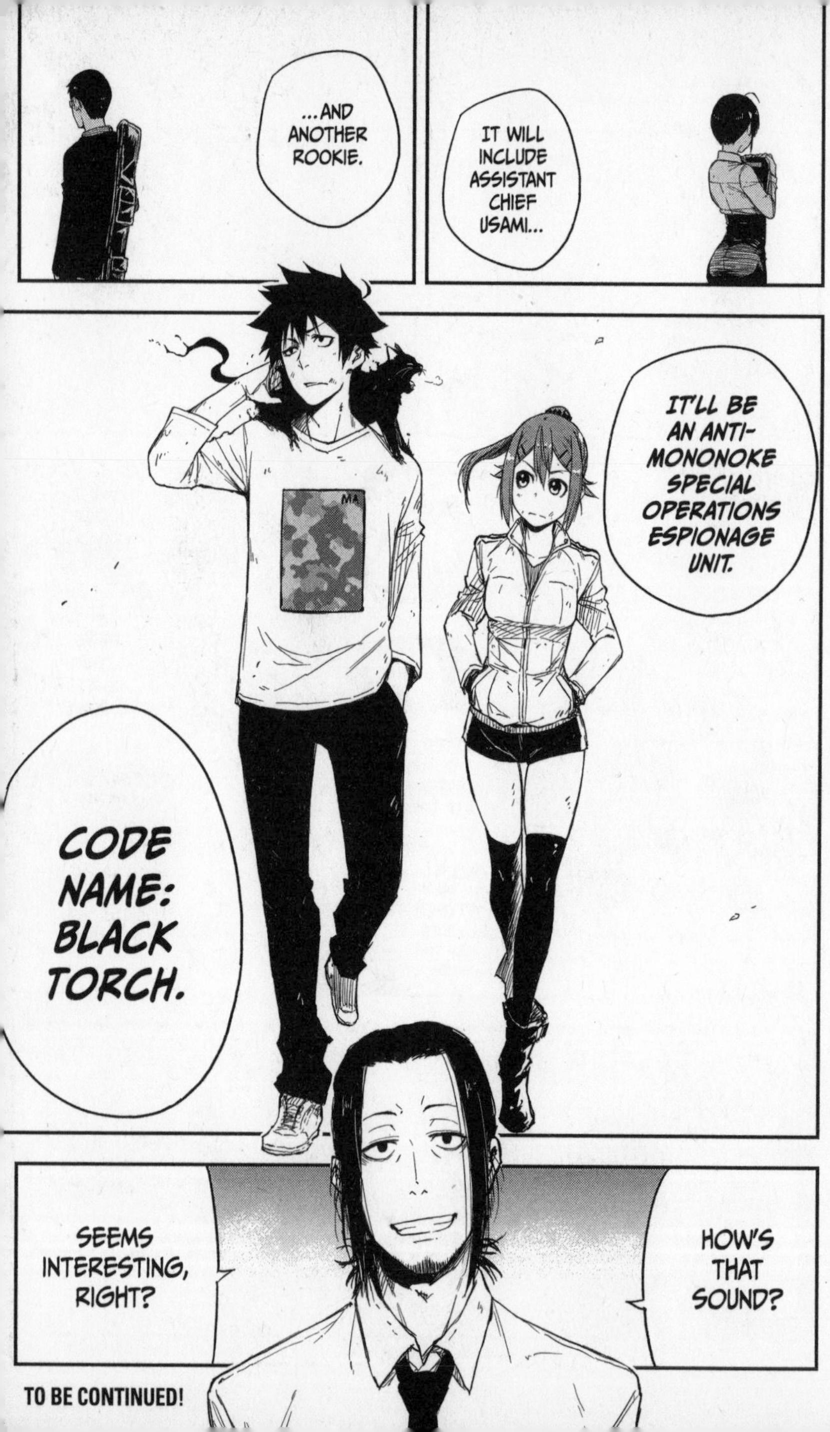
IT WILL INCLUDE ASSISTANT CHIEF USAMI...
...AND ANOTHER ROOKIE.
IT'LL BE AN ANTI-MONONOKE SPECIAL OPERATIONS ESPIONAGE UNIT.
CODE NAME: BLACK TORCH.
HOW'S THAT SOUND?
SEEMS INTERESTING, RIGHT?

TO BE CONTINUED!

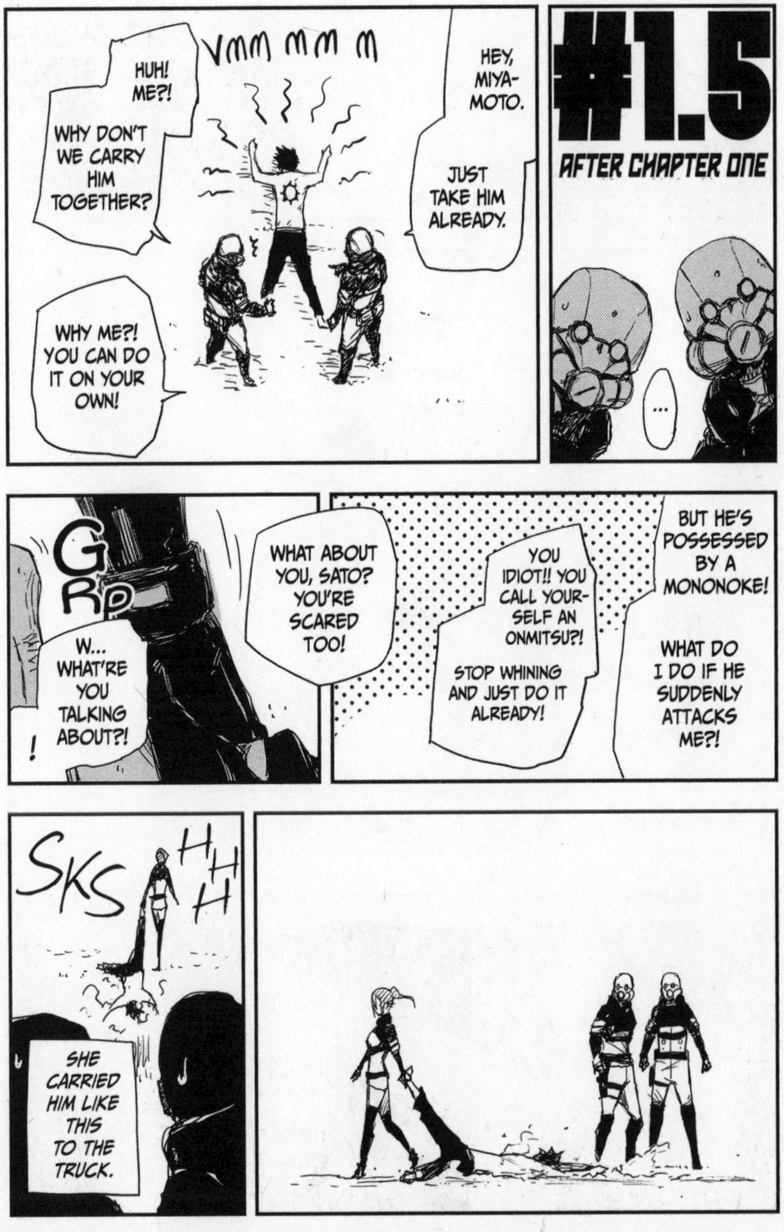
#1.5
AFTER CHAPTER ONE
...
HEY, MIYA-MOTO.
JUST TAKE HIM ALREADY.
VMM MM M
HUH! ME?!
WHY DON'T WE CARRY HIM TOGETHER?
WHY ME?! YOU CAN DO IT ON YOUR OWN!
BUT HE'S POSSESSED BY A MONONOKE!
WHAT DO I DO IF HE SUDDENLY ATTACKS ME?!
YOU IDIOT!! YOU CALL YOUR-SELF AN ONMITSU?!
STOP WHINING AND JUST DO IT ALREADY!
WHAT ABOUT YOU, SATO? YOU'RE SCARED TOO!
GRP
W... WHAT'RE YOU TALKING ABOUT?!
!
HHH
SKS
SHE CARRIED HIM LIKE THIS TO THE TRUCK.

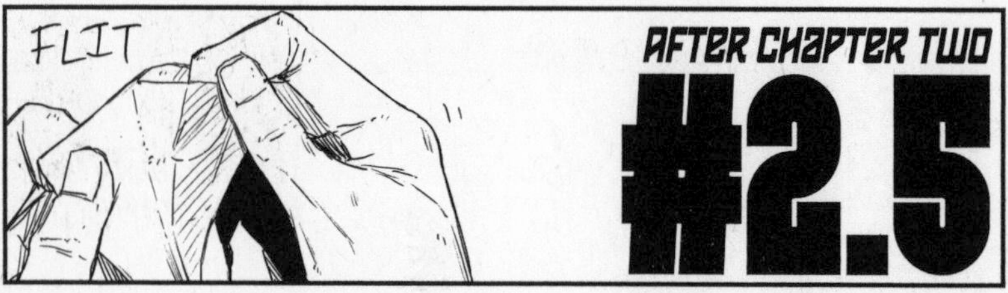
AFTER CHAPTER TWO
#2.5
FLIT

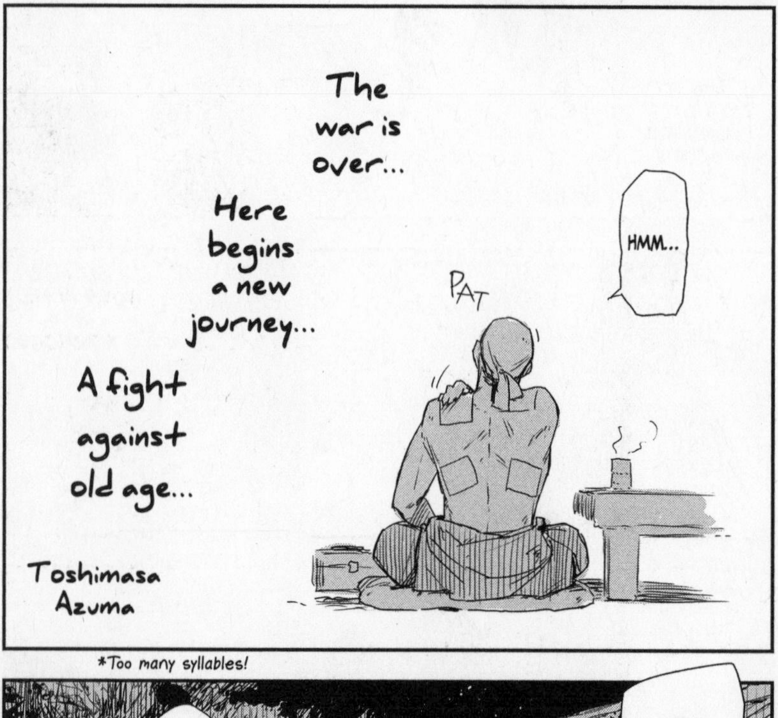
The war is over...
Here begins a new journey...
A fight against old age...
Toshimasa Azuma
HMM...
PAT

*Too many syllables!

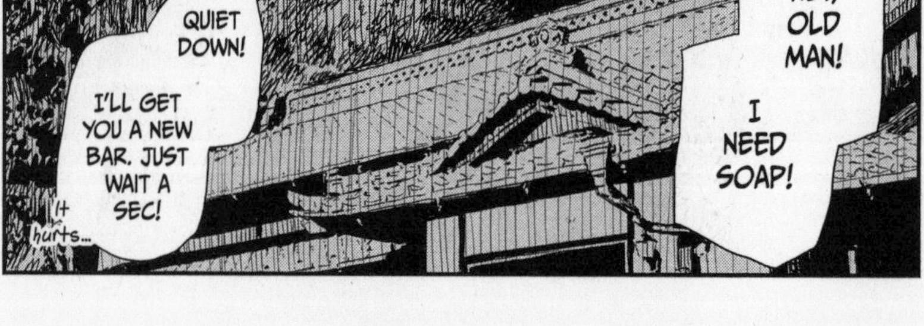
HEY, OLD MAN! I NEED SOAP!
QUIET DOWN!
I'LL GET YOU A NEW BAR. JUST WAIT A SEC!
It hurts...

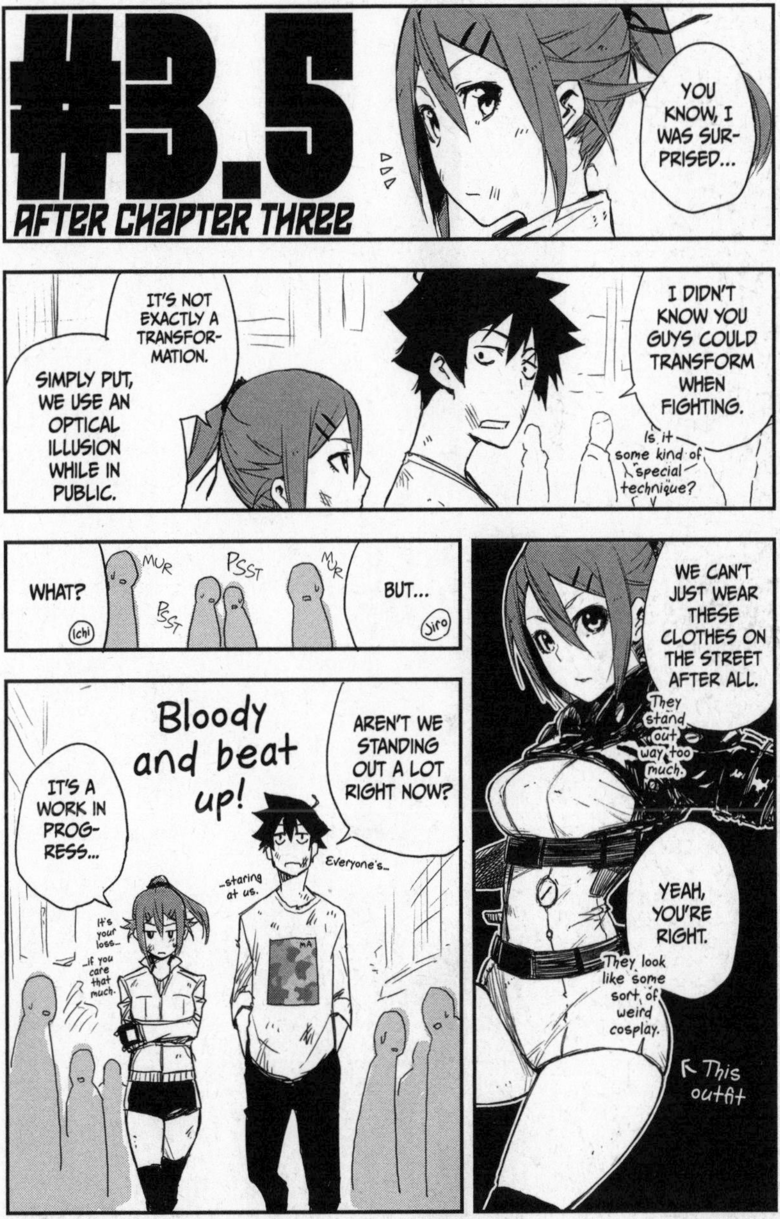
YOU KNOW, I WAS SURPRISED...
#3.5
AFTER CHAPTER THREE
I DIDN'T KNOW YOU GUYS COULD TRANSFORM WHEN FIGHTING.
Is it some kind of special technique?
IT'S NOT EXACTLY A TRANSFORMATION.
SIMPLY PUT, WE USE AN OPTICAL ILLUSION WHILE IN PUBLIC.
WE CAN'T JUST WEAR THESE CLOTHES ON THE STREET AFTER ALL.
They stand out way too much.
YEAH, YOU'RE RIGHT.
They look like some sort of weird cosplay.
← This outfit
BUT...
Jiro
MUR
PSST
PSST
MUR
WHAT?
Ichi
AREN'T WE STANDING OUT A LOT RIGHT NOW?
Everyone's...
...staring at us.
Bloody and beat up!
IT'S A WORK IN PROGRESS...
It's your loss...
...if you care that much.

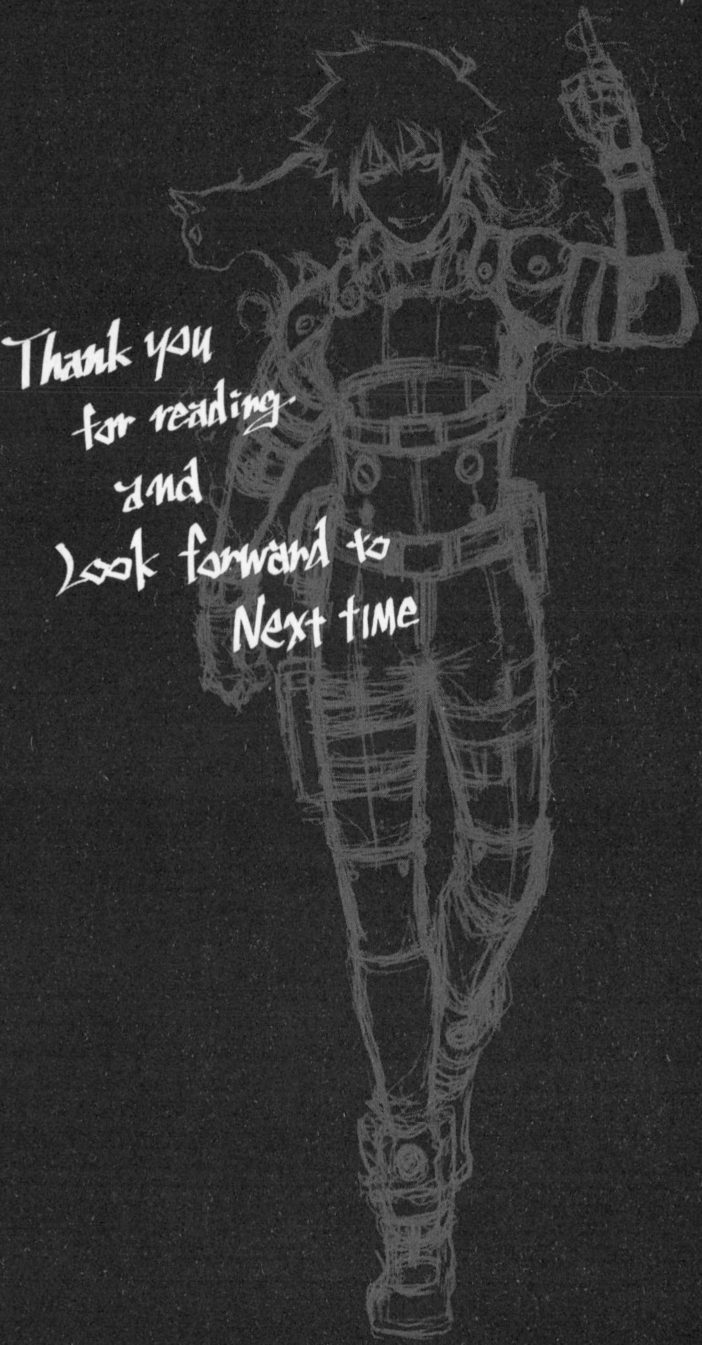
Thank you
for reading
and
Look forward to
Next time

POORLY WRITTEN AFTERWORD!

MY NAME IS TAKAKI.

IT'S NICE TO MEET YOU.

I WOULD LIKE TO EXPRESS MY THANKS FOR READING THIS FAR! THIS IS A SERIES ABOUT NINJA. THERE ARE SEVERAL REASONS I CHOSE TO WRITE A NINJA MANGA, BUT THE BIGGEST ONE IS THAT I THOUGHT THAT NINJAS WOULD WORK WELL IN A SCI-FI AND FANTASY SETTING.

ORIGINALLY, IT ALL STARTED WHEN I THOUGHT, "I WANT TO CREATE A MODERN-STYLE FIGHTING AND ACTION MANGA!" AND THEN I THOUGHT THAT I MIGHT AS WELL HAVE SOME KIND OF A THEME TO GO ALONG WITH IT. SO ONE IDEA LED TO ANOTHER AND I ENDED UP WITH NINJAS! NINJAS ARE POPULAR NOT ONLY IN JAPAN, BUT ALL AROUND THE WORLD, THANKS TO EARLIER CREATORS THAT MADE A LOT OF NINJA-THEMED MANGA, NOVELS, VIDEO GAMES, MOVIES, ETC...

NINJAS HAVE BEEN RE-CREATED AND REWORKED IN MANY DIFFERENT STYLES. THAT MEANS THAT EVEN IF MY INTERPRETATION OF THEM IS A LITTLE EXTREME, I THINK PEOPLE WILL CUT ME SOME SLACK... OR AT LEAST I HOPE THEY WILL...

THE NINJA IN THIS SERIES (ONMITSU) ARE A MIX OF CIVIL SERVANTS AND SPECIAL FORCES (KIND OF?) OPERATIVES WHO SECRETLY FIGHT AGAINST EVIL HUMANS AND MONONOKE. WELL, AS LONG AS IT WORKS WITH THE SETTING, I HOPE MAYBE THE GREAT NINJA MANGA ARTISTS AND NOVELISTS WHO HAVE COME BEFORE ME WILL CUT ME SOME SLACK. I THINK AS THE WORLD EXPANDS AND THE STORY PROGRESSES, I'D LIKE TO ADD CYBORGS, MECHAS, FORBIDDEN RITUALS, CURSED ITEMS—AND OTHER ELEMENTS TO THIS MANGA. AND IF ANY OF THOSE THINGS ARE ADDED TO THIS STORY, I HOPE YOU ALL THINK IT'S OKAY BECAUSE, HEY! IT'S A NINJA STORY!

WITH ALL THAT BEING SAID, I'LL BE EXTREMELY GRATEFUL IF YOU ENJOY THIS SERIES AND I HOPE TO SEE YOU NEXT VOLUME!

Tsuyoshi Takaki

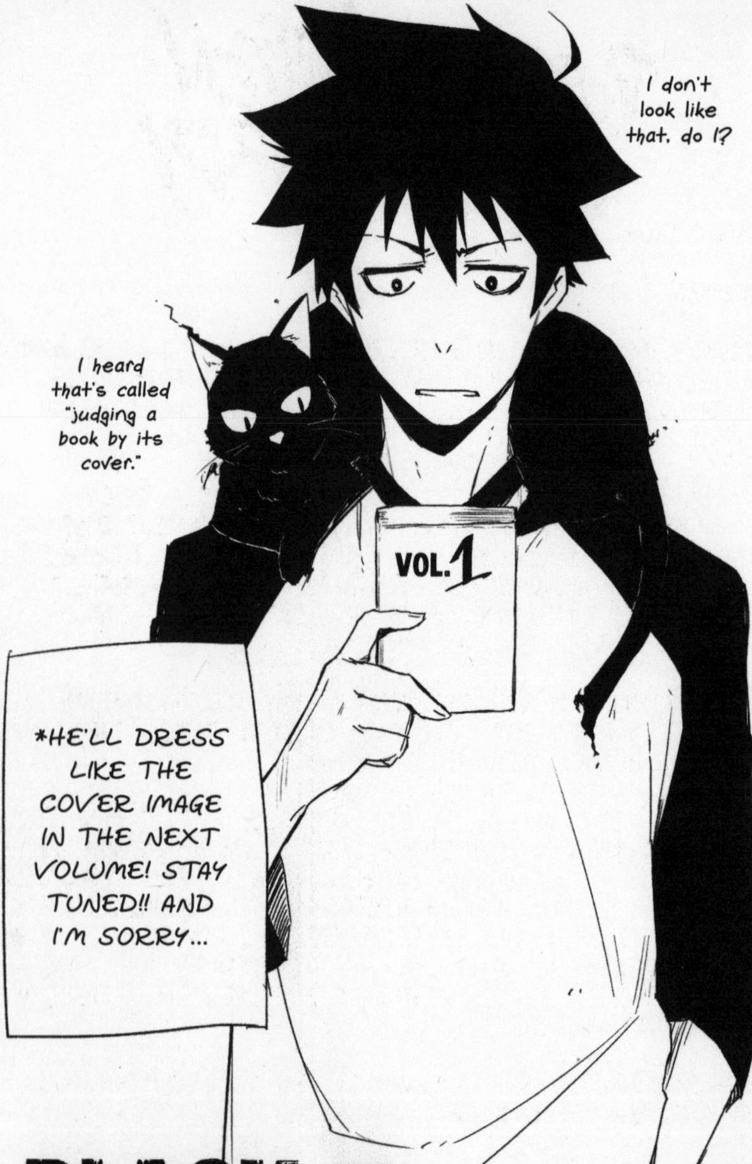
I don't look like that, do I?
I heard that's called "judging a book by its cover."
VOL. 1
*HE'LL DRESS LIKE THE COVER IMAGE IN THE NEXT VOLUME! STAY TUNED!! AND I'M SORRY...

BLACK TORCH 1

STORY & ART
TSUYOSHI TAKAKI

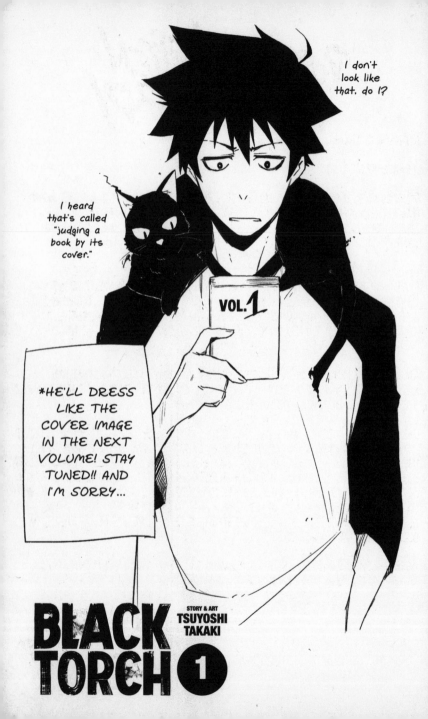

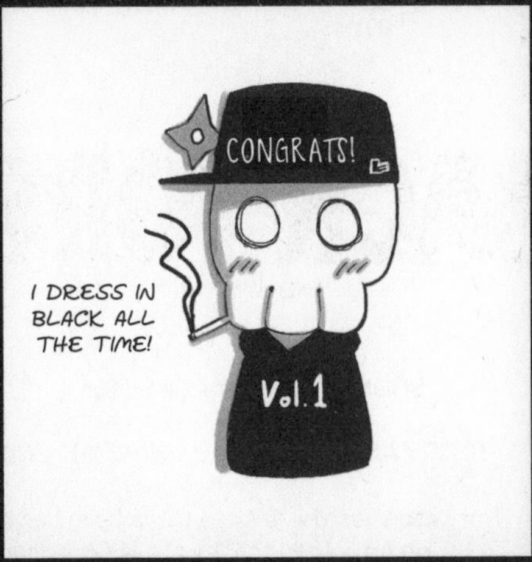
CONGRATS!
I DRESS IN BLACK ALL THE TIME!
Vol.1

TSUYOSHI TAKAKI

I'VE BEEN A FAN OF THE COLOR BLACK FOR A LONG TIME. IT'S A COLOR THAT CAN'T BE CHANGED BY OTHER COLORS. IT ALSO GOES WELL WITH EVERYTHING! I HOPE MY MANGA CAN BE LIKE THAT TOO. I HOPE YOU'LL ALL STICK WITH ME AND ENJOY FINDING OUT HOW THINGS GO.

Tsuyoshi Takaki published his first one-shot, *Freaks*, in *Jump SQ Crown* in Japan in 2016. He began serialization of *Black Torch* in *Jump SQ* later that year.